D1142061

Industrial change and regional development

Industrial change and regional development: the transformation of new industrial spaces

Edited by Georges Benko and Mick Dunford

Belhaven Press
(a division of Pinter Publishers)
London and New York

© New Industrial Spaces, 1991

First published in Great Britain in 1991 by
Belhaven Press (a division of Pinter Publishers),
25 Floral Street, London WC2E 9DS

All rights reserved. No part of this publication may be
reproduced, stored in a retrieval system, or transmitted by any
other means without the prior permission of the copyright holder.
Please direct all enquiries to the publishers.

British Library Cataloguing in Publication Data

A CIP catalogue record for this book is available from the
British Library

ISBN 1 85293 120 5

For enquiries in North America please contact P.O. Box 197, Irvington, NY 10533

Library of Congress Cataloging in Publication Data

Industrial change and regional development : the transformation of new
  industrial spaces / edited by Georges Benko and Mick Dunford.
      p. cm.
  Revised papers, chiefly translations from French, German, and
Italian, originally presented at a conference held Mar. 21–22, 1984,
at the University of Paris I—Panthéon-Sorbonne.
    Includes bibliographical references and index.
    ISBN 1-85293-120-5
    1. Industry—Location—Congresses.   2. Small business—Congresses.
  3. Regional economic disparities—Congresses.   I. Benko, Georges.
  II. Dunford, Mick
  HC79.D5I5   1991
  338.9—dc20   90–24902
                                                              CIP

Typeset by Witwell Limited, Southport
Printed and bound by Biddles Ltd of Guildford and Kings Lynn

Contents

List of figures

List of tables

Notes on Contributors

Giacomo Becattini was born in Florence, Italy in 1927. At present he is Professore di Economia at the Università di Firenze (Florence). He is an Honorary Member of Trinity Hall, Cambridge and a Correspondent Member of the Accademia Nazionale dei Lincei, and in 1986–9 he was Vice-President of the Società Italiana degli Economisti. He has published articles and written and edited books on economic theory, *Il concetto d'industria e la teoria del valore* (Turin, Boringhieri 1962), on the history of economic thought, *Marshall: Antologia di scritti economici* (Bologna, Il Mulino 1981) and on applied industrial and regional economics.

Pierre Beckouche studied at the Ecole Normale Supérieure and passed the agrégation in Geography. At present he is Maître de Conférences at the Institut d'Urbanisme de Paris at the Université de Paris XII at Créteil and a researcher in the CNRS (Centre National de Recherche Scientifique) Laboratoire STRATES at the Université de Paris I — Panthéon-Sorbonne.

Georges Benko is Maître de Conférences Associé at the Université de Paris I — Panthéon-Sorbonne and a researcher in Centre de Recherche sur l'Industrie et l'Aménagement (CRIA). He is a member of the editorial boards of the journals *Espaces et Sociétés* and *Society and Space*. He is the editor of *Les nouveaux aspects de la théorie sociale* (Caen, Paradigme 1988) and *Space and Social Theory: Towards a Postmodern Human Geography* (Ottawa, University of Ottawa Press 1991), and he has just completed a book entitled *Géographie des technopoles* (Paris, Masson 1991).

Paul Claval is Professeur de Géographie and Director of the CNRS Laboratoire Espace et Culture at the Université de Paris IV — Paris-Sorbonne. He is a member of the editorial boards of the journals *L'Espace Géographique*, *Urban Studies, Geoforum,* and *Tijdschrift voor Economische en Sociale Geographie*. He has published over 400 articles and more than twenty books including *Espace et Pouvoir* (Paris, Presses Universitaires de France 1978), *Les Mythes fondateurs des sciences sociales* (Paris, Presses Universitaires de France 1980) *La Logique des villes* (Paris, Litec 1981) *Géographie humaine et* *économique contemporaine* (Paris, Presses Universitaires de France 1984), and *La Conquête de l'espace américain* (Paris, Flammarion 1990).

Benjamin Coriat is Professor Agrégé de Sciences Economiques at the Université de Paris XIII — Villetaneuse and Director of CRIIF-LAREMI. He is an expert on high technologies and their impact on employment and work, and he is the author of *L'Atelier et le chronomètre* (Paris, Christian Bourgois 1979), *Alcool* (Paris, Christian Bourgois 1982), *La Robotique* (Paris, La Découverte 1984), and *L'Atelier et le robot* (Paris, Christian Bourgois 1990).

Mick Dunford is Lecturer in Human Geography in the School of European Studies at the University of Sussex. He is a member of the editorial board of *Espaces et Sociétés*. His main publications include *The Arena of Capital* (London, Macmillan 1983) written with Diane Perrons, and *Capital, the State and Regional Development* (London, Pion 1988). At present he is doing comparative research on the development of new technologies in Europe and is working on the regional implications of European economic and political integration.

Gioacchino Garofoli is Professore Associato in the Dipartimento di Economia Politica e di Metodi Quantitativi at the Università di Pavia. His main interests are in the spatial aspects of economic development and in regional and industrial economics. He has published many articles in Italian and foreign journals, and he has written and edited several books published in Milan by Franco Angeli including *Ristrutturazione industriale e territorio* (1978), *Industrializzazione diffusa in Lombardia* (1983), *Le Politiche di sviluppo locale* (1988), and *Modelli locali di sviluppo* (1990). At present he is editing a book entitled *Endogenous Development in Southern Europe* (Aldershot, Avebury).

Isabelle Geneau de Lamarlière studied economics at the Université de Paris I — Panthéon-Sorbonne and geography at the Université de Paris VIII. At present she is working in the Laboratoire Espace et Culture at the Université de Paris IV — Paris-Sorbonne and in the CNRS Théorie des Mutations Urbaines. She is preparing a doctoral thesis on the determinants of the location of the electronics industry.

Stefan Krätke was until 1989 a member of the housing and urban renewal research department at the Hochschule der Künste in Berlin. His main research interests are in housing and urban economics and in the approaches associated with the 'new urban sociology'. He has published numerous articles and books on new forms of housing finance and public housing, urban ground rent and the real estate market, and the relation between processes of social restructuring and the transformation of cities and urban regions. He has also carried advisory studies for the building and planning department of the West Berlin government.

Danièle Leborgne is an economist and works as a researcher in the CNRS CEPREMAP in Paris. She has written numerous articles and research reports. At present she is working on the development of the ideas of the French school of regulation and on their application to the analysis of industrial relations, industrial organisation, and their spatial (interregional and international) dimensions.

Alain Lipietz studied at the Ecole Polytechnique. He is an economist and a CNRS director of research and he works at CEPREMAP in Paris. He is a member of the editorial board of the journal *Society and Space*. His main publications include *Le Tribut foncier urbain* (Paris, François Maspéro 1974), *Le Capital et son espace* (Paris, François Maspéro 1977), *Crise et inflation: pourquoi?* (Paris, François Maspéro 1979), *Le Monde enchanté* (Paris, François Maspéro 1983), *L'Audace ou l'enlisement* (Paris, La Découverte 1984) *Mirages et miracles* (Paris, La Découverte 1985) and *Choisir l'audace* (Paris, La Découverte 1989).

Jacques Malézieux is Professeur in the Institut de Géographie at the Université de Paris I — Panthéon-Sorbonne, chargé d'enseignement of the Conférences de Civilisation Françaises at the Sorbonne and at the Institut d'Urbanisme de Paris at Créteil, and Director of the Centre de Recherche sur l'Industrie et l'Aménagement (CRIA). He is the author of numerous studies concerned with the character and the implications of the geography of industrial activities. His current research is on changes in the organisation of the productive system and the planning implications of the new geography of economic activities.

Claude Manzagol is Professeur de Géographie at the Université de Montréal. He is a member of the editorial board of the *Cahiers de Géographie du Québec*. He specialises in economic and industrial geography. His publications include *La Logique de l'espace industriel* (Paris, Presses Universitaires de France 1980).

Flavia Martinelli is Professore Associato in the Dipartimento di Analisi delle Strutture Territoriali at the Università di Reggio Calabria. She also teaches at the Centro di Specializzazione e Richerche per il Mezzogiorno at Portici, Naples. Her main research interests are in producer services, regional development, and Italy's underdeveloped Mezzogiorno. She has published articles in the *International Journal of Urban and Regional Research* and *Politica Economica* and has written reports for UNCTAD.

Eike Schamp is an economist and geographer. At present he is a Professor of Geography in the Institut für Wirtschafts- und Social Geographie at the Johann Wolfgang Goethe Universität in Frankfurt. His interests in geography are in the industrialisation of developing countries, and in particular of Central Africa, and in the spatial implications of technological change in industrialised countries.

Erica Schoenberger is Associate Professor in the Department of Geography and Environmental Engineering at the Johns Hopkins University in Baltimore. Her interests are in the investment and locational strategies of multinational corporations, the development of high-technology industries and regions, and industry–university relations. She has published her work in various geographical and regional science journals including *Economic Geography, Regional*

Studies, Society and Space, International Regional Science Review, Annals ofthe Association of American Geographers, Geografiska Annaler and *Acta Sociologica.*

Pierre Veltz studied at the Ecole Polytechnique. He is an engineer with a doctorate in sociology. He is Director of the Laboratoire Techniques, Territoires, Sociétes (LATTS), and Director of the Centres de Recherche de l'Ecole Nationale des Ponts et Chaussées. His main research interests are in contemporary trends in industrial organisation, the impact of computerisation, and spatial structures.

Preface

The 1970s and 1980s were years in which decline coexisted with growth and in which sharp recessions alternated with recoveries. At first academic research was focused on de-industrialisation, unemployment and regional decline. In the 1980s, however, more attention was paid to what was growing: high-tech industries, producer services and revitalised craft industries, and the 'new industrial spaces' in which these growth sectors were concentrated. What the contributors to this volume share is a wish to evaluate some of the main interpretations of these developments and to consider the implications of the experiences of the last ten or fifteen years for the final decade of the twentieth century.

Several of the authors consider the experience of the Third Italy. In these regions growth was centred around the development of small and medium-size specialised firms producing design-intensive goods for differentiated markets. The speed of their development in an era of slower growth led to the identification of these areas as some of the 'success stories' of the last fifteen years.

In recent years, however, an unparalled concentration and centralisation of capital has occurred. A second group of contributors deal with this paradox either directly or through analyses of the implications of the new technologies for the organisation of industry and of productive activities. While most of the authors identify the coexistence of divergent paths, differences remain concerning the relative weight of the small-scale and local on the one hand and the large-scale and global on the other.

The third theme is connected with the second. In the 1970s and early 1980s there was a view that processes of urbanisation and suburbanisation had given way to counter-urbanisation. In the more recent past more attention has been paid to the development of major metropolises whose positions as centres of economic control and wealth appear to have been reinforced.

What is clear from the coexistence of these opposed tendencies is that in the 1970s and 1980s there was considerable variation in the character and direction of development. There were also significant differences in the relative 'success' of different regions and countries. Attempts to explain these differences make up the fourth major theme addressed in this volume. The ways in which adaptation occurred, it is argued, were not determined by the new technologies but depended on politics. If this view is correct, it will also be politics that will determine the shape of Europe at the start of the twenty-first century.

The collection itself stems from a conference on New Industrial Spaces that Georges Benko planned and organised. The conference was partially financed by Plan Urbain, for whose help we are very grateful, and took place at the University of Paris I — Panthéon-Sorbonne on 21–2 March 1989. Initial versions of the chapters by Giacomo Becattini, Paul Claval, Isabelle Geneau de Lamarlière, Mick Dunford, Danièle Leborgne and Alain Lipietz, Jacques Malézieux, Claude Manzagol, Flavia Martinelli and Erica Schoenberger, Eike Schamp and Pierre Veltz were presented at this meeting. The final versions of the chapters were submitted between October 1989 and May 1990.

Once the volume had been planned and its contents agreed, Mick Dunford assumed most of the responsibilities for the editorial work, the revision of the chapters, and the preparation and submission of the manuscript to the publishers.

Giacomo Becattini, Stefan Krätke and Claude Manzagol prepared initial draft translations of their chapters which Mick Dunford corrected. Mick Dunford and Jenny Money translated the chapters by Paul Claval and Isabelle Geneau de Lamarlière from French, while Mick Dunford translated the chapters by Pierre Beckouche, Benjamin Coriat, Danièle Leborgne and Alain Lipietz, Jacques Malézieux, and Pierre Veltz from French, the chapter by Eike Schamp from German, and the chapter by Gioacchino Garofoli from Italian. All the authors provided helpful comments on draft translations of their chapters.

Gioacchino Garofoli, Grigoris Kafkalas and Diane Perrons read the introduction and conclusion and made many useful suggestions which we tried to incorporate in the final drafts. Susan Rowland of the University of Sussex Geography Laboratory produced all the illustrations and diagrams. In this work she showed remarkable initiative and imagination.

We are very grateful to the contributors not just for the chapters they have produced but also for their other stimulating contributions to the debates addressed in this collection. We would also like to acknowledge our debts to the CRIA and the Département de Géographie at the Université de Panthéon-Sorbonne and the School of European Studies at the University of Sussex for the stimulating academic environments in which our work was done. We would finally like to thank Iain Stevenson Andrée Blakemore, and Vanessa Harwood at Belhaven Press for their help and support in the production of the book itself.

G.B.B. and M.F.D

Part One: Introduction: Industrial change and regional development

1 Structural change and the spatial organisation of the productive system: an introduction

Georges Benko and Mick Dunford

1.1 The economic crisis, technological change and long cycles.

In the 1950s and 1960s economic growth accelerated relative to earlier trends in twentieth-century economic development. In the 'managed economies' of the West, in which national governments deployed sophisticated Keynesian strategies of macroeconomic management, economic crises were considered a thing of the past. Yet in 1974 the rate of growth slowed down, and rates of inflation and unemployment increased. All European countries were affected, even though there were significant differences in their economic situations. At first official reactions suggested that few difficulties stood in the way of renewed growth. For example, the majority of the authors of the McCracken report, commissioned by the Organisation for Economic Cooperation and Development (OECD), attributed the slowdown to the adverse expectations of economic actors, and argued that 'there is no fundamental reason' why, in more favourable circumstances and with improved policies, [these expectations] cannot be reversed'.

With the passage of time, however, growth was not restored. The economic orthodoxies that implied that it would were thrown into question, and a host of alternative interpretations of events were advanced. Some neoclassical writers identified the difficulties with market imperfections. These imperfections were thought to interfere with market equilibria and to disrupt growth which in neoclassical models are considered the natural outcome of rational individual behaviour in market economies. In particular the existence of irrational expectations on the part of consumers and wage earners, insufficient information, and the interference with market mechanisms associated with the actions of monopolies, trade unions, interest groups and governments were held to prevent markets from working. There was, in short, a lack of correspondence between neoclassical models of market economies and the actual structures of advanced industrial economies, and what was wrong was not the model but the real world.

From this diagnosis emerged the neo-liberal economic strategies that, in conservative, centrist or social-democratic forms, superseded the strategies of Keynesian welfare states in almost all countries. What was required, according to these views, was a programme of reforms that made economies closer to the idealisations of market models. Included were a range of measures whose character varied from one country to another: deregulation of monopolies, privatisation, legislation to limit the scope and effectiveness of trade-union action, and the commodification of welfare.

To account for the persistence of the crisis and its characteristics many other ideas and arguments were also put forward. Included were various theories of disequilibrium and post-Keynesian models. There was a revival of Marxist-oriented applied work concerned with the function of crises in the dynamic adjustment of capitalist economies and the role of the rate of profit as the key determinant of their development. In addition various theories of structural change were developed. Within the latter group fell two sets of explanations. The first was made up of Schumpeterian and neo-Schumpeterian views. The second comprised theories of regulation: 'les crises structurelles sont de retour', said Robert Boyer in his recent survey of theories of regulation, 'et les théories de régulation sont conçues pour en rendre compte' (Boyer 1986, page 8).[1]

1.1.1 Structural and technological change

In the 1960s and 1970s there were persistent sectoral differences in the rates of growth of output and productivity and in the rates of change of employment and prices. Some industries had rates that were two or three times the average, and others half the average. Over time, therefore, the shares of different industries in output and employment changed. These differences were closely related with changes in product and process technologies but were explained in two different ways. In the view of Kaldor (1966) the key lay in differences in the rate of growth of demand facing different industries, which led to differences in the rates of growth of output and, due to scale economies and the use of new generations of equipment, productivity. For Salter (1966), on the other hand, technical change was the cause of productivity growth, changes in the relative prices of goods and services, changes in demand, and changes in output. At the same time growth was spatially and temporally uneven. There were persistent differences in regional growth rates which were themselves connected with these structural changes (see Kaldor 1970 and Dunford 1988). In addition there were economic cycles, but the cycles were of limited amplitude, and the underlying trend was positive.

The depth of the 1970s and 1980s recession led some economists to rediscover the theories of long cycles in capitalist development developed in the inter-war years. Indeed the longer the slowdown continued, the more it resembled the long wave downswings of the 1830s, 1880s and 1930s, which were all periods of severe structural crisis and structural change in all of the world's market economies. In these periods some industries declined, while

Table 1.1 The growth of real output over the long swings.

Long swing	Years	Average annual percentage rate of growth of real output				
		United States	United Kingdom	Germany	France	Weighted average
IIA	1846-1878	4.2	2.2	2.5	1.3	2.8
IIB	1878-1894	3.7	1.7	2.3	0.9	2.6
IIIA	1894-1914	3.8	2.1	2.5	1.5	3.0
IIIB	1914-1938	2.1	1.1	2.9	1.0	2.0
IVA	1938-1970	4.0	2.4	3.8	3.7	3.8

Source: Gordon, Reich and Edwards 1982

others revealed a potential for dynamic growth. Unemployment levels were high, and divergent projects for fundamental institutional change coexisted. These crises varied in length but none lasted less than two decades. In between there were periods of relative prosperity and growth (see Table 1.1, which shows that with the exception of inter-war Germany the direction of change is the one which supports the long wave interpretation, and also Coombs, Saviotti and Walsh 1987).

These fifty-five year cycles, on which shorter (Kitchin, Juglar, Kuznets) cycles are superimposed, were named after the Russian economist, Kondratieff, who discovered them. In Konratieff's work these cycles were observed in analyses of commodity price movements rather than real indicators of economic activity. The causes were identified as cyclical movements in long-term fixed capital formation (major infrastructures such as railways and canals), which were themselves connected with cycles in the availability of investment funds (see Marshall 1987, pp. 20–5).

1.1.2 Schumpeterian and neo-Schumpeterian explanations of long waves

In his classic 1939 study of *Business Cycles* Schumpeter presented a multi-cyclical model of industrial capitalism and argued that its long-run development is characterised by fifty-five year waves of accelerated and decelerated growth. Schumpeter distinguished three waves: the 'Industrial Revolution Kondratieff' (1787–1842), the 'Bourgeois (or Railway) Kondratieff' (1843–1897), and the 'Neo-mercantilist Kondratieff' (1898–). In the view of Schumpeter each of the Kondratieff upswings were connected with the emergence and rapid expansion of new industries which were initiated when capitalist entrepreneurs turned inventions (which were considered exogenous) into innovations. Innovations offer monopoly profits and attract imitators and improvers. In a wave of entrepreneurial fever the innovations diffuse, the demand for related goods and services increases, and incomes increase in a wave of expansion, but surplus profits disappear due to increased competition. In the end the innovative growth impulses are exhausted, the confidence of entrepreneurs declines, and a downswing occurs. Schumpeter characterised this cyclical course of capitalist development as a process of 'creative destruction'.

Schumpeter's theoretical insights have stimulated an intense debate. If correct these ideas would have a major impact on the analysis of long-run economic growth. Whether or not the mechanisms he identified can generate long-term cyclical fluctuations in macroeconomic variables depends, however, on one of two factors. Either some innovations must be so large and discontinuous as to generate prolonged cycles. Major infrastructural investments with large multiplier effects may fall in this category. Alternatively innovations must occur in clusters connected perhaps with the establishment of new industries and technologies.

Schumpeter himself believed that clusters of innovations occurred. In the mid-1970s his ideas were given a new impetus when Mensch (1975) presented lists of innovations for various periods in the nineteenth and twentieth centuries and showed that these innovations were clustered in the deepest parts of long wave depressions. Mensch argued that his data showed a depression-trigger effect on innovation. In more recent research Kleinknecht (1990) showed that bunches or clusters occur in broader waves of major innovations in the downswing and in the early upswing phases of long waves.

The other principal neo-Schumpeterian explanation was put forward by Freeman, Clark and Soete (1982). What they proposed was a different causal explanation. In the first place it is not the number of separate innovations that matters but the interrelationships of innovations in technological systems that involve substantial inter-product and inter-process linkages. Several kinds of innovation can be identified (see Freeman 1988, pp. 9–11). Incremental innovations which produce a continuous flow of modifications to existing products and processes can be differentiated from radical innovations which involve qualitative shifts: examples of the latter include the development of nuclear reactors for electricity generation or the changeover from cotton to nylon. Incremental and radical innovations can occur in relative isolation. But where a constellation of technically and economically interrelated radical innovations that affect whole industrial sectors occurs, Freeman speaks of change in a 'technology system', and where changes in technology systems have pervasive effects on the whole of economic life and involve major changes in the capital stock and skill profile of the population, following Perez, he speaks of new 'techno-economic paradigms'. A new techno-economic paradigm is a set of best-practice rules and methods chosen from a range of technically feasible combinations of innovations. The diffusion of steam and electric power are historic examples, and innovations in microelectronics and computers a contemporary one. Second, it is the existence of clusters in the *diffusion* of innovations rather than clusters of innovations that is the critical cause of the upswing.

These ideas do offer significant insights into the development of capitalist societies. It leads to an interpretation of the post-war boom, for example, as 'the simultaneous explosive growth of several major new technologies and industries, particularly electronics, synthetic materials, drugs, oil and petro-chemicals, and (especially in Europe and Japan) consumer durables and vehicles' (Freeman, Clark and Soete 1982, p. 20), and to the view that one of the central factors shaping the events of the 1970s and 1980s is the development of information and communications technologies. At the same time the causal connections between technical change, structural change and economic growth help explain employment change at national and regional levels.

There is however a need to explain why new products and processes and new technology systems emerge at particular moments, why a new set of innovations do not occur as soon as a technological system matures, and why structural adjustment is so drawn out. Indeed one of the central difficulties with Schumpeter's concept of creative destruction is that it implies that the devaluation of old industries and products and a wave of investments in new technical and organisational innovations is automatic: a 'hidden hand' will lead to a way out of the crisis. The radical uncertainties that actors face at present, as well as the experience of earlier crises, suggest that the situation is far more complex.

To start to develop answers to some of these questions Freeman and Perez have argued that in years of crisis there is a mismatch between new technological developments and institutional and social structures (skill structures, management practices, industrial relations). The extent of the mismatch differs from one nation to another, with the result that some economies are far more successful than others. What results is a concern with institutional innovation which leads to some convergence of neo-Schumpeterian perspectives with theories of regulation and indeed with Marxist perspectives which focus in an immediate sense on long-run profit rates and in a more abstract sense on the dialectic of the forces and relations of production. Neo-Schumpeterian (and some Marxist) views tend however to be more deterministic than regulation approaches in so far as it is technological change that in the last instance determines institutional structures.

1.2 Theories of regulation

Theories of regulation were developed to explain processes of socio-economic development that exhibit significant spatial and historical variations. What, it is asked, lies at the root of the movement from regular growth to economic instability and stagnation? Why do phases of growth and crises assume different intensities and characteristics in different places, and why do phases of growth and crisis differ in character from one historical epoch to another?

In these theories capitalist development is viewed as a succession of phases of regular macroeconomic development/regimes of accumulation punctuated by crises as one order breaks down and new ones are established. The development of a regime of accumulation is a result of changes in the organisation of the forces of production/new technological trajectories and their correspondence with the evolution of social relations/modes of regulation and associated hegemonic structures (see Figure 1.1), while structural crises occur either when the stable reproduction of social relations does not take place, when models of development exhaust their potential, or when the development of the forces and relations of production are inconsistent.

A regime of accumulation is a set of regular dynamic relationships between (1) the valorisation and accumulation of capital, (2) the articulation of capitalist and non-capitalist sectors, (3) the distribution of income which

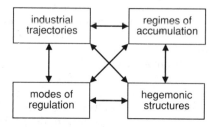

Figure 1.1 Theories of regulation: the key concepts

shapes the reproduction of different classes and social groups, and (4) the composition of social demand and consumption. While these regular relationships prevail, accumulation can proceed in a relatively coherent way, and the disequilibria that it constantly generates can be absorbed or put off (see Boyer 1986). Several schematic regimes of accumulation can be identified. In the nineteenth century a regime of extensive accumulation gave way to a regime involving a combination of extensive and intensive accumulation in which the investment of constant capital including investments in iron and steel, railway construction, and shipbuilding itself validated the growth of department 1. In the 1930s and after the Second World War in particular it gave way to a regime of intensive accumulation centred on the articulation of mass production and mass consumption (see Aglietta 1979, pp. 66–72).

There is a certain correspondence with neo-Schumpeterian views in so far as these regimes of accumulation can be linked with successive industrial paradigms or industrial trajectories (see, for example, Coriat's chapter in this volume). The emphasis is placed however more on transformations in the process of labour, the organisation of work, and the structure and distribution of skills (manufacture, mechanisation, scientific management or Taylorism, automation, and systemofacture) than on the development of new materials, products and sectors.

The central point of theories of regulation lies however in their emphasis upon the role of a mode of regulation. A mode of regulation denotes the concrete modes of expression of the fundamental social relations within which the strategies and actions of individuals and groups unfold. These social relations divide individuals and social groups and generate social rivalries, conflicts and contradictions. A mode of regulation is a set of social institutions or structural forms that codify these fundamental social relations and give a contingent material expression to social conflicts. These structural forms allow strategic conduct that expresses the underlying social contradictions. What is important about them however is that at the same time these structural forms temporarily transform these contradictions into simple differences and mediate, normalise, and regulate them (Aglietta 1979). In phases when these normalising tendencies prevail, and when the dynamic reproduction of social relations allows and supports the development of the forces of production, stable processes of economic reproduction occur.

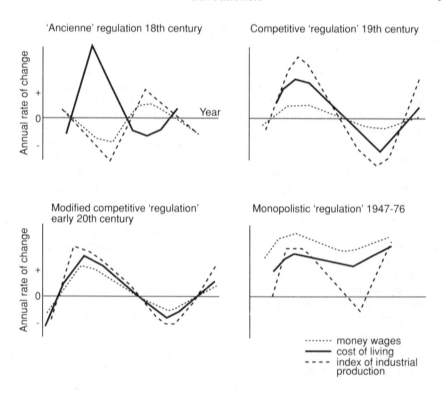

Figure 1.2 Stylised historical models of the regulation of employment and wages

Source: Boyer 1978

In capitalist societies the major structural forms identified are the monetary system, the wage relation, modes of competition and inter-firm relations, and the character and role of the state. The wage/labour relation, for example, has assumed very different forms in the course of capitalist development: a competitive regulation with very limited working-class consumption of capitalist commodities, a Taylorist regulation in which work was transformed without a commensurate change in working-class life styles, and a Fordist regulation in which new norms of consumption emerged in parallel with new norms of production (see Boyer 1986, pp. 49–50, and Figure 1.2).

A regime of accumulation is therefore the macroeconomic result of the operation of a mode of regulation within the context of a particular mode of industrialisation. The model of post-war development in western countries which is called Fordism is an example.

At the root of the Fordist development model was a revolution in the conditions of production and work (Taylorism and Fordism as principles of work organisation) in the consumer goods department (see Figure 1.3). As a result productivity increased. With increases in productivity went increases in the real incomes of the middle class, manual workers, clerical and shop workers, farmers and so on. Increased incomes resulted in a growth in the size of the market for consumer goods, a revolution in ways of life, and additional investment and growth in the consumer goods department. Intersecting this first virtuous circle was therefore a second. Increased investment in the consumer goods department led to increased orders for the capital goods department, while new machines and methods helped maintain a high rate of profit and accumulation. The view of Boyer is that these virtuous circles were dependent upon new monopolistic mechanisms of wage determination (see Figure 1.2). After the Second World War the rate of growth of real wages accelerated. Whether output increased or decreased, nominal wages went up, as did the cost of living, while increases in real wages matched the rate of productivity growth. Income growth was, in other words, made regular and less dependent on fluctuations in economic activity. The growth in the size of the wage-earning class and of indirect wages and transfer payments were further factors that contributed to this result, while new credit arrangements facilitated the acquisition of durable goods. The substitution of monopolistic for competitive mechanisms (which in the 1970s and 1980s were called 'rigidities') was therefore conducive to growth and one of the main reasons why the stagnation of the 1930s did not recur. At high rates of output growth the expansion of markets matched the growth of production capacities, as *ex ante* consumption and investment were equal to output for the economy as a whole and for its major sectors.

1.3 The crisis of Fordism

Towards the end of the 1960s and in the early 1970s growth slowed down. One influential account of the end of growth attributed it to the breakdown of mass production (Piore and Sabel 1984, pp. 165–93). In their view the demand for mass-produced goods stagnated as markets in advanced countries were, it was argued, saturated, while consumers sought goods that were more diversified and had a higher design content. In this situation smaller and more flexible specialised enterprises that made more diversified goods and services and that employed skilled craft workers started to gain a competitive edge and offered the prospect of a new model of development called 'flexible specialisation'.

Theories of regulation, on the other hand, are associated with a different view that identifies two major factors: (1) a supply-side crisis reflected in differential reductions in the rate of profit and rooted not in market conditions but in the system of value production and workers' struggles, and (2) a demand-side crisis which resulted from the internationalisation of economic life (as a result of the search for economies of scale) and the consequent weakening of the link between national growth and national demand management, and which made its mark with the rise of monetarism.

1.4 From Fordism to flexible accumulation?

In these phases of crisis, developments in the forces and relations of production are out of step, instabilities predominate, and a transformational TimeSpace

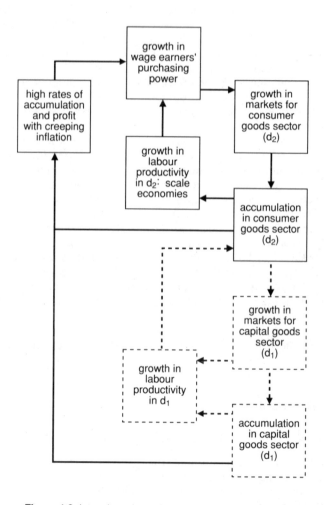

Figure 1.3 Intensive accumulation: the two virtuous cycles

exists in which social struggles determine new social and economic orders (see Wallerstein 1988). The directions in which social relations and the use of new technologies evolve and in which the strategies which are adopted depend on the struggles between different social and political forces and on the ways in which the objective laws of development of the prevailing social order operate in different technological, social and political contexts. With the breakdown of Fordism these directions of change were altered. In the 1960s attempts to promote structural change, increase the rate of adjustment to changes in economic conditions, and accelerate innovation were often centred around economic planning, the development of the public sector and the welfare state. In the late 1970s and 1980s, however, a different view assumed a dominant position in most advanced countries: a way out of the crisis required, it was argued, an attack on 'rigidities', deregulation, greater 'flexibility' and increased reliance on the market. (The goal was, in other words, to dismantle the institutions and the mode of regulation that were at the root of the post-war boom). At the same time some critical writers argued that increased flexibility is a fundamental characteristic of the post-Fordist era and went so fast as to identify a 'flexible' regime of accumulation.

In order to evaluate these judgements there is, first of all, a need to identify, differentiate and explain the trends in economic, social and spatial organisation that followed from the attack on rigidities and the search for greater flexibility. The trend towards increased flexibility is identified in the areas of production methods, employment contracts, wage determination, inter-firm relations and so on. Second, the extent to which these different developments are conjunctural or secular requires attention. Are some of these developments conservative and defensive reactions to the difficulties of accumulation and growth in the 1970s and 1980s? Can decentralised strategies and the pursuit of frequently myopic objectives lead to a new mode of regulation? Are there reasons for thinking that processes of innovation and competition which led at first to significant decentralisation will lead in the end to a further concentration and centralisation of capital? Is innovation and an acceleration in the development and use of new technologies consistent with a reinstitutionalisation of economic and social relations?

Some of these questions are considered in some detail in subsequent chapters. In the rest of this section our goal is to distinguish the different meanings of the word 'flexibility'.

1.4.1 Types of flexibility

1.4.1.1 Flexible production technologies

In the sphere of production and the process of labour the use of new technologies is reflected in the development and diffusion of machines and machine systems that are more flexible. With the development of electronics and information technologies, specialised machines (and specialised workers) can be replaced with machines that can perform a variety of different operations, can be quickly switched from one to another, are intelligent, and are computer-controlled and programmable: examples include CNC machines, CAD-CAM equipment, Flexible Manufacturing Systems, Electonic Data Interchange and computerised typesetting equipment, digital telephone exchanges and so on. (The speed and diffusion of these technologies is, it should be noted, uneven between and within sectors.) What is more, production can be controlled as it occurs: the allocation of work between work stations can be managed in real-time, as can the management of inventories and the scheduling of production. Technological flexibility therefore means that a machine's output (mix of products, design of products and volumes) can be varied and adapted to changes in the volume and composition of demand. In these special conditions of 'joint production' the life cycle of a machine can be delinked from the life cycle of a product, and (as long as overall demand is adequate) economies of scope[2] increase, with the result that the risks of investment are significantly reduced. At the same time the distribution of work can be varied in accordance with the progress of work on each machine, and so the intensity of use of the different machines in a workshop can be increased.

Whether these new technologies involve increased or reduced economies of scale is not clear a priori. Economies of scale exist when increases in output result in lower average costs. Several factors can produce this result. One is the existence of increasing returns to scale: doubling all inputs more than doubles output. Increasing returns are important when there are *indivisible* (single or multi-stage) processes of production with different unit levels and where large-scale processes are more productive. Another cause is the existence of high fixed costs, which, it should be added, may be a precondition for the introduction and use of economies of scope equipment.

1.4.1.2 Flexible industrial structures

In the past mass-production methods, available only when output was large, were more efficient than the best available processes for producing small levels of output. (In 1913, as Gartman (1979, pp. 201–2) shows, the stationary assembly of a chassis in the Ford Motor Company took 12 hours 28 minutes, whereas in 1914 after the introduction of a mechanical assembly line it required 1 hour 30 minutes.) Yet in most large industrial establishments and industrial firms what existed were multi-stage processes in which one part of the total process required inputs produced in another subprocess. In some cases the integrated process requires less of one input and is therefore a new process. An example is steel production where each stage involves reheating, if the processes are separated, and the integrated process requires less energy for heat. In most cases, however, multi-stage processes were just additions of separate operations. The organisational structure of production depends in part on the extent to which these different processes are integrated vertically within hierarchical organisations or are carried out by firms that are separated from one another in a *social division of labour*.

Scott has argued that the organisational structure of production depends on the relative weight of scale and scope effects, and has claimed that

as vertical disintegration (the social division of labour) moves forward, so production systems become steadily more externalised and hence, in organisational terms, more flexible. Vertical integration, by contrast, signifies increasing organisational inflexibility for it puts limits on the possibilities for combination and recombination of individual production processes.

(Scott 1988, page 25)

(Whether Scott is correct or not depends on whether or not large organisations are inherently inflexible. If the different parts of the organisation had greater autonomy and independence the combinatorial possibilities would increase.)

In the 1970s and 1980s average plant size fell in part as a result of the introduction of new productivity-increasing technologies and the decentralisation of production from larger to smaller firms. Average firm size also fell, but the causal mechanisms were very diverse: a significant wave of new firm formation occurred, and small and medium- sized firms were very dynamic. Increases in the numbers of small firms were however a product of a wide range of processes. Included were: (1) the decentralisation of functions such as the manufacture of components or modules or service activities from large firms to small and medium-sized dependent subcontractors, (2) the emergence of the industrial districts centred on networks of small and medium-sized firms, (3) the spin-off of small high-tech firms from larger research, development and design establishments, (4) the development of small and medium-size entrepreneurs and enterprises whose goal was the valorisation of local resources, (5) the development of small firms in areas of industrial decline and sectors where entry is easy as laid-off workers look for alternative sources of livelihood, (6) organised subcontracting to sweatshops and homeworkers, and (7) the survival in the interstices of underdeveloped societies of traditional artisans dependent on localised monopolistic markets.

The extent of the shift in the size distribution of firms varies however with the indicator used. The concentration of output is greater than that of employment. What is more, small output volumes often count against firms. On the one hand, the development of just-in-time systems and the need for increased quality control are associated with the substitution of one larger subcontractor for many smaller ones. On the other, a narrow range and small volume of output limits a firm's options and makes it difficult to sustain support services such as marketing and quality control on which the acquisition of contracts and adjustment depend.

1.4.1.3 The structure of capital

Scott's framework of analysis (which highlights the constantly changing organisational structure of production and the relations (market/non-market, material/immaterial, formal/informal) between industrial firms, service companies, research centres, groups and small and medium-size firms) has played a major role in recent analyses of new industrial spaces. What it underemphasises however is the structure of control and the financial role of groups in particular. A group is a collection of companies linked via hierarchical financial holdings under a decision-making centre — a parent company. It is the latter which develops global economic (productive and commercial) strategies on the one hand and financial strategies involving mergers, takeovers, and the acquisition and disposal of shareholdings on the other. All of these actions can be reversed. As financial units, as centres of economic control, and as centres of value production and appropriation, groups, they are therefore very flexible.

What is more, the ease of reallocation of financial assets and the greater risk associated with investments in physical assets are further factors shaping the decisions as to whether a firm should produce goods itself or purchase them from an independent supplier: strategies of fixed cost and risk reduction rooted in the rigidities of long-term and large-scale fixed capital investments therefore play a significant role in shaping processes of disintegration and productive decentralisation. In this case, however, strategies of decentralisation and the associated risk-averseness of the controllers of investment funds limit the fixed investments on which the realisation of the potential of the new technologies depends.

Increases in the share of banking capital and of other rentier and speculative incomes in aggregate surplus-value are related phenomena. At the same time the economic environment in which these fractions of capital operated was transformed as a result of the globalisation of the financial system and almost instantaneous transfers of money capital around the world's major financial centres. The increase in the role of these more fluid and flexible kinds of capital and the ease with which money can be moved around have played a significant part in the increase in economic instability and the rapidly oscillating fortunes of different parts of the globe (see Harvey 1989, pp. 160–72, and Swyngedouw 1989).

1.4.1.4 Flexible work practices

The debate about flexibility has focused in the main on work and employment relations. Two main kinds of flexibility are involved of which one concerns the organisation of work (functional flexibility) and one the market for labour (numerical flexibility). (On this distinction see Atkinson 1984, pp. 11–19 and Figure 1.4.)

Functional flexibility refers to the capacity of a firm to adjust the tasks performed by the workers it employs according to changes in demand, technology or marketing policy. This kind of flexibility is also associated with the development of 'new production concepts' (Mathews 1989) and new models of organisation that involve reliance on a group of skilled polyvalent core workers with full-time permanent status, as it is on these workers that the continuity of production and the maintenance of equipment often depends. These core workers are expected to be adaptable, flexible and if necessary geographically mobile.

1.4.1.5 Labour market flexibility

Numerical flexibility refers to the ease and speed with which firms can adjust the number of workers employed and the aggregate wage bill in line with fluctuations in demand and is associated with variations in the numbers of peripheral workers. Included in the peripheral category are two groups of people: (1) workers employed by subcontractors, specialised self-employed workers, and staff supplied by temporary employment agencies, and (2) the firm's own employees who do not have career status and can be laid off or re-employed according to economic conditions, who have temporary employment contracts or are part-time or casual staff, and who have jobs with high turnover rates where the numbers employed can easily be reduced by a policy of non-replacement.

In all capitalist countries there have in recent years been increases in the segmentation and polarisation of the working population (see, for example, Hakim 1990). Strategies of numerical flexibility are one of the causes of these trends, while increased functional flexibility and upskilling will have the same

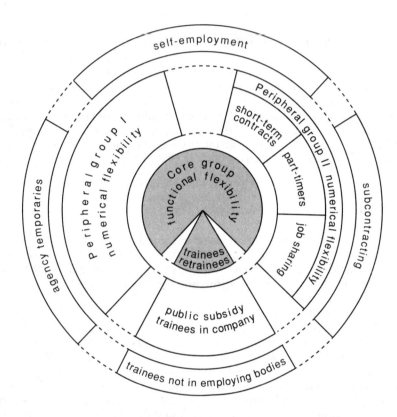

Figure 1.4 The flexible firm

Source: Alkinson 1984

effect unless they coexist with social and economic measures designed to allow all workers access to upgraded jobs. As a result the existence and the relative sizes of the different poles of a dual society will depend very much upon the goals, organisation and strength of trade union and other organisations defending the interests of wage earners as well as on the employers definitions of their own interests. (As Hakim (1990) shows, in Europe there are significant differences among countries that also reflect differences in the scope and extent of employment and labour laws.)

Strategies of functional and numerical employment flexibility are also associated with new wage structures. Wage flexibility and an individualisation of wages are reflected, for example, in attempts to establish a structure of wages and salaries that reflects the amount and type of work and the performance of each worker: one formula, for example, is the 'salaire trînome' in which a worker's pay depends on individual merit, the social minimum and the firm's results. In these circumstances inequalities in earnings between core sector workers and a marginalised population, dependent on irregular legal and illegal work and welfare, tend to widen (see Bluestone and Harrison 1988).

1.4.1.6 Modes of consumption

Changes in income distribution were reflected in an accentuation of inequalities and differences in consumption patterns and lifestyles. These inequalities stemmed from two major processes. One was the increase in income differentials itself: some households were able to consume exclusive commodities and sophisticated services, while others were forced to accept reduced standards of living, intensified 'consumption work' and informal self-production. At the same time there were parallel changes in household structures (including an increase in the number and a fall in the average size of households) that also contributed to the differentiation and pluralisation of lifestyles. The second was the increase in product differentiation on the one hand and the acceleration of product innovation and a shortening of product life cycles on the other. In these conditions 'the relatively stable aesthetic of Fordist modernism has given way to all the ferment, instability and fleeting qualities of a post-modernist aesthetic that celebrates difference, ephemerality, spectacle, fashion and the commodification of cultural forms' (Harvey 1989, p. 156).

1.4.1.7 Minimal state intervention

In the 1970s welfare state expenditure reached unprecedented historical levels. To finance this expenditure states had to choose levels of taxation, borrowing and deficit financing which capitalist interests and some sections of the populations of advanced countries were not prepared to accept. Towards the end of the decade neo-liberal forces mobilised sufficient support for the election of governments with programmes that included reductions in state intervention. Attempts were then made to accelerate cuts in public spending and moves in the direction of lower levels of state economic and social intervention (but not of defence- and law-and-order-related activities). Strategies of privatisation and contracting out of public sector activities were actively pursued as capitalist interests sought out new domains for the valorisation of capital. The logic of social policy was modified with the replacement of principles of welfare and of collective guarantees on behalf of the worse-off members of society with insurance, in which benefits would depend on an individual's ability to pay. Social benefits were increasingly targeted. Attempts were made to deregulate economic activities, and social and fiscal obligations and payments of private actors were reduced.

1.4.2 Ambiguities in the concept of flexibility

In this section we have insisted on the multi-dimensional character of flexibility, the differences in the content of the word flexibility, and the ambiguities associated with it. While some of the different types of flexibility (flexible production, flexible work practices, flexible employment, flexible wages, flexible social security arrangements, flexible inter-firm relations, flexible exchange rates) are inconsistent, the number of potential combinations and the specific forms flexibility can assume are very large. The existence of these differences makes the identification of particular models of flexibility premature. What is more, the ambiguities that surround the criteria of dominance make it difficult to demonstrate whether or not flexible models of development (or Fordism as an industrial model) characterise a social and economic order or an era. Is the relevant criterion the existence of dominant economic activities (measured in terms of value added) and of dominant actual employment practices, or of economic activities that are large and have propulsive effects, or of ideologically dominant visions of social and economic organisation?

There is secondly a need to distinguish between means, ends and consequences. As Boyer (1988, pp. 227–9) has pointed out, one of the aims of flexibility (which can be viewed as the speed of response of an economic system to disturbances or external shocks) is to increase its overall stability. It is important to recall that the need to respond depends on the magnitude and frequency of the disturbances. In addition there is a need to explain how rigidities do or do not affect other variables, and to show that the removal of rigidities will not create new endogenous disturbances.

In the 1970s and 1980s a wide range of imbalances and instabilities have characterised the development of the capitalist world. Of these some are connected with contradictions between the micro- and macroeconomic levels. Some of the 'schemes for introducing flexibility have sometimes become a euphemism for down-grading most of the rights of wage-earners' (Boyer 1988, p. 229). Yet 'considerable microeconomic flexibility can go hand in hand with notable macroeconomic rigidity... maximum flexibility is not [therefore] always the optimum' (Boyer 1988, p. 229). What Boyer shows is that while flexibility may make microeconomic sense for an individual firm and in some cases for a nation, it has ambiguous effects on productivity and effective demand, and it is not always the best solution for all countries. 'In a nutshell,' says Boyer (1988, p. 251), 'the pursuit of flexibility, a rational response to the crisis, may actually exacerbate it, by undermining international trade.' It seems therefore that the question as to whether or not the capitalist world will discover a stable new model of long-run development remains to be settled.

1.5 The new industrial space

In geography the discussion about Fordism and its crisis, about the development of information and communication technologies, and about the role of principles of flexibility in the quest for a way out of crisis gave rise to a vigorous debate about the role of paradigm shifts in shaping the economic, urban and regional geography of advanced countries. Out of this debate emerged the concepts of new industrial spaces and of regimes of flexible accumulation and the construction of post-Weberian theories of industrial location, while Sabel (1989) has identified the model of flexible specialisation with the re-emergence of integrated regional economies.

1.5.1 Theories of location

The study of the mechanisms that determine the location of economic activities has always been one of the major concerns of economic geography. In the 1970s these studies had to come to grips with the deindustrialisation of old industrial areas and industrial cities, the growth of services, the development of new production concepts and sectors, and new trends in the location of economic activities.

In line with established theories of location initial attempts to explain the geography of economic activities focused on location factors. What factors, it was asked, explain the attractiveness of areas of relative growth, the unattractiveness of areas of relative decline, and the location of particular establishments?

To provide a complete account, however, attention must also be paid to what is happening to industry itself (see Massey 1979 and Massey and Meegan 1982, where this approach was elaborated; see also Dunford 1977). The question as to where a plant is located depends on the structural character of the plant, while its characteristics are in part a consequence of its insertion into the economic and social division of space. Attention must therefore also be paid to the technological and economic characteristics and historical specificity of the industrialisation process on the one hand and the dynamics of firms and industries on the other.

In the 1970s these ideas led to new approaches. (The starting point was in some ways similar to that of product life cycle approaches to industrial location, but the view of the central processes of economic change was far wider.) In this work on 'industrial restructuring' and the 'spatial division of labour' several interconnected questions were posed: how is the structure of industry changing as employers adapt to changing market and competitive conditions, what determines which establishments survive and which close, what are the locational requirements and implications of new technologies and of restructured work and employment relations, and what impact do geographical conditions have on competitiveness? Quite clearly this approach shares the concerns of the location factor approach. Its distinctiveness, however, lies in the fact that it integrates them within a broader theoretical perspective and widens them: development is not just quantitative but depends on the social complexion of places. Within this framework, moreover, factors are considered interdependent rather than independent: for example, an enterprise that decides to introduce new technologies may seek regional aid to finance new investments, while the new methods of production may allow it to dispense with the old skills of unionised workers and recruit a new workforce. In this case the various location factors are interrelated and interdependent.

The third major approach focused not on individual location factors or on the location of industries and service activities but on the characteristics of places, of innovative milieux (Perrin 1989) and of territorial complexes of innovation (Stöhr 1986) viewed as complex and interdependent combinations of variables (local resources, knowledge, skill etc.), and on the factors which made some places more innovative and dynamic than others.

As with the location factors approach, however, insufficient attention was paid to the evolution of the productive system itself. The development of the notion of geographical industrialisation involves an attempt to move in this direction (see Storper and Walker 1990, pp. 125–52). On the one hand, territorial production complexes are seen as modes of industrial organisation that contribute in an active and powerful way to the dynamics of industrialisation. On the other, industrial structure and industrial organisation are viewed as short-lived and ever-changing results of a dynamic process of division and integration of labour and of creation and dissolution of establishments, firms and industries.

1.5.2 The geography of new industrial spaces

In the 1970s and 1980s there were significant shifts in the structure of the economic landscape. Quite dramatic structural changes occurred as the growth of some sectors slowed down or ended, and as new groups of growth sectors emerged. These differences in output growth rates along with differentials in productivity growth rates led to marked changes in the composition of employment. Variations in the competitiveness of economic activities in different regions led to differential rates of regional growth and an increase in spatial inequalities. Temporal instabilities were a cause of rapid changes in the rate and direction of development.

At some points there were tendencies to see these geographical shifts as involving a radical change of direction: a new regional and urban structure created in a new historical epoch. A phase of urbanisation and suburbanisation was giving way to a phase of counter-urbanisation, old industrial areas and industrial cities were in decline, and new industrial spaces had emerged.

In some ways these diagnoses identified significant trends. With the emergence of new growth sectors (in information and communications technologies, in designer industries, and in financial, management, legal and real estate services) and the greater competitiveness of some new industrial zones, one could identify: (1) areas centred on revitalised craft industries, (2) complexes of high-technology industries in areas such as Silicon Valley, Orange County and Route 128 in the United States and in many areas in Europe, and (3) metropolises with concentrations of producer services. Some of these activities exhibited strong agglomeration tendencies, and it was in these zones that some of the fastest rates of economic growth were recorded. Moreover in so far as differences in growth rates endure, the map of regional economic development is remade. At the same time, however, existing distributions exercise a strong inertial effect, new technologies can rejuvenate mature industries, the attractiveness of established centres is far from insignificant, and the scope for selective investment aimed at changing the structure and use of older areas is substantial.

Indeed in the case of the new industries of the information age one finds not just new high-tech developments in areas without significant previous industrial histories but also an integration of new activities into existing regional and urban structures. Zones of high-tech activities are often found, for example, in the suburban districts of metropolitan areas, in the gravitational fields of existing office centres, and in enclaves near users in old industrial cities (see Krätke's chapter in this volume).

What is also clear is that large metropolises are major nodes of physical and of computer and telecommunications networks, global centres of financial, commercial and management organisations concerned with the control of the valorisation and realisation of capital, and the focal points in a new 'space of flows' (see Castells 1989 and Part V of this volume). It is in these zones and in the complex hierarchical network of subordinate cities that surround them that service activities have expanded, and it is the differential development of these major cities that has played a major role in the creation of a new map of regional development.

1.5.3 The spatial organisation of IT industries

In order to explain the spatial logic of the information technology industries which are the leading edge of current capitalist development there is a need to draw on several of the sets of ideas identified in section 1.5.1: the sectoral and corporate logic of the new spatial division of labour and models of innovative milieux and geographical industrialisation (see Figure 1.5).

In the view of Castells (1989, pp. 71–6) the information dependence of IT industries implies the location of the information generation functions which command the chain of interdependencies in zones with high-quality scientific and technical labour and an innovative environment (leading universities, academic, government and corporate research and development centres, organisational synergies, sources of high-risk venture capital). At the same time as a producer of 'process-oriented devices' it is footloose and mobile, but its location must correspond with the spatial distribution of its users. In the third place the process of production of information-processing devices and equipment can be split into different stages of work with different labour requirements, while these stages can be located in different areas.

What results is, as Castells shows, a variety of spatial processes with a complex set of spatial outcomes. Included are (1) the development of high-level innovative milieux, (2) the dispersal of technical branch plants, (3) the offshore location of lower-level functions in areas with low production costs, (4) location inside the protected boundaries of major economic regions, (5) location in old industrial areas to exploit the 'mechatronics connection', and (6) with the decentralisation of some research and development and location near markets, the development of secondary milieux linked via interregional and international transport and computer networks. There is in short a dual process: the dynamic and uneven development of a socio-spatial division of labour within large groups and within strategic alliances among major corporations on the one hand, and the development around the nodes at which

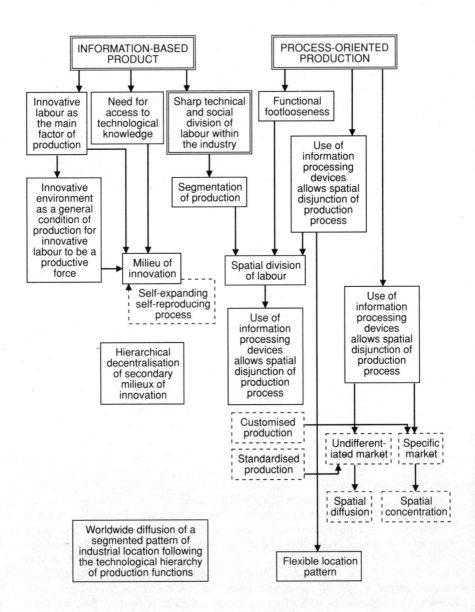

Figure 1.5 System of relationships between characteristics of IT industries and their spatial organisation

Source: Castells 1989

these groups locate of territorial clusters of activities and complex processes of territorial development on the other.

1.5.4 Capitalism in motion: social, economic and spatial change

In the world in which we live a technological revolution and a fundamental modification of the forces of production are transforming human work and life: with them have come remarkable increases in the productive capabilities of human societies and a dramatic compression of space and time (Harvey 1989). At the same time a structural crisis gave rise to attempts to restructure capitalist societies: a massive devaluation and restructuring of capital led to the reappearance of mass unemployment, the globalisation of economic life reduced the leverage of national governments and increased the commanding role of large corporations, and the attack on rigidities led to increases in social dualism and polarisation.

As we have suggested in this chapter, these restructuring processes were responses to structural challenges and were conditioned by the structural logic of a predominantly capitalist social order. The processes that were followed, however, were dependent on the economic, social and political conditions that prevailed in each country. There were therefore significant differences in the specific combinations of social relations that resulted and varied effects on the rate, character and quality of economic development and on the structure of space.

These processes of restructuring were also responses to the uncertainties and instabilities of the 1970s and 1980s : due to the risks of investing in fixed assets with specific uses and of offering long-term employment contracts there was a switch towards more liquid ways of holding wealth and a reduction in long-term commitments. These defensive reactions have shaped the development of new industrial spaces. However the polarisation that this course of action has induced and the suspicion that it is itself an obstacle to the creative use of the new technologies make the identification of alternative technological and social projects one of the goals of progressive social forces in the 1990s.

Notes

1. 'Structural crises are back, and theories of regulation were conceived to account for them.'
2. Economies of scope exist when the average costs of a multi-product firm are lower than the sum of the average costs of each product made separately. The development of multi-purpose machines and the existence of joint products gives economies of scope a special dimension. In the past economies of scope were said to exist when the integration of a range of different and separable processes within a firm reduced production costs (due to a fall in transaction costs that exceeded any consequent increase in organisation costs). The value of the concept lay therefore in the identification of the fact that the organisation of markets and market transactions is not costless.

Part Two: Social relations, industrial organisation and comparative economic development

2 Two social strategies in the production of new industrial spaces.[1]

Danièle Leborgne and Alain Lipietz

'Flexibility' — in many countries (in particular those in which the crisis of the industrial sector is most severe), and in many international reports (such as the ones produced by the Organisation for Economic Cooperation and Development), this word seems to be the key that is supposed to open the door to the world beyond the crisis. The 'flexibility' of machines, induced by the 'technological revolution', is invoked. It goes without saying that this technological flexibility 'must' be accompanied by 'flexibility' of wage contracts. One is enjoined to 'smash the old rigidities'. What is more, some theoreticians referring to approaches that use concepts of regimes of accumulation and modes of regulation forecast a 'regime of flexible accumulation' a regime that will without doubt beget flexible, post-Fordist and post-modern towns, and why not 'flexible' houses as well. The slum, the favella, are they not really an unchangeable fact of our times?

The buildings in Tokyo certainly have flexible foundations, to resist earthquakes. This flexibility is not the same as the flexibility of the slum. It is another kind of flexibility . . . The crisis of earlier models definitely calls for a 'change of direction'. But which direction? To this question regulation approaches do not provide a deterministic answer, and certainly not one that is determined by the 'technological revolution'.

They do show however that, in the crisis in which new technological possibilities intersect with a transformation of the international division of labour, specific *territories* (regions or nations) are already more successful than others. We shall try to identify some of the *social* characteristics of these successes and of these failures. We shall show that there are two main categories of policies leading to different results: *offensive flexibility and defensive flexibility*.

In the first section we shall summarise the analytical tools of the 'theory of regulation' and the analysis it provides of the crisis of the dominant model of the post-war period: Fordism.

In the second section we shall distinguish and characterise, in terms of industrial relations and forms of industrial organisation, three subgroups of ways out of the crisis of Fordism (all of which are 'flexible' but in different ways).

In the third section we shall identify three types of urban region, corresponding to these three models, and we shall determine what 'offensive flexibility' and 'defensive flexibility' mean.

2.1 Fordism and its crisis.

2.1.1 Basic concepts[2]

The reproduction of a commodity-producing capitalist economy is far from self-sustaining. In its development the conditions of production are transformed, as are the distribution of income and the preferences for various social uses of output. The evidence shows however that, over long periods, these transformations prove to be compatible, and that accumulation, economic growth, occurs without major disturbance. This kind of joint and compatible mode of transformation of the norms of production, distribution and use is called a *'regime of accumulation'*. This regime rests on general principles of work organisation and use of techniques that one might call a *technological paradigm.*

A regime of accumulation therefore refers to a recorded set of regular macroeconomic relationships. These regularities are themselves an invaluable guide for economic agents, in particular for investors. Nevertheless their initiatives continue to be threatened by a deep-rooted uncertainty about their future overall coherence. There is therefore a need for regulatory mechanisms. We shall call the collection of norms — whether implicit or explicit — of institutions, of compensatory mechanisms and of information systems, which constantly adjust the expectations and behaviour of individuals to the general logic of the regime of accumulation, *a mode of regulation.* These forms of regulation are concerned in particular with wage formation, the forms of inter-firm competition, and the mechanisms of money and credit creation.

But the establishment and consolidation of a mode of regulation are heavily dependent on the political sphere. In this sphere what matter are political and social struggles and agreements and *institutional compromises.* Social groups, defined by their conditions of daily existence, and in particular by the position they occupy in economic relations, do not in fact devote themselves to an endless struggle. No matter how wide the divergences in their interests and the inequalities in their conditions may be, over long periods of time these groups make up a nation in which power relations are perpetuated without major dispute. A stable system of relations of domination, of alliances, and of concessions among different social groups (dominant and subordinate) is called a *social bloc,* and a social bloc is *hegemonic* when it, in a more or less coercive manner, secures recognition of its plan of action as one that conforms with the interests of the great majority of the inhabitants of a 'territory'.

Inasmuch as the interests, whose consideration defines the issues at the centre of the consensus on which the hegemonic bloc is constructed and reproduced, are economic, a coherent triangle of relations between a 'hegemonic bloc', a 'regime of accumulation' and a 'mode of regulation' takes shape. The condition and the basis for the reproduction of a hegemonic bloc is clearly the existence of a regime of accumulation that is capable of producing the conditions required to satisfy social needs in conditions acceptable to the parties that belong to the bloc (including dominated groups). In its turn the mode of regulation (on which the realisation of a regime of accumulation depends) is no more than a set of routines, of what Bourdieu called 'habitus', and of compromises institutionalised in the very process of establishment of the bloc and which last only as long as the bloc itself supports them. We shall call this whole a *model of development*.

We have deliberately used the general term 'territory'. The question that arises is: in what geographical space is a unified model of development realised? We assume that three rough levels can be distinguished: regional, national and international (Lipietz 1977 and 1985a). The national level plays a central role as the hegemonic bloc is supported by the existence of the state, which ratifies and consolidates institutionalised compromises, asserts its monopoly of 'institutionalised violence', defends the currency, enforces legislation, and manages relations with other nations. But, as Gramsci showed when he introduced this concept, the hegemonic bloc can be *regionally* differentiated: it was not and is still not the same in the north as in the south of Italy, nor is it the same in the different states of Brasil or the United States.

In a symmetrical way to the case of regional hegemonic blocs, it is necessary to question the international compatibility of models of national development. In stable periods in the development of the world economy, an *international configuration* achieves this compatibility. It always involves the hegemony of a model of development adopted in one or several nation states which themselves are therefore considered hegemonic. This hegemony, based on the greater productive efficiency of their technological paradigm and the stability of their mode of regulation, is expressed not only in the advantages that dominant countries gain from international trade, but also in the rules that they are able to impose on what Keohane calls the 'international regime'.

2.1.2 The case of Fordism.

The dominant post-war model of development which shone forth from the Unites States is, after Gramsci, called 'Fordism'. As a regime of accumulation Fordism was the response that emerged at the end of the Second World War to the contradictions generated by the revolutions in the 'technological paradigm' that occurred in the first half of the twentieth century at the level of production forms, mainly in industry but also in the agricultural and service sectors: Taylorism and mechanisation.

Taylorist principles involve the fullest possible separation of the mental (research and development, design, and the 'scientific' organisation of work) and the manual aspects of work (unskilled operational tasks). To Taylorism

Fordism added the incorporation of the collective knowledge of the workforce into the machine system itself. To give an illustration, Fordism sets the 'organisation and methods office' against the 'assembly line'. The very rapid productivity gains that result raise the problem of effective demand in a particularly acute manner. The Fordist regime of accumulation is character- ised by not only a rapid increase in the volume of investment per head but also by a growth in per capita consumption. The expansion of these two outlets provides, internally within each nation, a counterpart for the productivity gains generated by the technological paradigm.

As for the mode of regulation, Fordism requires:

(1) stable forms of wage relation that ensures a division of productivity gains between capital and labour and regular incomes. The main structural forms are: collective agreements, the welfare state, and social legislation
(2) forms of relations between firms, banks and markets that allow firms to absorb the financial costs of a continuous transformation of their plant and equipment without perverse effects largely as a result of administered price setting practices. There is a tendency for industrial concentration to occur among multi-sectoral, vertically and horizontally integrated firms, with subcontracting of unskilled tasks to small and medium-size firms
(3) a specific form of money emission: credit money, issued by banks according to the needs of the economy, and under the control of the Central Bank, and
(4) a massive increase in the role of the state, which 'intervenes' in the regulation of the economy mainly through its regulation of the wage relation and the issuing of money, and *secondarily* through its discretionary budgetary policies. The role of other classic instruments of the interventio- nist state (planning, industrial policy, structural agricultural policy, and protectionism) also increases. This project and this capacity of the state to exert direct influence over the state of the economy and at any rate to guarantee the mechanisms of Fordist regulation make up what is at present (and incorrectly) called 'Keynesianism'.

In the countries where Fordism was dominant — and which were consequently the dominant countries — this model gave the *national level* a privileged role. In contrast to the classic age of imperialism, the markets for capitalist production were sought and organised essentially on a domestic basis. Leaving aside the countries of East Europe, the 'first international division of labour' largely excluded peripheral countries from trade in manufactures, reducing them to 'sources' of raw materials and immigrants. The mode of regulation of this world configuration was characterised by the hegemony of the United States. Included were its political and military hegemony, of course, and the hegemony of its technological paradigm and model of consumption, which allowed it to impose the rules of free trade (with some concessions, especially to the reconstruction of Europe and Japan, and then to the countries of the 'South'), and above all to impose its own credit money, the dollar, as the international means of exchange.

2.1.3 The crisis of Fordism: origins and periodisation

It is essential to understand that the crisis of Fordism, which developed in the 1970s, did not owe its origin to a single cause but to two sequences of destabilising events, each of which overdetermined the other. In particular it is incorrect to think that it was a matter of a new global 'crisis of under-consumption' (Piore and Sabel 1984, p. 254), and it is equally incorrect to argue, as liberals do, that it was a simple matter of a 'supply-side crisis' (inadequate profit rates) and that a restoration of profits is 'therefore' all that is needed to find a way out of the crisis. In practice the development of the crisis must be understood as articulations of 'internal causes' (the crisis of the model of development itself, principally on the supply side) and 'external' causes (the internationalisation of the economy which jeopardised the national management of demand) (Glyn *et al.* 1990; Lipietz 1985a).

Several phases can be distinguished in the articulation of this twofold set of events. The model of development along with the international configuration started to crack at the end of the 1960s. At first the productivity gains generated by Taylorism started to slow down, in spite of an increase in the capital–output ratio. The reasons for this phenomenon are many, but they can be reduced to the main principle of Taylorism. An increasingly educated working class was asked to work without thinking, which was both inefficient (from the point of view of the capitalist) and intolerable (from the point of view of the wage earners). As purchasing power continued to increase at the earlier rate, rates of profit fell, and rates of investment followed. Unemployment started to rise, putting pressure on the finances of the welfare state. The increase in oil rents accelerated this first sequence of events: crisis in the organisation of work – investment crisis – crisis of the welfare state. However, from 1973 to 1979, the security nets of the mode of regulation in crisis were fully operational. Up till 1979 the lax issue of money (in particular of dollars) and the support given to domestic demand prevented a repetition of the collapse of the 1930s. Increasing inflation concealed the underlying conflicts.

This first phase of the crisis even allowed the newly industrialising countries to spring up. Credit was plentiful, and demand was still increasing in the North; some countries in the South got into debt in order to industrialise, with the intention of exporting in order to repay the loans. Various regimes of accumulation were adopted ('primitive Taylorism' and 'peripheral Fordism'). International organisations and banks encouraged them in this action.

But with the approach of 1979 the political, financial and industrial élites in the North had to accept that 'Keynesian' policies of support for demand were not resolving the supply-side crisis, that of profitability. Profits were not restored, inflation was accelerating dangerously, and the value of the over-issued dollar fell rapidly. Then, as a result of the second oil crisis, 'monetarist' ideas were adopted: 'Reduce wages. Dismantle the welfare state. Tighten credit. There will be some victims, but the firms which manage to invent a new model of development will survive.' From 1979 to 1982 the shock was terrible. The world recession triggered off by the monetary authorities in the first countries converted to 'monetarism' (Great Britain and the United States) spread to the rest of the world. It superimposed a demand-side crisis on the supply-side crisis, bringing to light the second sequence of events that generated the crisis: the absence of international regulation.

To balance its trade, each country had to reduce its wages more than its neighbour in order to export more and import less. To balance its capital account, each country had to increase its rates of interest more than its rivals in order to attract mobile funds. In 1982 this war of 'competitive recession' was on the verge of recreating the crisis conditions of the 1930s. In particular it was paralysing the European Community, a free trade zone without a common social policy. The newly industrialising countries trapped between rocketing interest rates and markets that were drying up were seized by the throat.

In August 1982, in the face of the imminent catastrophe foreshadowed by an increase in the number of major bankruptcies and Mexico's decision to suspend loan repayments, the world monetary authorities, in particular the American Federal Reserve Bank, put an end to this second phase. The United States resumed a policy of domestic expansion and easy credit. The recovery was extended to the rest of the world. In contrast to the first phase this recovery was not accompanied by renewed inflation, and profits started to increase again. The 'supply-side' crisis seemed over. But very sharp differences appeared.

First of all, over the years, two diametrically opposed approaches to tackling the 'supply-side crisis' were established. Some countries (the United States, Britain and France), rather than introduce innovations in the field of work organisation, restored profits and eliminated inflation by attacking the status of workers and the gains they had made. Others, mainly Japan and Northern European countries, on the other hand, managed to combine the revolution in electronics with the questioning of Taylorism. This second group of countries was shown, in the 1980s, to have chosen the more competitive course of action: they had large trade surpluses.

These surpluses worsened the crisis of the international order. The United States financed its expansion by means of a gigantic budget deficit, while (after 1986) Britain's was sustained by wage increases. No longer competitive, these countries accumulated enormous trade deficits that had to be financed by loans. Interest rates started to rise again, all the more so as Third World debt was not reimbursed. Certainly the newly industrialising countries of South East Asia like South Korea, whose industrial structures were transformed with success, gained from the growth of the American market and started to repay their debts. The case of Latin America (especially Brasil) and of the rest of the Third World was however different. The banks had in fact progressively to write off a part of their debts, but these write-offs were offset by new tensions over interest rates.

At the end of 1986 the accumulated imbalances threatened the success of this third phase. Rapid increases in the rate of interest on loans cannot in the end be sustained by productive capital. This tension resulted in the stock market crash of October 1987. The crash was immediately stemmed by a stream of issues of new money, which led to a dramatic fall in interest rates — American growth was able to continue, as was world growth, with the growing risk of renewed inflation (a little like 1979). The fact is that a passage to a fourth phase is very difficult to achieve and, despite more and more frequent stock market crashes, this situation continues to prevail at the beginning of the 1990s. It is necessary to eliminate the American deficit without allowing the onset of a recession, which would be as catastrophic for the world as a whole, for the Third World in particular, and even for Japan and South Korea as that of the second phase.

2.2 The challenge of international competition: the invention of new forms of organisation of work

Our analysis allowed us to examine and interrelate the two main aspects of the crisis: the 'demand side', and the 'supply side'. The 'demand side', that is the erosion of the conditions that allowed 'Keynesian states' to stimulate growth by increasing domestic demand, does not yet have a satisfactory solution. And there will be no solution until new international agreements contain the law of the jungle that rules in the field of exchange rates, rates of interest, and also national variations in wage levels. In fact, over the course of the crisis, there were phases when the growth of the United States and the abundance of Eurodollars allowed world expansion (1975–9, 1983–?), and phases when North American 'monetarism' plunged the world into depression.

But, as we have also just pointed out, the countries of central and of peripheral Fordism did not all respond to the crisis in the same way. West Germany, Japan and Korea advanced on the new map of the international division of labour, while the United States, the United Kingdom and France lost ground, and Brasil, which set off like an arrow, is experiencing serious difficulties. Within countries interregional relations were also profoundly changed. As we shall show, a country's successes and failures are expressed in the development of *urban areas* with profoundly different internal dynamics.

In the world configuration of the Golden Age of Fordism, and even in the first phase of the crisis, the growth of world markets guaranteed all countries and all regions that gambled on growth a permanent positive sum game. Today, however, it is necessary to struggle to *conquer* markets whose size is sometimes increasing and sometimes decreasing. Even the growth of a country's domestic market is subordinated to the growth of its share of the world market as a result of balance of payments constraints. This rule can be bypassed through borrowing (as in the case, in the past, of Brasil and the United States and the United Kingdom) but at the risk of setting off a spiral of cumulative indebtedness.

Leaving on one side the problem (which can nevertheless not be avoided (Lipietz 1989)) of the organisation of a progressive international order, we shall concentrate on the capacity of a territory (nation or region) to face international competition.

The latter seems to be a matter of 'adaptation to the new technologies' and of the well-known need for 'flexibility'. In reality, as our former studies have suggested (Leborgne and Lipietz 1988), these 'adaptations' can vary a great deal. *Several models* have taken root, and they imply several possible hegemonic models. First of all we shall summarise the results of our analysis of the different forms of wage relations and of inter-firm relations that are developing today, as well as of their spatial implications. Then we shall show that these differences are associated with political and cultural differences.

2.2.1 The false promises of the 'new technologies'

The erosion of the technical efficiency of Taylorism, as it appeared at the end of the 1960s, was in fact a result of social factors. The Fordist worker is in principle *not involved* in the course of the process of manufacture. Responsibility resides with technicians, engineers, and the organisation and methods office. This non-involvement generates resistance and rebellion. In the Fordist system the latter can only be avoided via excessive automation. The 'electronic revolution' seemed to offer a solution.

The main characteristic of the current technological revolution is the invasion of the microprocessor and electronic interfaces, not only into new products, but also into the process of labour itself: microelectronics redefines the very meaning of automation.

First of all microelectronics provide the devices required to make the movement of machines more complex. In this regard electronics are only an extension of earlier trends in mechanisation: increases in productivity, and increases in the volume of capital per head. Their effect on profitability is not determined.

But above all electronics enable equipment to be made more flexible. In other words they make it theoretically possible to change, even automatically, the mode of operation of standardised machines. Flexible machines, which are at least as expensive as, if not more expensive than, rigid Fordist equipment, also require continuous use though not necessarily in the production of a single product. The profitable use of a flexible machine is possible with several short runs selected from a range of *differentiated* products aimed at smaller, segmented markets.

Still more important is the fact that the management of the workshop can itself be modified with the introduction of electronics. Computer-assisted manufacturing significantly increases the possibilities of controlling in real time the in-process stocks required for each operation. Stocks can be controlled in accordance with the production needs of the workshop, while the latter can be optimised in the light of the levels of intermediate and final demand. This 'just-in-time' principle can be extended to the relations between workshops in an establishment, between the establishments of a single firm, and between firms and their subcontractors.

But these 'advantages of the new technologies' are not without disadvantages. Machines can cost a great deal, and the virtues of machines (it is assumed that machines never get tired and never go on strike) are counterbalanced by the fact that they do break down. The down-time of an automated workshop made up of thirty to fifty industrial robots could be as high as 30 to 50 per cent unless manual operatives are able, on the spot, to assume responsibility for operations that are interrupted. This fact raises the issue of the involvement and skills of the workers.

Still more severe are the limits to flexibility. Contrary to a common overestimation of the extent of a new 'industrial divide' (Piore and Sabel 1984), the flexibility entailed by electronics does not necessarily imply the end of the tendency for the technical and financial concentration of capital to increase. In fact the flexibility of equipment is limited to a narrow range of related products. Moreover the implementation of this flexibility is a very complicated task that requires a great deal of simultaneous real-time activity on the part of the design, maintenance and manufacturing staff. Finally the machine system itself can be made obsolete as quickly as the range of products for which it was initially designed. This fact significantly reduces the advantages of flexibility.

The 'electronics revolution' therefore worsens rather than resolves the problem that underlies the crisis of the Fordist paradigm: the problem of the *involvement* or *non-involvement* of the direct worker. It is at this point that 'future models of development' start to differ.

2.2.2 Three types of industrial relations.

The first alternative path could end with the total removal of all initiative from the direct operative and with the triumph of production engineers and the organisation and methods office. The tendency could be for the workshop to become completely automatic, perhaps with a few blue-collar workers for some materials handling and cleaning tasks, and a few white-collar technicians to adjust the process. This result may be the dream of the majority of employers who remain faithful to the principles of Taylorism. It would be a matter of a *deepening* of the Fordist industrial paradigm, and not a way out of it.

The alternative is quite clearly the choice of technical systems that are less sophisticated but that require the real-time involvement of the direct operatives. The goal is to encourage the workforce, not just to involve itself voluntarily in the permanent adjustment and maintenance of equipment, but to do so in such a way that improvements could be incorporated systematically into the hardware and software. The knowledge acquired through learning-by-doing in the daily maintenance of the productive process should be amenable to formalisation and assimilation by the methods office and production engineering staff. In fact the problem is to *reconnect what Taylorism has separated: the manual and intellectual aspects of work.*

Industrial relations of this kind could seem to be more efficient than earlier types (Aoki 1986). But involvement and skill increase the autonomy of workers, and this independence was the 'hidden' reason for Taylorism. It is therefore necessary for management to give something in return.

The first alternative involves an *individual* compromise: in return for the worker's involvement he/she gets a share of the advances a firm makes in the form of bonuses, career advantages, and so on. The other alternative is collectively *negotiated* involvement. A trade union offers the involvement of its members in the struggle for increased productivity and high standards in exchange for control over working conditions, redundancies, and the distribution of productivity gains.

At the moment none of these three ways (A: continued polarisation,

B: individually negotiated involvement, and C: collectively bargained involvement) has emerged as a new hegemonic model, a new paradigm of industrialisation. They coexist within most countries, within firms, and even within plants.

2.2.3 The 'flexibility' of the wage contract.

The nature of the compromise that is finally negotiated will have profound implications for the regime of accumulation. But even without entering into a study of the macroeconomics of possible regimes, one can see straight away that much will depend on the *stability* of the *wage contract*. We touch here on 'the other' classical theme of the 'flexibility' debate.

This flexibility, which allows employers to recruit and lay off workers as they see fit, is proclaimed as necessary by many spokespersons for the employers. Its imposition is one of the aims of monetarist policies. A definitive attack against the 'excessive rigidity' of the Fordist type of wage contract would, it was argued, open the path to a new regime of accumulation. In order to outline the different possible models, we must consider, therefore, not only the three typical forms of labour process reorganisation, but also two typical forms of employment contract (I: rigid, and II: flexible). Of course what is more likely is the development of a *segmented* labour market. However an investigation of alternative future scenarios requires an examination of the most distinct combinations of alternatives.

Here one must be cautious. There is sometimes a tendency to imply that there is a link between the 'flexibility' of the new technologies and the flexibility of the wage contract. No such link exists. Before the war assembly-line workers had a 'flexible' contract, and sometimes very independent, multi-skilled workers already benefited from very 'rigid' collective agreements. What the character of the wage contract will be tomorrow depends on the social struggles of today (and, of course, on the traditions of the past). But are flexibility and rigidity compatible with any form of reorganisation of the labour process? At this stage of historical experience we can only consider the logical implications of different combinations and evaluate their initial results.

The first combination (skill polarisation with rigid contracts) is the point of departure for Fordism. It can be assumed that it will continue to predominate for a while, with a 'natural' evolution towards the second (skill polarisation with flexible contracts aimed at reducing wage costs). This scenario (a further development of Taylorist principles in conjunction with automation and fewer 'Fordist' gains for workers) can be called the *neo-Taylorist path* of technological and social development. It leads to very unsatisfactory social structures, with a polarisation of skills, a dual labour market, and a dual society. It is a future that is possible but not very nice. It is the path that seems to have been the majority choice for North American, British and French capitalism.

On the contrary, the combination of 'collective involvement with flexibility' seems quite simply inconsistent, an exercise in wishful thinking on the part of employers. The combination of 'collective involvement with a rigid contract' may seem, when compared with the previous one, a utopian dream on the part

Table 2.1 The new wage relations

Work organisation	Non-involvement	Negotiated involvement	
	Polarisation of tasks	Individual	Collective
	A	B	C
Nature of compromise			
I: rigid employment contract	Continuation of the Fordist model	Participative employers' path for a stable core of employees	Participative path with compensation for all workers
II: flexible employment contract	Liberal employers' path without compensation	Liberal and participative employers' path of 'corporate culture' type	Incoherent
Type of model	Neo-Taylorist	Californian	Kalmarian

of the workers. However this dream of a 'new deal' for the twenty-first century (Lipietz 1989) seems to be shared by some employers, not only in Sweden but also in Japan, Germany and Northern Italy. Models of development of this kind are likely to display the properties of stability of Fordism, with the employers profiting from technological trends that are less capital-intensive and more productive, and the workers being granted greater job security, higher wages and/or shorter working hours. Let us call this family of models 'Kalmarian'.[3]

What remain are the cases of 'individually negotiated involvement'. The difficulties of the 'rigid' variant (the voluntaristic way of involving workers) can be removed by taking into account the possibility of differentiating wages in accordance with the individual contributions of workers. Combined with the 'stick' of job loss in the flexible variant, this 'carrot' may lead to a sort of recommodification of the wage relation, which seems to be directly in line with the ideological fashion for market regulation. Let us call this class of models 'Californian' (see Table 2.1).

The evidence has quite obviously already settled the matter: Kalmarian models crush, commercially, neo-Taylorist models. The grey zone of Californian models (under which we are inclined to include Silicon Valley, San José dos Campos in Brasil, and the Third Italy) is the only one that provides arguments (often vague) for those who associate the 'flexibility of the wage relation' with 'competitiveness'. It is necessary in fact to examine each of these experiences more closely, but let us turn instead to a third form of 'flexibility': the relations among firms, which we call *industrial organisation*.

2.2.4 The forms of 'vertical near integration'

The classical form of industrial organisation in the Fordist model was the intra-firm division of labour between workshops, in accordance with Taylorist principles (I: production engineering and the organisation and methods office, II: the skilled manufacture of machines, and III: unskilled execution as, for example, in the case of assembly lines. So sharp was this division that the division between workshops could assume the form of a division between establishments, a 'spatial disintegration', and even a division at level III between final producers and subcontractors, a *vertical disintegration*. This set of divisions led to the theory of *branch circuits* (Lipietz 1974 and 1977, Lafont, Leborgne and Lipietz 1980). The new technologies offer new possibilities in the area of industrial organisation, largely as a result of the computerised management of flows of information and products, the flexibility of machines, the standardisation allowed by high-precision automated manufacturing, the modular design of products, and automated assembly of sub-assemblies. (On what follows see Leborgne (1987 and 1988).)

The segmentation of labour processes into modules and the integrated management of the sequence of modular stages allow the transformation of sequential batch processes into continuous flow processes and the continuous production of differentiated goods. The optimal management of integrated modular processes would seem to call for greater vertical integration of firms. But flexible automation (which permits the continuous production of differentiated goods) and computerised management of flows (which reduces 'transaction costs', that is the costs of establishing a market relation between two stages in a process of production) in effect presents new possibilities for vertical disintegration. The new solution that is emerging is the *specialised firm*, producing a limited range of differentiated (final or intermediate) goods. It is at this level that the management of quality, innovation and time economies is optimised.

In fact automation leads to a proliferation of specialised know-how and to an extension of the divison of labour. Moreover flexible production constantly increases the importance of control over a sequence of short series. However the complexity of the integration of modular tasks increases more than in proportion to the number of links in the chain: as a result some technical disintegration allows tighter control over costs and quality. Then computer-aided management of external flows, that is of flows between firms, along with greater precision in manufacturing, allows the major firms to coordinate just-in-time subcontractors. What results is a *network of specialised firms*.

To these *technical* reasons for disintegration must be added economic and financial *pressures*: the importance of *pooling the risks* of research and development, of high-technology fixed assets, and of fixed assets in general among *several* owners of capital. The deverticalisation of large groups into networks of specialised firms, or the grouping of firms into networks of this kind may be an answer to this challenge: it is known as *vertical near integration* (Houssiaux 1957; Enrietti 1983).

Vertical near integration (VNI) involves stable relations between suppliers and their clients, customers that account for a large share of their suppliers' turnovers, an extension of the domain of subcontracting from design to marketing, and non-commodity forms of inter-firm relations that range from subordination to partnership. It implies a generalisation of non-market relations between firms: strategic alliances, transfers of technology, joint research programmes, 'joint ventures', and so on. When the 'subordination' of subcontractors predominates (subcontractors have little initiative and do little applied research) we shall refer to *weak VNI*: it is the old tendency of Fordism. When, on the other hand, specialised firms have control over the development of their particular expertise and develop relations of partnership with their customers we shall refer to *strong VNI* or 'oblique near integration'.

But over which spaces will networks of these kinds be organised? Today one can observe two polar forms of VNI which correspond, naturally, to weak VNI and strong VNI.[4]

In the case of the United States, VNI is established by processes of geographical decentralisation and recourse to specialised firms *in other countries*: in Japan (for high-skilled, high-technology tasks) and in Third World countries for unskilled and even for semi-skilled tasks (Scott 1987). Let us call this form '*territorially disintegrated near integration*'. It results in marked deindustrialisation, a weak diffusion of high-technology innovations within national industries, and so on.

On the contrary '*territorially integrated near integration*' is realised as a network within a single national, or even regional, space. Macroeconomic multiplier and accelerator effects remain internal to the country, which retains control over the diffusion of innovations from one sector to another through direct intra-regional relations. It is the typical model in the Po Valley in Italy, in many German *Länder*, and so on.

2.3 Territorial blocs and new models of development.

The facts *already* show that certain territories (countries or regions) have advantageous combinations of a certain model of industrial relations (capital-labour relations) and a certain model of industrial organisation (inter-firm relations). The forms vary, of course, from one sector to another even in a single region (Lafont, Leborgne and Lipietz 1980). But experience shows that a 'hegemonic model', a particular combination of social relations of this kind, has a good chance of prevailing at regional or national levels. A model of development is in fact by its nature located in a particular territory: social relations of that sort, which prevail in social space, tend to spread from one sector of activity to another. This diffusion is a product of the fact that a model must take the shape of a territorial hegemonic bloc, a set of norms of social and cultural behaviour and of mental frameworks that are condensed into a compromise institutionalised at the national or regional level (Lipietz 1985b).

2.3.1 Three types of urban region

The neo-Taylorist path, as a descendant of the Fordist model whose classical tendencies were analysed in a sequence of studies from Lipietz (1974) to

Noyelle (1982), results in processes of territorial disintegration: activities at each of the three levels of skill are located in three types of region with subcontracting more and more common at the lower levels of skill (except for the final downstream assembly operations). It can be considered as the weakest form of VNI: the mediocre quality of the links in the hierarchy of firms reflects the poor quality of industrial relations within the firms. In these circumstances it is normal for territorially disintegrated VNI to prevail.

Agglomerations of subcontractors are consequently formed around major firms or in low-wage zones in order to maximise external economies of transport and minimise transaction costs. Zones of this kind can be observed in South East Asia (Scott 1987), and it is areas of this sort that enterprise zone policies are seeking to encourage in deindustrialised regions. But they can also emerge spontaneously. They correspond to *specialised productive areas* in the typologies of Garofoli (1986) and Courlet (1987). Specialised productive areas are recently formed agglomerations that have weak relations with the pre-existing regional social formation. They are monosectoral, and export-oriented, with weak intra-regional, inter-firm relations.

High-level service sector tasks (research and development, design, finance, and so on) are concentrated in the 'nodal centres' of a few metropolises or, more precisely, in their city centres, with a complete hierarchy of secondary urban centres, 'specialised tertiary areas' of 'back office jobs' (Nelson 1986).

Now let us consider the spatial manifestation of the Californian way. Its fundamental characteristic is the involvement of workers on an individual basis (with bonuses, career advantages, and the fear of redundancy as incentives). Involvement means more professionalism and more 'face-to-face' (non-hierarchical and non-market) contacts. But market regulation still prevails in the Californian models whether in industrial relations or in the exchange of products. Consequently vertical disintegration tends to become the dominant form of industrial organisation. But the need for face-to-face contacts and professionalism entails spatial concentration in zones that (again with reference to Garofoli's terminology) we shall call *local productive systems*. A local productive system is also monosectoral and export-led, but there is an intra-sectoral specialisation of firms, and therefore a tendency for *local* vertical near integration to develop among the firms. It requires a local (and probably longstanding) supply of industrial skills. The origin of the firms may be external or (through spin-off) internal. The classic example is of course Silicon Valley, Santa Clara, the earliest example of a technopole supported upstream by the 'supply of skills' from Stanford University and downstream by defence contracts. There is a large number of local productive systems spontaneously created on the basis of older traditions and regional know-how in Italy, Germany and elsewhere. The experience of South East Asia shows that state intervention and the organised diffusion of technological know-how allow a transition from a neo-Taylorist, specialised productive area to a local productive system (Scott 1987).

The class of Kalmarian models rests not only on the involvement of workers but also on collective, non-market negotiation of this involvement. Trade unions and employers' organisations, as well as political administrations at all levels, are therefore involved in the mode of regulation. There is no longer any

Table 2.2 The organisation of work and urban regions

	Wage relations		
	A	B	C
Industrial organisation			
Weak VNI	Specialised area for unskilled tasks	Specialised area for unskilled tasks	Unstable
Strong VNI	System area for high-level services in a nodal urban centre	Local productive system	System area

doubt that this class of models (examples are found in Sweden, and to some extent in Japan, Germany, Northern Italy and in a few American states such as Michigan) exhibits the highest levels of performance from a capitalist point of view.

It is certainly possible for an establishment isolated from its spatial context to adopt Kalmarian industrial relations. That situation is probably unstable. As intra-firm industrial relations are based on skill and cooperation, there is a good chance that the principles of industrial organisation will be based on a dense web of partnerships between firms, trade unions, universities and local administrations. In Garofoli's and Courlet's typology the spatial expression of this complex is called a *system area*. In this case VNI takes the form of a multi-sectoral, diversified and territorially integrated network of specialised firms and principal firms. In effect, the deployment of Kalmarian models in *system areas* requires and consolidates a social consensus: the formation of an innovative territorial hegemonic bloc.

Table 2.2 summarises this discussion. As is clear, all of these models share a tendency to favour *urban agglomerations*. The reason why lies in the way in which vertical near integration strengthens the market and face-to-face character of relationships between establishments. Both market and face-to-face relations imply proximity. Rural establishments will, of course, continue to develop, but will be less important. However urban areas may experience very different rates of growth.

2.3.2 Defensive flexibility and offensive flexibility

What are the determinants of these divergent developments? The determinants are, of course, inherited from the past, but this inheritance is reflected through the prism that results from the formation of a territorial social bloc which, through the struggles and compromises that define it, influences *all of the actors* and determines a territory's destiny. The formation of blocs of this kind is at present under way: for the moment one can only speak of 'politico-cultural projects' whose goals are the constitution of these blocs, and of the practices of actors that tend to establish them.

Just as the 'flexibility' of machines, of work relations, and of inter-firm relations can be interpreted in different ways, so do the territorial policies and projects conducted in the name of 'flexibility' correspond to emerging social blocs that are quite different from one another. To simplify matters we shall distinguish the discourses and practices of 'defensive flexibility' and 'offensive flexibility'.

Justification for this distinction would require forays into the fields of political science, the social sciences, law, history, etc. and, as well as a multidisciplinary inquiry, would call for further conceptual developments. Above all the distinction is a hypotheis which clarifies some recorded facts to which we shall refer in note form.

The defensive option	*The offensive option*
The (labour) 'flexibility' gained is used negatively, or the 'removal of rigidities' is imposed to defend threatened markets.	A capacity to develop new technologies in accordance with prospects for the development of new markets is implemented through negotiation.
It is a short-term view of 'adaptation to the constraints of competition and to the new technologies'.	It is a medium- to long-term view of the collective interests of a large proportion of the territorial community.
Its goal is the formation or maintenance of a bloc of entrepreneurs and asset owners.	Its goal is the formation or maintenance of the hegemony of a bloc of entrepreneurs and productive groups.

The implications for the workers are:[5]

The destruction of the social gains that made the wage contract more rigid through the development of temporary contracts, the weakening of labour law, and so on:	The development of training, of multi-skilling, and of the initiative of workers in a context of stable wage contracts:
neo-Taylorist model.	Kalmarian model

. . . for capital are:[6]

Non-involvement of financial capital of local origin with local industrial capital.	Significant investment of local savings in local productive enterprises.
Opportunistic (short-sighted) rela-	Partnership between large firms and

tions between large firms and small subcontractors.

specialised firms.

weak VNI

strong VNI

. . . for institutions are:[7]

Tense and unstable relations between a central state which makes the major macroeconomic decisions and delegates the management of the social consequences to the regions, and regions which constantly demand central state support. Central state support assumes the form of *ad hoc* plans which are reviewed when there is a change in political control.

Stable agreements (even if their implementation is conflictual) at appropriate territorial levels for the establishment of networks for the exchange of information and discussions between the state, trade unions and firms about research, the definition and constant adaptation of the territorial project, and so on.

. . . at the ideological level are:[8]

'The imperative of modernisation' is proclaimed, and the defence of former social gains is called 'archaic'.

The existence of differences in the interests of capital and labour is denied ('everyone is in the same boat in the face of international competition').

Modernisation is implemented, and the social problems it creates are discussed.

Differences in interests are taken into account, and mutually advantageous compromises are negotiated (sometimes after long conflicts).

. . . at the legal level:[9]

Earlier territorial agreements that disallowed 'social dumping' are torn up, competition among workers, subcontractors and sites (inside and outside of the spatial area) increases.

Enterprise or establishment agreements are negotiated on an *ad hoc* basis.

The rules of the game are decided at the highest territorial level (national or continental) in bipartite or tripartite agreements, (involving employers, trade unions, and political administrations), outline laws, and sectoral collective agreements. Within this context enterprise and local agreements mobilise existing human resources.

These attitudes take root in the
Fordist traditions that are on their way out

A Fordism which gave greater importance to low labour costs,

A Fordism which gave greater importance to know-how in engi-

unskilled work, unskilled juvenile and female workers, and immigration.

neering and in skilled manufacture.

. . . in the balance of social forces

A trade unionism that is defeated after a state of tension over the former compromises or that allows employers to direct 'redeployment'. Employers relocate to circumvent social gains.

A trade unionism which mobilises the relation of strength established in the past to influence the new model of development. Employers seek to compensate for social gains by negotiating over the involvement of workers.

Their effects

The destruction of obsolescent industrial sites, and the loss of existing technical culture and know-how. Increasing dependence of the regional productive system on imports. Loss of control of the domestic market.
A polarisation of the productive system around certain niches or 'competitive poles', and the abandonment of some sectors because they are 'archaic'.

Negotiations anticipating reconversions. The mobilisation, adaptation and reuse of existing know-how.
An increase in the density of intra-regional, intersectoral and intra-sectoral relations. Control of the home market for certain filières.
An inter-sectoral diffusion of know-how, of applied research, and of growth.

. . . and in the forms of urban growth

A specialisation of metropolitan system areas in high-level tertiary activities, with a dual social structure in these areas.
The survival or development of specialised productive zones in low-skilled industrial or tertiary activities.

The development of system areas with industrial and tertiary activities.

The transition of specialised productive zones to local productive systems.

Some symptoms

The mythology of the 'small firm'.
A multiplication of projects for the creation by administrations of 'technopoles'.

An inrease in the density of networks of specialised firms around emerging multinationals.
The formation of system areas or local productive systems through an

increase in the density of relations of
partnership between firms, universities and administrations.

2.3.3 The limits and risks of 'offensive flexibility'

The results of territorial projects based on 'defensive flexibility' are, in France
as in Britain or in the United States, only too well known.[10] The industrial
success of Japan, Germany, Sweden and Northern Italy must not, however,
lead us to overlook their limits.

First of all offensive flexibility covers without doubt a variety of models.
There are already important differences in the areas (regional or national) in
which 'flexible-offensive' social blocs have been formed. A 'national' offensive
flexibility is more consistent than a 'regional' one. Neither German nor
Japanese regions are homogeneous, but the regional differences between
Emilia-Romagna and, for example, Sicily may in the end undermine Italy's
growth. More generally the heterogeneity of the positions on modernisation of
Europe's social blocs and, in practice, the absence of a 'European social space'
have hampered the European Economic Community for years (Leborgne and
Lipietz 1990).

Second, within a single territory the scope of Kalmarian agreements may be
more or less wide. There is not a great difference between Sweden and Japan
when one confines oneself to large firms and the inner circle of suppliers in
VNI networks. But differences in living standards, which are already
significant for wage earners as a whole, become glaring when one moves
outside this inner circle. Sweden and Japan have the same (very low) rates of
unemployment, but in Sweden women have a social independence which
makes them look for permanent full-time work, whereas in Japan they
disappear from the labour market upon marriage. Similarly old people are
forced into the 'marginalised side' of Japan's dual society, whereas Sweden is
an extremely homogeneous society.

This difference in the models of development rests in part on a profound
macroeconomic difference, and reinforces it. It is what Aoki (1990) calls the
'dilemma of a workers' democracy'. In Fordist models, in fact, we saw that the
state and/or bipartite national agreements ensured that the size of the domestic
market increased in line with productivity gains. The compensation offered to
workers in exchange for their acceptance of Taylorism, in the form of increases
in purchasing power, involved a *division* of the fruits of the growth of
aggregate productivity (or, in Marxist terms, of *relative* surplus-value).

On the contrary a firm or a region which, due to superior social organisation, produces more or produces less dearly than the rest of the world (or, in
the extreme, produces what the rest of the world does not produce), and which
as a result increases its market share, can guarantee its workers full employment, and even can give them wage increases.[11] In this case all it is doing is
handing over quasi-rents, profits based on the difference between its costs of
production and those of the world market (which, in Marxist terms, are extra
surplus-value). The reproduction of these quasi-rents occurs through 'invest-

ments of form' in the training of personnel, the negotiation of compromises, research and development, and so on. It encourages the cooperation of firms in the same region, a sharing of the costs of technological research, strategic alliances, and so on. This result (in which contradictory class interests and inter-firm competition seem to disappear) seems doubly paradoxical in relation to neo-classical theory and also to Marxist theory (Scherer 1970). It ceases to be so if one considers these alliances and territorial compromises as both the condition and result of a quasi-rent situation in world competition. In other words, in the absence of a global policy for the growth of demand (or for a reduction in working hours), social policies on the supply side (Kalmarian) that are based on explicit agreements among private actors but that are *not generalised at the political level* are as a matter of course confined to a minimal number of participants (firms, wage earners and territories). It is possible to guarantee full employment for a 'core group of wage earners' but on the condition that all the new jobs generated by the technical and commercial dynamism of the firm or of the firms grouped in a strategic alliance are reserved for them.

'Offensive flexibility', in the absence of a more general political agreement, can thus lead to a 'yeoman democracy', a wage earners' democracy for skilled workers of the kind that Piore and Sabel (1984) commend, but that will leave, for example, 'women slaves' in the shadows, a dual society divided on the basis of differences in gender, race or age. Already in Japan there is a tendency, which is typical of trade unionism in hegemonic countries (formerly Britain, followed by the United States), for workers to behave as 'labour aristocracies'.

2.4 Conclusion

On the basis of a crisis of the Fordist wage relation, monetarist policies have amplified international macroeconomic disorder. Two groups of territories stand out due to the differences in their results. In these two groups, two conceptions of flexibility have been implemented in the areas of capital–labour relations and capital–capital relations.

The ruling social blocs in the first group (Britain, the United States, France . . .) have practised a 'defensive flexibility', giving priority to a deregulation of the wage relation, an accentuation of the division between 'designers' and 'manual workers', the most modest forms of subcontracting, and the development of urban areas with narrow specialisations existing alongside a few metropolises where high-level tertiary activities contrast with small service trades that have no social protection.

The ruling social blocs in the second group (Scandinavia, Germany, Japan, and Northern Italy) have practised, in different degrees and leaving on one side a varying proportion of the population, offensive flexibility. They have accepted a new compromise in workplaces, exchanging the involvement of workers in the struggle for quality and productivity for various social guarantees and advantages. They have managed to organise forms of partnership between enterprises, trade unions, educational institutions, and local administrations. The increase in the density of inter-firm relations has allowed the consolidation of urban areas forming flexible and diversified productive systems.

With regard to these successes, people often speak of the 'cultural context' and of 'social effects'. We have tried to go a little deeper into the *policies* that are based on this culture and that further it. But it is necessary to keep in mind the fact that, in many cases, the policies of 'offensive flexibility' exclude large sections of the working classes. In every case they operate at present as a strategy for strengthening some territories *vis-à-vis* other territories and other nations. If they indicate directions for a progressive solution to the crisis, they are not in themselves sufficient. New conceptions of solidarity and democracy in urban societies and in the international economic order still remain to be defined.

Notes

1. An earlier version of this chapter was presented at the International Sociological Association Conference, Rio de Janeiro, 26–30 September 1988.
2. The basic concepts of the regulation approach used here were put forward in Aglietta (1976), Boyer (1986), Boyer and Mistral (1978), Coriat (1979), Delorme and André (1983), Lafont, Leborgne and Lipietz (1980), and Lipietz (1979, 1983, 1985b and 1985c).
3. In our 1987 paper we took up the terminology of Messine (1987): neo-Taylorist, Californian and Saturnian. The inability of General Motors to develop the 'Saturn Project' in largely neo-Taylorist geographical surroundings led us to choose the term 'Kalmarian' inspired by Rianne Mahon (1987).
4. The contrast between these two forms of spatial deployment of VNI is very striking in the industrial equipment goods sector (numerically controlled machine tools, robotics). It is true that this sector can itself be considered as a 'microcosm and the core element' of industry as a whole (Leborgne 1987): a core element because in it are developed new norms of production, and a microcosm because the sector itself becomes a scale model of the dominant principles of industrial organisation.
5. In the offensive option the imperative of modernisation and/or the introduction of new technologies provide trade unions with an opportunity to engage in protest actions aimed at securing from employers a reduction in working hours, the maintenance of employment, and compensation for the reorganisation of worktime, and at countering employers' offensives aimed at making the employment contract more flexible. This case applies in West Germany, Italy and Sweden.

   In the case of West Germany reference can be made to the strikes and actions of IG Metall in metal manufacturing, and to the collective agreements signed in the chemical industry (*La Note de l'IRES*, no. 12, 1988). Zachert (1988) indicates in particular that with the new technologies many workers 'fell without a parachute' (with respect to the system of job classification). Consequent trade-union action resulted in the signing of a collective agreement on 'the security of the level of wages'. A collective agreement, which is also of interest for its consequences for the areas of know-how and training, was signed on 3 March 1978 and which applies to the region of Baden-Württemberg, protects workers (in all sectors) aged 50 to 55 with a certain length of service in an enterprise. The latter received guarantees that their wage would not fall, even in the case of transfer, and that they would keep their job. They can only be made redundant for misconduct.

   As far as Italy is concerned reference can be made to the negotiation (in the 1983 textiles agreement) of flexible working hours which accompanied a reduction in worktime without a proportional reduction in wages (Chiesi cited in Bachet 1986) and, more generally, to the draft agreement with IRI (Industrial Reconstruction Institute), the main management body of the largest of the state holding companies. Through this agreement signed in December 1984 the trade unions obtained the right to intervene in the preparation of modernisation projects in the framework of joint consultative committees. This agreement opened the possibility (in principle) of examining alternative courses of action and of involvement in the management of employment (training, redeployment, organisation of worktime, organisation of work . . .). In 1986 ENI and EFIM (the other two nationalised groups) adopted this same agreement (*La Note de l'IRES*, no. 11, 1988), whose aim was, through a policy on information, to promote a 'new culture' in the enterprise. If practice falls short of what is envisaged on paper, it is nonetheless the case that new spaces have opened for trade unions and that this type of agreement is spreading to the private sector. Overall in the private sector, sector-level collective bargaining, far from being abandoned in favour of plant-level bargaining, is being strengthened.

In the case of Sweden recall the Progress Agreement of the employers' organisations, trade unions and executives' organisations (SAF, LO and PTK respectively) which was signed in April 1982 and which is discussed in Mahon (1987).

In the countries that are instances of the 'defensive strategy' (the United States, Britain and France), on the contrary, employers successfully used the introduction of new technologies to worsen the employment contract. In France the February 1986 Delebarre Law, stripped of its 'constraints' (sector-level negotiation and reduced worktime), became the 1987 Seguin Law. These laws are concerned with easing restrictions on redundancies, authorising womens' night work (and, as everyone knows, this legislation was to apply essentially to the textile and food-processing industries in which conditions of work are the most unpleasant and wages the lowest), and authorising irregular hours of work.

If, with respect to the Auroux Law of 1982 on the rights of workers in the enterprise, one can agree with Jeammaud and Lyon-Caen (1987) that 'the project of democratising labour relations drew its legitimacy from a value whose restoration was spectacular and which was made more sovereign than ever: productivity', which is not specific to France, these laws did not have the repercussions intended by their proponent (Borzeix and Linhart 1988).

In so far as Britain is concerned reference can be made to the works of Maurau (1988) and Okba (1988) which highlight the growing importance of temporary work, the destabilisation of the trade unions through the attacks of Mrs Thatcher's governments, and the current development, under the aegis of Japanese capitals, of single union deals beyond the sphere of influence of the Trades Unions Congress.

6. The same dichotomy between West Germany, Italy, Japan and Sweden on the one hand and France, Britain and the United States on the other is also found when one examines the density of relations between finance capital and industrial capital and the content of different forms of partnership. To cite just the case of Japan, the financial environment of firms is as follows. Interest rates are very low, large groups are industrial, financial and commercial conglomerates, and small and medium-size firms can obtain credit from sixty-four regional and local banks that specialise in this type of lending. To these banks it is necessary to add numerous, exclusively local mutual and co-operative credit associations. In Germany the closeness of local banks and small and medium-size firms in the framework of the Länder is emphasised in many studies. In Sweden the development of industry was a result of the diversification of the banks. In Italy, if the relations between industrial capital and finance capital are not as organised as in Japan or West Germany, it is

nonetheless necessary to point out that local savings banks have close relations with small and medium-size firms and that they play a part in the creation of regional centres whose role is to provide services (research, marketing, advice) to small and medium-size firms: it is the case in Emilia-Romagna in particular.

In the second group of countries, outside of the large firms which have 'the confidence' of the banks, small and medium-size enterprises (SME) have difficulties in finding finance. In the end this finance assumes the form of 'venture capital'. In France small and medium-size enterprises have difficulties in recovering money that is owed to them: a factor in very many bankruptcies. Mayer (1988) eloquently sets out the disadvantages that small and medium-size industries (SMI) suffer and that are due to the functioning of the financial system itself. As for the content of partnerships, in France for example, in the best of cases it is a matter of large firms selling services to SME. 'It is the contribution of the group to the national effort which avoids social tensions and eases consciences . . . Our research centres can work on the margin for some SME, bring their knowledge to those who want it'. These remarks were taken from an aricle in the May/June 1987 issue of the journal *PME-PMI Magazine* which under the title 'PME: profitez de l'aide des grandes' ('SME: take advantage of the assistance of large enterprises') compiles a list of the different kinds of partnership. The latter are pure market relations, and have nothing to do with the non-market relations which underpin exchanges under vertical near integration and which resemble those that Renault has introduced (*La Lettre de Machine Moderne*, 4 April 1985), and that FIAT has used for a number of years (Enrietti 1983).

7. In the regions that are typical of offensive flexibility, employers' associations make use of the region to further their strategy and develop, through their initiatives, bipartite or tripartite cooperation with banks and local and regional authorities. This case applies in Italy, in West Germany and in Japan. In the case of Japan one can cite the 1978 'law for the stabilisation of sectors in crisis' which was renewed in 1983 (Laumer and Ochel 1986). This law, which was exemplary in its formulation and implementation, dealt simultaneously with the problems of excess capacity, modernisation of the whole of the industrial fabric, and retraining of wage earners.

In the regions in which defensive flexibility prevails, policies directed at firms are developed, mainly on the initiative of the administrative authorities. It is frequently the case in the United States with the renewal of 'regional policies' implemented at state level, and it is the case in France with the creation of technopoles and with the policy of 'contrats de plan' (planning agreements) and 'contrats Etat-Région' (government–region agreements) (whose application is heavily dependent on fluctuations in political control). In addition it is necessary to point out that difficulties stand in the way of the process of decentralisation in France, which stems from the laws of 1982, and that it is more a matter of deconcentration — in practice the role of the Prefect remains paramount — than decentralisation.

8. In West Germany the trade union IG Metall launched its manifesto 'Der Mensch muss bleiben' (People must remain) in 1984, and adopted a position on the role of people in the modernisation process. Later it started a poster campaign against the inauguration of Saturday work (a child said 'On Saturday, Daddy is mine!'). In France, in the face of the extent of the deregulation of the labour market, and realising the extent of the constraint that it places on the processes of modernisation, a group of modernist employers reacted and addressed other employers in the report 'Modernisation mode d'emploi' (Modernisation as a method of employment). In Britain 1986 was declared 'Industry Year' in order, it was said, to reconcile society and industry, as if the idea that 'manufacturing matters' merited interest for just one year.

9. See note 5.
10. In our study (Lafont, Leborgne and Lipietz 1980) we had already noted this divergence in the development of relationships between car manufacturers and equipment suppliers and between customers and machine-tool firms in several European countries.
11. One can see at present that countries whose superior productive efficiency ensures a trade surplus (Japan and South Korea) can implement a policy of increasing domestic demand without risk.

3 Industrial trajectories and social relations in areas of new industrial growth.[1]

Mick Dunford

3.0 Introduction

In the late 1960s and early 1970s the model of development that had underpinned the growth of Western capitalist economies broke down. At first attempts were made to reconstruct and preserve the older social order. Towards the end of the 1970s, however, the elites of these countries concluded that a transformation of the institutions and structures of advanced capitalist societies was required. What triumphed in the United States and United Kingdom in particular were neo-liberal projects centred around arguments in favour of markets, private ownership, and competitive capitalism and against managed, welfare capitalism.

In the 1980s the focus of attention switched towards the crises of Third World countries trapped between the downturn in world trade, their indebtedness to international financial institutions, and the dramatic rise in interest rates, while at the end of the decade what was highlighted in the West were the difficulties of socialist countries: nationalism, democratisation and the realisation that the command mechanisms and institutional structures of the socialist world were incapable of a further satisfaction of human needs and of directing a transition from extensive to intensive economic growth.

As a result of these developments it has been argued that the 1970s and 1980s represent a turning point at which the advance of social-democratic politics and of proto-socialist elements in the West was halted or thrown into reverse gear, as more market-oriented modes of capitalist development gained ground, while in the some parts of the socialist world a re-establishment of capitalist social relations is on the agenda.

The breakdown of earlier models of development was connected with the emergence of a new industrial trajectories centred on information and communication technologies. In practice the implementation of new technologies and the diffusion of the new paradigm from leading-edge sectors proved difficult and slow due to mismatches with existing institutional frameworks. There was therefore an experimental search for combinations of technological and institutional innovations. (Different sets of social relations shape the speed, extent and character of innovation and innovation diffusion, while the particular combinations that emerge determine the rate, character and quality of economic development.) In its turn the search for new institutional and social structures was connected with the establishment of new political alliances and strategies, and what underlay all these developments were contradictions in the development of the forces and relations of production.

The present phase is therefore one of crisis and transition and of changes in what Wallerstein (1988) calls structural TimeSpace. At these points instabilities predominate, and a transformational TimeSpace exists in which we all are able to exercise fundamental moral choice and choose a new order. The world is confronted in short with a transformational moment: new models of development are required, and they involve the development of new technologies, new social relations and institutions, new hegemonic structures, and new macroeconomic mechanisms.

The advocates of neo-liberal ideas who have been so dominant in the last decade or more often suggest that the outcome of this transformation has already been determined. In practice, however, neo-liberal projects as with any project for the restructuring of social relations are contested in a constant war of manoeuvre, and so the actual course of events depended on the political and social situation in each country. The range of responses to the crisis was therefore far wider and the situation far more fluid than some writers suggest. What I hope to show, however, is that an examination of differences in the relative success of new industrial spaces in the West gives little support to neo-liberal claims. Successful adaptations to the crisis depend, it will be argued, on an increase in the socialisation of economic activities and the development of more organised models of capitalist development. The reason why is that unregulated market mechanisms and the myopic pursuit of individual self-interest are dysfunctional. Arguments for social justice and for a more rational model of development seem therefore to come together in favour of a further movement in the direction of a supersession of capitalist social relations, even though what happens in practice will depend on the constant renegotiation of change among economic, social and political forces and movements.

3.1 The dialectic of the forces and relations of production.

3.1.1 Which new social relations?

Capitalism, of course, is characterised by two fundamental social relations. In the first place it is a system of commodity production in which goods and services are produced for sale on the market: decisions about what to produce, how much, when and where are made not in accordance with a social plan but are the decisions of private and autonomous individuals, and the social validation of these decisions is determined a posteriori through the sale of the products they make on the market. Incomes similarly depend on the market validation of the activities of individual producers.

In opposition to the market stands a planned system. Where a social plan is agreed, decisions about output and employment are made *ex ante*. In general resources are used more fully, inequalities tend to be smaller, and instabilities are less pronounced. But in so far as all output is validated in advance and on completion sold to trade organisations, producer interests can play a dominant role, and it is difficult to ensure that all goods and services are of a satisfactory standard. Moreover where full employment is guaranteed and where shortages of goods and services exist, sanctions and material incentives to work are weak.[2]

Capitalist societies are distinguished, however, not just by the existence of the commodity relation but also by the fact that work itself is structured by the wage relation and the property relations on which it depends. Under capitalism the means and objects of production and consumption assume the form of private property, can be exchanged for money on the market, and are concentrated in the hands of a class of landowners and capitalist employers along with the money wealth against which the production conditions are exchanged. On the other side of the social divide stands a wage-earning class that is separated from the means of production and the product of its work. In order to work and secure a claim over a part of the social product members of this wage-earning class must sell their labour power to capitalist employers.[3]

A supersession of capitalist social relations therefore implies, it seems, a movement away from (*ex ante*) market methods of allocation, a transformation of private property into 'universal' socialised property, and a transformation of the wage relation and of the separation of the producer from the means of production (a decommodification of the wage relation, the establishment of rights to work and workplace democracy, and new ownership relations).[4]

In modern capitalist societies not all of the process of social reproduction is structured by capitalist social relations. Many goods and services are not commodities, not all work is performed by wage-earners, and some property is collectivised (see Dunford 1988: 11–12 and Figure 3.1). In the course of capitalist development the boundaries have shifted. After the Second World War that shift occurred at the expense of the capitalist sector, but under neo-liberal governments there has been an attempt to extend commodification and private ownership.

In recent years governments have sought to increase the size of the capitalist sector, and influential accounts of the uses of new technologies and of changes in employment practices and industrial organisation suggest that there will be an increase in the sphere in which markets, private ownership and the wage relation predominate. The search for wage and employment flexibility has led in the direction of a recommodification of the wage relation. Small firms have increased in numbers and have assumed a far more important role. State enterprises have been sold off, and state intervention in economic life has declined with a consequent increase in the role of markets and of private initiative.

There is also, however, evidence of different paths of change. In some

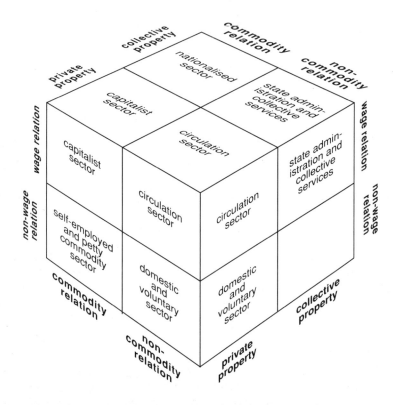

Figure 3.1 The social relations of capitalist production

countries there has been an extension of the rule-governed and regulated character of markets. In addition there is some evidence of developments which seek to overcome some of the instabilities and uncertainties characteristic of market economies. The development of strategies of vertical integration, for example, involved a substitution of hierarchies for market relations.[5] In the more recent past capitalist enterprises have sought to gear production to orders received (even if equipment must be installed in advance), to allow sales to determine in advance what is produced, and to transfer or pool risks and uncertainties with other firms. Similar factors underpin the increase in the dominance of commercial capitalists whose knowledge of market conditions is most developed. The integrative character of information technologies also leads in the direction of a substitution of cooperative and collaborative non-market relations for market relations (see Veltz, Chapter 10).

It seems therefore that not all change is in the same direction. Some of these developments may be short-run rather than secular. What is more their social content is far more complex than it seems at first sight. These contradictory and inconclusive developments raise therefore two general questions. What kinds of institutional organisation are more appropriate to the new industrial paradigm rooted in electronic technologies, automation and flexible systems that have applications in all spheres of work and life? Will new technologies lead to societies that are more market-oriented or more organised?

3.1.2 Social relations and uneven development

In many countries dynamic sectors (centred around electronics and information technologies: electronic components, computers, telecommunications, office automation, consumer electronics, and defence electronics) are located in new areas of growth, away from older industrial areas, while differentials in the success of strategies for the revitalisation of traditional sectors and the development of new 'designer' industries are a major source of unevenness among the latter. Other areas owe their growth to their role as centres of producer services (see, for example, Scott 1988c).

In this chapter I shall consider a small number of areas whose growth is connected with the development of electronics industries: Silicon Glen in Scotland, Rhône-Alpes in France, and the Cambridge phenomenon in England (on Scotland and Rhône-Alpes see Dunford 1988 and 1989).

The character, speed and direction of development of high-tech industries differ in quite significant ways from one area to another. The organisation of work, and the size, structure and interrelationships of industrial firms all vary from one place to another as does the role of the state. New technologies do not impose new sets of social relations. The success of different sets of technological and social choices will however be reflected in unevenness in the character, speed and quality of development, while what happens in areas that are more dynamic will in the end have an important impact on ones whose growth is slower. The coexistence of different courses of action raises in short a set of issues that are geographical and geopolitical.

Which type of strategy is adopted is, however, a question of politics and not simply a result of technological imperatives or the operation of the abstract laws of economics. A nation could choose a conservative course and sustain it over a significant number of years, especially where the costs can be shifted on to minorities on whom the coherence of the dominant electoral bloc does not depend. In so far as other nations adopt different courses, uneven development will occur and the economic and geopolitical role of the countries that stagnate will decline. Uneven development is in other words one of the mechanisms through which the development of the forces of production is carried forward under capitalist social relations, and an index of the success of different types of adjustment.

Institutional changes determine not only which countries will grow and which will lose ground but are also one of the factors shaping the quality of development and of life. In an interdependent world, however, what happens in one area is not independent of what happens in another or of the global context of development. Where the increases in productivity associated with more progressive sets of social relations are substantial, the threat of compe-

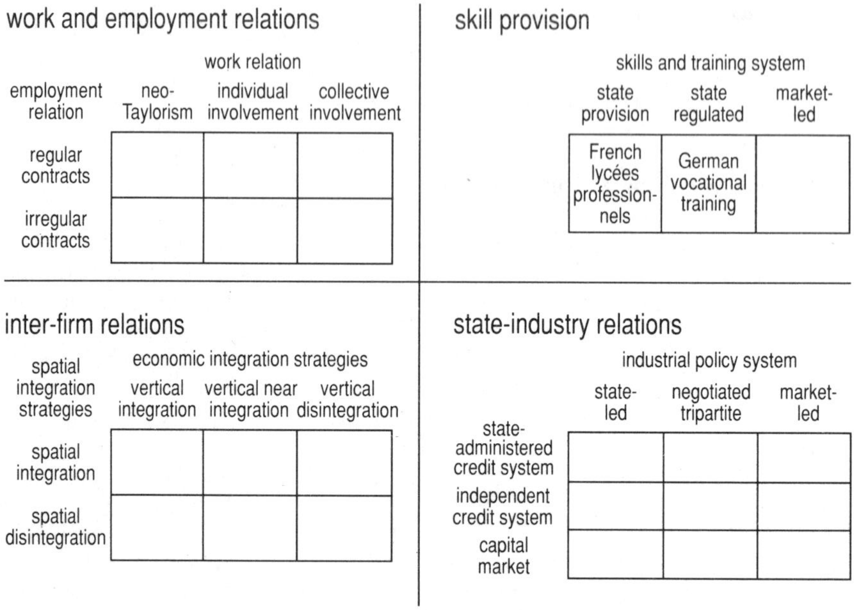

work and employment relations

employment relation	work relation		
	neo-Taylorism	individual involvement	collective involvement
regular contracts			
irregular contracts			

skill provision

	skills and training system		
	state provision	state regulated	market-led
	French lycées professionnels	German vocational training	

inter-firm relations

spatial integration strategies	economic integration strategies		
	vertical integration	vertical near integration	vertical disintegration
spatial integration			
spatial disintegration			

state-industry relations

	industrial policy system		
	state-led	negotiated tripartite	market-led
state-administered credit system			
independent credit system			
capital market			

Figure 3.2 Social relations and social strategies in areas of new industrial growth

tition from more backward areas is limited, but in other cases social advances will be held back.

Notwithstanding these qualifications a question that arises once again is the following: with the new developments in the forces of production which societies will do better and in which will the quality of development be greatest: societies that are more market-oriented or societies that are more organised?

In this chapter my aim is to contribute to an answer to the questions I have raised. To do so some of the differences in the development of high-tech industries will be examined. In part the differences observed are a product of different environments, histories and cultures. Others, however, are a result of differences in the mechanisms of industrial change. On the one hand there are differences in sectoral specialisation and in the roles of the enterprises in different areas in wider divisions of labour (Massey 1984). On the other there are differences, on which I shall focus, rooted in the choices that are made concerning the character of the wage relation, the acquisition of skills, the relationships among firms and among activities, and the role of the state.

This second set of differences can in fact be viewed as elements of different experiments in the construction of new institutional structures and new modes of regulation. A mode of regulation is of course multidimensional: it involves methods of wage and income determination, credit mechanisms, market structures, and so on. In this chapter only four elements will be considered: the wage and employment relation, inter-firm relations, state–industry relations, and vocational education regimes (see Figure 3.2). In each case there is no new hegemonic set of answers and no new flexible model of development. Instead there is a series of adaptations to crisis and a series of experiments whose outcomes have yet to be determined.

3.2 Wage and employment relations and local development

In their work Leborgne and Lipietz (1988) argued that the way in which work is organised and the character of the employment contract are important factors differentiating local economies. With respect to the organisation of work three broad principles were identified: neo-Taylorism, individual involvement and collective involvement. In the case of neo-Taylorism, a single most efficient method ('the one best way') is identified and methods of production standardised. At the same time a sharp division is drawn between mental and manual work: manual jobs are for the most part unskilled, while skills, knowledge and control over the speed of work are concentrated in the hands of scientists and managers. Innovations depend on the activities of the organisation and methods office and normally entail the development of more complex machines.

The major alternative is for employers to seek a more active involvement of workers. Instead of using new technologies to rationalise mass production and deskill workers, jobs that are more varied and have a higher skill content are designed. Workers are given jobs that are more responsible and autonomous, and all of the workforce is involved in the search for increased efficiency and quality. Strategies of this kind enable a reduction in the volume of capital per head, and play an important role where firms are seeking to move in the direction of high quality, diversified and customised goods.

The existence of involved and multi-skilled workers does however require a new kind of industrial relations. In the view of Leborgne and Lipietz there are two models. One is the Japanese-style individual bargain where increases in efficiency are shared out in the form of individual bonuses and career advantages. The second is the typical Swedish model of collective involvement negotiated with trade unions. Under this model skills and wages would be higher and the distribution of income more even.

With respect to the employment contract, Leborgne and Lipietz distinguish regular and irregular contracts. Irregular contracts involve reduced job security and a more widespread use of temporary workers, contract workers and subcontractors: in all of these cases the commodity character of the employment relation and of the wage is reinforced. What tends to prevail is a mixed situation: secure core workers are surrounded by a group of insecure peripheral workers employed so as to make a firm more flexible with respect to the numbers and types of workers it employs (Atkinson 1984).[6]

None of these three models is dominant. Within countries, firms and even plants elements of each coexist. In Scotland where the development of the electronics sector was a result in the main of the arrival of inward investors making standardised products with large-scale production methods, processes of production are in the main Taylorised. As a result relatively few skilled manual jobs exist, and the skill structure is polarised with, on the one hand, many unskilled operatives and, on the other, highly qualified and individualistically involved production and test engineers.[7]

In Grenoble the different skill profile is mainly a result of the different composition of employment: with a high share of jobs in education and research, high-quality scientific jobs with their very different conditions of work and employment are much more significant than in Scotland.[8] In universities and research establishments scientists and technicians have secure jobs, and in many cases trade unions and professional organisations negotiate collective improvements in conditions and terms of work. The small high-tech firms sector is however closer to what Leborgne and Lipietz call a 'Californian model': individual involvement predominates, while employment contracts tend to be irregular as key workers move frequently from one firm to another. In Grenoble however there is some evidence that the organisation of manufacture in some firms where there was a juxtaposition of research and development, design and production involved greater reliance on strategies of responsible involvement. The most striking case was Télémécanique which as early as the 1960s introduced autonomous groups. In large French firms such as Thomson, however, Taylorism tends to predominate.

Nonetheless the existence of different skill profiles is significant as the development potential of these models is rather different. Cities such as Grenoble or Cambridge with their higher skill profiles and with skills that are less firm-specific are more able to adapt and innovate should investors whose decision-making centres lie elsewhere decide to pull out and are more able to spin off new firms.

3.3 Strategies of economic integration and industrial structures: markets versus hierarchies

A second set of variables concerns the relationships among firms and their spatial strategies. In several studies Allen Scott (1986b and 1988c) opened up the question as to the circumstances in which the competitive edge lies with networks of small firms related via market transactions or with vertically integrated corporations whose interrelated activities are organised hierarchically. Scott uses the term vertical disintegration to refer to the first set of relations among economic activities, and vertical integration to describe the second. Leborgne and Lipietz, on the other hand, add a third set of inter-firm relations which they call vertical near integration: in this case the ownership of the constituent firms is decentralised, but stable non-market as well as market relations link the firms into interdependent hierarchical systems (Leborgne and Lipietz 1988).

Standard (Coase-Williamson) analyses of these developments involve a consideration of several factors.[9] In recent debates about vertical integration and disintegration most attention has been paid to the role of economies and diseconomies of scope. Suppose that economies in the costs of a firm can be divided into three elements: (1) economies of scale which depend on the volume of output and the scale at which a single step in the process of

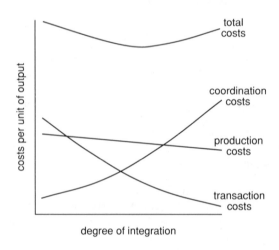

Figure 3.3 Strategies of integration and the structure of costs

production occurs and which determine production costs, (2) economies of scope which depend on the range of related products and services a firm makes and provides and the number of distinct processes of labour it operates, and (3) economies of diversification which depend on the advantages and disadvantages of a firm diversifying into unrelated processes and products (conglomerate strategies).

Economies of scope are related to the size of the range of products a firm makes. This range depends in part on the extent of vertical integration upstream/backwards into activities supplying inputs and downstream/forwards into activities involving further transformations of the commodities it produces, and on conglomerate strategies. In the first case the scope of a firm depends on a series of 'make or buy decisions' which depend on the relative size of internal and external production costs and the constituent elements of the costs of organisation of economic activities: costs of coordination which increase as a firm integrates upstream and downstream, and transaction costs which increase with reductions in vertical integration and an increase in the volume of market transactions (see Figure 3.3 and also Del Monte and Martinelli 1987, pp. 8–10). With the development of flexible machines, however, increased scope can also stem from increases in the mix of products or the number of designs made with particular machines. There is no doubt that these ideas help explain processes of economic integration and disintegration. What this framework overlooks however is the fact that the goal of capitalist production is not to minimise costs but to maximise the rate of profit.

If finally one combines these strategies of economic integration with decisions as to whether different economic activities should 'be spatially concentrated or spatially dispersed around major physical and telecommunications networks one arrives at the typology represented in Figure 3.2 (see also Leborgne and Lipietz, Chapter 2).

3.3.1 Vertical disintegration, vertical integration and vertical near integration

In recent years many authors have suggested that an earlier dramatic concentration and centralisation of capital was giving way to more disintegrated systems of industrial organisation involving complex inter-firm linkages: large firms were adopting conscious deconcentration strategies involving an increase in the use of satellite subcontractors, specialised niche markets offered innovative and traditional small firms a space in which to operate that was sheltered from competition of large corporations (see, for example, Brusco and Sabel 1981), and industrial districts made up of networks of small firms underwent fast growth. In these districts increases in the size of the market and in the volume of sales, moreover, created the conditions in which new specialised firms could develop and survive through the exploitation of economies of scale in particular steps in the process of production as long as sufficient integrated firms decided to externalise production.

However, the competitive advantage of strategies of flexible specialisation and of networks of small firms depends on very specific conditions. On the one hand, it depends on market demands that are static, irregular and differentiated: in these conditions, as Benjamin Coriat (Chapter 7) has shown, the advantages of almost instantaneous switches from one product to another exceed the advantages of scale, and product differentiation allows the appropriation of monopolistic rents. On the other, start-up costs must be limited. In the initial phases in the development of new technologies a subset of these conditions prevails: initial experimentation with products and processes involves low entry costs, there is a very rapid process of product succession, and monopolistic niche markets exist. In these circumstances small high-tech firms can flourish.

If, however, these conditions do not obtain, the advantages of vertical disintegration will diminish. Indeed several factors suggest that the role of scale and of large industrial and financial groups on the one hand and of non-market relations on the other will be greater than the advocates of a new industrial divide suggest. In some sectors the development of strategies of product renewal or product succession (from, for example, compact discs to compact video discs) allows a dynamic reuse of equipment that reduces the risks of volume production, allows the adoption of strategies of cost reduction through the search for scale economies, and involves the development and extension of oligopolistic mass markets (see Coriat, Chapter 7). In addition modularisation allows the survival of traditional mass production: modules or components are mass produced, while differentiated final products are assembled in flexible production islands.

The new technologies also involve immense investments in research and development which in some sectors are a stimulus to mergers and joint ventures. In order, for example, to recover the research and development costs of new generations of digital switch telecommunications equipment a firm will need to achieve a sales volume that exceeds the size of individual national markets in Europe. What is more, research and development is associated with major scale economies. Three-quarters of the cost of a modern telephone exchange is software, whereas ten years ago three-quarters of the cost of the previous generation of exchanges was hardware. But software has a special property: the first copy is very expensive, but the second is almost free. Instead of the erosion of scale economies used to justify privatisation and deregulation there are strong increasing returns to scale which justifies public provision and public investment (see Costello, Michie and Milne 1989, pp. 98–9).

Indeed in many cases the development of more disintegrated structures is a product of the development of networks of large and small firms. In years of crisis conjunctural circumstances and in particular the desire to avoid strategies that tie up resources in inflexible projects and to pass the risks and costs of devalorisation onto others lead large firms to transfer certain activities to smaller subcontractors: a path of this kind is, however, in the end self-defeating as the costs of supplies comprise a high share of the costs of large groups. In these circumstances a more cooperative course of action is more rational.

The growth, secondly, of telematic networks, systemofacture and just-in-time methods involves attempts to overcome some of the contradictions of market mechanisms and to organise and plan inter-firm relations.

3.3.2 Integration strategies in electronics and the development of technopoles

In the electronics sector vertical disintegration was an important characteristic of the early development of Silicon Valley in the United States and also appears to characterise the development of the ZIRST (*Zone pour l'innovation et les réalisations scientifiques et techniques*) and Grenoble where small firms were spun off from research institutes, universities, and in particular from SEMS (*Société européenne de mini-informatique et de système*) and also of Cambridge.

In the case of the United States these developments were, however, closely related with the early stages in the life cycle of electronics products and the fact that entry costs were low. At first the companies in Silicon Valley adopted strategies of territorial integration: from the producers of final goods downwards inputs were sourced from other small and medium-sized local firms creating a dense and complex network of local market transactions. Towards the end of the 1960s, however, the key firms had grown in size and were integrating vertically. In addition defence markets had declined in relative importance. With these developments went a trend towards territorial disintegration as several major American semiconductor firms sought to decentralise some stages of manufacture and assembly. One of their preferred destinations was Europe and in particular Scotland where inward investments were welcomed. (The Germans were indifferent, while the French tried to keep American companies out.) Scottish development may thus be seen as a joint product of these strategies of vertical integration and territorial disintegration on the one hand and of Scotland's attempt to attract inward investors on the other.

However, not all stages of semiconductor production were decentralised. In Scotland the most important activity was wafer fabrication. Wafers, made in Scotland to circumvent the 17 per cent EC tariff on semiconductor devices, were sent to South East Asia where assembly and test operations were concentrated, and the finished products were imported back into Europe, while research and development and mask-making remained in the United States. Scottish plants were in other words simply one part of an international division of work within vertically integrated American semiconductor firms (see Table 3.1 and Henderson 1987).

In the case of Grenoble mechanisms of endogenous growth were however much more significant: a whole series of new firms emerged in the main from the CENG and, directly and indirectly, the universities of which some of the most important were EFCIS and Télémécanique-SEMS (see Figures 3.4, 3.5 and 3.6 and Dunford 1989).[10] As in the case of EFCIS, however, growth resulted in the vertically integrated Thomson group's takeover, while integration resulted in the end in disinvestment.[11]

In the case of the new technological enterprises that developed on the ZIRST at Meylan near Grenoble, however, one is not dealing with firms that are likely to emerge as major producers but with what Gilly called a technico-scientific system. While these firms do develop products and services for sale on the market, industrial production is not a major concern. In many cases revenues depend to a very significant extent on research contracts which embed the firms concerned into upstream networks of a non-market kind, and so vertical disintegration in the sense of a substitution of market transactions for hierarchical ones or the growth of small market-oriented firms is not the central mechanism of change. Vertical near integration is nonetheless a more accurate description of the structure of the ZIRST. As Leborgne and Lipietz (1988) suggest, it responds to a dual 'imperative': the need to exploit economies of scope through the integration of research and development and production and marketing on the one hand and the need to exploit the advantages of specialised firms on the other.

These 'technopoles' (Gilly 1987, pp. 785–7) are a product of a separation of research and innovation from the process of production and the development of organic links between science and production through the development of an intermediate technological sphere in which scientific and industrial knowledge and logics are fused. This intermediate technological sphere is made up of research centres, innovative small and medium-sized enterprises, service companies and subsidiaries of large groups that comprise a productive system. The productive system itself is characterised by principles of interdependence and hierarchy: on the one hand a series of scientific, technological, economic and financial interdependencies exist, while on the other relationships are asymmetrical and involve relations of domination and dependence.

A technico-scientific system (Gilly 1987, pp. 787–90), of which the ZIRST is an example, is a local productive system that is centred on relationships between centres of public research and mainly small and medium-sized new technological firms. In these areas technologies from different areas of science

Nature of operation and labour processes

Company	USA	Scotland	England & Wales	Germany	France	Ireland	Switzerland	Japan	S. Korea	Taiwan	Hong Kong	Singapore	Malaysia	Philippines	Thailand	Indonesia
Motorola	c, rd, w, a, t, ms, m	w, a, t		w, t	w, t		d, r, m	w, d	a	a	d, t, r, m		a	a		
National Semiconductor	c, rd, w, a, t, ms, m	d, w	r, m								a, t, m	t, d, m, r	w, a, t	a	a, t	a
Fairchild	c, rd, w, a, t, ms, m		d, r, m		w, t, m			w, d, a, t	a, t	d	t, m	a, t, m	a	a		a
Texas Instruments	c, rd, w, t, ms, m				w, t, r			w, d		a		a, t, m	a	a		
General Instrument	c, rd, w, t, ms, m	w	d, m, r		m					a, t			a			
Hughes	c, rd, w, a, t, ms, m	w, a, t (ms)	d, r, m								(a)			(a)		
Burr-Brown	c, rd, w, a, t, ms, m	w, a, t, d														
Siliconix	c, rd, w, t, ms, m		a, t, m							a	a, t, d					
Teledyne	c, rd, w, t, ms, m										a, t					
Advanced Micro Devices	c, rd, w, t, ms, m					w					m	t, m	a	a	a	
Silicon Systems	c, rd, w, t, ms, m											d, a, t				
Sprague	c, rd, w, t, ms, m									a	r, t, m			a		
Zilog	c, rd, w, t, ms m					w					d, r, m			a, t		
Burr-Brown	c, rd, w, t, ms, m, a	w, a, t, d						a, t								

key:
c – corporate control   rd – research & development   d – design centre   ms – mask-making
w – wafer fabrication   a – assembly   t – final testing   ( ) – operation under sub-
r – regional headquarters   m – marketing centre   contract arrangement

Source: Henderson (1987).

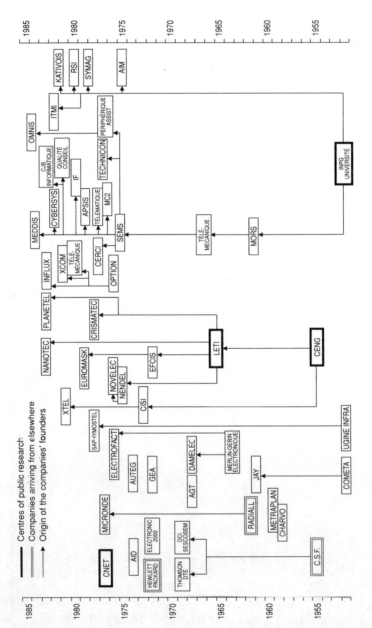

Figure 3.4 The development of Grenoble's electronics sector

Source: based on Champ and Fradet 1985.

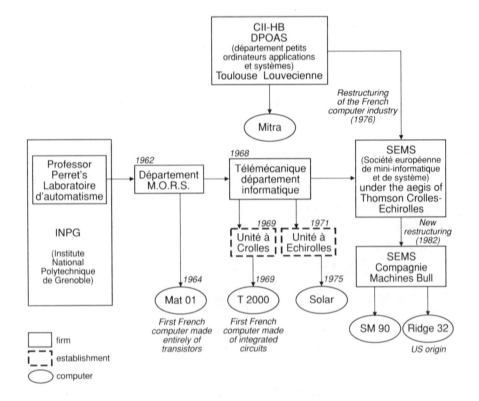

Figure 3.5 The development of SEMS

Source: based on Hurtado 1984.

represented in local universities and research centres are combined to create new technological clusters that arise from new industrial applications of generic technologies such as electronics and telecommunications; examples include robotics which brings together mechanical engineers, electronic engineers and artificial intelligence specialists on the one hand and the development of hardware and software on the other. Areas of this kind depend on the development of local research and education for ideas and skills, the development of clusters of new technological firms and the activities of local authorities and other local actors, and within them new types of social compromise emerge.

A technico-productive space (Gilly 1987, pp. 787–90) is a product of the relationships between new technological enterprises and the sphere of production where these enterprises, other small and medium-sized firms and industrial groups implement industrial applications and seek to valorise innovations. In these areas large groups are dominant. While large groups do act as

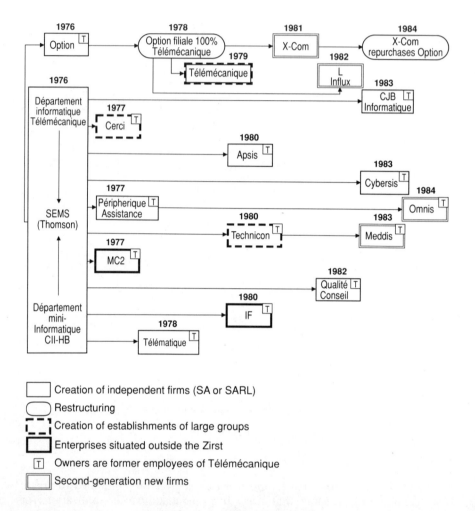

Figure 3.6 Spin-offs from SEMS, 1976–84

Source: based on Hurtado 1984.

a source of spin-offs, use is made of technopoles as a source of innovations, and with acquisitions new technological firms are incorporated into vertical, hierarchical relationships with the group's headquarters and financial centre. (The groups themselves have two characteristics. One is their financial flexibility that allows them to switch resources in accordance with the profitabilities of different courses of action. The second is the integration of innovations, production and markets into technological clusters and trajectories centred on particular generic technologies which give them considerable upstream and downstream flexibility. Changes in group strategies and related investment and disinvestment decisions will however have a major impact on the development of technopoles.)

Integration creates a dependence of the technopoles on metropolitan centres, and through the relationships a group has with a variety of different technopoles links them into a hierarchical network. As a result of the international character of the markets they serve and the critical relationships of local research and educational centres with national government programmes technopoles emerge as places that are integrated into national and global networks. With internationalisation national systems of regulation disintegrate and national solidarities and identities weaken: in these circumstances national productive systems fragment into a mosaic of local economies, and inequalities increase, and in the absence of new international solidarities a sense of belonging to smaller and more localised communities grows. The economies that result are differentiated therefore not just in accordance with their internal structure (sectoral specialisation, the organisation of production, the character of the wage relation, inter-firm relations and so on) but also with the character of their insertion in the national and international economic and political order (see Gilly 1987 and also Ruffieux 1987).

In England small and dynamic high-tech firms selling very specialised products in particular high-profit niche markets are the foundation of the Cambridge phenomenon (see Segal, Quince and Partners 1984), yet what one finds is a set of firms whose small size places limits on their growth potential. In a survey of a small sample of twelve Cambridge firms John Grieve Smith and Vivien Fleck (1987) observed a predisposition to stay comparatively small, to remain independent of external finance and large firms, and to avoid the human and organisational difficulties associated with growth.

A minimisation of involvement in direct manufacture and an emphasis on the assembly of bought-in components bought from abroad or from foreign multinationals as well as an averseness to external finance means that these firms have no chance of emerging as major producers or of making a major contribution to the national industrial base. (It does however keep down capital requirements, ease the redeployment of resources, limit managerial efforts devoted to activities with which the founders were unfamiliar and allow the maintenance of more informal and less hierarchical organisational structures.) What is more, the lack of resources places limits on the research and development required to develop successor products when low-cost producers appear, and so survival will depend on access to new developments in fundamental research. (The small firms surveyed have a high proportion of research and development staff. But much of the research and development is to adapt their products to work with new hardware systems and to develop new applications for them.)

What is clear from these examples is that the growth of small firms is often a stage in the development of larger firms that assumes increased importance in years of fundamental technological change. In other cases new technological enterprises have developed whose goal is not production and which, if successful, risk takeover and whose long-run survival otherwise depends on a constant renewal of close relationships with research centres. Vertical disintegration in these growing sectors does not offer much potential for growth, whereas vertical near integration does.

3.4 State–industry relations and industrial structures: politics and markets

While small firm growth is a common characteristic of technopoles, the Silicon Valley model cannot be imitated as the emergence of small firms as major international competitors increases in difficulty with the move from the initial stages of innovation to the further development of new technical paradigms. With the increase in entry costs into the field of semiconductors, for example, countries wishing to challenge the Americans could not rely on small firms. The up-front investment required to finance a new wafer fabrication facility today amounts to at least £200 m.: £100 m. for equipment, and £100 m. for research and development. In the late 1960s when entry was easy and Silicon Valley at its strongest the corresponding sum was £5 m. It helps to explain why the only new entrants into main-stream (commodity) chip production in the last decade have been the major Japanese electronics firms which have had the resources to finance such ventures. The Japanese also benefited from a major state-led programme of collaborative research and development targeted at breaking into the market.

Within the capitalist world, however, there are important differences in the character and extent of state intervention in industry. Almost all nations rely at least in part on state intervention involving, as with MITI in Japan, major national programmes of a sectoral or global character, and state-supported research and development. Even in the United States, the defence sector, in effect, runs an industrial strategy for high-tech industries. Indeed it has been estimated that some 20 per cent of federal spending (£8 000 m.) goes to electronics, and pays for 35 per cent of electronics-sector activities (Stoffaes 1984).

Institutional structures and strategies give different weights to interventionist and neo-liberal ideologies and methods. Zysman (1983 pp. 7 and 91–3) has distinguished three technical-political strategies aimed at shaping national development: state-led, market-led and negotiated tripartite.

Consider the French case. After the Second World War French industry was modernised through what might be identified as a 'third way' lying between market-led capitalism and the socialist command mechanism. Under this model the state is the central actor in the economic system not only looking after macroeconomic equilibria but also accelerating, encouraging and supporting private initiative where it can, and replacing it when it fails. Until recent years political debate involved arguments concerning the relative merits of this mixed economy and socialism, understood as involving nationalisation, economic planning and self-management. In 1983, however, within two years of the election of a socialist government, political discourse had shifted, with the left championing the new mixed economy and the right moving, at least at the level of rhetoric, in the direction of neo-liberalism.

In countries such as the United Kingdom where state interventionism was less important, many sectors such as gas, water, electricity and telecommunications were under the control of public monopolies, while a major defence sector was developed in the private sector through state orders. Under the neo-liberal influence of Margaret Thatcher's three administrations, the dividing lines between the public and private and non-market spheres have undergone substantial redefinition as a result, in particular of the wholesale privatisation of several public utilities.

Variations in the role of the state are a result of a variety of factors including the structure of industry, administrative organisation and the character of the ruling political coalition. Also important, however, are the mechanisms through which money and credit are allocated, as they shape not only corporate strategies but also the capacity of the state to act. According to Zysman (1983, pp. 18 and 55–75) three varieties of financial system can be identified: a capital market with market determined prices, a credit-based system with critical prices administered by the state, and a credit-based system in which financial institutions are dominant.

Selectivity and discretionary control over the use of credit are essential instruments for a state seeking to guide industrial development (see Zysman 1983, pp. 75–95). Where a capital market dominates state interventionism is likely to find itself blocked. In the second type of financial context, executive discretion is considerable and state-led industrialisation facilitated, while in the third, the state has some discretion through negotiations with institutions supplying industrial credit.

In the French case the financial system was state-controlled and adjustment state-led. In the United Kingdom what predominated was a cosmopolitan capital market and an ambiguous industrial development mechanism. Attempts by UK governments to establish an interventionist framework and to shape industrial adjustment were unable to overcome the obstacles the financial system placed across the path of interventionism. Since 1979, however, a market-driven path consistent with the character of the country's financial mechanisms and the strength of rentier interests has been followed.

Over and above these differences which are rooted in the differences in economic structures, political frameworks and hegemonic blocs there are common elements rooted in mode of operation of capitalist societies. In particular in all epochs of crisis capitalist entrepreneurs seek more fluid ways of holding money wealth, while indirect costs associated with land and other kinds of speculation increase. In the 1960s the share of banking capital in value added increased, as did rentier incomes. In the 1970s the concepts of an aggressively assertive economic liberalism and of rentier perspectives, which reflected the interests in particular of the holders of money capial, gained ground, and in some nations achieved a hegemonic role. The ascendancy of these concepts was however not just a result of the increasing weight of their usual advocates such as commercial capitalists and financiers, owners of small enterprises, and individuals with incomes made up of interest, rents and dividends (van der Pijl 1984, pp. 8–20). Owing to the difficulties of accumulation the concepts of economic liberalism also gained ground in the ranks of industrial capitalists. The differences in the French and UK cases are therefore differences of degree and in the relative weight of different social classes rather than differences of kind.

These distinctions nevertheless play an important role in explaining the differences observed in the development of the UK and French electronics sectors. Successive French governments have adopted strategic plans for the national electronics sector, and these interventions have played a major role in the development of French technopoles. In the case of the United Kingdom the attempts at intervention in the 1960s and 1970s gave way to disengagement in the 1980s (see Table 3.2) and a very strong emphasis on the attraction of inward investment which itself is an important determinant of the different character of high-tech development in the United Kingdom.

3.4.1 Grenoble and French government ambitions in the electronics sector

In the late 1970s only one-half of the integrated circuits consumed in France were produced in that country, while in the case of MOS circuits French production was minimal. As in the United Kingdom, markets were dominated by the US companies many of which had emerged from the 1960s benefiting from the twin advantages of defence contracts which underwrote leading-edge research and development and a venture capital market which was prepared to finance new and relatively unknown enterprises. What resulted was, as Sciberras identified in relation to the United Kingdom, a 'big league/little league' phenomenon in the semiconductor market: firms which were established at the leading edge had the advantage of knowledge and experience which others found impossible to replicate. Many European firms had in consequence given up the battle and withdrawn to niche markets (Sciberras 1977; Dosi 1981).

As Sciberras pointed out, the only way to overcome these learning-curve disadvantages was a concerted (and long-term) strategy on the part of the companies concerned (and their governments) to make major investments in research and development and equipment, deliberately planning to break into the market with the next generation of technological developments. It was precisely such a strategy that underlay the Japanese VLSI (very large-scale integration) programme of the mid-1970s which enabled them to break US hegemony in the 1980s.

French plans were less ambitious than the Japanese and concentrated on catching up rather than leaping forward (which perhaps explains why they were less successful). In 1977 the French government introduced its first Plan Composants (Components Plan) for the years 1978–82 with an expenditure of over FF600 m. (£69 m.)

Thomson was at the centre of these plans (see Table 3.2 and also Table 3.1). Thomson was to take over EFCIS from the CEA (since EFCIS was the main centre of MOS technology in France) and FF220 m. (£25 m.) were to be ploughed into research and development and new manufacturing operations. As a result of this investment EFCIS grew spectacularly. Between 1978 and 1981 its revenues increased from FF31 m. (£4 m.) to FF250 m. (£23 m.). As well as the support for EFCIS, Thomson was given a further FF100 m.

Table 3.2 State intervention: aid for and reorganisation of the French, German and UK electronics sectors

	1968	1970	1973	1975	1976–8	1978	1978–9	1979–80	1980	1981–2	1983	1983–4	1984
France	State fosters SECO (Thomson) and COSEM (CSF) merger to create SECOSEM. Thomson given major state support.	EFCIS created as joint venture between Thomson and CEA	Creation of UNIDATA (computers) as a joint venture of CII, Siemens and Philips. (Government attitude uncertain.)	UNIDATA fails. State supports merger of CII and Honeywell-Bull.		Thomson takes over semiconductor division of LTI and SILEC.	State supports joint ventures of Saint-Gobain and National Semiconductor, Matra and Harris, Thomson and Motorola. Saint-Gobain enter CII and Olivetti. Support for RadioTechnique (Philips). 5 poles of production.			CGE, Thomson, Saint-Gobain, CII-HB (named Bull) nationalised. Majority government stake in Matra.		Concentration of Thomson, Saint-Gobain and CGE's computer activities with Bull. Thomson takes over Saint-Gobain/National Semiconductor joint venture (Eurotechnique) and semiconductor activities of CGE. Of 5 poles only 2 remain. Saint-Gobain withdraws from Olivetti. CGE takes 10% share in Olivetti.	
Federal Republic of Germany		Creation of DATEL. Joint venture of state, Siemens, AEG-Telefunken and Nixdorf in computer applications.	Creation of UNIDATA. State in favour.	Siemens takes over large computer division of AEG. Approved by state.			Rescue of AEG-Telefunken by a joint consortium of banks. Indirect Federal support.	Plans for the establishment of a joint research laboratory of the 3 major firms and public agencies (Berlin Synchrotron Projekt.)			Semiconductor division of AEG merged with Mostek (United technologies) in a joint venture. Telefunken taken over by Thomson.		Joint research in Germany of ICL, Siemens and Bull in computers and IT. Philips takes over Grundig after Bundeskartelamt's disapproval of Thomson's bid.
United Kingdom	Mullard (Philips) takes over its joint venture with GEC. Series of mergers results in ICL. 10.5% state-owned.				NEB buys shares in Ferranti (computers, semiconductors, defence electronics) and in various small and medium-sized firms in software, industrial and consumer electronics.	NEB creates INMOS (VLSI memories and MPUs). Wholly financed by state.			Conservative government sells ICL and Ferranti to private sector.				State sells its 75% share in INMOS to Thorn-EMI. STC (25% owned by ITT) tries to acquire ICL.

Source: data for 1968–80 from Dosi 1981, p. 94, updated.

Table 3.3 The Plan Composants of 1978–82: version 1

	Shareholders	Factories	Public aid (m.)	Employment
Eurotechnique	SGPM: 51% National Semiconductor: 49%	Rousset (Bouches-du-Rhone) start: January 1981	FF100 + FF80 (FDES)(Total investment FF400)	200 (600 in 1985)
Thomson EFCIS	Thomson: 50% CEA: 50% (Technical agreement with Motorola)	Grenoble (Isère)	FF220 (Total investment FF670)	460 (700 at end of 1980)
Thomson Division Semiconducteurs	Division of Thomson-CSF (Agreement with Motorola)	St. Egrève (Isère)	FF100	5000 (of whom 1000 outside France)
Matra-Harris Semiconducteurs	Matra: 51% Harris: 49%	Nantes (Loire-Atlantique) start: 1981	FF150 (Total investment FF200)	100 (540 in 1985)
RTC	Philips: 51%	Caen (Calvados)	FF100	NA

Source: Augoyard, Champ and Fradet 1982, p. 14.

(£12 m.) to expand its activities at St. Egrève (Grenoble) where it manufactured semiconductors under licence from Motorola. By 1980 some 40 per cent of French integrated circuits output, valued at FF650 m. (£66 m.) was made by Thomson at its two sites in Grenoble.

In the early 1980s sectors such as military electronics, telecommunications and aerospace, where there had been major and sustained state support in the shape of spending on research and development and state orders, were doing well, whereas in others (consumer electronics, office automation, industrial electronics, dataprocessing and components) the French industry was weak. In this second group the concept of a national industrial strategy was either non-existent or unsustained and fragmented (dataprocessing and integrated circuits).

With the election of a socialist government all the main French groups in electronics were nationalised, and the state returned to a strategy of national champions with CGE specialising in telecommunications equipment, the Compagnie des Machines Bull in computers, CGE and Bull in office automation, Thomson and Matra in military electronics and components, and Thomson in consumer electronics. Investment was much greater than under earlier programmes and intervention was extended to the whole of the electronics sector, including the making of materials and machines in upstream sectors. In components additional resources were invested in indigenous companies. Investment occurred in the main research establishments in

Table 3.4a Inward investments handled by Locate in Scotland

	1981–82	1982–83	1983–84	1984–85	1985–86
Enquiries received	320	377	442	281	288
Visits to Scotland	116	140	199	124	142
Investment decisions	32	49	54	69	58
Jobs created	4 600	4 760	3 446	8 169	4 663
Jobs safeguarded	2 400	1 146	3 460	1 274	3 554
Project costs £'000	237 370	211 231	166 541	689 170	561 840
Assistance offered £'000	20 451	24 738	16 931	41 304	41 491
Expansions of companies already in Scotland	19	18	22	33	27
New starts	13	31	32	36	31

Source: Locate in Scotland 1986.

Table 3.4b Offers of regional selective assistance in Scotland in 1984–85

	Number of offers	Value of grants (£m.)	Associated project costs (£m.)	Associated jobs created or safeguarded
All plants	274	77.60	861.40	24200
overseas-owned	58	46.40	438.70	10200
Electronics	42	37.80	333.40	7800
of which:	23	32.40	270.30	6800
overseas-owned				

Source: Industry Department for Scotland 1986.

Grenoble (LETI and CNET), though EFCIS was a victim of asset swaps through which Thomson acquired new capacities, the 1985 acquisition of Mostek, and the merger with the Italian state-controlled firm SGS-Ates. (In 1989 SGS and Thomson acquired Inmos: Inmos was set up by the National Enterprise Board, and developed the transputer, but in the early 1980s it was sold off to Thorn-EMI and starved of long-term investment until the French/Italian takeover.)

3.4.2 Scotland, inward investment and the UK government's electronics strategy

In the case of Scotland, the Scottish Development Agency (SDA) set up in 1974 has played some part in helping indigenous companies. Its electronics industry strategy launched in 1979 focuses mainly, however, on attracting inward investors.[12] In 1984–5 and 1985–6 investments worth over £500 m. a year were attracted to Scotland (see Table 3.4a). Table 3.4b indicates that nearly 40 per cent of that investment was in electronics and that over 80 per cent of electronics investment was foreign-owned.

Inward investors in the main are seeking access to EC markets, but are also attracted by government financial assistance: automatic regional aid, and discretionary selective assistance which the government uses to cap bids from

Mick Dunford

Table 3.5 The growth of major countries' electronics markets, production and balance of trade, 1976–86 (£'000 m. adjusted by GDP deflators)

	Markets		Production		Balance of trade	
	1976	1986	1976	1986	1976	1986
Japan	17.50	47.50	28.66	78.26	11.16	30.76
US	73.00	175.00	75.44	167.74	2.44	-7.26
Italy	5.80	10.70	5.12	9.22	-0.68	-1.48
France	11.20	18.90	11.27	18.71	0.07	-0.19
FRG	12.30	26.70	13.47	27.38	1.17	0.68
UK	8.30	20.50	8.12	18.24	-0.18	-2.26

Source: National Economic Development Office 1988, p. 7.

Table 3.6 Electronics sales and employment growth of major companies by country, 1976–86 (average annual percentage rate of growth)

Companies	Real sales growth	Employment growth
Japanese	7.60	4.70
US	6.60	4.50
European	4.40	0.20
UK	2.60	-1.40

Source: National Economic Development Office 1988, p. 7.

other countries (see Table 3.4b which shows how overseas companies were the major recipients of selective assistance in 1984–5).

The development of Silicon Glen is regarded as one of the outstanding successes of a targeted, strategic regional policy. In Scotland, however, the industrial output and employment are dominated by multinationals whose local linkages are limited.[13] Inward investors establish production sites but research and development, design and marketing are under-represented. At a national level, moreover, support for inward investment conflicts with the development of a national presence in these sectors.

Scotland's success in attracting inward investors, the limited spin-offs, and the relative weakness of national firms outside of the defence field are in part a result of a national project that differs sharply in consequences and character from the more interventionist strategies of successive French governments. What Table 3.5 shows is that in the United Kingdom a high rate of growth of the domestic market was associated with a relatively slow growth of domestic output and a sharp deterioration in the country's trade deficit. The share of major UK companies in sales fell from 40 to 31 per cent as an increase in the share of imports was accompanied by an increase in the share of UK production of non-UK companies. In 1982–6 the sales of UK companies increased 50 per cent, imports increased almost 100 per cent and UK output of non-UK companies increased over 125 per cent. UK companies, as Table 3.6 shows, grew slowly (see also NEDO 1988).

What distinguishes these two models are two factors. One is the extent to which the central state welcomes and finances inward investments. As a result of state support, inward investors have a significant advantage over the indigenous firms they displace, while the absence of indigenous firms and the consequent lack of knowledge of new systems and methods place domestic user industries at a disadvantage.

The second factor differentiating these two models is the existence of industrial policies in favour of indigenous industries. Included are high levels of state support for collaborative civil research and development, the identification of independent international standards, cheap long-term finance, and public-sector procurement initiatives as well as education and training schemes. Measures of this kind are advocated by the National Economic Development Office (NEDO) but not accepted at a governmental level. In the French case, on the other hand, similar measures were at the centre of the state's industrial policies.

In the United Kingdom the weakness of indigenous firms has contributed to the comparative underdevelopment of the information technology sector and a dependence on inward investments. 'On present trends,' said a NEDO report in 1984, 'the UK will not have an independent broad-based IT industry by the end of the decade. It will have a mixture of inward investment, UK-owned companies employing licensed technology, and specialised niche and applications companies' (see National Economic Development Office 1984 and also Blackburn and Sharpe 1988).

3.5 Skills, vocational training and the development of the electronics sector

The skills and human resources of a society are another major determinant of its development potential. Skills are not, however, an independent variable but stand in a reciprocal relationship with other economic decisions. Whether new technologies are used for diversified high-quality production or rationalised mass production depends, for example, on the skill profile of the population, while a society associated with high skill levels will tend to have high wages, a relatively even distribution of income, relatively equal life chances and an effective social welfare system.

In order to provide skills three broad strategies exist. On the one hand, there are market-oriented approaches in which individual self-interest is relied upon to get individuals to invest the time, effort and money required for the acquisition of marketable qualifications to which firms can add job specific skills. A second approach is centred on the view that work and learning should occur in conjunction with one another and involves the social imposition and regulation of vocational training schemes agreed in tripartite negotiations. The German vocational training schemes are an example of this approach. In the third place vocational education can be provided by the state. In the French case, for example, most engineering training is provided in publicly funded vocational schools (or lyces professionnels), and with the exception of a small number of apprenticeships decisions about the provision of places are made by the Ministry of Education.

Skills and training comprise another area in which unregulated market mechanisms are, in fact, self-destroying and under-developing. High skills are a collective resource whose existence is a precondition for productive activities whether public or private. As Streeck (1987) has shown, however, the provision of skills is subject to a prisoners' dilemma problem where the optimal outcome for all requires cooperative coordinated behaviour of all but where, for individuals, cooperation is too risky and the potential rewards of non-cooperation are too great.

Self-interest on which market models rest cannot therefore be relied upon to achieve the desired results. The problem of skills is in fact not one that stems from the inappropriateness of financial rewards but is a result of market failure. The reason why is that individuals acquire fundamental skills when they are young and when they are least able to accept the long deferral of gratification that is the essence of an investment since it presupposes certainty about what one will value in the years to come and this certainty is itself a product of an individual's social and personal identity which in young people is in process of formation. (This critique is of course much more fundamental than that of institutional economists who highlight the uncertainty of the returns to training and the consequent need for institutional reinforcement via, for example, state provision.) Young people whose personal identity has not yet been formed lack 'the crucial properties and capacities needed for rational decision-making of a neoclassical kind' (Streeck 1987).

As a result, moreover, of the existence of a free contract job market firms invest less in training than is in their own interest. The reason why is that skills are a collective resource. A firm's investment adds therefore to a pool of skills on which others, including its competitors, can draw. Various factors qualify this situation, but in general firms tend to provide firm-specific skills. Transferable and non-transferable skills are however interdependent, and so a firm that confines itself to the creation of non-transferable skills will under-develop them. Knowledge also, on which a more active involvement of workers depends, is kept from them in part for similar reasons. A market-oriented approach which is weak in creating dedicated skills will, concludes Streeck, fall far short if it is asked to create skills as cultural resources which will appear to rational decision-makers as excessive qualifications. Yet the central role of generalised and polyvalent skills and the need for skills that can be used in as yet unknown ways transform skills into cultural resources of central import-ance.

The alternative approach that Streeck favours involves a reintegration of learning and work, a treatment of learning as socialisation and as an obligation, and the social regulation of firms. In the view of Streeck enterprises in the West as in the East should be places of learning as well as places of production. But if the acquisition and development of skills can only occur in conjunction with work within the firm, and if the firm does not have the rational motivation to fulfil this role of its own accord, regulation, of the kind embodied in the West German vocational training system, is required.

Skill shortages exist in all societies but are most acute in the United States and United Kingdom where market models prevail. In West Germany and in Japan with their community and corporate institutions shortages are less severe, as they are in France where state intervention is the order of the day.

In a recent study Ray (1988) pointed out substantial differences in the training and roles of electrical (and mechanical) craft workers and technicians in France and Britain. Over three-quarters of French electricians hold the equivalent of a City and Guilds Part II certificate or better compared with 44 per cent in Britain. The most striking differences occur, however, at skilled worker level. What is also important, however, is the fact that in Britain electrical technicians are employed in laboratories, drawing offices and as junior managers whereas their French counterparts are also employed on the shop-floor in process control and maintenance functions.

In 1984 over four times as many gained craft qualifications in France as in Britain: 32 000 against 7 000. At technician level the French trained half as many again: 14 000 against 9 000.

France is now level with Germany in numbers of craftsmen trained each year in electrical work (while ... France trains only half as many mechanical craftsmen as Germany) . . . In 1975 Britain trained around half as many as France to craft and technician standards . . . [In 1975–82 the rate of expansion was similar in the two countries] . . . By 1987, despite the financial support provided to apprentice training by the YTS subsidy, numbers qualifying in Britain were 60 per cent below the peak of 1982, having declined even more sharply than employment in the industry (Ray 1988, p. 64–5).

In 1987 the French lead had increased from a factor of two to a factor of three: the French trained three times as many qualified craftsmen as Britain to standards which are as high and often higher than equivalent British qualifications.[14]

What is clear is that the skill profile of the workers in the French electronics sector is much higher than in the United Kingdom. In the United Kingdom, however, more attention has been given to shortages of professional IT staff with graduate level qualifications: in 1985, in comparison with the difficulties encountered with experienced professional IT staff, shortages at the technician level were considered relatively minor nationally (see Connor and Pearson 1986) and in Scotland (Firn and Roberts 1984, p. 302–3).[15] Skill requirements interact, however, with the volume of employment and the profile of jobs: the evidence on skill structures seems to indicate significant differences in the quality of jobs and in the character of the work relationships in the French and Scottish electronics industries.

3.6 Conclusions

In Grenoble and Cambridge growth was very dependent on the skills and scientific advances that flowed from investments in education and research, and in the French case from the decisions to decentralise important publicly funded research laboratories such as the CEA and the CNET. But whereas Grenoble firms such as EFCIS and Télémécanique-SEMS were caught up in national industrial policies aimed at strengthening the national electronics sector, in the United Kingdom industrial policies were weaker and major national firms did not emerge. Instead inward investment was sought. In

Central Scotland this factor along with central government grants, the existence of skills and the cheapness of labour at the scientific, technical and shop-floor levels were important factors in attracting inward investors. What Scotland attracted was production jobs. Jobs in research and development and decision-making centres remained in the multinationals' home countries. What resulted was a productive system that was dependent on non-domestic multinationals, and a much weaker national electronics sector.

While they are in no sense sufficient, national industrial strategies and influence over the credit mechanism seem on this evidence to be essential conditions for the development of independent national and European firms and an industrial structure that embraces research and development, design, marketing and production. In the United Kingdom the dominance of rentier interests is, however, a major obstacle to the establishment of a developmental state on which such a course depends.

There is also strong evidence to suggest that market mechanisms cannot ensure an adequate supply of skilled workers: on the supply side private actors offer insufficient training owing to free-rider problems, while on the demand side young people lack the crucial properties, capacities and information on which rational decision-making depends.

There is however an important interdependence between skills and the organisation of work. Taylorised work does not require skilled and actively involved operatives, whereas strategies of worker involvement do. Whether the economic results of these two paths differ is a question I have not considered and on which systematic evidence is lacking. In their work, however, Leborgne and Lipietz argue that the enterprises and areas that have been most successful in recent years have adopted strategies of worker involvement. What is clear, however, is that high-productivity, high-wage and high-quality jobs are far superior to deskilled ones.

As far as industrial structures are concerned the development of areas of new growth in electronics provides little support for models of flexible specialisation or the view that we face a new order in which vertical disintegration and an increase in the role of market relations will predominate. In electronics large integrated firms are dominant. Where an explosion of small firms occurred it was connected with innovative breakthroughs and with the development of new technological enterprises: with the passage of time some of these firms grow into major producers, others are taken over, some will operate in networks established around large groups and the rest will face difficult problems of adaptation and survival, while new developments in science will lead to the appearance of new generations of new technological enterprises.

At the outset the question was posed as to which societies will do best: societies that give enterprises and markets a free hand or societies that impose socially enforced social obligations on them? integrated companies, independent small firms or integrated networks of firms? societies whose enterprises use new technologies to deskill or enterprises that seek more consensual management styles? societies in short that are more market-oriented or societies that are more organised? In this chapter we have posed these choices in terms of choices concerning the organisation of work, the differing strategies of economic integration and views about the role of small firms as well as differences in state industrial policies and in approaches to the development of skills. Which choices are made depend in part on economic circumstances. Abstract economic laws always work their way out, however, in particular institutional and political contexts, and choices about the organisation of economic and social life depend also on political factors. The evidence considered in this chapter does suggest, however, that not only the quality of development in a region but also a region's competitive success will be greater in areas where development is more planned and organised and less market-oriented.

Notes

1. An earlier version of this chapter was presented at the Conference on Self-management and Social Protection in the Urban Settlement and the Enterprise held at the Institute of Management, Moscow on 25–30 September 1989.
2. Involved in development of socialist mechanisms are two elements. One is the development of self-management and of new kinds of social property and socialist democracy. The other issue concerns the dominance of producer interests. In a recent article Paul Cockshott and Allin Cottrell (1989) suggest how a computerised socialist resource allocation mechanism could combine values with market clearing prices: the use of the ratio market-clearing price/labour value as an adjustment indicator should encourage a shift of resources in line with consumer demand. What is more an enterprise can only secure a high market clearing price/labour value ratio if it either produces attractive goods and services or uses efficient production methods to reduce labour values. Wage reductions and work intensification are, Cockshott and Cottrell suggest, ruled out.
3. As Mészáros (1978, p. 19–20) argued: 'capitalism is that particular phase of capital production in which 1. production for exchange (and thus the mediation and domination of use value by exchange value) is all-pervasive, 2. labour-power itself ... is treated as a commodity, 3. the drive for profit is a fundamental regulatory force of production, 4. the vital mechanism of the extraction of surplus-value, the radical separation of the means of production from the producers, assumes an inherently economic form, 5. the economically extracted surplus-value is privately appropriated by the members of the capitalist class, and 6. following its own economic imperative of growth and expansion, capital production tends towards a global integration, through the intermediary of the world market, as a total interdependent system of economic domination and subordination.' In post-revolutionary societies, continues Mészáros, only the extraction of surplus-labour survives, while its regulation is political and not economic. In this transitional phase, the rule of capital prevails, and yet its self expansion is undermined by the job control and lack of active involvement of workers. One result is that there is a risk that the process will be thrown into reverse gear.
4. The development of communism is not, for Marx, a 'state of affairs' but a 'real movement' and a 'dynamic principle' of change (see Avineri 1971, p. 221–2). Involved are two stages, identified in the 1844 Economic and Philosophical Manuscripts and in the Critique of the Gotha Programme. In the first instance, private property is abolished objectively through its transformation into 'universal property' or the property of all, and all members of society are made into wage-earners. (In the second stage it is abolished in its subjective form as objective human labour, as is the division of labour on which it depends.) At a political level Marx

envisaged a 'revolutionary dictatorship of the proletariat': in this order individuals *qua* individuals are dominated by structures (the class to which they belong) over which they have no control.

5. Within the Marxist tradition there is a view that with the development of capitalism directly allocated labour is substituted for market-allocated labour. What Engels in *Anti-Dühring* identified as the 'contradiction between socialised production and capitalist appropriation . . . [which] presents itself as an antagonism between the organisation of production in the individual workshop and the anarchy of production in society generally' (Engels cited in Mandel 1986, p. 8) results in an extension of the rational planned organisation within large factories and large firms and a reduction in the scope of market principles. Auerbach, Desai and Shamsavari (1988, p. 71–2) have criticised this view. The rise of large firms cannot be explained fully either by the gains associated with volume economies of production or advantages in the generation of new technologies. As conglomerate structures predominate financial factors may be most important. In any case, they argue, the ratio of value added (or sales less purchases from other firms) and sales for US firms has remained stable after its increase in 1880 to 1920. A great deal of these transactions involve, however, not impersonal market relations but the relations of large core firms with a constellation of subcontractors.

6. Irregular contracts are not a new phenomenon in capitalist societies. Over the last few decades irregular work has been more important in some sectors (services in particular) than others, for some groups of workers (women, immigrants, young people and unskilled workers) and in the upswing of economic cycles. In the 1970s and 1980s many commentators suggested that irregular work (where workers were employed by a firm with which they had no direct relationship (subcontract work, self-employment, agency, freelance, homeworkers, outworkers) or in which workers were employed on fixed term contracts) was on the increase as companies sought to adapt employment to sales and minimise their wage bill. In the United Kingdom statistical evidence for a major shift is limited. The working population is made up of two-thirds 'permanent' and one-third 'flexible' workers. Anna Pollert (1988) has suggested, however, that a structure of this kind has deep roots in the past, and that recent variations are a product not of management strategies aimed at a transformation of the employment relation but of (1) redundancies and lay-offs in the late 1970s and early 1980s, (2) sectoral changes of which the most important was the growth of the service sector in which female part-time jobs were numerous (In 1981–6 employment of part-timers in Britain increased by one-third of a million, while full-time employment fell by one million. From 1983 employment growth was based entirely on an increase in female employment in the service sector which was almost entirely made up of part-time work. In the public sector 'two-fifths of the manual workforce . . . consisted of part-time workers in 1984 compared with just over a quarter in the private services sector' (Millward and Stevens 1986, p. 207, cited in Pollert 1988)), and (3) state-led deregulation and its corollaries of privatisation, changes in the employment structure of the public sector services, and youth training schemes.

7. In Scotland the proportion of craftsmen and skilled operators is conversely low. A polarised skill structure is a common characteristic of electronics manufacturers. In Scotland, however, research and development staff are under-represented, and so the ratio of managers and highly qualified technical staff is, at 18 per cent, comparatively low. Some non-Scottish companies have set up research and development and product design departments, and, in the case of some smaller companies, UK headquarters in Scotland. Eighty per cent of scientific and technical jobs are, however, in design engineering and in production and testing. Where a

design capability has been developed it is typically restricted to the customisation of US products to meet European specifications.

8. In 1983 Grenoble had 1 per cent of the French active population. Yet 14 per cent of French graduates in electrical engineering qualified in the city, 10 per cent of research jobs in the *filière électronique* were found there, and 3 per cent of industrial jobs in the French electronics sector were located in the city and its region.

9. Vertical integration can stem from monopolistic strategies, strong technological interdependencies of the kind found in most process industries, gains associated with increases in amounts of information that a firm has, attempts to reduce uncertainties such as delays in deliveries, and transaction costs associated with the 'contractual skewedness that derives from asymmetric information flows, the existence of uncertainties and opportunistic behaviour (see Del Monte and Martinelli 1987, p. 6).

10. In 1976, Télémécanique was taken over by Thomson and the founders left the firm and moved to set up a series of small companies on the ZIRST at Meylan. Subsequently this type of development snowballed. Many other engineers left SEMS, its successor firms and other electronics concerns, and set up their own small firms in specific crénaux (see Figure 3.4). In 1986 there were 121 mostly small firms on the ZIRST employing about 3,316 people. Two units dominate: Merlin Gérin and the CNET (Centre national d'études des télécommunications) employing 800 and 300 people respectively. Of the rest 70 are small and medium-sized, high-tech firms, and 49 are service companies. In Grenoble there was a significant spin-off of new firms from universities and research institutes. Other large firms were, however, more important for the local electronics sector. Oakey, Rothwell and Cooper argue that in the United Kingdom and United States the links between high-technology small firms and universities are minimal: in Silicon Valley many of the earliest firms were spin-offs from universities, but after 1970 the founders of new firms were in the main individuals who had come to California to work for large local firms. Spin-offs depend therefore on the existence of large firms. In Silicon Valley moreover are located the large firm's corporate headquarters: large concentrations of research and development staff, high-level managers, and key engineers working on prototype development are the source of spin-offs. Inward investment strategies that attract 'screwdriver' operations, and science parks that prevent the installation of large firms will, therefore, not encourage spin-offs. In the United Kingdom fast-growing small firms did not make the transition into new large firms: many were acquired by foreign firms and were made into satellite plants. Much of the explanation of the lack of growth by new small firms in the British semiconductor industry of the 1960s and 1970s was their absorption into large multinational electronics firms, where subsequent innovation and employment growth was unimpressive compared with the growth of independent American semiconductor firms of this period. As Oakey concludes, 'a core of large firms is essential to lead high technology sectors of British industry, act as a source of new firm spinoff enterprises, and compete in the high research and development investment and mass production areas of high technology production where only large firms can survive' (Oakey 1989).

11. In 1982 SEMS was transferred to the Compagnie des Machines Bull, and in 1988 a decision to end production in Grenoble was announced: all that was to remain was research into Unix systems. It was decided to close the plant at Crolles and to limit the activities at Echirolles to research and the making of preproduction machines. Jobs were expected to fall from 800 in 1987 to 450 at the end of 1990. Work was to be concentrated in Bull's plants at Angers and Villeneuve-d'Ascq (Frappat 1988).

12. As far as the SDA was concerned, the goal of seeking inward investors in new sectors represented a change of direction. The original industrial role of the SDA was to help regenerate indigenous companies in traditional industrial areas and to help fill a perceived 'equity gap' (see Radice 1978). With the election of a Conservative government state entrepreneurship associated with the development agencies and the National Enterprise Board ceased to be acceptable, and a question mark was placed against the Agency's survival. As a result the Agency changed in character, role and personnel, while its critics argued that much more attention should have been paid to the use of new technologies to modernise existing industries.

13. Over 80 per cent of employment in the Scottish electronics industry is generated by the multinationals, and only 12 per cent of their total supplies and 17 per cent of their main inputs come from Scotland. Only 5 per cent of Scottish production in electronics actually comes from firms with headquarters in Scotland and only 15 per cent from other UK firms. Most of the major plants in Scotland are part of integrated global operations. In many cases raw materials are imported, processed and exported, mainly to the United Kingdom and European markets, though some companies make products for US, Japanese or other world markets. These decisions are taken, however, not in Scotland, but at headquarters in the United States or Japan.

14. One of the consequences of the greater flow of skilled workers is that French firms have been able to move much faster in the direction of new flexible computer-controlled manufacturing systems that require shop-floor work teams which have a wider range of and more sophisticated skills and which are able to perform devolved maintenance, planning and quality-control tasks (see Ray 1988, p. 66-7).

15. In the Scottish Office 1981 Electronics Manpower Discussion Paper a 25 per cent increase over the 1980 level of student intake into university and college B.Sc. courses in electronics-related subjects was recommended. This increase was over and above the projected 50 per cent increase in B.Sc. awards in electronics and electrical engineering in 1979–85 (that selectively reinstated the cuts made in higher education in 1981). Also recommended was an increase in the intake to courses producing electronics technicians. What was implied was, in other words, a diversion of resources within higher educational institutions in order to favour technological subjects. In 1986, however, the view of the Scottish Development Agency and the Scottish Office was that no serious shortage of skilled manpower existed although there were some specific shortages of newly qualified, experienced and some specialised engineers. The major difficulties were connected not so much with the supply of graduates but with flows into and out of Scotland and the industry. In 1980–85 Scotland made a net gain of graduates at the newly qualified level. Only one-third of entrants into degree courses, however, entered electronic engineering as newly qualified graduates. Of the entrants who did not enter the industry a very high proportion dropped out of courses at the end of the first year. In the face of this situation various options are likely to be considered. One is to alter the amount of fundamental mathematics contained in degree courses. A second is to seek to increase the 'quality' of applicants for electronics engineering: differential grants are one mechanism considered as capable of attracting school-leavers away from the humanities and social sciences. In Scotland as in the rest of the United Kingdom, what emerges clearly is the wish of the government institutions to act so as to divert educational resources towards vocationally determined ends, but to act in reaction to developments in the economic sphere instead of in anticipation of them and to place most emphasis on market incentives. In Grenoble the availability of skills resulted from the concentration of research institutes and the existence of education at a range of levels from the two-year electronics programmes of the IUT, CUEFA and the Centre FPA to the five-year programmes of the INPG and universities (see Dunford 1988, p. 18).

Part Three: The Italian Industrial Districts

4 The Italian model of spatial development in the 1970s and 1980s.[1]

Gioacchino Garofoli

4.1 Introduction: the models of post-war spatial development: from spatially concentrated development to diffused development

Centre- periphery relations are constantly changing dialectical relations that progressively alter the relations between spatial systems as well as relations within them. The relations within a country are not constant (in the medium and long term the positions of the various regions change), and deterministic laws of development (such as the theory of circular and cumulative causation and the hypothesis concerning the life cycle of regions and of urban development) are unacceptable.

In the end it should not be forgotten that spatial dynamics (the spatial distribution of productive establishments, the growth of large cities, migration processes . . .) are powerfully shaped by the specific international role of a country: the different positions countries assume in the international division of labour involve different processes of demographic and/or employment growth in large cities. It is this fact that explains, for example, why there are variations in spatial development in different parts of the world, not only between developed and underdeveloped countries, but also among and within advanced countries. The analysis of these phenomena has stimulated the interest of researchers in regularities and in similarities and differences in development (see, for example, the works of Drewett 1980 and 1985, Fuà 1980, and also Van Den Berg *et al.* 1982), even if it is difficult to arrive at general theories that adequately explain these phenomena.

Analyses of the Italian case in the period from the end of the Second World War until today indicate the presence of different models of spatial development. There was in fact a change from a model of progressive spatial concentration of production (especially industrial), of income and of population to a model of spatial diffusion of the processes of development and industrialisation which progressively affected regions at intermediate levels of development.[2]

It must be emphasised first of all that all periods of intense development led to increased spatial differentiation at all scales of observation (from international to regional inequalities, centre–periphery differences, and contrasts between town and country). The phases of intense development and of major quantitative changes involve an increase in the strength of migration flows and processes of urbanisation, and result in socioeconomic developments that radically change urban forms and profoundly modify centre–periphery relations. In periods of slower development, however, there are, on the one hand, opportunities to rationalise the city and the organisation of space. On the other hand, the development of peripheral areas is not strongly conditioned, and in general a transformation 'without fractures' (of the mode of production and the organisation of society) is allowed.

The 1950s and 1960s, and the years of the Italian economic miracle in particular, witnessed a growing spatial concentration of production, with flows of capital and labour towards the most developed areas. Many factors contributed to this result. The key variables were, however, the types of technological innovation introduced (which were largely embodied in large plants which required minimum levels of production to guarantee high levels of productive efficiency) and the modes of operation of the labour market (the release of the labour force in the countryside in the northern regions, and the migration flows from the other regions kept the labour market 'loose' and gave the demand side a leading role, with the consequent limitation of wage increases). In these conditions it was advantageous to enlarge existing plants rather than construct new ones and hence to search for ever greater economies of scale. The large multiplier effects that were created in advanced regions (especially in the sequence of interactions: industrial development » employment growth » development of construction » growth in income » and so on) in a phase of intense development must not of course be forgotten.

The diffusion of ideologies of modernisation from the large city, from the modern sector and from large firms had, moreover, very important effects not only on private actors (firms and families) but also on public actors.[3]

In the early 1970s the spatial tendencies of the model of development were reversed with the implementation of widespread strategies of productive decentralisation in a search for greater social and productive flexibility in the face of changes in relations of class strength in large enterprises and in large metropolitan areas. Above all, strategies of decentralisation involved a search for a labour force with lower costs of reproduction (see Garofoli 1978).

'However, the major spatial redistribution of productive activities that followed had only weak links with productive decentralisation because it was essentially a result of processes of industrialisation that were largely autonomous in that they were based more on the birth of new firms and new entrepreneurship than on the movement of externally controlled productive establishments. With the initiation of a phase of productive decentralisation there were nevertheless profound changes in the mode of organisation of industrial production. These changes demonstrated the opportunities for small-scale, highly specialised, high productivity production, and as a whole were accompanied by a high level of productive flexibility and the opportunity to change customers and commercial partners and to introduce small but continuous technical adjustments and process innovations (see, for example, the evidence in Brusco 1975).

4.2 The model of spatial development in the years 1970–80

4.2.1 Diffused industrialisation and small firms: the main features of the Italian model in the years 1970–80

In Italy the 1970s witnessed the start of several processes that profoundly changed the structure of production and its spatial organisation and that are probably also destined to have effects on the future development of the country. First of all two important reversals of previous trends must be underlined:

(1) There was a reversal of trends, which I have already mentioned, in industrial location that gave rise to a switch from a spatial concentration to a spatial 'diffusion' of productive establishments.
(2) There was a reversal of the trend for the average size of firms and plants to increase and of the progressive convergence on the industrial structure of European countries.

As a result of the developments I have just mentioned the model of Italian development of the 1970s and 1980s assumed further characteristics that differentiated it both from its own past and from other countries. To be specific:

(3) There was an increase in the role of small firms, with a rapid growth of new firms especially of small and medium size (see Table 4.1) which distinguished the Italian case even more than in the past.
(4) There was an increase in specialisation in sectors conventionally called 'traditional' as a result of the marked growth of employment and output in traditional sectors which itself stemmed from the questioning of previously accepted assumptions about the need to develop modern sectors. These changes in specialisation resulted in a progressive divergence in the structure of output and foreign trade from those of other European countries. (On the differences between the structure of Italy's foreign trade and that of other European countries see Modiano 1984.)
(5) There was a progressive decline in the role of prices as a determinant of international competitiveness and hence also in the role of production costs and wages. (See the results of the analysis of the international competitiveness of sectors conventionally called traditional in Modiano 1982 and 1984.)
In the end two features of the Italian model of the last fifteen to twenty years emerged as fundamental. One was the process of diffuse industrialisation, especially in the regions with intermediate levels of development, but also in the regions in which development occurred earlier. (On the process

Table 4.1 The distribution of manufacturing employment by size of firm in 1951–81 (in percentages)

Year	1–9	10–19	20–49	50–99	100–499	over 500
1951	32.1	14.1	8.0	20.4	25.4	
1961	28.0	18.8	10.1	21.6	21.5	
1971	23.4	8.5	12.5	10.2	22.4	23.1
1981	22.8	12.4	13.7	10.1	21.1	19.8

Source: elaborated from ISTAT's Industrial Censuses.

of diffuse industrialisation in Lombardy see Garofoli 1983a.) The other is the proliferation of small firms, which is linked with the formation of a new class of entrepreneurs, remarkable for their independence and innovativeness.

4.2.2 The increasing spatial articulation of the Italian economic system

In the 1970s the spatial articulation of the Italian economic system was profoundly changed with, on the one hand, significant industrial development in some 'peripheral' areas, and, on the other, processes of deep crisis and restructuring in the 'central' areas of the country. Overall the dichotomous differences between advanced and backward regions were reduced. The relative distances between regions were in other words modified, especially as a result of the faster growth of the 'middle regions' of the centre and north-east of the country (see Table 4.2 and Figure 4.1). Moreover there was a decline in the importance of the traditional division of the country into large territorial divisions (North, Centre and South) in that the differences within these large areas started to assume more significance than (or at least as much as) the differences between regions (see Figure 4.2).[4]

The fact that processes of this kind were in motion had already emerged in the debates of the late 1970s and early 1980s about, first of all, productive decentralisation and, subsequently, peripheral development and the role of small firms.

Studies of various areas had in fact clearly shown the new organisational and spatial order that the Italian industrial system was assuming. Several trajectories of particularly intense development (the central and north-eastern regions, the 'Adriatic development path, the 'peripheral' areas even within regions of older industrialisation) had already been identified, as had some forms of organisation of production based on systems of small firms which were very closely related one with the other and which gave rise to an increasing division of labour between firms especially in very localised spatial units ('system areas' and/or 'industrial districts').

To comprehend these substantial changes in productive and spatial organisation a series of extremely important questions were naturally raised (and are still stimulated by the results of the last census).

It suffices to think of the following questions. Is the process of spatial 'diffusion' 'physiological' in character or not? How prevalent are the 'auton-

Table 4.2 Changes in the number of local units and industrial employment in the Italian regions in 1971–81 (in percentage rates of change)

Region	Local units	Employment
Piemonte	47.6	-2.3
Valle d'Aosta	51.8	1.3
Lombardia	49.0	3.5
Liguria	20.4	-4.5
Trentino-Alto Adige	43.9	17.9
Friuli-Venezia Giulia	60.4	9.6
Veneto	83.6	27.4
Emilia-Romagna	48.2	26.7
Toscana	40.1	13.8
Umbria	60.6	37.4
Marche	74.5	51.8
Lazio	35.9	28.6
Abruzzi	24.7	47.8
Molise	14.3	67.8
Campania	19.1	25.8
Puglia	13.6	31.1
Basilicata	24.9	38.8
Calabria	-1.8	20.9
Sicilia	10.6	15.3
Sardegna	44.1	20.2
Italy	42.7	14.4

Source: adapted from comparable data based on the ISTAT's 1981 Industrial Census classification (see ISTAT, 1974 and 1985).

omous' characteristics of peripheral development and to which models of development do the regions of diffuse industrialisation give rise: is development 'endogenous' or 'exogenous'? Will new strategic functions eventually appear in 'central' areas, and what shape will the new system of relations among areas assume? Obviously the replies to these questions were critical determinants of the different interpretations of the spatial diffusion of industrial development.

4.2.3 The spatial features of industrial development in the 1970s and 1980s

Before confronting the question of the interpretation of the phenomenon, it seems useful to recall briefly the major characteristics of the process of transformation which is under way and which, in the last instance, caused the spatial redistribution of industrial activities.

The most important differences with respect to the forms of development in the preceding period seem to be the following (Garofoli 1983d):

(1) *productive depolarisation* with a substantial reduction in the importance of traditional industrial 'poles' (see Table 4.3);
(2) *non-metropolitan growth* both from an economic and a demographic point of view;
(3) *deindustrialisation* in the more developed areas (particularly in

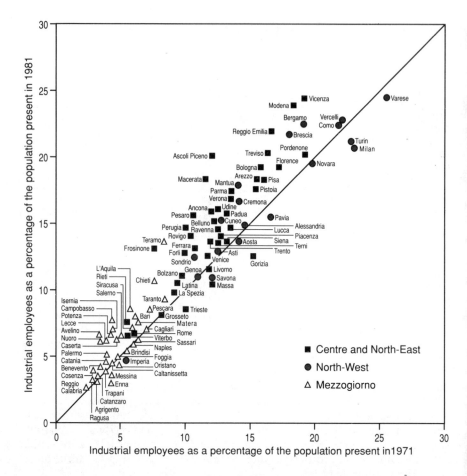

Figure 4.1 The ratio between industrial employment and population in the Italian provinces in 1971 and 1981

metropolitan areas), followed by a process of *counterurbanisation* that resulted in a block on urban growth in large cities, especially in the North;

(4) *delocalisation and spatial decentralisation* of industrial production which had an effect both on urban and peripheral areas;

(5) *peripheral demographic growth* that involved areas that were not contiguous with traditional zones of urban concentration (see Figure 2.3);

(6) *productive deconcentration* with a reduction in the average size of firms and plants as a result of major processes of vertical disintegration and decomposition of productive cycles; and

(7) *the formation and development of local productive systems* that were highly specialised and made up of a multitude of firms with dense productive interrelations in a relatively small spatial unit.

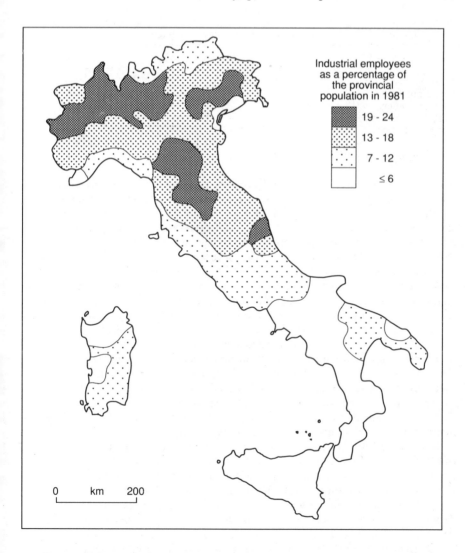

Figure 4.2 The territorial articulation of the industrialisation process in Italy in 1981

Source: Becattini and Bianchi 1982.

4.2.4 The causes of the spatial model of the 1970s and 1980s

In the last section several possible explanations of Italian spatial development were identified. In my view it is not possible, to attribute a physiological character to the process of relative spatial diffusion that has occurred in Italy in recent years and to deem, therefore, that it is destined to continue[5] and to

Table 4.3 The spatial concentration of industrial employment: the share of national employment in the main industrial provinces in 1971–81 (in percentages)

	1971	1981
Milan–Turin–Genoa	24.6	20.1
First 3 provinces	26.0	21.9
First 5 provinces	32.1	28.2
First 10 provinces	44.9	41.3

Source: adapted from comparable data based on the ISTAT's 1981 Industrial Census classification (see ISTAT 1974 and 1985).

extend progressively to areas that are less and less developed (consequently allowing a progressive elimination of regional imbalances). The spatial redistribution of productive activities should be seen in fact both as the result of several specific contradictions of the preceding model of development and as a consequence of several particular conditions which are both internal and external to the areas involved in the process of 'diffuse' development, and which obviously are not necessarily destined to endure.

As far as the more general question is concerned, it does not seem as if the spatial redistribution of industrial activities can be interpreted as a phenomenon that is entirely exogenous nor as a phenomenon that is simply endogenous to the areas of recent industrial development. In fact the spatial redistribution of industry is not a result of a decentralisation of capital or a hierarchical decentralisation controlled by medium and large firms in 'central' areas. It is instead a product of the valorisation of local resources in peripheral areas that gives rise to decentralised development (Dematteis 1983). The new spatial organisation of the Italian industrial system was in fact a result of the emergence of local entrepreneurship in areas at intermediate levels of development and not of the interregional mobility of firms.[6]

The 'spatial' diffusion of industrialisation cannot therefore be interpreted exclusively as a reversal of the advantages of a spatial concentration of production, which in the long run produces contradictory effects and increases the costs of reproduction of the labour force. Nor can the process of 'valorisation' of peripheral areas be explained by exogenous variables: it is not dependent on the outside world, on decisions made, in other words, by large firms in central areas that use peripheral areas to develop a productive system of the 'branch-circuit' type (to use the well-known term introduced by Lipietz 1980; see also Damette 1980).

In the Italian model of the 1970s endogenous processes of development did, on the contrary, play a major role, even if these processes were accelerated by favourable external conditions. However the latter operated exclusively as 'catalysts' of or permissive conditions for the process of development, and were not its cause (Becattini and Bianchi 1982). It was as if local development was largely autonomous. The endogenous development factors in areas of diffuse industrialisation are specific to particular local social formations and depend on a system of social relations and a series of socio-economic variables that are favourable to this type of industrialisation and that, in the last instance, facilitate the emergence of a new small and indigenous entrepreneurship. (For

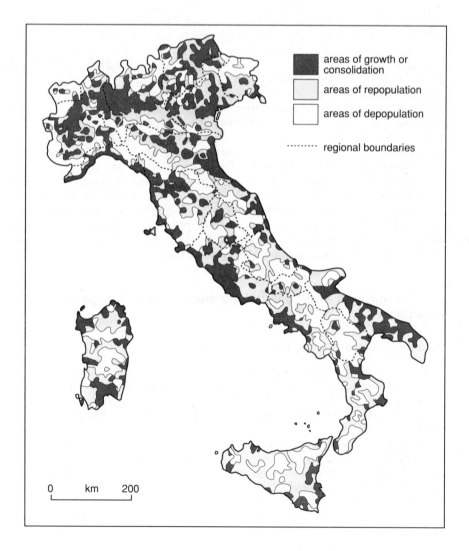

Figure 4.3 Italian demographic change 1961-81

an identification of these variables see Garofoli 1983d, and in particular Bagnasco and Pini 1981 and Paci 1980 and 1982.)

Among the external conditions that favoured a spatial diffusion of industrialisation one should not however forget (besides those already mentioned) the role of new technologies which are diffused horizontally into various sectors (of which microelectronics and computing are the most important). These new technologies are no longer 'embodied' in large plants, but are technically capable of being split up, and hence are particularly suited to small firms and plants (see the arguments put forward by Friedrichs 1982 and Sabel 1982 and 1983), and particularly appropriate for the needs of small-scale production and flexible specialisation (resulting in particular, as Brusco (1982) has shown, in a reduction in the cost differentials between standardised production and flexible, small-batch production). Other important external factors were the progressive crises of standardised production which enlarged the domain of specialised production (see the arguments put forward by Sabel 1982 and 1983 and Piore and Sabel 1984) and allowed the reduction of barriers to the entry of new firms, which facilitated decentralised and flexible production and the access of small firms to national and international markets.

To summarise, small firms and 'diffuse' development are not synonymous with crisis and/or backwardness and with the 'economic dependence' of areas that experience this kind of industrialisation, but are rather characteristics of a new mode of production organisation which is somehow original (which, in other words, gives rise to a new and autonomous 'development path') and which often, at least in more established local productive systems, has deeply rooted characteristics of autonomous development.

4.3 The process of diffuse industrialisation and the system of small firms

4.3.1 'Self-centred' versus 'extraverted' development

The degree of autonomy of the process of development is particularly important for territorial systems of small firms with extensive interrelations both between the firms and the various local productive sectors and between the productive system and its environment (see Becattini 1984b and Garofoli 1984a and 1989).

In these cases what is in fact extolled is the relation between the economic system and its environment on which are founded *economies that are external to the firm but internal to the area* and that, in the last instance, depend on the network of productive and socio-cultural interdependencies established at a local level (Garofoli 1983c). It is these *external economies* that make possible the adoption of different productive techniques, organisational processes, and strategies (and different rates of innovation and of diffusion of technologies) in the various areas that produce the same commodities independently of (or, at any rate, with a loose dependence on) simple relations between the relative prices of 'factors' and of the employable inputs (Garofoli 1984a).

To illustrate the difference that exists between models of *extraverted development* (that are dependent on decisions taken outside of the area) and models of *self-centred development* (that are based on variables controlled from within the area), all that is required is an analysis of a typology of local development models and of 'territorial clusters' ('ispessimenti localizzati') of firms. Obviously the key variables that underpin the two models differ. The local specificity of the model, the close interaction between the economy and its environment, and the capacity to 'guide' one's own process of development are clearly much greater in (if not exclusive to) the second model. Clearly this fact must not absolve one from the study of the characteristics and prospects of models of development that are largely dependent on exogenous variables and from the explanation of the advantages of 'territorial clusters' of firms even in these situations. Nor should one forget that very often local productive systems, which have now achieved a high degree of autonomy with respect to the outside world and which increasingly valorise endogenous variables, originated from phenomena connected with the spatial decentralisation of production (and which hence were controlled by firms that were external to the area). In the medium to long term, however, these systems were able to bring to life relations with the local environment, developing interrelations in the process and priming processes of industrial growth based on local resources and local entrepreneurship.

4.3.2 The structural characteristics of local productive systems

I have just shown that the determinants of the local productive system are, on the one hand, the relations between the economy and its environment and, on the other — in the realm of economic relations in the narrow sense — the relations among firms.

Limiting the analysis exclusively to economic relations,[7] the following structural characteristics of local productive systems can be identified (Garofoli 1981 and 1983a):

(1) an extensive division of labour between firms in the local productive system which gives rise to a dense network of intra- and inter-sectoral input–output relations;
(2) very strong productive specialisation at the level of firms and plants which circumscribes the field of activities, stimulates the acquisition of specialised knowledge, facilitates the introduction of new technologies, and in the last instance increases the economic independence of the firm and of subsystems within the area;
(3) the multiplicity of local economic actors (the 'plurality' of protagonists) that leads to the use of methods of 'trial and error' with a high probability of some people finding satisfactory solutions to the problems of the productive system (and with the immediate consequent imitation of this solution by the other actors);
(4) the progressive development of an efficient information network at the level of the area which guarantees a wide and rapid circulation of information about markets, the alternative technologies that can be used, new raw materials, components and semi-finished goods that can be used in the cycle of production, and new commercial and financial techniques, which contributes to the transformation of the knowledge of each single actor into the 'common property' of the area;
(5) the diffused professional knowledge of the workers within the area as a result of the transmission from one generation to another of knowledge about the production cycle and techniques used;
(6) the diffusion of 'face-to-face' relations between actors (especially between

the suppliers and users of intermediate goods and services to firms) which favour a cascade effect in the transmission of technological and organisational improvements through the system of firms, and which increase the overall efficiency of the local system. The advantages of these relations are greater in face-to-face contacts between innovators and the users of an innovation in local systems characterised by the presence of an industry making machine tools for the production of the goods typical of the area.

As the local productive system reaches a sufficiently high level of development, of division of labour between firms, and of productive integration, a definition based on the marketable goods of the sector in which it is specialised becomes ever more narrow: the system progressively extends into industries and market sectors that differ from the initial ones, generating a phenomenon that *apparently* and superficially could be considered the consequence of a process of *despecialisation and productive diversification* but that in reality should be interpreted as a *strengthening and deepening of the original productive system*. In fact productive interrelations within the area and among firms belonging to different market sectors are made more dense, thereby giving rise to *increasing intersectoral integration* within the local system (Garofoli 1983c).

All these developments are in fact a consequence of the progressive emergence and growth of productive sectors that are closely related to the sector of original specialisation, and are directly stimulated by it, often with more developed technological and economic characteristics (higher levels of value added, higher levels of productivity, and higher capital–labour ratios), with a greater capacity for technological innovation, and with a greater degree of control over the market: The combined effects of these processes shifts the local productive system 'upwards' into higher positions in the regional and international divisions of labour, moving it progressively further away from the areas and firms that are purely imitative, and hence increasing its capacity to defend itself in the face of external competition (from firms located in other areas whether in the same country or abroad).

As the local productive system is made more complex, making external economies to firms ever more important,[8] and once the valorisation of the resources specific to the area is extensive, the process of development at last assumes all the characteristics of a model of self-centred development. In fact the development process becomes completely endogenous when all the resources used are predominantly local (local entrepreneurs, locally trained workers with a high level of skill, locally accumulated financial resources, and innovative technologies introduced in the local area).[9] At this point the local system may be in a position to manage its own process of development and change, even if it, clearly, does not imply that the survival of the local system is guaranteed.[10]

The conditions for survival are in fact dynamic. The model is in fact one of continuous change (and not of simple adjustment) both in interrelations internal to the area (relations between firms, and interrelations with the environment and with local institutions) and in external relations (with the market, with other areas with which it competes, and with other spatial systems) with the obvious influence that all of these elements have on the position of the local system in the spatial division of labour. Change and innovation are therefore the conditions of survival of the local system.

If the latter is correct, it follows that there is a need for a strategy of transformation of the local system which requires a capacity to understand its relative position and to forecast medium- and long-term developments. These capacities are ones that it is difficult for individual small firms to have, and so, on the one hand, the need arises for supra-firm levels of decision-making and, on the other, there is an opportunity to introduce appropriate interventionist policies whose goal is to develop further the relationships between the economy and local institutions.

4.3.3 Strategic variables for the consolidation of local models of development

The fundamental condition for the consolidation of local models of development (especially in the cases of local productive systems and of 'territorial clusters' of firms) is the adoption of an ever more 'systemic' structure that strengthens the economic bonds between firms and the relations with the local environment so as to make local specificity the fundamental factor of location and development.

The variables that determine the consolidation of the local system are both endogenous (and hence controllable from within the area) and exogenous.

Included among the variables that can be controlled from within the local system are certainly the following:

(1) Technological and organisational innovation which increasingly assumes, in systems of small firms, the form of a continuous process, with a cumulativeness and an interdependence in the effects of a large number of technological changes, each of which is small. The innovative process is therefore incremental in character (à la Rosenberg) rather than discontinuous (à la Schumpeter). Technological innovation in local systems is not however the exclusive result of processes of spatial diffusion, but very often is itself the product of the local system, especially in cases in which the production of machine tools for the manufacture of the good typical of the area is present. Movements in the technological frontier introduced in the area therefore determine the consolidation and survival of the local system.

(2) The information system. An efficient and rapid circulation of information, timely knowledge of market conditions, and the diffusion of information about technologies and inputs are in fact the foundations of a correct evaluation of the prospects of development of local firms;

(3) The capacity to control the market. The strengthening of the marketing capacity of the system of local firms is one of the determinants of the autonomy of the local system and at the same time a constant source of opportunities to introduce new products.

(4) The forms of social regulation that operate outside of the market and that depend on an advantageous integration of local institutions, local society, and the local economy (see Sabel and Zeitlin 1982, Bagnasco and Trigilia

1984 and 1985, Bagnasco 1985 and Zeitlin 1985). Just consider the critical role (in the development of firms and of the local system) that can be performed by centres of quality control, technology centres and centres of services to firms established on the basis of agreements between local public bodies and consortia of firms; centres of professional training and school-industry liaison institutes; and institutions that regulate competition between firms, aiding the introduction of new products and processes rather than competition based on costs of production and, indirectly, on labour costs.

Of the variables that determine the capacity of local models to succeed the exogenous ones clearly cannot be forgotten. Consider, for example, the role played by the crisis of markets for standardised mass-produced goods (Sabel 1982 and 1983) that facilitated the success of the model of 'flexible specialisation' and of 'small-batch' production (Brusco 1982 and Sabel 1983) and by the new technologies that have already been mentioned (microelectronics, computing, numerically controlled machines, and so on) that are more suited to small-scale activities (Friedrichs 1982 and Sabel 1982 and 1983).[11]

4.4 Concluding remarks and suggestions for appropriate development policies

The first series of conclusions concerns the specificity of the model of Italian development of the last fifteen or more years. First of all, does it represent a new model of development without historical precedents? In the second place, is there a single model of development (the 'Italian model') or are there several (in different spatial contexts)?

In aggregate terms (reflecting on the development experience of the central and north-eastern regions of the country, but also of significant parts of the north-western regions) it seems possible to argue that the development model of the 1970s and 1980s is a new model with several characteristic features that differentiate it from the development models previously pursued in the advanced regions of Italy and from those currently in operation in the Italian Mezzogiorno and in other European countries. If, on the other hand, one subsequently disaggregates the analysis and studies different local and regional cases, one can identify, over and above many conditions and modes of behaviour that are similar, the importance of specific situations, and one also discovers models of behaviour (of firms, institutions and local authorities, and society as a whole) that differ from one area to another. One can speak therefore of local models of development that follow different and in some ways original paths.

It is even more difficult to answer the question about the uniqueness of this model of development. One can certainly argue that in recent years in Italy the model of flexible specialisation, connected with the use of multi-purpose machines and highly skilled and specialised workers (Sabel and Zeitlin 1982), and with large possibilities of modifying products and breaking into different markets, has reached a high level of 'sublimation'. It is a model that offers an alternative to standardised mass production based on large economies of scale, on single-purpose machines and on repetitive work. When these distinctions are made a historical precedent for this mode of organisation of industrial production is identifiable in the English (and also in the French and German) 'industrial districts' of the late nineteenth and early twentieth centuries which Marshall accurately described. But the distant origins of this model lie in protoindustrial structures and in the first phases of the industrial revolution in certain countries (especially Italy, Germany and, to a lesser extent, France) where processes of spatially diffuse industrialisation involving close interrelationships between agriculture and industry, especially in so far as the creation of family incomes was concerned, occurred mainly in non-urban areas.[12]

A second series of remarks can be made with respect to the possibility of setting in motion a process of industrialisation in a backward area, in order to attempt to discover whether it is better to start a process of industrialisation through 'territorial clusters' of firms rather than one based on different sectors that are not related one with another and/or one based on local demand. At this point the problem shifts to that of *how and when* it is possible to valorise local resources and the specific qualities of an area in order to set in motion a process of local development with a specific identity. This question clearly requires reflection on the role of external and internal *agents* in allowing local development to start. In this respect what are particularly useful are reflections on the conditions that underly the establishment of local productive systems, on the specific mechanisms at work within them, and on their modes of development.

A final group of problems concerns the strategic perspective that should be adopted *vis-à-vis* the processes of development and change in areas of diffuse industrialisation and, especially, in territorial systems of small firms. The fundamental choice lies in fact in the contrast between a perspective that is liberal and very optimistic about the possibilities of development processes based on small firms (and that is therefore opposed to public intervention and actually sees in this type of development a sort of 'market vengeance') and a perspective that is more pessimistic or that at least scrutinises this model and seeks to identify the specific conditions that underly the success of this type of industrialisation and at the same time the weaknesses that can block the realisation of the dynamic conditions on which competitiveness depends. The limited size of firms, the modes of access to entrepreneurial roles, the difficulties in constantly identifying appropriate new technologies and in moving the frontiers of knowledge, the narrowness of the market for the supply of specific and valuable services, the difficulties of controlling the final market, and above all the lack of an appropriate strategy for the local system lead to the identification of specific kinds of local public support and appropriate instruments. (Consider, for example, the experience of technology centres and of agencies for the diffusion of services to firms established in some typical industrial districts.)

These considerations demonstrate therefore the possibilities of interventionist policies at a local level (which hence should no longer be confined to spatial planning, civil infrastructure provision, and the supply of social services, but should also be concerned with the economic sphere, and especially with industrial policy matters) which can make up for the inadequacies of national economic policies.

In fact it is only at the local level that one can identify the specific needs that must be met to strengthen and consolidate spatial systems associated with diffuse industrialisation and that one can plan and introduce (after a wide debate and the direct involvement of local social forces and institutions) coherent interventionist policies with a view to eliminating the 'points of weakness' of the process of diffuse industrialisation and of local productive systems.

These possibilities do not alter the fact that a fundamental review of the modes of management of national economic policies (and in particular of labour and industrial policies) is called for. In fact it establishes the need for economic policies that are sufficiently disaggregated spatially and sectorally so as to take account of wide sectoral and spatial differences within the Italian productive system and hence to respond coherently to the needs of the heterogeneous models of regional development that coexist. This need should be quite obvious especially once one is convinced of the obsolescence (both from an interpretative point of view and from the viewpoint of policy discussions) of a single model and, hence, of the need to follow original development paths (see Fuà 1983).

Notes

1. The work on which this chapter is based was carried out in the framework of a research project on 'L'articolazione territoriale del sistema economico italiano negli anni '70' financed by the Ministry of Public Education.
2. This development does not mean that regional inequalities have been reduced but simply that the sharp North–South divide has been modified as a result of the development of the intermediate regions, the slowdown in the growth of the more advanced regions, and the progressive differentiation of the economic structure and development potential within the Mezzogiorno. For an analysis of the development of regional imbalances from 1973–5 onwards see Garofoli (1984b and 1987).
3. In the case of private actors think of the spatial diffusion of organisational typologies and productive techniques, the spatial diffusion of models of consumption, and the progressive homogenisation of social and cultural behaviour in different regions. In the case of public actors it is sufficient to recall the policies for the industrialisation of the Mezzogiorno which, in those years, prioritised large industrial plants, modern capital-intensive technologies, and sectors with high labour productivities, substantially importing the industrial model developed in more developed areas and countries (see Garofoli 1983d).
4. The map of industrial development was overturned and henceforth revealed an intricate mesh of highly industrialised and less industrialised areas even within each territorial unit (North-West, North-East, Centre and South) and each region. For example, the supposedly homogeneous character of development in the 'industrial triangle' disappears: within it all the types of development identified in Figure 4.2 are found. In a similar way highly industrialised zones are henceforth identifiable in some (often large) areas in the Centre and North-East.
5. It is in fact impossible to foresee the future effects on the spatial distribution of

productive activities of technological innovations, of modifications in the structure of markets and in models of consumption, of transformations of the financial system, of spatial policies, and of infrastructural investments. It is possible to envisage both scenarios that will advantage the centre and scenarios that may continue to advantage the periphery (see the analysis of these questions in Garofoli 1986a).

6. The limited scale in quantitative terms of processes of relocation in Lombardy as well as the small distances moved are demonstrated in De Blasio and Riva (1984).
7. On this occasion therefore the typical characteristics of the peripheral social formation on which the productive flexibility of systems of small firms is based are not considered. On these factors see Bagnasco (1977) and Bagnasco and Pini (1981).
8. When the economies of agglomeration exceed the diseconomies of urbanisation, location in the area continues to be advantageous. This situation should prevail even in the presence of increasing costs for the setting up of productive establishments and insufficient levels of infrastructure provision and transport facilities (see Garofoli 1983a, Chapter 4).
9. Clearly this situation does not mean that the local system is closed to the outside world. One of the specific characteristics of these systems is related precisely to high and increasing levels of international openness. What is more, the conditions for the efficiency of the local system are specifically guaranteed by its active involvement in international markets.
10. Many foreign industrial districts have, for example, passed through crises that were often irreversible. See the remarks made later in this chapter and Garofoli (1983b).
11. In conclusion one should not forget the growing importance of the inter-sectoral diffusion of innovations which facilitates the introduction of innovations outside of the firms and sectors that invest in research and development (Momigliano 1982 and 1984) with its obvious influence on the innovative capacity of small firms.
12. It is however possible to notice similar phenomena as a consequence of recent processes of industrialisation in rural areas and the creation of 'territorial clusters' of small firms in Southern Europe, especially in Spain (see Vasquez Barquero 1983 and Granados 1984), but also in Portugal (see Lewis and Williams 1984) and in Greece (see Kafkalas 1984).

5 The industrial district as a creative milieu.[1]

Giacomo Becattini

The question to which this chapter tries to sketch some sort of answer is whether the 'Marshallian Industrial District' (MID) can be considered a creative milieu. The obvious answer would seem to be yes, because the MID could not survive the competition from other forms of organisation of the production process (such as the traditional large firm, or the new network firm) unless it were creative. In a sense, an MID is either creative or it is not a (true) MID. This statement is presumably the logical conclusion of the analysis of MIDs. However in order to persuade ourselves we shall have to make a detour through the rather remote territory of de Bono's psychology of creativity.

5.1 The psychology of creativity

The analysis of creativity goes beyond any specific discipline, and requires a cooperation of many talents: psychologists, biologists, artists, and poets, all have something to say on the matter. That 'creativity' remains beyond all analysis is a romantic illusion that must be abandoned. Creativity may not be learned, but it can certainly be encouraged and promoted.

(Medawar 1969, p. 88)

This is all. Very well, but how?

Edward de Bono, the well-known Cambridge psychologist, who is, on this occasion, my main source of inspiration, gives us a precious hint. He writes: 'If we manage to come to a deep understanding of what prevents the emergence of new ideas, whether in general or for some given person, it becomes possible to increase the capacity for having new ideas.' [2]

A 'new idea' will not necessarily be a totally new idea, an absolute newcomer in the world of thinking; it could more simply be a new way of connecting pieces of knowledge that are already well known. The result of these 'connections' may be absurd or useless, as is often the case with the lunatic or with children, or may be logical and useful, as happens with recognised inventors. What counts, however, in the case of generic creativity, is the ability to make unusual connections. Because of the conditioning power of the system of ideas which prevails at any given place and time, it is not at all obvious that some individual can be quite free to reorganise ideas in an order which differs from the received one, without considerable effort.

From an abstract point of view, there exist at any given time infinite possibilities for rearranging knowledge and the language in which it is expressed. Any possible rearrangement is a candidate for the title of a 'new idea'. Among the innumerable recognisable candidates for the title of new ideas, only a few will pass the tests of consistency, elegance, utility, and so on, which a given society (or parts of it) at a given historical time deems should be passed for an idea to gain admission to the select club of 'sound new ideas'.

No analytical dissection, however radical, of the cultural heritage of a given historical group of people can describe completely its latent generative power. Indeed it possesses a partially indistinguishable, embryonic reservoir of truly new concepts, whose latent existence will be recognised only after they have come into the limelight. Before that, they constitute a shapeless potential with unforeseeable implications. Combinatorial activity involving ideas conti-nuously draws and feeds material from and into this 'tank'.

One can then think of some sort of 'generic creativity' which might be expressed by means of a measure of the ability of an individual, or a group, to combine the stock of ideas which exist at a given time, in a certain place. This generic creativity will remain quite independent of whether the product of such activity is then socially adopted. One can also think of a 'goal-oriented creativity' [3] that expresses an 'efficient' combinatorial ability, that is, one resulting in products which pass the particular tests which some of the (territorial, scientific, artistic, and other) communities one belongs to have adopted.

5.2 The development of creativity

5.2.1 Schooling and creativity

Who should provide for the formation of a large 'goal-oriented creativity', and how? It might be thought that scholastic education should fulfil this task. In fact, even though one can say that the problem has always been well known to pedagogues, the educational system has great difficulty in solving it. The main obligation of the educational system is to transmit, quickly and efficiently to new generations, that knowledge possessed by past generations which is considered sound. This task is obviously of great importance for humankind, but, from our point of view, it has serious drawbacks. The transmission of an amount of knowledge, which increases exponentially, to a growing mass of people, in a period of time per learner which is necessarily limited, requires the employment of highly 'economical' methods. The bulk of knowledge, and especially of scientific knowledge, is consequently reduced to textbook knowledge, and 'passed on to' new generations by means of procedures which are thought to allow for orderly and speedy learning. The amazingly positive effects of this process of incessant systematisation of knowledge have been stressed widely, and I shall not deal with them.[4]

Since received knowledge is also needed to prepare individuals for the activities which are available in a given society, knowledge must be transmitted in such a way that its 'usefulness' can be easily, quickly, and possibly 'objectively', checked. This requires some standardisation, both of content and of methods.

Again, it is not my intention to disregard the advantages of these procedures for the transmission of a large and growing mass of information and ideas; but nor should we disregard the narrowing effects on the mind that usually go with them, because of the exclusion of the unheard of and the uncodified. Despite some exceptions, all of the knowledge acquired at school is tightly packed into well-defined and potentially closed disciplinary structures, which are conceived of as the 'natural forms' of that knowledge. The wide but rigid knowledge that results reveals its limitations whenever it is called upon to disentangle real phenomena, 'unstructured' and essentially 'trans-disciplinary' as they are: hence the frequently denounced separation between school and life (de Bono 1971, p. 15)

A limitation of these methods of transmitting knowledge which may be less direct, but is nonetheless important, is the increasing rigidity of thought that they may create in the mind of the learner. This type of rigidity does not concern the content of learning or the way it is 'packed', but rather the proposed procedure for its application, that is, for putting scholastic knowledge to work in order to act in the world. This procedure involves a number of canonical steps. First of all, one specific field within organised knowledge is singled out for attention. Since no problem exists outside of a context of organised notions, one must first of all select the subsystem of notions with which to operate. The second step consists in 'taking the flesh off' the concrete situation which suggests the problem, according to the analytic style appropriate to the field selected. If, say, some situation is to be treated as an economic problem, then it should be formalised in terms of scarce means and multiple ends that can be compared. It is then that the method of solving problems which specialists in the field have devised can be applied. If no solution that satisfies the standards of that field of research can be obtained with the help of this procedure, the problem must be reformulated, reallocated, or discarded. This procedure is far from being specific to scientific research. It permeates all areas of human behaviour. And quite rightly so. However, it should be observed that, from our point of view, the most creative phases of the process are those of 'taking the flesh off' the problem, and of reformulating it in the case of failure. The rest of the process is essentially mechanical in nature and potentially could in fact be delegated to a computer (de Bono 1971, pp. 11–13).

The usual outcome of this process of conditioning the mind of the learner is that, while the learner is engaged in the acquisition of well-tested procedures and notions, he progressively loses, in the view of many psychologists (de Bono 1987, p. 210) the combinatorial ability (the generic creativity) he used to have in his early infancy, and obviously gains the advantage of greater information and combinatorial ability (goal-oriented creativity) which the social environment he belongs to accepts as sound.

From the point of view we adopt here, the net effect of 'scholastic education' often is a substantial reduction of the individual's ability to react to unexpected situations by recombining the stock of knowledge he has access to at the time. Indeed the 'success' of the teacher is measured in practice more by his ability to transmit correctly notions and procedures that are socially approved of, rather than by the percentage of intellectually mature and autonomous individuals he is able to produce. Any failure of an education process — construed in this wider sense — is therefore usually imputed to the insufficient 'natural endowment' of the learner, rather than to the mental cramp induced in his mind by the sterile 'formalism' of teaching.

A population, which is in this sense 'highly educated', may end up in a position which is not very different from that of a highly specialised animal species, that is, a population which is well adapted to a very specific environment. If the environment changes significantly, the species runs a risk of extinction. With an increasingly turbulent social environment, a more or less 'highly educated' population (that is, a population possessing more specialised knowledge), may lose its position of comparative advantage in favour of those who have retained greater generic combinatorial ability, possibly at the price of a more limited stock of knowledge. The rigid application of a wider set of conceptual and linguistic tools may yield results which turn out to be inferior to those that result from a flexible use of a narrower set.

We can conclude then that school, in the absence of a redefinition of its purpose, does not seem to be a structure capable of producing 'goal-oriented creativity' compatible with the acquisition of the knowledge which is nowadays necessary for acting in the world.

The situation could of course change if teachers were selected and trained with that target in mind. At present, however, the actual situation in schools — everywhere, I believe — is such that the creative teachers who are necessary to educate tomorrow's creative teachers and the day-after-tomorrow's creative men do not exist. But even if they did exist, our society is organised in such a way that their qualities would be sought and captured by better-paid and more prestigious posts than teaching (where the prestige of teaching is what this society confers).

5.2.2 The social environment and creativity

The school is, however, not the only factor which affects the formation of a style of thought. Family and playing environments, the neighbourhood, the 'gang' for the young, the working environment for the adult, and the mass media for everyone produce stimuli and constraints that are no less powerful than those produced by schools. Many of these environments are less directly concerned than the school with efficient and accurate transmission of received knowledge, and are oriented instead towards the construction and diffusion of practical knowledge. They are thus an endless source of 'dialectic' terms and notions, that is of terms and notions whose meaning is partially obscured by 'semantic penumbras' (Georgescu Roegen 1966, p. 25–55). These environments have then two effects: they enrich, or, as others would say, contaminate, language — which disciplined knowledge would otherwise tend to make 'rigorous' and sterile — by means of the use of 'vague' but 'pregnant' terms, which hybridise seemingly clear and well-defined ideas, and may encourage the development of techniques of thought which are less strictly 'vertical'.[5]

These environments leave greater room for what is commonly termed intuition and imagination. In them, therefore, a fund of undifferentiated thought is used and, at the same time, stimulated. But since no conscious design lies behind the development of this knowledge, frictions and contradictions which can be easily detected and condemned by scholars obsessed with clarity, will inevitably follow. A sense of proportion, *savoir faire*, connoisseurship, are just a few members of a wide family which, in the best cases, result from the combination of formal education with the stimuli, constraints and opportunities which come from the rest of social interaction. These qualities are however all claimed to be intellectually inferior, so as not to be a threat to the prestige of formal knowledge. In this way the separation of and opposition between the two 'worlds of knowledge' is perpetuated, and the superiority of formal knowledge over any other kind of knowledge is consecrated.

To sum up, while it remains clear that formal knowledge is the main tool man has to further his cognitive enterprises, the point I wish to make here is that the canonical superiority of formal knowledge in the world of today is a threat to mental flexibility which, in the wider perspective of the survival of humanity, is no less important.

5.2.3 Creativity and social and economic reform

The general theme of creativity belongs to the psycho-pedagogical sciences, but social scientists and economists in particular are directly involved with what I have called 'goal-directed creativity'. What is involved is not only the opportunity cost of the economically measurable resources required for different education systems — which is a classical theme in the economics of education (Blaug 1958, volume II, pp. 168–201) — but also the direct effects on the educational process of different ways of organising the processes of production and social distribution of goods: many of these effects are implicit, and nearly all of them are yet to be explored. There are forms of organisation of the process of production which involve great physical stress or largely repetitive movements, and which are therefore a threat to the very basis of creativity. Consequently, if creativity is regarded by some societies as a valuable asset, these societies should curb or even forbid those forms of organisation of the process of production which involve physical stress and tedium, and at the same time promote research and investment into the production of means of mitigating human fatigue, and methods of production capable of eliminating excessive repetitiveness in human activities.

Furthermore, since institutions link the production process to the educational process, the production process should not dominate the institutional structure to the point of producing institutions which inhibit creativity.

The battle for creativity, then, is not a strictly pedagogical battle, but is rather a commitment to social reform which involves society as a whole. There will be an evaluation of effects, both direct and indirect, on man and on things, of any conceivable reorganisation of the institutional structure, and in that evaluation the economist will certainly have his say.

5.2.4 The process of production of knowledge

A very popular attitude among economists is that the flow of inventions which have economic value — the only ones they are usually interested in — may be considered, as far as economic research is concerned, to be a function — however complex — of the investment devoted to pure and applied research.

The process of production of new knowledge, as well as any other, is interpreted along the lines of the classical idea of a black box with inputs entering one side and outputs exiting from the other. This pattern of thinking yields well-tested results in the case of a transformation of things into things, but it is less appropriate for an interpretation of the production of services, and is quite misleading, I believe, in our case. The reasons behind a different and at least seemingly erratic yield of new ideas from given inputs are such as to baffle a formal method of this sort.

A different framework from the one mentioned above is then required for the very special process of production of new knowledge. In this case the starting point will have to be mental blocks and the waste and delays that result, the accumulation of potential, qualitative jumps, and finally the vicious and virtuous circles which come out of them.

I believe that a wide and intensive study of the 'technology' of the psychological process of production of new knowledge may throw some light onto the so-called paradox of instruction, which involves the withering away of combinatorial abilities that accompanies growth in the stock of knowledge and the fostering of 'goal-directed creativity'.

I dare say that devoting resources to the study of these problems may be much more efficient in determining whether a country will flourish or decline, than devoting a high proportion of national income to scientific-technological research *tout court*.

5.2.5 Institutions, knowledge and creativity

The issue I am dealing with arises because society does not concern itself with extracting from its own institutional system any result which can be interpreted as a mix of some amount of knowledge, goal-directed creativity and generic creativity. The following questions must therefore be asked: what kind of mix can be obtained from an accidental combination — with respect to our problem — of the institutions found at different times and places? Conversely, what kind of institutions should be promoted in order to achieve specific results in terms of that mix? Better still, does the MID, in particular, provide an efficient combination of these elements?

The problem is, I believe, new, and I intend here only to draw, so to speak, its contours.

5.3 The characteristics of a creative milieu

5.3.1 The coexistence of different competences

In the following pages I am going to present a mixture of arguments drawn from the little specific literature I know and from my own personal experience of research and life. I realise that the resulting combination of ideas will appear arguable to everyone (as well as to myself), and even repulsive to some. However it seems to me that the principles of the 'analysis of creativity', formulated by Medawar, suggest that my own mix may be of some use.

It seems to me that the features which a territorially defined environment should have, in order to be a source of creative processes, should include at least the following.

First of all, different 'competences' should coexist. Each competence, that is, each system of knowledge concerning some specific object, which has been acquired by study or experience, has effects that shape the psychology of the bearer: practice takes the form of, say, a 'typical approach'. Just as many professions have a reputation for involving a particular 'bent', many competences have their own typical approach, that is, a method of presenting and solving problems which is well established and recognisable by the 'professional'. Such an approach does not float in the air of pure logic, but is a child of historical circumstances, and thus differs from one 'competence' to another (such as engineering and medical approaches) and even from one cultural tradition to another (such as Eastern and Western Medicine).

5.3.2 The interaction of competences

The coexistence of different 'approaches' creates the conditions for a number of challenges in the formulation of any given problem.[6] In establishing a creative environment, the mere coexistence of different competences, however, does not suffice. The help of a 'linking primer' is needed. Different institutions which act as links between competences obviously exist. One example is the market, with its network of exchanges and its plexus of contracts, which puts competences acquired by different individuals to work. But what matters in our case is not so much the institutions which make use of competences as they have developed, or which increase their specialisation, as the institutions which make competences interact dynamically, and which appeal to and liberate their latent and embryonic power to create the possibility of a storm of challenges. Human subjects must make contacts and must be sufficiently open to make use of the approaches of others. People must meet in the no-man's — and everyone's — land that lies in between particular approaches with an attitude which is ultimately playful.

Obviously this condition could not be satisfied if the approaches were totally specialised and there were no communication between them. Naturally this situation is not found: the problems which arise in different specialised areas can be reduced to a relatively limited number of broadly defined logical structures. What I mean by 'broadly' is that there are many methods of comparison — besides the traditional formalised one — which may reveal analogies between problems which seem very different. This way of posing the problem of creativity emphasises the advantages of dialogue, both because it promotes the advance of the whole frontier of knowledge by allowing for a transmission of solutions from one field to another, and also because it implies, and indeed requires, a different style of reasoning: a style that is looser and more pliable than the ones which characterise single competences. Part of the agility of thought, which was frozen by the 'educational' process and social routines, is thus recovered. The conversation is then construed no longer as an instance of pure communication of knowledge, but as a genuine act of creation of knowledge, or of the conditions for knowledge.

5.3.3 Institutions and the interaction of competences

The institutions which best allow this 'loosening' are informal or quasi-formal. The actor involved does not therefore perceive them as a part of the formal process of acquisition of his competence. At the same time, however, he sees them as not far, in some sense, from the place and the process of acquisition of that competence. The actor, say, takes a break of one or a few hours from his work and, still deeply involved in his own problems, may meet up with others interested in seemingly different problems. The fact that the worker is outside of the working place (in the strict sense) helps to create a 'convivial atmosphere' [7] which favours the communication of problems, or parts of them, and possibly — with greater or lesser awareness — of hypotheses for their solution.

A solution which is still in *statu nascendi* — if I am allowed to use this expression — is often rich with hints which are potentially useful even outside of the particular field in which they were generated. These hints are often discarded, and thus lost, as the 'true' solution is approached. The waste products of the 'problem-solving activity' may turn out to be useful for the 'problem-finding activity'.[8]

There is more: it is almost certain that, in the conditions I have asssumed as to exist, the various participants will struggle to describe their own problems in terms which allow them to communicate and explain them to one another. The essential traits of the problems will thus emerge through an approach which is not the typical and incommunicable one of any given competence. In other words, it becomes possible to perceive and utilise various stimuli coming from thinking and living practices which are otherwise very remote one from the other with the help of a sort of *ad hoc* language. A kind of brain-storming will result, which stimulates a recombination of everyone's stock of knowledge.

A classical example is the High Table in Oxbridge colleges. In this case the structure is indeed institutional, and thus, in a sense, formal. But it is also so much a part of the common life of its members that it no longer looks so: contacts occur in such a relaxed and convivial atmosphere as to reduce significantly the role of inhibiting factors.[9]

5.3.4 Creative environments

Ultimately, the coexistence of competences and the existence of catalysts define an environment (a formal or informal institution) where random spurs to recombine knowledge are planned, rather than left to . . . chance. It is a question of creating a mechanism which can integrate well-known specialised machines for the formation and transmission of knowledge (research and school), and which continuously 'trains' the natural individual's creative abilities, without interfering too much with the functioning of the machines themselves.

It will be remarked that this function is already performed by games and hobbies. This is true. However, what is sought in our case is more than a 'scientifically constructed' pastime, since its results must end up on the 'markets' for things or ideas, which have their own social criteria for ratifying 'utility'. What is sought is an environment which is carefully designed to produce an active combination of goal-oriented scientific and/or commercial research and the mental meandering of the imagination, an area where mental energies can be restored, where intellectual saturation can be overcome, and where, on the basis of the knowledge of an adult, a child's 'freshness' is reacquired and yields socially approved results. I realise that these expressions contain some emphases which are hard to justify rationally. I believe however that there is something in them which deserves to be said, even though it cannot be proved.

5.3.5 Creativity and the characteristics of a population

It is difficult to imagine that the specified conditions have their effects independently of the characteristics of the available human materials. Intuition and experience (which I know are not always a reliable guide) tell me that it is necessary to have populations with some basic features, such as mental curiosity as an end in itself, a strong tendency to socialise, a bent for using analogies as reasoning processes, and a moderate tendency to overvalue an individual's own possibilities of success. I cannot imagine these conditions being found amongst a population made up of specialists gloomily locked inside their own competences, or of hyper-critical people who are over-conscious of the risks involved in any course of action. However, it must be said that some of the features that are suitable may develop strongly — though possibly not start from scratch — in the course of the functioning of a creative environment.

5.4 The Marshallian industrial district

5.4.1 A definition of the Marshallian industrial district

After this long detour through the maze of the psychology of creativity, it is now possible to come back to the problem with which I am mostly concerned, that is, whether the MID is a creative milieu.

The expression 'Marshallian Industrial District' has been used fairly widely in the last few years, but it has not, as yet, been well defined. Therefore I need a provisional definition to specify what I intend to discuss. I shall use the term MID to refer to a socio-territorial entity which is characterised by the active coexistence of an open community of people and a segmented population of firms. Since the community of people and the population of firms live in the same geographical area, they will crisscross one another. Production activities and daily life overlap. The community is open because the industrial nature of the district and the related problems of increasing returns imply incoming and outgoing flows of goods and people. The population of firms is segmented in the sense that different phases of the process of production are divided between the firms, each of which specialises in one or a few phases.[10]

5.4.2 Intra-district values and relations

The relationships linking people in the MID exist on two intersecting planes. At one level they are perfectly fluid. The choice which dominates the economy of the MID is between doing and buying (preferably in the district). As a result, any customary link which produces quasi-rents for some tends to crumble. At the same time, however, because of the redefinition of customary links, other links take shape. Exchange relations and hierarchical relations intertwine and alternate with no discontinuities. The district is at the same time the realm of the most lively competition,[11] and the realm of cooperation, custom and informal institutions.

No small entrepreneur would play a game which is potentially as destructive as the one described above, if the community did not have rules (mainly unwritten ones) which allow those who played fair and were beaten to play again. There is thus a network of values and institutions which is invisible to the economist, but quite visible to the sociologist and the anthropologist, and which holds this society together, and makes it a sort of community.[12]

5.4.3 The coordination of activities in the district

Although by definition the presence of big firms in the MID is not ruled out, the MID requires that large firms do not polarise the overall process of production and induce small firms to go bankrupt or be taken over. The function of coordinating the overall process, which cannot be performed impersonally by the district market, nor by the large firm that is missing, are fulfilled by particular agents whose job it is to link external markets and internal production capabilities, taken in a very wide sense. In the Italian case the most typical figures are the buyers and the *impannatori* of Prato. Although these agents differ, they all incessantly design and redesign the product and, to a lesser extent, the process, according to the features of the external conjuncture and the internal situation of the district. In a sense, they extract from the local cultural stock (which includes technologies, but much more besides) all the new ideas it contains. By doing so, they guide and stimulate the combinatorial instinct of all the other agents in the district.

5.4.4 Social and occupational mobility in the MID

Socio-culturally the district is characterised by great mobility. Very frequently individuals move from a position as a wage-earner to self-employment or a position as a small entrepreneur, and vice versa. Products and, to some extent, processes are changed once a season at least. Partners and employees, or, conversely, co-workers and employers rotate continuously. Yet the more one changes, the more one remains in the same socio-cultural environment. The immanent conflict between different social roles leads the individual to consider himself as an autonomous agent, able to gamble with his own destiny. The individual hence has an attitude of self-help towards the difficulties of life and work.

5.5 The MID as a creative milieu

5.5.1 Single sector industrial districts and creativity

If a single branch dominates in the district, it might be assumed that different competences will not coexist. If, say, the textile branch, is the only one that exists, a 'textile culture' might be assumed to dominate local culture in an oppressive manner. In part this is indeed true. But if one considers the concrete process of production, one realises that there are phases of production in a textile district which involve cultures which are different from the textile culture in the strict sense, such as mechanical, chemical, mercantile, and other cultures.

An even deeper examination also reveals that competences in different phases of the textile cycle itself may show great differences. Consider, for instance, the differences in the approaches of the spinner and the weaver, which are both potentially scientific and technological, and the approaches which characterise other phases of the textile process, such as the drawing of patterns on material which is artistic and handicraft-like. Hence the coexistence of different competences is in fact fairly common even in a district where a single branch dominates. Every trade, says Alfred Marshall, is a window on the world, and the district is a microcosm and an endless generator of different trades.

5.5.2 Competition and cooperation

The strongly competitive atmosphere which pervades the MID puts brakes on the possibilities of every single 'phase-entrepreneur' sharing freely his problems with colleagues involved in the same phase (for example, spinner with spinner). But this constraint does not prevent him from discussing problems with entrepreneurs of different phases, with his workers and with the *impannatore*. This continuous recombining of the technological stock of the MID produces both a constant stream of innovations from the bottom upwards and a stimulation of the tendency to innovate.

The intrinsically 'colloquial' structure of the MID produces a constant synergic interaction between 'problem-solving' and 'problem-finding'.

5.5.3 The *impannatore* as a source of combinatorial and creative activity in the MID

The role of catalyst is played in the MID by the *impannatore*, or by similar figures. To earn his living he must break up and continuously recombine in new ways the production process of the MID. His earnings are the price the market pays for this special activity. In order to survive and grow the *impannatore*, or his functional equivalent, must prevent the MID from settling into any definite immutable pattern.

The unrelenting innovative activity of the *impannatore*, conceived as his characteristic answer to the conditions of uncertainty surrounding the district, creates and consolidates a *forma mentis* which is very malleable and versatile. Its normal result is a comparatively high proportion of 'district skill' over 'firm skill'. *The MID is a place where there is the maximum of versatility compatible with the specialisation required by the prevailing degree of competition.*

The mix between goal-oriented and generic creativity and the stock of knowledge prevailing in the MID involves a high level of goal-oriented creativity at the price, presumably, of a lower (average and overall) stock of knowledge. The MID is a 'spontaneous' creative milieu whose inner logic we should understand in order to run it appropriately. Together with a remoulded school and 'cultural' cities, it can help us move towards the ideal institutional mix to which I alluded earlier in this chapter.

When the combinatorial attitude, the symbol of which is the *impannatore*, is dampened, the end of the MID is in sight. Hence the MID ends up functioning like a machine which allows random factors to shower continuously on to solidified forms of competence.

In order to survive the competition from other MIDs and those production machines which are better financed, and which — presumably — make rational use of scientific and technological knowledge, that is, large and network firms, every single MID is forced to become a favourable ground for spontaneous creativity.[13]

My conclusion is provisional, both because I do not know the specific literature on creativity well enough, and because the issue of the industrial district has not yet been explored sufficiently. But if a conclusion is to be drawn, mine will tend to give a positive answer to the question posed : the current MID, as depicted in this chapter, is a creative milieu.

Notes

1. What is stated in this chapter owes much to frequent discussions with foreign and Italian scolars. In particular, I wish to thank Marco Bellandi, Gabi Dei Ottati and Fabio Sforzi of the University of Florence and the IRPET (Florence) for their acute comments. I alone remain responsible for what is stated in the text. An earlier Italian version of this chapter appeared in Benedetti (1989, pp. 19–33).
2. Compare with de Bono (1971, page 21). The fact that I draw heavily on de Bono's ideas obviously does not mean that I use them correctly. It goes without saying that I have tried to do him justice; but I must also add that I have not refrained from 'developing' his ideas in the directions which suited my purposes.
3. I shall bear the responsibility for the coinage of such expressions.
4. See, for a very effective treatment of the advantages of a scientific organisation of knowledge, Georgescu Roegen (1966, pp. 11–16).
5. On the contra-position between vertical thinking and lateral thinking, see of course de Bono.
6. De Bono writes: 'The usefulness of an outside view of a problem is not only that special experience from a different field can be brought to bear, but also that the outsider is not bogged down by the particular way of approaching things that has developed in those closest to the problem' (see de Bono 1971, p. 133).
7. For this idea I have been inspired by Michael Polanyi (1978, chapter 7).
8. On the distinction between 'problem solving' and 'problem finding' see de Bono (1987, pp. 34–6). See also Getzels (1988) and Dillon (1988).
9. On the relevance of these factors in the creation of a convivial atmosphere see, as one among many examples, Breit (1987, pp. 647–8).
10. For the sake of brevity, I shall refer for these definitions to some papers of mine included in Goodman, Bamford and Saynor (1989) and Pike, Becattini and Sengenberger (1990).
11. The notion of competition assumed here is the one defined by Marco Dardi (1990).
12. On these somewhat paradoxical and seemingly self-contradictory aspects of a 'community market' see Dei Ottati (1987).
13. On the comparison of the chances of innovation in industrial districts and the results of R & D in large firms, see Bellandi (1988).

Part Four: Flexible production, large firms and spatial organisation

6 Oligopoly is alive and well: notes for a broader discussion of flexible accumulation

Flavia Martinelli and Erica Schoenberger

6.1 Introduction

In the literature on flexibility, which has focused more specifically on the phenomenon of flexible specialisation, a rather monolithic picture has been drawn of the nature of the current restructuring of production following the crisis of Fordism. In this chapter, we propose to raise some questions about this phenomenon and its interpretation, to widen the discussion and to re-equilibrate the debate. We believe that the restructuring process currently under way is still a very open one which affords the possibility of numerous permutations of the industrial and spatial structure. The consistent emphasis on the Third Italy, Silicon Valley and other unusual or even unique spatial/ industrial formations has led to an obscuring of the broader meaning of flexible accumulation and its multiple modes of expression.

In the course of the chapter, we shall argue that oligopolistic structures of production are quite compatible with increasing flexibility, and that flexibility is not a characteristic specific to small-scale, non-hierarchical, integrated production complexes. Similarly, we shall seek to show that the implications of flexibility for labour processes and labour markets are likely to be quite mixed. Attention will also be drawn to certain contextual features such as the concentration of financial capital and control over markets, and we shall emphasise the importance of keeping in mind the fact that the multiple dynamics underlying the recent increase in the flexibilisation of production will themselves evolve over time.

The thesis of flexible specialisation was originally concerned with a production system organised on the basis of small, vertically disintegrated and highly specialised firms, knitted together in a dense network of market-based interactions, within a more or less clearly defined territory. Though regulated by market processes, successful industrial districts of this sort are also characterised by a high degree of recognised interdependence and collaboration among firms. This feature sets the districts dramatically apart from the hierarchical and market- power-based, inter-firm relations traditionally associated with large-scale, vertically integrated, oligopolistic enterprises.

The main proponents of this thesis have, indeed, acknowledged its specificity in sectoral, territorial, political and sociological terms (Brusco 1982; Bagnasco 1983; Storper and Scott 1989; Scott 1988c; Sabel 1982 and 1989; Sabel, Kern and Herrigel 1989).[1] But while these specificities and limitations are acknowledged, in much of the work on flexible specialisation there persists a kind of implicit syllogism whose first premise is that, for a variety of reasons, flexibility in production is now necessary for competitiveness. The second premise is that the specialised network of small, disintegrated firms is inherently more flexible than the large, vertically integrated firm by virtue of its greater organisational malleability, allowing the various independent elements of the production system to be continually recombined as circumstances require.

Taken together, the almost unavoidable conclusion is that the large, vertically integrated firm, though not headed for extinction, is under increasingly severe competitive pressures which it is, by virtue of its size and organisation, ill equipped to handle. In this light, the flexible specialisation model is tendentially generalisable far beyond its geographical and sectoral origins. Moreover, the route to competitiveness and survival for the large firm may be an organisational and managerial restructuring that progressively erodes hierarchical and power-based relations both within the firm and between the firm and its suppliers (Sabel 1989; Sabel, Kern and Herrigel 1989).

While we are inclined to accept the first premise of the syllogism, we believe that it is less obvious that large, vertically integrated firms are inherently hindered from reorganising their production along flexible lines. Furthermore, the large firm may be able to achieve this flexibility without relinquishing many of the key attributes that have traditionally set it apart from the small firm, including large-scale financial resources, market power, and enhanced geographical mobility.

A second reason for insisting on reconsidering the role of the large corporation is that, as the discussion about flexible specialisation filters out of the academic and into the political and policy realm, we must expect that the cautions concerning its limitations as a model will be progressively elided. Any vulgarisation of the model will almost certainly promise more for it than even its original proponents intended. There is hence a need to re-equilibrate the debate.

We shall argue that while the flexible organisation of production is a major underlying feature of the new accumulation regime, the actual social and spatial forms of such an organisation are multiple and do not coincide uniquely with that of small-scale, competitive industrial districts. More importantly, we believe that no substantial rupture in the long-term trend towards a hierarchically structured production system will necessarily occur with the new regime.

6.2 The indeterminacy of flexibility

Underlying the notion of flexible specialisation, there are a number of different analytical issues that are often blurred and presented as being necessarily linked in a particular way. In other words, flexible technologies, vertical disintegration, small-scale production, market-based and competitive inter-firm relationships (albeit tempered by trust), and reskilling of the labour force (up to and including a return to craft production) all come together in a cohesive package (compare with Wood 1989). In what follows we shall briefly consider some of these factors and stress how they can evolve quite independently of one another.

6.2.1 Technology

The technological basis of the flexible specialisation model is the general-purpose machine which can be adapted to the production of a variety of product types. Among other things, this type of machine provides a crucial link with the reskilling/craft hypothesis since general-purpose machinery often requires skilled and knowledgeable workers. Similarly, many kinds of general-purpose machines are within the reach of small firms and can be used for small-batch production, and so there is a link between technology and the scale of operations.

It can be noted at the outset that programmable automation technologies allow high volumes of output to be increasingly diversified and internally differentiated. In this way, economies of scale are still obtainable from large-volume but unstandardised production. Flexible automation, then, provides a major alternative to the kind of production process envisaged in the flexible specialisation thesis. Moreover, the high cost of this technology still presents barriers to entry by small firms. To justify an investment very large volumes of output aggregated across product types are required. The continued import-ance of scale economies, of course, presents capacity utilisation problems in the face of unstable levels of demand (Schoenberger 1989). However, the flexibly specialised industrial complex also requires continued market growth for its maintenance and reproduction (Brusco 1982; Nuti 1985a).

6.2.2 Organisation of production and industrial structure

By organisation of production we mean the way a work process is broken into distinct phases (each using a certain type of more or less flexible equipment and a certain type of more or less skilled labour), and the way these phases are related to one another. The flexible specialisation literature is mostly con-cerned with vertically disintegrated production organisations and, hence, with small, highly specialised and interlinked firms, each responsible for a particular phase of a broader production process. This highly refined and coherent division of labour, whose individual components can easily be recombined on the basis of competitive market relationships, allows for flexibility of output in terms of both product mix and volumes.

The flexible organisation of production, however, is not necessarily coincident with flexible methods or technologies in production. In many production phases, single-purpose dedicated machinery is used and overall flexibility is achieved only by varying the mix of suppliers and their output volumes.

Furthermore, small size is not necessarily identical to vertical disintegration. Many small firms are actually substantially vertically integrated.[2] Moreover, as already suggested, large integrated firms can achieve flexibility in product mix on the basis of programmable automation technologies. Finally, large firms can also externalise certain phases of production through subcontracting to small firms, but these linkages may be hierarchical rather than competitive.

On the advantages of internalisation versus externalisation of phases there is by now a wide literature (see Williamson 1980, 1986; Scott, 1988c; Contini 1984) and we shall not review it here. Nevertheless, two advantages of a disintegrated productive organisation can be highlighted, even assuming that, from a purely technical point of view, the same flexible organisation of production can be carried out within one firm or across firms.

First, in the disintegrated system, the costs and risks of uncertainty are spread over a larger number of producers. It is possible that the advantages of such an organisation will be securely enjoyed only by those firms at the top of the chain, since they can raise and lower output levels while shifting the costs involved on to their subcontractors and suppliers. Moreover, in the case of large firms externalising phases, many suppliers are 'captive', that is, they do not have substantial market alternatives for their output. Thus there is reason to suppose that vertically disintegrated flexible production is quite compatible with hierarchical and exploitative relationships among firms. Or, in other words, the production system can be fragmented but control, in principle, can remain quite concentrated.

A second major contribution to flexibility of vertical disintegration is its ability to take advantage of, indeed promote, labour-market segmentation. Small firms are generally less unionised and, as in Italy, may be exempted from some statutory labour regulations. But large, integrated firms can also reap the advantages of labour-market segmentation through spatial strategies which allocate different segments of the production process to different geographical labour markets.[3]

Our argument is not that vertical disintegration, small scale and specialisation have nothing to do with flexibility but that the forms of flexibility identified with these characteristics are not necessarily of a market-competitive nature. Furthermore, these methods are also available to large, vertically integrated corporations, although they may have to reorient their management strategies significantly as a result.

This point is part of the argument put forward recently by Sabel (1989) who suggested that large firms are converging towards the flexible specialisation model by reorganising their production and management structures. There are numerous examples of the sort of restructuring that he describes, including closer and more egalitarian relationships with suppliers. Yet the flexible large corporation remains very large indeed and threatens to grow even larger in the face of the current boom in mergers and acquisitions. Hewlett-Packard provides a good illustration of a managerially decentralised firm that has nurtured close collaborative relationships with suppliers (Saxenian 1988). At the same time, it has just bought Apollo Computers for upwards of £500 million which will make it the world's largest supplier of computer workstations (*New York Times* 1989).[4] In this sense, changes in management strategies do not erase the differences in capabilities and behaviour between large and small firms. Deconcentration or decentralisation in one sphere of operations may coexist with concentration or centralisation in another. The key point about large corporations may be that they have a range of organisational strategies at their disposal and they can deploy them with a high degree of flexibility and simultaneity.

6.2.3 Labour

Another issue is the impact of flexible technologies and organisations on labour, particularly with regard to skills. The flexible specialisation thesis proposes that, in contrast to the deskilling trend of the Fordist assembly line, flexibility provides significant possibilities for labour reskilling.

Flexibility with regard to labour can mean two things: (1) flexibility in quantitative terms as a function of fluctuations in demand and output; and (2) flexibility in qualitative or 'functional' terms, that is, in the way workers are assigned to different (multiple) tasks within the production process.

The first type of flexibility is certainly an important attribute of smaller firms, where labour regulation is less strict and the work-force often more pliable. However, large firms also have a wide array of internal solutions to match labour supply with production fluctuations (temporary lay-offs, more or less covered by institutional compensations, as well as paid overtime).[5] Externalising phases through subcontracting is also a widely used strategy to ensure this type of flexibility, but this of course means that labour adjustment is merely displaced down through the hierarchy of firms.

Flexibility in the deployment and redeployment of workers within the production process and the assignment of workers to any number of specific tasks (Atkinson 1987) seem to be in distinct contrast to the Fordist one machine/one job/one worker approach.[6] The question still remains, however, whether functional flexibility implies broadly based reskilling and revalorisation of craft production, as opposed to multi-tasking. Flexible organisation of production can, in principle, be associated with widely varying skill levels. Even in industrial districts, while some phases do have a high skill or craft content, many others are narrowly defined, repetitive, and substantially deskilled. In the case of flexible automation, the situation is, if anything, still more uncertain (Gertler 1988; Kelley 1989; Cavestro 1989; Schoenberger 1989b).[7]

The great attraction of the flexible specialisation thesis is the tendential upgrading of skills and reinforcement of craft traditions in the flexibly specialised industrial district. This upgrading is thought to be a product of the technology in use and the particular division of labour regulating these complexes. However, as we have seen, the link between technology, division of labour and skill content appears indeterminate (compare with Walker 1989). In any event, it appears that flexibility *per se* is not inherently linked with any particular model of the labour process.

6.3 Industrial districts and new industrial spaces revisited

Having argued for the relative independence of technology, the organisation of production and labour *vis-à-vis* flexibility, we can briefly review the specifities and generalities of the few cases currently presented in the literature under the rubric of 'new industrial spaces'.

The distinctive characteristics of these examples are the spatial agglomeration of small, specialised, independent firms and the significant inter-firm linkages which tie them together on the basis of competitive market relationships. In this section, we propose to review three of the most commonly considered cases of flexible organisation: the Third Italy 'industrial districts', high-technology complexes, and business services. Two issues will be stressed. The first concerns the uniqueness of many of these industrial/spatial formations and hence the question of the sectoral and geographical generalisability of the model. The second concerns the evolution of these cases over time, and hence the question of their reproducibility *in situ*.

6.3.1 The Third Italy

The literature describing the Third Italy phenomenon is by now quite extensive and does not need to be described in detail here (see Garofoli 1981; Brusco 1982; Sabel 1982; Fuà and Zacchia 1983; Piore and Sabel 1984; Becattini 1987; Scott 1988c; Bellandi 1989; and for a critique, Amin 1989). Suffice it to recall that Italian industrial districts concern mostly traditional industries (textiles, clothing, leather and footwear),[8] and must be interpreted in the light of both macro factors (that is, the particular economic conjuncture of the 1970s) and local specificities.

With regard to the first aspect, the crisis of vertically integrated industrial organisations in these sectors, which were confronted with increased labour conflicts while being ill equipped to face an increasingly diversified demand, must be emphasised. But while domestic rationalisation of capacity and internationalisation of investment were implemented in most Western countries, in Italy a very different pattern emerged.[9] Partly as a consequence of strategic externalisation by large firms, partly as a spontaneous process of local development based on the existence of particularly favourable labour market conditions and original nuclei of craft production, a number of regional systems of small, highly specialised and interlinked firms developed. The competitiveness of these districts lay in the lower costs of labour, the flexibility that could be attained with regard to an increasingly diversified product demand, and the external economies that spatial agglomeration afforded.

The lower cost of labour was achieved in two ways. The first was via the lower absolute level of direct wages due to the small size of firms, the evasion of social security payments, and the exploitation of even lower-wage and less protected home-workers. Second, savings were achieved through quantitative employment flexibility that was permitted by the relative absence of labour-conflict and labour-market rigidities. The smooth functioning of the system hinged also on the fact that workers could engage in multiple job-holding (maintaining, for example, ties to the agricultural sector) and could mobilise the entire family into various segments of the labour market, both formal and informal, thereby lowering the costs of reproduction and ensuring a non-institutional form of unemployment compensation.

Furthermore, this characteristic division of labour, while reducing the costs of production via economies of specialisation, provided additional flexibility by permitting the continual recombination of specialised phases, according to the needs of the market. In addition, the risks of market variability were spread over the whole system of firms rather than confined to one large firm. Agglomeration economies, in the form of diffused skills, information and services, further increased the competitiveness of such a system.

However, other features need to be highlighted. First of all, in these industries, the technology in production is quite traditional. The use of small computers for administrative functions has diffused, but only the largest firms, or those with a direct link to the market, have extended it to design, certain phases of production, and inventory and sales management (Martinelli 1988). Overall, flexible automation technology is not a major feature of Third Italy industrial districts.

Secondly, it is certainly true that skills constitute an important component of the Third Italy's success, especially knowledge about materials and processes, as well as certain manual skills. But it is also true that for a number of production phases, the division of labour implies many unskilled, repetitive and narrow tasks (from sewing on buttons to attaching labels), which do not require lengthy training and are most often decentralised to low-wage home-workers.

Thirdly, even if labour conflict is low, the working conditions of the majority of employees are quite unfavourable. The weakest units of the disintegrated system (small workshops, home-workers, and so on) bear the costs and risks of fluctuations in the market. If barriers to entry are low, the mortality rate is also quite high (Contini and Revelli 1986). Moreover, even if the lack of job security (implying a high degree of income variability) and low social security coverage are compensated by the particular socioeconomic structure and the local patterns of social reproduction, in the final analysis the industrial district thrives on a high degree of worker exploitation and/or self-exploitation (by individuals who might be thought of as 'sweated entrepreneurs' whose independence is quite precarious given the high rate of firm mortality).

Finally, the success of these organisationally fragmented districts rested on strong demand growth (Nuti 1983 and 1985a; Brusco 1982). The hypothesis that Italian industrial districts are not necessarily durable, once the macroeconomic conditions that fostered them cease to hold, is supported by recent trends. The key change is precisely in demand, which begins to falter because of competition from newly industrialising countries, the fall of the dollar exchange rate, and the revitalisation of national industries in some Western countries. The immediate consequences have been closures and lay-offs, but more importantly, the beginning of a reconcentration process (Martinelli 1988; Nuti 1985a; Bursi 1985 and 1987; CITER 1987 and 1988; NOMISMA 1988).

This reconcentration does not operate at the level of production, which remains fragmented, but in phases before and after material production. Increasingly, the most strategic functions of management and finance are concentrated in the hands of fewer and larger firms,[10] with a direct link with the market, and at the head of an increasingly structured tree-like system of quasi-captive suppliers, not unlike large firms in other sectors that have strategically decentralised production. This strengthening of hierarchical relationships occurs mostly through informal contractual agreements, but in some cases also through outright financial control.

These types of relationships existed in the past, but were diluted by the multiplicity of opportunities (that is, many customers, many suppliers) allowed by a growing demand. The reasons offered for the reconcentration process are, first, the need for better quality control in the face of rising competition from newly industrialising countries, and second, the need to attain economies of scale in finance, design, marketing and distribution, and to improve control over output markets (Martinelli 1988).

In conclusion, many industrial districts of the Third Italy appear to be a highly specific historical and geographical form of flexible accumulation. Moreover, there is increasing evidence that this model may itself be unstable, with rationalisation of capacity and reconcentration of finance and strategic functions. In some segments of these industries, such as textiles, there are also signs of renewed vertical integration, with highly flexible automated machinery in several industrialised countries. Therefore questions arise not only concerning the model's generalisability to all of the industries it concerns, but also about its capacity to reproduce itself *in situ*, beyond the particular macroeconomic conditions that fostered it.

6.3.2 High-technology complexes

High-technology industry has become a central focus in this debate both because of the way the industry is itself organised and because its products are so deeply implicated in the increasingly flexible production process of a wide range of industries. Inevitably, Silicon Valley and its nearest relatives have been singled out as exemplars of the new model of industrial/spatial organisation.

Again, the stress has been on a highly advanced division of labour, implying a fragmented, externalised, but tightly interconnected industrial complex (Scott 1988c). Silicon Valley has indeed been a veritable hotbed of new firm formation. Among the hallmarks of the valley are an extremely specialised labour force with a high degree of mobility among firms, a feature which constitutes another form of labour flexibility for those sufficiently qualified to take part. Furthermore, the continuous proliferation of new, niche-market firms embedded in a web of shifting customer–supplier relationships anchors the flexibility of the production complex and, no doubt, contributes to its innovativeness (Scott 1988c; Saxenian 1988).

Yet, these characteristics do not encompass the entire high-tech sector. Silicon Valley and its relatives provide only one model of high-tech-based regional development and, perhaps necessarily, not the most widely diffused one. Other models include technical branch plants, quite self-contained vertically integrated firms, and lower-level assembly regions (Glasmeier 1988). Moreover, there are strong reasons to doubt that the Silicon Valley model is generalisable, if only because its own success tends to foreclose similar development possibilities in other regions (Scott 1988c; Massey 1985). Among other things, this is a reminder that flexible specialisation also reproduces spatial inequalities, although in new forms.

Secondly, continuing fragmentation is by no means the only organisational story in the industry. There are increasing signs of a parallel tendency to consolidation and integration effected by mergers and acquisitions, equity investments by large firms in smaller partners, joint ventures, technology-sharing agreements and the like. In this sense, both formal and quasi-integration are at issue. Indeed, according to some analysts, the global semiconductor industry provides a very strong example of increasing flexibility in output, continued fragmentation of the manufacturing base, and a trend to large-scale corporate integration (Santo and Wollard 1988).

This integration is being promoted by a number of factors, One is a financial consideration, related to the rapidly rising costs of entry in an increasingly capital-intensive and highly internationalised business. New, state-of-the-art fabrication facilities, for example, now cost between $50 and $90 million, compared with under $400 000 in the early 1970s. Soaring R & D costs for products and processes exacerbate this problem. Intel, for example, spent $100 million over three years to develop its new 80386 microprocessor (Santo and Wollard 1988). The need to stabilise markets by internalising them to some degree, and technological factors, such as the blurring of boundaries between components and systems and the need to protect proprietary technology also contribute to this integration (Schoenberger 1986; Santo and Wollard 1988). Strategic manoeuvrings, particularly with respect to consolidating market positions via, for example, international joint ventures or attempts to establish internationally recognised standards to which other firms must adapt come into play as well.

Thus the organisational trajectory of high-tech sectors is not uniquely or even primarily in the direction of fragmentation and disintegration. Its development may reflect a broader kind of flexibility that allows firms to confront different kinds of market and/or product contingencies via different organisational combinations.

Given the relative newness of high-tech industries, we should be wary of premature judgements concerning their eventual organisational and spatial configurations. After all, the early history of the automobile industry also exhibited a startling degree of fragmentation with large numbers of small competitors and various technological options vying in the field (Mutlu 1979).

6.3.3 Business services

Business services constitute another 'new' industry with quite specific development patterns, organisational features and locational requirements which are
nevertheless rapidly evolving (especially in the organisational and technological consultancy areas). Their product is highly variable and often substantially
customised. The most advanced services have a high immaterial content (that
is, know-how and information) which generally requires close contacts and,
frequently, a high degree of cooperation between supplier and client.

These characteristics imply that business services (1) can be organised on a
small scale, and are highly specialised and skilled, and extremely flexible and
interdependent; (2) tend to cluster together to exploit agglomeration economies; and (3) are heavily market-oriented and tend to locate in or near
existing or developing centres of accumulation and control. These activities
closely follow the hierarchical structure of cities at a global and regional level
(Martinelli 1989a and 1989b). Such locations also provide ample pools of both
skilled (technical and professional) and less skilled (clerical) labour.

These organisational and locational dynamics may be perfectly explicable by
existing theory. Moreover, the characteristics described are evolving. Although
the customised nature and market orientation of many business services help
maintain a structure of independent small firms serving niche markets,
concentration in the industry has always existed and is actually increasing
(UNCTC 1988; Noyelle 1988; Sauvant and Zimny 1987). In management and
accounting consultancy, for example, the 'Big Eight' are expanding their
operations on a global scale (Stevens 1981; Moulaert *et al.* 1988). Moreover,
they are broadening their product range, encompassing new information
technology services (Moulaert *et al.* 1989). Intra- and inter-sectoral concentration through acquisitions and mergers is also occurring (Niada 1988; Rock
1987; Booz-Allen and Hamilton 1988), paralleled by intra-corporate vertical
decentralisation and deconcentration of less skilled functions to low-wage,
peripheral areas in the more mature service sectors (such as insurance) (Nelson
1986; Baran 1985).

The picture is thus quite diversified and does not especially lend itself to
generalisation. The flexible, small-scale, spatially integrated specialisation
model concerns only certain segments of the industry which are themselves
evolving. Developments in information technology are actually favouring
industrial concentration (UNCTAD 1985; UNCTC 1988) and eroding the
initial competitive edge of small firms.

What is definitely the case is that business services concentrate in central
locations, close to existing centres of accumulation. Their impetuous development has changed the economic base of many cities, but their pattern of
location and organisation is not greatly different from older service industries
which have always created 'central business districts'.[11]

In sum, these three examples of flexible specialisation exhibit, in the first
instance, a high degree of variability amongst themselves. In explaining their
different manifestations a great deal depends on the specificities of industry
and place. Moreover, their evolution over time may be tending to alter their
observed dynamics in significant ways. In particular, there is the distinct

possibility that oligopolistic structures may be tending to reassert their dominance in the process of accumulation, even in these special cases.

6.4 Flexibility and large corporations: oligopoly alive and well

Given the specificities and limitations of the flexible specialisation model, it seems appropriate to refocus attention on the still-dominant actors in the world economic system: large corporations and industrial-financial groups. These organisations remain the major locus of contemporary accumulation and change, and, hence are the main agents shaping the economy and space.

Industry has always experienced waves of concentration, punctuated indeed by periods of fragmentation, often associated with the rise of new sectors and technologies. But the wave of acquisitions and mergers of the last few years is unprecedented. Originating in the United States, it has now reached Western Europe, partly spurred on by strategic repositioning in the face of the approaching 1992 deadline for the integration of the EC market (Booz-Allen and Hamilton 1988; McKinsey 1987; Cecchini 1988; Niada 1988; Onida and Viesti 1988).

Several characteristics of this latest wave are worth noting. First, it concerns both mature (oil, chemicals and food) and newer sectors (electronics, telecommunications and business services). Second, as opposed to the conglomerate fever of the 1960s, there is some evidence of a prevalence of intrasectoral concentration, extending to families of closely related products (Niada 1988). Third, acquisitions are carried out not only by large multinational groups pursuing a strategy of globalisation, but also, as in Italy, by smaller, national or local firms, attempting to strengthen their market positions (NOMISMA 1988).

There are a number of factors propelling this trend. Acquisitions provide a rapid means of consolidating and enlarging markets, especially at an international scale.[12] Indeed, whatever the virtues of independence for smaller firms, they may not be able to resist the power of large firms simultaneously seeking an outlet for investment and the establishment of global market shares. Acquisitions also allow large firms to combine sales in niche markets with mass-market outlets.[13] They also help to achieve scale economies in certain strategic functions (R & D, distribution, marketing and advertising) and corporate synergies across complementary products.

It is worth stressing that the various types of restructuring strategies (such as acquisitions, joint ventures, externalisation and so on) can be pursued concurrently. More importantly, while they lead to a growing concentration of capital and control, they do not necessarily translate into concentration of operations. Production can remain physically fragmented for labour market as well as for output market reasons. In many cases, acquired companies remain quite autonomous in their operations and management, although integrated into a wider corporate strategy. Especially in intra-sectoral concentration, plants and firms in various locations may continue to produce their traditional products for their traditional markets, while benefiting from greater corporate resources in, for example, finance, marketing and distribution.[14]

Given this array of restructuring mechanisms, analyses which emphasise new technological and organisational features solely at the level of material production miss an important part of the picture. Perhaps one of the problems of the flexibility debate so far is precisely that it has focused on the organisational and spatial dynamics of the economic system purely as a production system. But under capitalism, production is really a means to another end: the further accumulation of capital. Different scales of analysis are involved (Cooke 1988; Contini 1984), and these differences make fragmentation of production perfectly compatible with organisational and financial integration. In this sense, the various forms of restructuring that are taking place allow large firms to reproduce the flexibility available in the Marshallian industrial districts, as Sabel suggests (1989), but the massive financial resources and imposing market positions of these corporations still set them irrevocably apart from the flexibly specialised small firm.

It is therefore necessary to ask some questions about the actual loci of accumulation and the flows of control within the overall production system. The type of inter-firm and intra-firm transactions, and in particular the existence of unequal power relationships and hierarchies among firms and between firms and workers, remain crucial issues.

Even in the flexibly specialised industrial districts these questions are quite pertinent as the dynamics of accumulation influence the future evolution of the districts themselves. The presumption that in these highly fragmented and inter-linked complexes the distribution of profits and market shares is determined on a competitive basis is weakened if one considers the emergence of some organisations dominating the others by virtue of their position as financiers, marketers, designers or coordinators of production (Brusco 1982).

In sum, the fragmentation of the production system must not be confused with a fragmentation of capital and control and a generalised resurgence of atomistic and competitive entrepreneurial forces. The focus of the recent literature on flexible specialisation as an organisational–territorial model has accorded a privileged position to the small, the specialised and the spatially integrated. While this picture may be accurate in some cases, it must be clear that the model forms only a part of a broader and more complex process.

6.5 Flexibility and the regulation model

The regulation approach suggests that, due to several circumstances, we are moving away from the previously dominant Fordist regime of accumulation towards what some have described as a new regime of flexible accumulation, although the eventual outcome remains a subject of debate (Aglietta 1979; Boyer 1986b; Lipietz 1986; Jessop 1990; Harvey 1988 and 1989; Schoenberger 1988; Moulaert and Swyngedouw 1989). In any case, this restructuring is still in process and its precise outlines are still unclear.

The growing need for flexibility is determined by several interrelated factors. These include the growing contradictions within the preceding regime arising on the one hand from increased labour resistance to the conditions of work and life under Fordism and on the other from greatly increased competition within a context of market stagnation in the capitalist West. As a consequence, firms have sought ways to strengthen their grasp over increasingly uncertain markets through reductions in production costs and a more diversified and flexible product base.

Among the various possible features of the new accumulation regime, two major characteristics merit particular attention. The first is the increased flexibility in the organisation of production, whether intra- or inter-firm, which is translated into an increasing fragmentation of the productive system but is perfectly compatible with a growing concentration of capital and control. The second is the growing precariousness of the labour force, reflected in a progressive erosion of its acquired statutory and contractual protections (where these existed). These features entail a spatial structure of production which is far from monolithic and certainly encompasses more than the very particular notion of 'new industrial spaces'.

6.5.1 Fragmentation of production and integration of control

The increased fragmentation of the advanced economies' productive system is demonstrated by the fall in average employment size of establishments in many sectors. This decline, however, must not be interpreted solely as the result of a renaissance of small-scale, craft-based firms where entrepreneurship blossoms and quasi-perfect competition rules. Other processes are also at work: (1) the substitution of capital for labour; (2) the strategic fragmentation/externalisation of productive activities (intra- or inter-firm); and (3) the acquisition of formerly independent firms, often followed by rationalisation and the elimination of overlapping capacity, without otherwise altering the locational structure.

The organisational flexibility achieved through these various mechanisms does depart substantially from the rigid, integrated organisation of Fordism. However, while promoting fragmentation of the productive system and even lowering the average size of productive units in terms of employment, these processes do not diminish the actual market and financial power of the large firms that are implementing these changes. Counter to the decline in the physical concentration of workers under one roof typical of Fordism, one must acknowledge the continuation — and even acceleration — of the concentration of industrial and finance capital.

This combination of increasing fragmentation of the productive system on the one hand and increasing concentration of capital and control on the other may be one of the most distinctive features of the new regime of accumulation. Crucial issues in this regard, to which more analysis must be devoted, are the type of inter-firm relationships and the loci of decision-making, control and accumulation.

6.5.2 The precariousness of the labour force

A second key feature of the new regime of accumulation is the erosion of the power of organised labour and the dismantling of important protections acquired after decades of struggle. This weakening of organised labour is partly achieved by means of an increased segmentation of the labour market, which breaks the rigidity in the use of labour inherited from the Fordist regime and the collectively acquired work rights gained by unions. We believe that this increased precariousness of labour is a major underpinning of the new mode of regulation (see also Moulaert and Swyngedouw 1989).

The particular features of this process vary from country to country (even from region to region), depending on historical circumstances, labour culture and the pattern of industrial relations. In Italy, the conquests of the labour movement and, in particular, the rigidities introduced by the Statuto dei Lavoratori in the structure of the primary labour market have been undermined in several ways. Both the development of the Third Italy's small-scale industries and the strategic deconcentration of production implemented by large firms in other sectors were aimed precisely at lowering the cost of labour and increasing the flexibility of its use by breaking the shop-floor resistance characteristic of large plants.[15] Moreover, the crisis and lay-offs of the 1970s have severely reduced the strength of unions in the primary labour market itself.

In the United States, the increasingly precarious position of labour is reflected in a number of factors. Unionisation rates, for example, have declined sharply from their Fordist peak, as large numbers of workers have been expelled from the traditionally unionised sectors. New-growth industries (high-tech and services) have proved, on the other hand, remarkably resilient to organisation. Furthermore, particular groups of workers who form a growing segment of the active labour force (women, minorities and undocumented workers) have remained largely unorganised. In contrast to many European countries, the aggregate unemployment rate in the United States has been relatively low for some time, but the scale of unemployment is partly due to a sharp rise in temporary and part-time employment. Wage rates have remained virtually stagnant despite low unemployment (Uchitelle 1988). The progressive occupational and income polarisation of the labour force is further evidence of its weakened position (Harrison and Bluestone 1988).[16] In the face of all these pressures, even unionised workers have acceded to demands for far-reaching changes in work practices.

More generally, the erosion of workers' acquired rights, together with the diffusion of an entrepreneurial ideology of self-reliance (promoted by, *inter alia*, the Thatcher and Reagan administrations), while allowing greater flexibility on the part of capital, increase the exploitation of labour (often disguised as self-exploitation). Everyone is encouraged to think of him or herself as a 'free professional', if only because there is no alternative. In this context, the flexibility in the use of labour gained by capital is no longer an exclusive attribute of small firms.

6.5.3 A new mode of spatial organisation?

Whether these features of the developing regime of accumulation translate into a specific spatial form is debatable. Some factors may promote a certain degree of regional reconcentration (Sabel 1989; Schoenberger 1988). Included are a greater dependence on agglomeration economies in some sectors and the need for more flexible and more rapid adjustment of the productive system from product design through manufacturing which may be more easily achieved if these various activities are closer together. Speeding up the flow of goods within the production system (as with just-in-time) may also promote a more clustered spatial pattern. Spatial concentration may also be more possible given the precarious position of labour in many traditional industrial regions, making it less imperative to search for cheaper and more compliant labour in distant regions.

At the same time, the pressures for increased internationalisation of production are also growing. In this sense, we may expect to witness quite contrary tendencies working in parallel. It may be that a flexible regime of accumulation will also entail more flexible spatial relationships, with intensi-fied competition among places for the favour of industrial development (Harvey 1988 and 1989). At the least, any trend towards regional reconcent-ration will make the development problems of lagging regions and the gap between centre and periphery more urgent.

6.6 Concluding remarks

In conclusion, we wish to stress three points. The first is that small is not necessarily beautiful, as even the small relies on the exploitation of labour and is frequently associated with low-wage, low-skilled and deadening work. Second, small firms do not necessarily represent the leading edge or the major feature of the new regime of accumulation. Third, therefore, the view that oligopoly is alive and well may be a more appropriate guide to analysing the emerging patterns of industrial and spatial restructuring.

The search for flexibility may indeed translate into a fragmentation of the productive structure, but does not coincide uniquely with the model of flexible specialisation. Moreover, placed in a historical perspective, the rise and good fortune of small firms assumes a more conjunctural connotation. The 1970s and 1980s were years of severe economic dislocation (oil shocks, slow growth, debt crises, inflation and social unrest), in which large firms had to face changed macroeconomic conditions and to restructure rapidly. They were slowed down, however, by strategic uncertainty, by organisational and technological rigidities, and by sheer size itself. Small firms, less burdened by labour conflict and more agile, were able to face the crisis and adapt more rapidly. They therefore 'held on' and even prospered in a time of transition during which large firms were undergoing severe difficulties. But if large firms can successfully restructure their operations, which we believe to be the case, then they may be in a position to reassert their dominance over the space-economy.

Notes

1. Brusco, for example, takes care to delimit the kinds of industries to which flexible specialisation may be most applicable and discusses the different kinds of labour processes and labour market dynamics that can be distinguished (Brusco 1982; see also Scott 1988c). The socioeconomic preconditions for flexible specialisation in the Third Italy identified by Bagnasco, which feature an incompletely proletarianised labour force with continued ties to the agricultural sector, certainly appear to have a high degree of historical and geographical specificity (Bagnasco 1983). Rather particular social and historical conditions also underlie the emergence of 'high-tech' industrial complexes in California (Storper and Scott 1989; Scott 1988c). Sabel acknowledges the continued existence of large, vertically integrated firms while proposing that they are tending to converge organisationally with their small, flexibly specialised counterparts (Sabel 1989; Sabel, Kern and Herrigel 1989). In earlier work he has also emphasised the rather unusual political circumstances surrounding the emergence of the Third Italy (Sabel 1982).

2. This is true even in certain 'craft' industries. In the South of Italy, for example, small firms in the footwear industry (Nuti 1990) and in electronics (Del Monte and Martinelli 1988) exhibit a very high degree of vertical integration, compared to their North-Central counterparts.

3. Intra-corporate geographical deconcentration can also facilitate quantity adjustments as plants in areas with weaker labour organisation bear the brunt of output fluctuations (Clark, Gertler and Whiteman 1986).

4. While many recent, large acquisitions have been followed immediately by asset sales to reduce debt, the resulting industry structure may not be remarkably more disintegrated. When Kohlberg, Kravis, Roberts engineered its highly leveraged buyout of RJR-Nabisco, for example, it immediately sold $2.5 billion worth of assets to BSN, a huge French food and beverage company (*Business Week* 1989). Similarly, IBM, which failed in its effort to synthesise the computer and telecommunications businesses via its purchase of Rolm in 1984, eventually sold Rolm to Siemens, the German electrical engineering giant (*New York Times* 1988).

5. By institutional compensations we refer to such mechanisms as the Cassa integrazione in Italy or negotiated supplementary unemployment benefits in the United States.

6. It must be stressed, however, that functional inflexibility was a product of social and historical, rather than purely technical or organisational dynamics. In the US case, it was an important feature of collective bargaining agreements designed to protect the position of individual workers and particular skill categories. Also in Italy, the outcome of the late 1960s shop-floor conflicts was a particularly rigid structure of work categories and rules. In Japan, by contrast, workers have long been subject to repositioning throughout the factory, even within a mass-production environment (Monden 1981).

7. If we posit a set of criteria for what constitutes skilled labour, a major one would be accumulated, specialist knowledge (a *métier*). A second would include acting on, or at least understanding, the whole of the production process. A third is the autonomy and level of responsibility of the worker, that is, the possibility and capacity to solve problems and develop one's own approach to accomplishing the work (in contrast to machine- or organisation-set tasks). In the context of flexibly automated, large-volume production, workers are typically responsible for the operation of a number of machines. However, 'multi-task' work does not necessarily mean skilled work.

8. In some cases they also include the machine-tool industry, mostly oriented to the traditional industries cited.

9. At the end of the 1970s, Italy was the greatest world exporter of clothing and footwear products, whereas all other Western countries were net importers.

10. In terms of sales rather than the number of employees.

11. At present, these districts may have expanded into adjacent, more suburban areas, but this expansion may have to do with land use and labour-market issues rather than new locational requirements.

12. 'The first reason for the recent wave of acquisitions derives from the narrowness of the British market which is only 4 per cent of the Western market. Such a share is too small to sustain the growth of a large chemical group . . . This could have been done through a strong policy of direct investment, but it would have been too slow a process. Therefore, we decided to act through a series of acquisitions' (Imperial Chemical Industries, cited in Niada 1988).

13. 'Our strategies are two. On the one hand, we aim at making our company number one in a sector we believe strategic, that is, that of large-scale household appliances. The other strategy is that of exploiting niche markets, that is, smaller, but not less important markets' (Electrolux, in Niada 1988).

14. This may, however, also be subject to change. According to the Cecchini report (1988), with concentration, there will be some rationalisation of capacity. The heads of a number of corporations concur, stating that some restructuring in the relative specialisation of different units is likely to reduce duplication of effort (see Niada 1988).

15. Firms with fewer than twenty-five employees are exempt from much of this labour legislation. Significantly, unions are now addressing the issue of labour protection in small firms.

16. Furthermore, under the Reagan administration, Federal labour policy, particularly in-so-far as the orientation of the National Labor Relations Board was concerned evinced a decided shift in favour of business (Clark 1989).

7 Technical flexibility and mass production: flexible specialisation and dynamic flexibility

Benjamin Coriat

The long crisis that has unfolded in front of our eyes has stimulated — and has already validated — many new developments in the technical foundations and supports of the accumulation of capital. The old productive order centred on the large Fordist firm and mass production, if it has not disappeared, has undergone major and vigorous changes of great significance. These changes have reached a point where it is possible to argue, without exaggeration, that, through changes in the technical foundations of accumulation, there has been a *reorganisation of the industrial economy as a whole*. New principles are at work and are reshaping it.

To start to outline the implications of this 'second transformation' for industrial organisation, I shall concentrate on the characterisation and the effects of the *new information technologies on productive processes*. In order to accomplish successfully the objective of identifying and setting out the new principles which are at work in the mass-production system, I shall divide this chapter into four parts.

In the first I shall characterise the new technological trend which is reshaping the productive apparatuses of the developed capitalist countries. I shall defend the thesis that a there is a *new technological trajectory* based on the two principles of integration and flexibility. The latter will be defined, and its content will be specified.

An analysis of the economic meaning of its effects can then be undertaken. I shall show that the new categories of equipment that take advantage of the productive use of electronics and computers combine the *classical effects* of technical progress with some other (largely renewed) effects. Of the latter the most important are due to the fact that a basic productive unit with flexible machines can get access to the advantages traditionally associated with *multi-product firms*.

If, on the basis of these initial arguments, one proceeds to *dynamic* analysis, some new properties of flexible technologies can be identified, mainly as a result of a reconsideration of the classical notions of 'learning and experience curve effects' and the specific content that technological flexibility is able to give them.

With the help of the categories and tools of analysis set out in earlier sections it will then be possible to identify the overall significance of the changes that the system of mass production is experiencing.

In a final section I shall spell out the points I have established and the perspectives that can inform further research.

7.1 A new technological trajectory

If one accepts that what is new about automation is the emergence of a category of *programmable* machines,[1] the thesis I wish to advance for consideration can be presented in a few words. It involves several interdependent propositions that can be summarised as follows.

7.1.1 A socially determined trajectory ...

In industrialised countries technological development — especially in so far as process innovations are concerned — follows trajectories that are determined. The notion of a technological trajectory comes in the main from the work of Nelson and Winter (1982) and Dosi (1984). In this chapter I shall give it a slightly different meaning.[2] I shall define it as a series of *successive and cumulative goal-oriented innovations* with the socioeconomic conditions in which these trajectories are formed giving rise to a process of *selection of innovations*.

More specifically, the hypothesis is that in the case of programable automation two sets of phenomena 'determine' and 'select' innovations:

(1) The relative exhaustion of Taylorist and Fordist methods of work organisation as sources of productivity growth. In particular numerous studies[3] came to the same conclusion: as the methods of *equilibrating* production lines involved *far too much dead and unproductive time*, studies of the productive use of electronics and computers would seek to identify new ways of reducing 'dead time' in production.
(2) The *new characteristics assumed by the demand that a firm faced* in the crisis. Demand became far more unstable and diversified, and so everywhere or almost everywhere the demand for standardised, mass-produced goods was replaced by differentiated demands for limited runs of products whose characteristics varied from one batch to another. Put another way, on top of cost competition, which continued to have its own implications, was superimposed *competition over quality* in the sense that keeping and winning a market today increasingly involves meeting a demand that is specific and differentiated.

These two sets of phenomena, which also constitute new *long-run constraints on accumulation*, are the major determinants of the direction in which technological change occurs. It is in this sense that the new technological trajectory that I have just briefly outlined can be considered 'socially' determined. It is a matter of responding both to the crisis of 'work' of the 1970s and to the new characteristics of inter-firm competition.

7.1.2 ... centred on the principles of integration and flexibility

In practice the new long-run constraints that I have just mentioned stimulate and favour the emergence of new production engineering paradigms that involve in brief:

(1) A search for *integration* as a new way of achieving productivity gains. The 'integration' aimed at involves a new optimisation of the sequence and duration of production activities with a view to maximising the density of work and reducing labour time and the duration of operations. Still more generally, integration involves all the methods whose goal is to *convert dead time in production into time that is actually productive*, whether the dead time relates to workers, the rate of use of machines, or the time in which raw materials and semi-finished goods are stored (on this point see Coriat 1983).

In essence integration relies on different organisational alternatives aimed at production in '*hidden time*'. Note that the actual exploitation of the potential advantages of integration presupposes the introduction of *organisational innovations* in the arrangement of production lines: trolleys whose route and speed can be varied and controlled, complex computer-controlled circulation of parts that breaks with the unidimensional character of traditional Fordist lines, and so on. In this sense integration offers new ways of achieving 'organisational economies' which in their general form are designated, after Liebenstein, as the *effects of X efficiency* (I shall reconsider this point in Sections 7.2 and 7.3).

(2) An attempt to increase the *flexibility* of production lines to facilitate adaptation to the unstable, volatile and differentiated character of market demand in an era in which the importance of quality considerations in competition increases. To give a succinct definition one can say that in a technological sense flexibility depends in the main on the programmable character which the new information technologies have allowed machine tools and handlers to be given. The arrangement of a line of machines and handlers endowed in advance with a variety of different and alternative modes of operation allows them to be used to produce, *simultaneously* if necessary, and automatically, a variety of different pieces or products from a simple shape or a given input. Starting with this general characterisation of technological flexibility, various more specific attributes can be added. For the basic essentials I shall draw in this chapter on the distinctions made by Gerwin and Leung (1980). In a remarkable article they identified the following five dimensions or types of application of technological flexibility:

(i) Design change flexibility refers to the possibility of modifying the process in accordance with the particular characteristics that can be introduced in the same basic product.

(ii) Mix flexibility has to do with the possibility of producing simultaneously, on the same line, different and alternative products that have certain basic elements in common.

(iii) Part flexibility concerns the fact that the process as a whole can be made more simple or complex at low or no cost through the addition or subtraction of productive operations.

(iv) Volume flexibility denotes the possibility of altering the quantitative output of the line in accordance with variations in demand.

(v) Routing flexibility refers to the capacity to route the product via segments of the process that are free or underemployed.

Of course other distinctions are possible. However in subsequent sections of this chapter the reader will discover that the categories proposed by Gerwin and Leung are particularly useful for a consideration of the *economic* meaning of these new technological developments as opposed to their technological character.

No matter how they are presented it is in general these two characteristics of *integration* and *flexibility* that are considered the new features of the new generation of automatic devices.

The issue which interests me above all is the extent to which these two properties of integrated-flexible automation modify the mode of operation of the mass-production system. In the absence of well-argued and substantiated theses, the most diverse points of view have been expressed. These positions can be grouped into two extreme positions.

(1) In so far as it allows an adaptation to differentiated and variable demand, flexibile automation is, it is argued at one extreme, in a position to face up to the new characteristics of demand, and is able to establish the conditions for a coherent new macroeconomic growth model. At present some time is considered necessary for completion of the transition to a new phase of growth. This point of view is the one that emerges in particular from current neo-Schumpeterian perspectives whose variants can differ quite sharply (see, for example, Freeman 1984 and Mensch 1979) but which envisage the onset of 'hyper-industrialisation' after a phase of stagnation.

(2) For others, on the other hand, who lie at the other extreme, the new technological trajectory corresponds to a new trajectory in the area of *industrial organisation*. The end of the system of mass production is proclaimed, as is its replacement by another economic order based on *flexible specialisation*. This thesis assumes its most powerful form in the the work of Piore and Sabel (1984).

In all of these cases, however, the changes identified are of considerable significance. To develop my own reply to the question I have asked, which in its general form involves asking *what are the overall changes in the system of mass production as a whole* — within which the new technologies emerged — that will result from the new technologies, a clear idea of the *modus operandi* of these technologies is needed. I have therefore chosen to focus first of all on *the content and nature of productivity gains* associated with the new technological current. To make the argument more clear I shall draw a distinction between static (Section 7.2) and dynamic (Section 7.3) analysis.

7.2 The gains from integrated-flexible automation : a static approach

In the world of statics[4] integrated-flexible automation is, I shall argue, the source of two sets of potential benefits:

(1) *classical productivity gains* which rest, however, on new (technological) foundations; and
(2) *productivity gains whose source and nature differ* from those associated with earlier generations of automatic machines.

7.2.1 Integration: a new source of 'classical' productivity increases

One method of analysis — which is by far the most common — involves investigating the economic effects of programmable automation using the *same tools and concepts* as are used to analyse *inflexible automation*: Detroit-type automation whose archetype is the transfer line developed in the 1950s. This method of analysis is not wrong. It is just very limited in that it overlooks the very aspects of programmable automation that are associated with flexibility. The major initial points that can be made, on the basis of this restrictive approach, which is concerned only with the integrative properties of programmable automation, are as follows.

7.2.1.1 *A lowering of the cost frontier ...*

To identify the greatest 'efficiency' contribution of programmable automation the emphasis is placed on certain attributes of *integration*. Thus productivity gains are explained by:

(1) a reduction in 'dead time' and a more intensive use of living labour power, and
(2) a higher rate of use of machine tools, which
(3) are combined in the general techniques of work in 'hidden time' which aim to convert into productive time unproductive time linked with the organisation of manufacture.

In the end it is a better optimisation of the relations between *circulation time and operating time* that is at the root of these gains. It is also for this reason that I argue that *organisational economies* à la Liebenstein can be invoked in this case. Indeed these effects can be expected to be all the more powerful because *work* organisation is — in contrast to the implicit hypothesis of Liebenstein (see, for example, the overview of his research in his 1966 article)

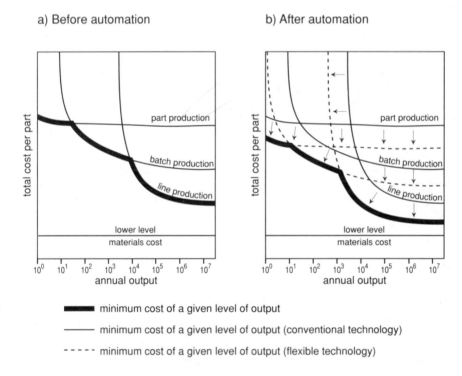

a) Before automation

b) After automation

minimum cost of a given level of output

minimum cost of a given level of output (conventional technology)

minimum cost of a given level of output (flexible technology)

Figure 7.1 Programmable automation and the lowering of the cost frontier

Source: Ayres and Miller 1983.

— no longer their only source. As soon as account is taken of the *organisational* economies which the application of computers to the management of production allows, the effects of improved work organisation can be combined with the *effects associated with the organisation of production* (on this point see Section 7.4).

No matter therefore how long the run considered, a point-by-point comparison reveals potential advantages for programmable automation. Figure 7.1 is explicit on this point. It shows how the switch from one productive arrangement (inflexible automation) to another that is more efficient (programmable automation) results in an overall reduction in factor inputs for the same quantity of output.

7.2.1.2 ... *modified by a lengthening of production cycles*

The productivity gains that result from programmable automation are, as the different studies carried out insist, only potential. Various preconditions must be satisfied for this potential to be realised. Everything hinges on a paradoxical effect of programmable automation. On the one hand programmable (as opposed to in flexible) automation involves an *increase in average production costs*, at least at constant output levels. In general there are three reasons for this increase:

(1) the purchase and installation of programmable automation is more expensive than inflexible automation,
(2) structural maintenance costs (parts, tools and workforce) are greater, and
(3) as the labour 'saved' is in general relatively unskilled labour, the savings in labour costs do not offset the increase in capital costs.

It is therefore only because it allows the *multiplication of cycles of work* (a change to shift work and/or weekend work, as, for example, in the car industry) and the lengthening of the series produced in a given clock hour that programmable automation becomes more profitable than inflexible automation. Only in these conditions are average and marginal costs lower with programmable than inflexible automation.

This consequence is very important. It shows that the development of programmable automation is seriously constrained and limited by the size of the market and the demand a firm gets. This conclusion is moreover the same as the one drawn by David in the conclusions to a long article on the conditions for the diffusion of robots:

In the curent state of robot technologies and for the foreseeable future fixed costs are high in comparison with net cost reductions, so that the introduction of robots is only profitable beyond a certain scale of production that I shall call the 'minimum scale' required for mechanisation and automation. (David 1986)

7.2.2 Flexibility: a new source and kind of productivity growth

Under this heading fall the developments that really are *specific* to the generations of technologies based on programmable automation. Flexibility and the advantages associated with it are — at least in part — quite new in the history of techniques.

The 'economic' gains associated with flexibility, while often difficult to identify with precision, can be approached in two ways: on the one hand from the purely static point of view of arguments about the intensity of use of installed capacities, and on the other from that of arguments that deal with the notions of economies of scope and range. In this article I shall deal with them separately.

7.2.2.1 A better use of installed capacities: flexibility and 'static' economies of scale

This argument, which is identified most often, has already been presented in detail (see Bultel 1983; Coriat 1983; and Boyer and Coriat 1986). I shall therefore pass over it quickly. Just let us recall that, in so far as a firm with flexible equipment can — in less time and at lower cost — follow fluctuations in the qualitative side of demand (by adapting to the different varieties of a product that are demanded), it is in a position permanently to operate close to *the point at which its installed capacities are saturated*. A rigid firm has no choice but to forgo those sections of demand that it cannot satisfy without expensive and time-consuming rearrangements of its production lines.

From an economic point of view not only do flexible technologies thus appear to reduce the risks of investment. A fundamental consequence is that the general conditions for profitability for a firm with flexible equipment are significantly modified. Note in passing that it is on this point that the argument of David (1986) just cited seems inadequate. The profitability of programmable automation does indeed require — in general — a 'minimum scale'. But allowance for flexibility means that this 'minimum scale' can be achieved by the *simultaneous production of a variety of products* and that the conditions for profitability are modified. It is a point that David neither recognises nor discusses.

7.2.2.2 Economies of scope, and economies of range

Half-way between these 'static' scale economies that I have just discussed and genuinely 'dynamic' scale economies, a third set of arguments can be introduced. The arguments involved concern the notion of economies of scope which emerged from different studies by Baumol, Panzar and Willig (the main points are set out in their collective 1982 publication).[5] To appreciate the meaning and in particular the relevance of these ideas for the question I am examining, several remarks are necessary.

It should be noted first of all that the notion of 'economies of scope' was introduced by Baumol, Panzar and Willig in relation to the cost functions of a *multi-product firm*. The intention was to identify a type of scale economy that is found specifically where a multi-product firm produces joint products. In this case the source of the productivity gains lies in the fact that certain inputs can be used simultaneously to make different products. There are economies of scope if the average costs of the multi-product firm are less than the sum of the average costs of each of the products made separately. If $y1$ and $y2$ are two joint products, and $c(y)$ is the general cost function, the condition of existence of economies of scope is that:

$$c(y1,y2) < c(y1,0) + c(0,y2)$$

In this case the relative magnitude of the economies of scope (sc) is given by the equation:

$$sc = [c(y1,0) + c(0,y2) - c(y1,y2)] / c(y1,y2)$$

If one intends to move from the cost functions of multi-product firms[6] to the cases of flexible technologies and automation, several further remarks are needed.

(1) As a first approximation the notion of 'economies of scope' does indeed seem capable of direct application to flexible production lines. Among the inputs the *machines* at least are common and their profitable use depends on the production not of one but of several products.

(2) Note also however that it is no longer just a matter of an advantage which results from the possibility of more fully saturating a *given* amount of

installed capacity. The advantages that economies of scope provide go
further. They lie in the fact that a firm that invests in flexible equipment can
also adopt an 'offensive' strategy centred on the search for scale economies
by choosing a higher level of capacity than it would if it had to install
inflexible automatic machines. What is more, it can do so with less risk in
asmuchas the technological flexibility it acquires allows it to produce for a
'multiproduct' market.[7] Apart from certain economic limits,[8] there are
technological constraints on these strategies of anticipation. They rest on
the degree of differentiation of the products that a given flexible technology
allows one to consider. One can thus distinguish, for example, between:

(i) Economies of scope in the strict sense. The latter allow one to consider a
high degree of product differentiation and in the limit the *supply of
different products*. However their production must at least have a
'technology' input in common.
(ii) Economies of range which correspond to a scaled-down version of
'scope' economies in which the differentiation that can be achieved is less. It
involves the adaptation of technical systems to handle differences in the
simple external *characteristics* of a product in the sense of Chamberlain's
(1927) theories of monopolistic competition or Lancaster's (1966 and 1975)
theory of consumption.

In an earlier article (Boyer and Coriat 1986), in which the categories
proposed by Gerwin and Leung (1980) were used, a distinction that is
analogous in principle was introduced when we differentiated the *flexibility of
products*, involving a high level of differentiation, and the *flexibility of range*,
involving a low level of differentiation.[9]

As I shall show in detail, these different sources of productivity can be used
in new and contrasting strategies of valorisation of capital. However before I
identify these strategies, I must complete the analysis of the potential
productivity gains associated with programmable automation by taking into
account the dynamic effects.

7.3 The transition to dynamics

If one introduces the notion of 'economic time' and argues in terms of periods
which themselves include the effects of scale economies and volume increases,
new potential gains from programmable automation can be identified.

7.3.1 The reuse of equipment and dynamic economies of fixed capital

These advantages hinge on whether or not a large part of equipment can be
reused when one changes from one product or model to another. (In the car
industry, for example, with a change of model some 70 to 80 per cent of
equipment should, in the view of observers, be reusable.) The advantages that
result consist of an immediate advantage and a very real indirect advantage.

The immediate advantage that a reuse of a substantial part of the earlier capital stock allows is the reduction in the costs of capital investment over the different generations of products made with it. (With flexible machines 'reprogramming' and a resetting of interfaces suffice, whereas inflexible automatic machines are not reuseable.) The other advantage, which is related to the former but is analytically separable, is the possibility of avoiding a certain amount of 'overinvestment'. Due to the shape of demand curves at different periods in the product's life cycle, a firm with rigid equipment which intends to maintain a presence in the whole of the market cannot avoid overinvestment over time and over successive generations of models.

In the article cited, Bultel (1983) summarises the argument on the basis of two graphs. In a rigid system, cumulative investment creates an ever increasing gap between installed capacity and market demand for different models at different moments in their life cycles. In a flexible system cumulative investment and demand can converge so that installed capacities are not — or remain slightly — excessive.[10]

7.3.2 The effects of learning and experience: a reconstruction of the learning curve

Here perhaps one touches on the propostions that have the most far-reaching consequences. In order to make the argument as clear as possible I shall once again proceed by stages. I shall first summarise the meaning of the concepts of learning and experience in general, as applied therefore to classical technologies and products. Afterwards I shall propose a new meaning relevant for the technologies of the information age.

To start with, remember that learning curves involve the establishment of a relation between average costs and the cumulative volume of output obtained from an installation whose capacity is assumed fixed and constant (see Figure 7.2 for a formal account of the measurement of learning-curve effects).

Empirically it has been shown that the rate of decline of unit costs is a direct function of the proportion of direct labour (measured in hours of work of 'direct workers') included in the productive combination. The slope of the learning curve varies with this share. Numerous empirical studies support these conclusions (see, for a synthetic account, Abernathy 1978 and Hirschman 1985). However, the establishment of the *theoretical foundations* of the learning curve is a much more difficult task. In this area it is without doubt Arrow (1962) who has carried out the most systematic study. His main conclusions concerning the *source* of learning curve effects can be summarised as follows:

(1) 'learning is a product of experience in that it can only occur as a result of the attempts made to solve a problem',
(2) 'a second generalisation . . . is that learning associated with the repetition of a problem that is essentially identical is associated with strong increasing returns' but these advances can only be temporary, and
(3) 'to get continuously improved performance requires that the situations that

Traditionally the 'experience' curve establishes a relationship between unit costs, C, and cumulative production, N. It states that each time experience (cumulative production) doubles, costs can be expected to fall by a fraction, a, where, typically $0.2 \leq a \leq 0.4$. Mathematically

$$C = C_0 N^{-b}$$

where $N = \int_0^t Q(t')\, dt$, $b = -\ln(1-a)/\ln 2$, and annual output $Q = \dfrac{dN}{dt}$

Ayres (1985) assembled the results of a series of empirical studies of very old and classic products (such as the Model 'T' Ford) and of new products of the electronic era (such as disc drives and integrated circuits). The data are far from exhaustive. However the trend that emerges is for more powerful experience curve effects. This unexpected result poses problems of interpretation.

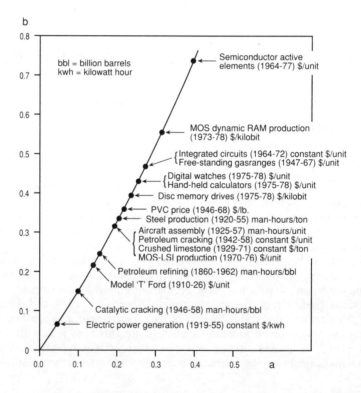

Figure 7.2 Experience curves for old and new products

act as stimuli must themselves evolve regularly rather than be repetitive' (Arrow 1962, p. 138).

These three propositions established by Arrow have to do with the psychological and social foundations of learning curve effects. They indicate hypotheses concerning the *origin* of the gains from learning but do not provide an operational method of measurement. In practice the notion of learning must undergo several redefinitions to make it useable.

If one focuses on microeconomic uses,[11] learning-curve effects (attributable only, as we have seen, to increases in the efficiency of the direct labour force) were extended and incorporated into the wider concept of experience-curve effects. The latter include not only increases in the efficiency of direct work but also increases associated with indirect work, organisational improvements, and even the small technical improvements to which a new technology always gives rise as and when control over it increases (see Abernathy 1978).

Note also that, *if one adds to experience-curve effects the effects of classical economies of scale* corresponding to increases in capacity, one gets, through a further extension of the concept of experience, what orthodox microeconomics calls the *long-term productivity curve*.

With the help of the tools whose origins and content I have just briefly outlined, experience curves — or, more exactly, long-term productivity curves — have been pieced together to show, over the course of time, substantial reductions in production costs. The gains seemed so large and so certain that the systematic research into their use led to real firms' strategies of what was called 'descent' along experience curves. The classic case is that of the Model 'T' Ford. From 1909 to 1923 its costs were reduced, according to Abernathy and Wayne (1985), along a curve by 85 per cent (or 15 per cent for each doubling of output over some fifteen years). Experience curves exist for almost all the large manufactured products of the typical sectors of Fordism.

If one turns now to the new products of which the majority are — at least in part — manufactured in flexible installations, what lessons can one draw?

Let me start with an obvious fact. It is naturally very difficult to establish a clear empirical account of learning- and experience-curve effects for these products. In spite of the lack of a suffficiently long temporal perspective, one preliminary study by Ayres (1985) is nevertheless available. Ayres compared the experience-curve effects for the classical products of Fordism and the new products that typify the era of computers and electronics (see Figure 7.2). Although partial, the results are all the more remarkable in that they give rise to a hypothesis that was somewhat unexpected: far from fading, experience curve-effects are more pronounced for new products than for the canonical products of Fordism. While hypothetical because of the fragility of its statistical foundations, this result deserves further attention and several comments.

Observe, first of all, that this result is paradoxical: if one holds to a strict definition of learning-curve effects, *the slopes ought to be much smaller*, because the proportion of direct workers is smaller. There are however strong reasons why the hypothesis suggested by the data Ayres collected should be taken seriously. Taking account of what I have argued so far, two sets of theoretical propositions can be found to support it. As matters that affect technologies that are integrated and flexible these two propositions concern what I shall call *organisation effects* on the one hand and *interaction effects* (or iteration effects) of processes and products on the other.

7.3.2.1 Integration, paths and organisation effects

As I pointed out earlier, the productive use of microelectronics makes possible, in particular, 'path' effects which allow a new optimisation of production and circulation time. This optimisation is the distinctive new contribution made by the introduction of the methods of production *integration* that flexible technologies allow. Considered from this point of view as technologies of organisation, computing and microelectronics allow the very great potential that progressive *learning* offers to be highlighted. In this sense the advantages that appear at the level of comparative statics (see section 7.2) are much more evident at the level of dynamics. And the X-efficiency effects that Liebenstein attributed to systems of work organisation can be attributed to the current generations of automatic machines by relating them on this occasion to the organisational resources that the productive use of computers and electronics provides. In this way therefore one can start to explain the existence of large experience curve effects from current generations of technologies, and one is led to anticipate them.

7.3.2.2 Design change and mix flexibility: the process/product interaction or iteration effects

The other explanation is connected with the *programmable* character of the new technologies. In the framework of static analysis of section 7.2 I indicated its importance with reference to the concept of *economies of scope and range* which can be exploited with these technologies. In a dynamic context the potential gains seem much greater as soon as one takes into account not only process but also product engineering. What flexible technologies allow is a costless (or low-cost) adaptation to the *combined development of process and product*. A brief account of the history of Ford's cars provides a clear illustration of what is involved. The key point lies in the fact — cited forcefully by Abernathy and Wayne (1985) — that any strategy for rapidly descending the experience curve (through- scale and learning-curve economies) that implies standardisation and repetition comes up against a fundamental limit: *the absence of a capacity to face change* without incurring costs and without major reorganisation. Abernathy and Wayne (1985) cite two facts:

(1) The first relates to the specific shape of the experience curve. Experience curves for very long periods include changes in model and in essential instruments, and one can see that with each major change the experience curve rises more or less sharply according to the significance of the reorganisation that the new development requires, before descending once again. In practice a long-term Fordist experience curve is therefore made up of several stepped segments with the curve (marked as a solid line in Figure 7.3) rising at each point where a major change occurs prior to further reductions.

(2) The second important fact cited by Abernathy and Wayne concerns a key episode in the history of Ford: the 1930s when Ford was definitively supplanted by General Motors. In essence General Motor's strategy was,

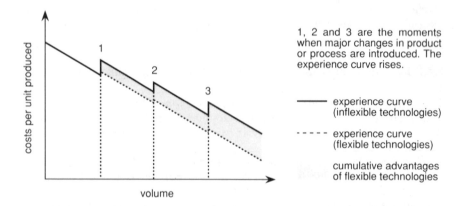

Figure 7.3 A comparison of experience curves for inflexible and flexible technologies

Abernathy explains, one of product differentiation and market segmentation. Ford could not follow this path. The River Rouge plant which had been constructed in accordance with the principles of hyper-specialisation proved far too rigid to accommodate the necessary product changes and diversification with which Ford had to proceed to counter General Motor's new strategy. In the end Ford had to *close the River Rouge plant for nearly one year* and to carry out a global reorganisation of its installations as well as changes in a large number of its tools and machines so that it in its turn could supply the market with differentiated products.

These two sets of facts allow the dynamic advantages of technological flexibility to be specified. In essence flexible technologies offer the possibility of *joint modifications in process and product engineering that over time allow the long-term learning curve to fall regularly* without the sharp upward jumps that rigid arrangements cause when there is a change of product. The area between the broken and the solid lines in Figure 7.1 indicates the long-term experience curve advantages of flexible as compared with inflexible technologies.

Having reached this point it is now possible to attempt to proceed to an overall view of the changes in the system of mass production that the new technologies introduce.

7.4 Technical flexibility and mass production: new principles and new productive arrangements

To identify the new productive arrangements that are emerging, I shall draw a sharp distinction between 'static' strategies, which draw in the main on the gains from economies of range and scope, and dynamic strategies, which rest on 'inter-temporal' perspectives on the valorisation of capital and which endeavour to take advantage of the gains from line production and the new kind of experience-curve effects that I have described.

7.4.1 Economies of scope : the principle of flexible specialisation

The systematic exploitation of *economies of scope* — whether it involves the implementation of what I have called design change (range) or mix (product) flexibility — is the first key way in which the hegemony of the canonical Fordist model is broken.

In the new world whose contours are shaped by the instability of mass production, the flexible firm, smaller in size than the classical Fordist firm, does indeed appear to be a new actor in a class of its own.

In all of the markets in which demand is unstable and rapidly changing, or in markets whose products face rapid obsolescence, the theoretical capacity of a flexible firm, even of a small one, to adapt almost instantaneously to product changes makes it in principle possible for it to outperform a classical Fordist firm. All that is required is that the advantages obtained from *economies of scope* exceed those obtained from *economies of scale* in the strict sense.

To be more precise one can say that, with respect to the *valorisation of the capital invested*, flexibility allows a *strategy of differentiation* that has two aspects:

(1) *a strategy of passive differentiation* involving a simple adaptation of the goods and services a firm offers to identified changes in the composition of demand, and
(2) *a strategy of active differentiation* which is characterised by the fact that the firm takes the initiative and regularly launches products with new features that *substitute* for older ones (see Figure 7.4(1) and (2)).

To illustrate these ideas several examples of these strategies of differentiation can be given. Quite intentionally I shall choose examples from the sectors for which mass demand and consumption exist. The first type of case is the shoe industry. In France more than 400 firms share the market, and none of them has a large market share. Moreover demand varies a great deal, is diversified and unstable. Due to seasonal factors and fashion considerations the whole range of products must change every six months. Each range is, on average, made up of six basic products (shoes for a man, woman, child, sport, and so on) each with different sizes and colours.

In a world of this kind the advantages that can be obtained from a strategy of valorisation based on flexible specialisation are obvious. Whether it involves *passive adaptation* (with the firm 'specialising' in the models and variants that are most in demand on the market) or *active differentiation* (with the firm, after considering revealed demand, attempting to promote a new product), differentiation is a means of earning monopolistic rents.[12]

In the clothing industry (see, for example, Dubois and Barisi 1982) the same types of behaviour have been identified for that part of demand characterised by seasonal or fashion-related fluctuations. Similarly the special 1987 issue of the *Cahiers du centre d'études de l'emploi* on the theme of 'Firms and products' contains many studies of the different methods of adaptation of firms to changes in demand and quality. More generally in Piore and Sabel (1984) there are also examples drawn from very varied situations.

Over and above the illustrations that can be given, the important point is the following. At a conceptual level, it is this kind of firm (average in size, but with flexible equipment, which exploits different possibilities for differentiation, and if the case arises enters relations of cooperation and partnership with other similar firms) that Piore and Sabel have in mind when they refer to the transition to a model of *flexible specialisation* that is expected to *succeed and substitute for mass production*. As this thesis has caused a great stir, I shall dwell on it for a moment. But after paying tribute to this pioneering work — which has acted as an important stimulus to research — it is necessary to show its limitations. For even in its modified and most developed form (see Piore 1987) the thesis is very restrictive and, for that reason, finally inadmissible if its goal is to cover all of the changes which are at present affecting mass production.

On analysis it can be seen to depend on a series of interrelated hypotheses which finally lead to the key hypothesis on which the validity of the *model* implicitly depends. This key argument is that, from a dynamic point of view, strategies centred on economies of range and scope are triumphing or will triumph over those that endeavour to draw on economies of scale. In other words the hypothesis is that products for which *demand is growing sufficiently and is sufficiently stable* for a strategy centred on a search for scale economies and long runs to win out do and will not exist. Thus in his 1987 article, which is based on surveys of the uses firms make of information technologies, Piore reconsidered the initial theses of the model of flexible specialisation. By classifying the results of the surveys, he distinguished six types of situation, of which three came under the model of flexible specialisation, and three under flexible mass production. But afterwards the author reaffirmed the strategic superiority of flexible specialisation, with the forms of flexible mass production he identified being characterised as *unstable* and as no more than 'transitory' moments in the forward march of flexible specialisation.

Finally Piore and Sabel's model rests on the hypothesis that quality factors (rapid adaptation to changing demand) everywhere and always outweigh price factors. In other words it rests on the repeatedly stated idea that the demand a firm faces is for products that have short life cycles and are mutually substitutable or exclusive. If these interrelated hypotheses (products with a short life cycle, quality considerations are more important than price considerations, and so on) cease to be valid, then the conditions of existence and efficiency of flexible specialisation will have dissolved.

This conclusion can be demonstrated by relaxing just one of the hypotheses of the model. Suppose, for example, that there is a market made up of a collection of — complementary or substitutable — products *for which demand is increasing*. To focus our minds think, for example, of the market for compact discs which will be considered in a moment (with several thousand units sold in 1982, 370 million in 1987, and sales of one billion expected in 1990), video cassette recorders, and microcomputers, which are all new products for which there is a strong increase in demand. In the Piore and Sabel model such a market can be served only through a *multiplication* of flexible production units. But this case which involves a choice between a multiplication of small firms and a large firm is the very one that is used in the textbooks to demonstrate the existence and superiority of scale economies in the classical sense of the effects of the amount of capacity installed.[13] The lack of realism of the solution that the model of flexible specialisation suggests is indicated by two arguments of which one is empirical and one theoretical.

Theoretically, first of all, in the strict context of the cost functions of a *multi-product firm*, the conclusion is clear. The relevant case is that of scale economies of the 'trans-ray' type analysed by Bailey and Friedlander (1982). The latter result from the addition of the economies of scale of specific products and the economies of scope (see Bailey and Friedlander 1982). Where output is increasing everything depends on the relative importance of the *economies of scale of specific products* and the *economies of scope*. Once the former are large and greater than the second it will be more efficient to produce in two specific plants with longer runs the two joint products formerly made with a flexible technology.

In practice — and it is the empirical argument with which one can oppose Piore and Sabel — firms in sectors with increasing demand really do adopt strategies that involve a search for scale economies and the cost reductions that scale economies allow. There is a nuance that will be examined in a moment: although governed by long runs, organisational and technological choices allow process–product iterations that encourage certain kinds of product development and adaptation to demand.

The conditions on which the validity of the model of flexible specialisation depends do therefore appear to be established — a market of stable size but where the product composition is changing — and clearly limited. If demand is increasing (even if it is qualitatively unstable) large-scale production has the edge.

Considered from a macroeconomic pont of view (as it is a level that Piore and Sabel explicitly consider), this model, which rests exclusively on the principle of flexible specialisation in the sense I have outlined, appears much more of a productive model of *adjustment to slow and unstable growth* than a way out of crisis.

The model of flexible specialisation does offer new possibilities for capital valorisation à la Chamberlain through product differentiation and the search for niche markets. It does, therefore, certainly allow the most dynamic individual firms to develop by constantly recreating (small) *monopolistic rents*, but it lacks the generality that Piore and Sabel claim for it. To finish, let me add that the hypotheses concerning macroeconomic interlocking that Piore and Sabel postulate (increase in the number of medium-sized flexible firms and relations of partnership among them) seem, besides their normative character (Proudhon's artisans' republic is explicitly invoked), very fragile in all those cases where increasing demand even for differentiated products is the order of the day.

Thus while rejecting the hypothesis of a new macroeconomic model based on flexible specialisation which itself is seen as a result of the new techological trajectory, it does seem possible to retain the principle of flexible specialisation as one that is at work and can be applied in certain competitive conditions and in certain conditions relating to the life cycles of products and the characteristics of demand.

To this principle of flexible specialisation, however, it now seems possible to oppose a quite different principle: that of dynamic flexibility.

7.4.2 Economies of experience and the principle of dynamic flexibility

The first question that arises concerns the specific content of the principle of dynamic flexibility. It is clear from the earlier discussion that the distinctive feature, which marks it out and distinguishes it from flexible specialisation, is that it is centred around *a systematic pursuit of economies of scale and the advantages of long runs*. Having made this point, a more detailed exploration of the content of the principle of dynamic flexibility can be undertaken. To do so I shall start with Klein's (1986) initial definition which Cohen and Zysman (1987) extended in a remarkable way. Klein arrived at his formulation as a result of observing the behaviour of certain Japanese firms. The definition he proposed was the following:

Dynamic flexibility ... in contrast with static flexibility does not arise from the production of more than one product (for example cars and light trucks) on one production line although the Japanese also follow this practice. It is concerned more with the design of production lines capable of rapid adjustment in response to changes in product and process engineering.

This observation of considerable significance is however, it seems to me, somewhat under-theorised by Klein when, at the end of his argument, he concludes that: 'The central objective of dynamic flexibility is to make rapid changes in the technology of production with a view to reducing costs and, as a result, increasing productivity' (Klein 1986). The weakness of this short extract lies in the fact that Klein reduces the principle of dynamic flexibility simply to the search for lower costs.

I shall provide the notion of dynamic flexibility with a content that is both more precise and wider. Making use of the different arguments set out in the analysis of the dynamic advantages of technological flexibility (see section 7.3), I shall argue that the principle of dynamic flexibility depends in the main on *economies of interaction (or preferably of iteration) between process and product which themselves are mobilised in a strategy whose goal is to take advantage of economies of scale and size*. To make the point clearer, I would say that whereas the principle of flexible specialisation is intended to take advantage of the possibilities of *instantaneous adjustment* that technical flexibility allows, the principle of dynamic flexibility is implemented where there are longer time horizons and there is an integration of policies of *product evolution* and *scale economies*. Strategies of cost reduction and a search for 'dynamic' differentiation through modification of the characteristics of products are therefore combined in the characterisation of dynamic flexibility.

The importance of a redefinition of this kind and an extension of the concept *on the basis of the new content of the effects of organisation, learning and experience* is that they allow one to take into account other hypotheses concerning the development of the life cycles of products and the strategies of valorisation associated with them. Without making any pretence to exhaust the range of possibilities, and in order to illustrate the argument, I shall distinguish two major strategies of valorisation of capital: (1) *a strategy of valorisation through extension of the life cycle of the product,* which can be compared with (2) a strategy of valorisation through *renewal* of the life cycle. Figure 7.4(2) deals with (1) and (2) in the context of these strategies.

7.4.2.1 A strategy of valorisation through extension or lengthening of the product life cycle

While systematically making the most of scale economies the firm acts on the interaction between process and product to change the product composition of its output and/or improves its cost or quality with the result that new customers are won and the product's life cycle extended. The firm focuses more on process or product improvements depending on the magnitude of the price elasticity of demand for its products on the one hand and the impact of quality improvements on the other.

The Japanese firm Matsushita illustrates amongst others this type of strategy.[14] This firm which sells throughout the world (under the National trademark) accounts alone for some 30 per cent of world sales of video casette recorders. There is hardly any need to point out that this output is not produced in small flexible enterprises, but in very long runs in plants which each employ several thousand people. The policy followed in organising production involves the application of three sets of principles:[15]

(1) The first principle involves a complex choice between different types of production lines according to the nature of the products to be made, their respective markets and the phase of production. Matsushita combines:

(i) rigid production lines (automated or not) for the standardised parts of products and some components,
(ii) specific assembly lines for final products with a very large market distinguished according to export norms and the share of the market conquered, and
(iii) multi-purpose lines for products destined for export markets that are quantitatively smaller (in order to benefit from line production while allowing some variation in the product made).

(2) The second principle involves a *permanent search for product innovation.* Several developments are involved: miniaturisation, design, the ergo-nomics of moving parts (automatic controls, digital switches, readability of information, etc.), the addition of new features (remote control, winding speed, automatic programme search, extension of time horizons for programme selection, and so on) and a search for improved recording and reproduction quality: at present recording relies on mechanical contact which leads to progressive cassette wear.

1. Flexible specialisation (capacity maintained)

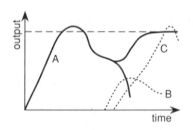

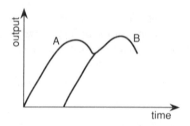

1. Passive differentiation
A, B and C are varieties for sale on the market. The firm follows changes in the composition of demand.

2. Active differentiation
The firm reacts promptly to the fall in demand for product A by launching a new product B. A strategy of permanent innovation of short life cycle products.

2. Dynamic flexibility (increased capacity)

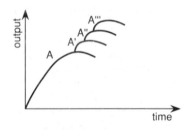

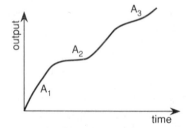

3. Differentiation by extension
The firm extends the life cycle of a product by periodically launching varieties A', A" and A"' of the same product, or by making the varieties that are in demand. The firm's flexibility allows it to take advantage of scale economies.

4. Differentiation by renewal
At the moment when there is a significant inflexion in the demand for the product A_1 the firm proceeds with the launching of a second generation of the same product (A_2) which incorporates an important process or product innovation.

Figure 7.4 Technological flexibility, product life cycles and strategies of valorisation

(3) The last principle is that the product innovations that I have just described are immediately taken up on the production lines. Organisational flexibility (multi-skilled operatives, autonomous work groups, etc.) and technical flexibility (especially in the machining of some parts) make possible this constant product–process iteration, which I have identified as one of the elements of dynamic flexibility, and which allows a constant search for cost

reductions, along with a capacity to adapt to fluctuations in demand, or with the continual release of new variants, allowing a continuous extension of the product life cycle.

In this last case and in many others (Philips is no different) the form of production is that of *flexible mass production*. The advantages of long runs are extended by means of qualitative product differentiation.

7.4.2.2 Strategies of valorisation through 'renewal' of the life cycle of the product

In this case another variant of flexible mass production which entails more intensive research and development than the last model is involved. A firm faced with a weakening in the demand for a product is supposed to be in a position to renew demand by means of (process and product) innovations whose impact is sufficient to allow significant reductions in prices and/or major quality improvements, and as a result to attract an enlarged circle of customers.

An almost perfect illustration of this type of strategy is provided by an investigation of changes in the market for records in which 'major' innovations have succeeded one another at an accelerating rate. Three phases can already be identified. In the first, which started in 1982, compact discs and laser readers appeared and were substituted for 'good old' vinyl discs and record players. Substitution was rapid, as the market for compact discs (370 million units sold in 1987, and 405 million sales expected in 1988) has already overtaken that for vinyl. However these events are only the start of the story. What is of interest for us are subsequent developments. It was estimated that the product life cycle would not peak until 1990. Yet in 1988 the product that will renew the market was launched: the compact video-disc (CD-V) and a corresponding laser reader. One of the characteristics of the new product is that it will absorb the existing market for compact discs (CDs). CD-V readers are able to play CDs, and open up a new market at the same time. The CD-V will know how to read sound, but will also connect with television and transmit images. What is more, a compatible medium will allow the reuse and conversion of current CD readers into players that can transmit images.

In all one has a perfect example of a strategy of renewal of a product (from CD to CD-V) which is centred on the existing CD market in order to extend and widen it. The CD-V reuses the market created by the CD. The key point for the present discussion is however that the equipment used to make CDs can be reused to make CD-Vs, as the sound standard in CD-Vs is the same as in CDs. What is more it is the same establishments (in France PDO at Louviers, Lor Disc at Saint-Michel-sur-Meurthe . . .) that at present make CDs that will make CD-Vs.[16] It is therefore an perfect example of the 'dynamic' reuse of equipment linked to the life cycles of products which are renewed and interlock. Philips and Sony who are the two major producers of CDs will use the same licence for the CD-V.

In these cases there are markets for very long product runs, demand is increasing, and innovation is rapid. At same time there are continuous and substantial reductions in price. These products are typical of the configurations in which only an addition and combination of the effects of long runs and effects of scope can ensure that new or existing firms can enter, maintain or enlarge their position in the market. These cases are typical examples of situations in which flexible mass production seems a requirement, and which the implementation of the principle of dynamic flexibility makes possible.

A further characteristic of the conditions of valorisation associated with this type of firm deserves mention. It involves the forms of competition: in contrast with the case of flexible specialisation which comes under analyses of monopolistic competition, the firms involved in flexible mass production evolve in a world of oligopolistic competition. Their capacity and cost strategies reconstitute the principle of barriers to entry — and oligopolistic rents — which characterise large-scale production.[17] This fact gives further encouragement, if there is a need for it, to these firms to assume the risks — and seek the advantages — of a strategy of dynamic flexibility, always supposing that the nature of the markets and of demand do not make it a pressing need.

7.5 To conclude: the future of mass production

To conclude I shall offer several replies to the initial question: *what reorganisations of the mass-production system are implied by the development of flexible technologies?*

The main points that I have tried to make can be summarised in the following propositions:

(1) *At the level of productive forms integrated-flexible automation seems as if it can at one and the same time:*

(i) favour the appearance and guarantee the survival of a new type of firm that concentrates on medium runs. On the basis of the possibilities for technical flexibility that it possesses it can secure its survival either by exploiting its capacity to *adapt instantaneously* to changes in the composition of demand (passive differentiation) or by systematically promoting 'new' short-life products (active differentiation). In every case, however, the survival of firms of this kind depends on the characteristics of demand and of product life cycles. The latter must be short and/or strictly dependent on quality (wide but segmented markets) rather than price factors.

(ii) revitalise firms making long or very long runs. In this case the risks inherent in volume production and large capacities are tempered or reduced by the possibilities offered by flexible technologies of 'extending' or 'renewing' the life cycle of products. In this situation the large firm can provide for the development of the mass market by giving priority to the exploitation of the effects associated with product–process iteration which allow differentiation in a context of cost reducing strategies. These firms focus their attention on markets in which demand is increasing.

(2) *At the level of the conditions of valorisation and forms of competition* the

firm can apply two principles: *flexible specialisation* and *dynamic flexibility*. To complete the picture several details can be added:

(i) in the case of flexible specialisation, I have shown that in essence it rests on strategies of differentiation à la Chamberlain that allow the appropriation of monopolistic rents. If pursued to the limit such strategies end up as logics of valorisation that entail a *creaming off* of the most rewarding components of demand. For the firm the logical course of action is to make use of its ability to modify the composition of its output in order to offer combinations of products that maximise inter-product rents. In its most extreme form what results is a new kind of *predatory* behaviour involving a systematic creaming off of markets. These considerations lead us a long way from the virtues that Piore and Sabel attribute to the model of flexible specialisation.

(ii) in the case of dynamic flexibility the principle can be characterised more precisely by saying that in essence it implements a principle of '*intertemporal* valorisation' (compared with flexible specialisation which relies on *instantaneous* product changes). Considered from the point of view of the nature and origin of the productivity gains, which are its fundamental motivating force, everything hinges on the renewal of the *content*, and of the effects of organisation, learning and experience that flexibile organisations allow.[18] The paradox — more apparent than real — is that, in spite of the role of systematic cost reducing policies, the firm that is organised in accordance with the principle of dynamic flexibility ultimately recreates the conditions of *oligopolistic* competition. Research and development and capacity effects create barriers to entry that are analogous to the ones created by the classical large Fordist firms. The different forms of *flexible mass production* do appear however to be the *appropriate solution* in markets in which demand is increasing.[19] At this point I find myself in agreement with one of the main arguments of Cohen and Zysman (1987) which makes dynamic flexibility one of the major traits of the current technological revolution.

(3) *With respect to the mass-production system as a whole* the conclusion is that *technological flexibility*, as such, *does not imply its dissolution nor is it in a position, on its own, to ensure its revival.*

The change is of a different nature. Technical flexibility allows the systematic implementation of two principles of valorisation based on flexible specialisation and dynamic flexibility which I have deliberately contrasted in these pages. Moreover these new forms do not necessarily rule out the survival of earlier forms of mass production. Certain *product engineering strategies* can allow complex combinations of classical long production runs (for modules or standard product components) and of assembly with flexible technologies that allow a differentiation of the supply of the final product. Diverse strategies are therefore possible on the basis of the implementation of complex principles governing the externalisation of functions, industrial subcontracting, and cooperation and partnership, in addition to or in conjunction with different modes of implementation of flexible and/or classical mass production.

The examples of this type of strategy are legion. Whether one considers cars and office automation equipment many standard parts are made in very long runs sometimes in dreadful working conditions (in free-trade zones in Hong Kong or Taiwan, for example) prior to assembly in flexible production 'islands'. Note that from a theoretical point of view these types of organisation — old-fashioned long runs and flexible final assembly of components — should be the more efficient the further downstream the differentiation of the product can be pushed. Tarondeau (1982 and 1986) speaks in this manner of *retarded differentiation* and analyses its advantages.

If, therefore, there is no doubt that industrial organisation as a whole is changing, it is at present much more difficult to say which of the productive or organisational forms will play a leading role in a reconstructed mass-production system. One point does however seem certain: the shape that the system of mass production will assume in the future will critically depend on the institutional arrangements that surround the wage relation. Of these the most important are the ones that determine the creation and distribution of primary and secondary incomes. The stratification of the wage-earning class, the components of domestic demand, and the forms of insertion of each national economy into the international division of labour will also clearly have a decisive effect on the structure of new productive forms.

Considered from a macroeconomic point of view, technological flexibility is finally highly ambivalent. As far as the conditions of valorisation of *individual capitals* are concerned it offers both principles of *adaptation to slow and unstable economic growth*, and principles of *revitalisation of volume production for products whose demand is increasing*. The question as to which institutional arrangements will allow a new coherence between new forms of production and consumption is more than ever the key on which an eventual renewal of stable and fast economic growth will depend.

Notes

1. The word programmable automation refers to the current generation of automatic machines. Based on the productive use of computers and electronics these pieces of equipment have two properties: they can perform several operations and, to different extents, are capable of adapting to variations in their environment. Their fundamental attribute is therefore said to be their 'flexibility'.
2. I intend to define the notion of a technological trajectory in terms of a macroeconomic and macrosocial perspective. In the case of Nelson and Winter (1982) the rejection of the hypothesis of 'perfect' rationality and the introduction of 'search' behaviour on the part of the firm, while opposing standard neoclassical accounts, does not allow one to avoid the definition of trajectories that depend on the world of *methodogical individualism*.
3. See, for example, Emery (1969), Emery and Trist (1972) and Davis and Taylor (1972). I tried to set out these ideas systematically in Coriat (1979).
4. The 'static' framework envisaged in this section is so defined by two assumptions. On the one hand the potential advantages of programmable automation are identified by relating them to the advantages classically obtained from inflexible automation. On the other I abstract from economic time: neither capacity nor volume increases are taken into account in this section. (They are considered in the dynamic analysis in Section 7.3.)

5. On this point see also the remarkable article by Bailey and Friedlander (1982) and Azoulay's (1987) critical presentation of their argument as applied to flexible technologies.
6. In their article Bailey and Friedlander (1982) define other categories of scale economies that apply to multi-product firms. Involved in particular are the notions of 'ray' and 'trans-ray' scale economies. I shall refer to them later.
7. This hypothesis is explicitly envisaged and discussed in Bailey and Friedlander (1982).
8. In this case *economies of scope must exceed the so-called 'specific products' economies of scale associated with each of the products which contributes to output.* This argument is important. It will be re-examined and developed in Section 7.4.
9. In the article cited (Boyer and Coriat 1986) *design change (range) flexibility* and *mix (product) flexibility* were related respectively to the concepts of *differentiated* production and *varied* production.
10. Tha *macroeconomic* effects of a situation of this kind are analysed in Boyer and Coriat (1986).
11. On the introduction of experience curve effects into macroeconomic models see in particular, in addition to Arrow (1962) who has already been cited, Kaldor (1961). This task is also attempted in Boyer and Coriat (1986).
12. These ideas are drawn from an investigation conducted by Azoulay. The results were published (Azoulay 1987) in the *Cahiers du GERTTD*. In the same publication there is a study by Saillard of subcontracting in mechanical engineering which provides a typical example of 'passive adaptation'.
13. See, for example, Gold's excellent 1981 survey.
14. The following observations were formulated after a November 1986 visit to and survey of the Matsushita plant at Okayama in Japan. I would like to thank in particular Professors Hirata, Yagi (of the University of Kyoto) and Nomura (of the University of Okayama) for the excellent conditions they provided for my work and stay in Japan.
15. These remarks are provisional. They result from the visit to the Okayama plant and the interviews with the manager in charge of production as well as from discussions with Professor Nomura in which they were developed further.
16. For a brief but clear account of these changes see the supplement 'Affaires' of *Le Monde* for 30 January 1988.
17. Note that some contemporary developments in the theory of competition — associated with what it has become customary to call the theory of contestable markets — presume that flexible technologies make possible an easier exit from a sector and will therefore re-establish conditions of non-oligopolistic competition even in markets in which large firms have very large market shares. It goes without saying that my own view is different. For a critique of these theses of the theory of contestable markets see Azoulay (1987).
18. In this chapter I have intentionally concentrated on the potentialities of *technical* flexibility. It goes without saying however that important learning and experience curve effects can be obtained from the different method of mobilising labour through forms of organisation based on *cooperation* rather than on specialisation (see, in this respect, Aoki 1986).
19. It appears to be an *adequate* form and not a 'transient' one as Piore (1987) suggests. I make this point in order to indicate clearly the differences in the positions we have reached.

8 Towards a spatial reorganisation of the German car industry? The implications of new production concepts.[1]

Eike Schamp

Structural change is the normal state of affairs in industrialised countries. However, current changes are interpreted as something quite new in that the structure of the social as well as of the spatial division of labour is changing.

The new economic structure that is identified most often in current research is the one that the concept of flexible specialisation describes. In addition a fundamental reorganisation of spatial production systems is anticipated. Two possibilities that have been identified are that there will be a reregionalisation of production (Junne 1985) or a reconcentration of production (Läpple 1986). An important cause of structural change is, for example, the logistical principle of 'just in time' that is used in certain sectors of industry. Quite early on it was supposed that this principle would require the proximity of suppliers to their customers (see, for example, Estall 1985 and Meyer 1986). However, the assumption that reconcentration will occur is based on the idea that a regional production system did once exist in the German car industry. When one speaks of regions, one means an area of average size with a diameter of little more than 150 kilometres. New vehicle manufacturers like Ford in Cologne (1925), BMW in Munich (1928), and VW in Wolfsburg (1938) developed away from the regions in which their respective suppliers were located (see Figure 8.1). These regions were above all the traditional metal-working regions like, for example, Württemberg, the Bergische Land and Thüringen. One might suppose that the thesis concerning the reconcentration of the motor vehicle production system applies in particular to Daimler-Benz due to its location at Sindelfingen in Württemberg. There are however indications that even there no reconcentration

[1] The research on which this paper is based was financed by the Deusche Forschungsgemeinschaft (German Research Council).

is at present taking place (Richter *et al.* 1988). In what follows I shall therefore question the thesis of a renewed concentration of the motor vehicle production system and of a new polarised production complex (Scott 1988a). Indeed if one allows for the fact that most productive establishments are locationally fixed in the short run, one realises that in these concepts are ideas that relate in the main to the long-run development of the spatial configuration of Western industrial economies. Implicitly the partial steps that are identified at present in the industrial world are taken as indications of an entire new spatial organisation of production that will appear in the future.

The car industry is reputed to be a forerunner in the introduction of flexible automation. In fact it is especially suited to a critical discussion because:

(1) throughout the world in the 1980s car firms altered their ideas about production. With these changes the industry sought to respond in a far-sighted manner to the expected stagnation of sales and changes in consumption patterns;
(2) in the traditional producing countries the industry must hold its ground in the face of new lower-cost producers through the achievement both of market flexibility and cost reductions;
(3) in the past it developed a unique production system (*filière*) made up of many suppliers and subcontractors who were frequently small in size and a few producers who were often large. In West Germany the subsector composed of the suppliers of parts and accessories is especially important: the German car industry has about ten times more suppliers than the Japanese (Weissbach and Weissbach 1987, p. 18).

At present, however, ideas about the character of flexibility and its importance are widely debated. On the one hand there is doubt about the general validity of the principle of flexible automation (see, for example, Gertler 1988). These doubts must of course also have implications for debates about the spatial reorganisation of industry (compare with Holmes 1986). On the other hand one can point to the unique trajectory of each national and regional production system. The differences that exist lead, however, to uncertainties as to whether regional phenomena can provide pointers to general processes.

In what follows I shall adopt a sceptical position and ask whether there are signs of a new spatial organisation of the car industry in West Germany. Several limits on the scope of the answer must however be noted: I shall confine myself first of all to the production of motor cars, because the new ideas about production were introduced above all in this market sector. Second, I shall avoid a consideration of the international role of the German car industry. The German locations of Ford at Cologne and Saarlouis are, for example, closely integrated into a European-level system of production (Dicken 1986). I shall concentrate much more on the territory of West Germany, and there I shall consider in particular the relations between all the producers of vehicles — foreign as well as German — and their suppliers.

The distribution of the German car industry shown in Figure 8.1 has developed slowly. Its major features date back to the 1950s and 1960s and hence to a period that is often designated as the age of Fordist mass

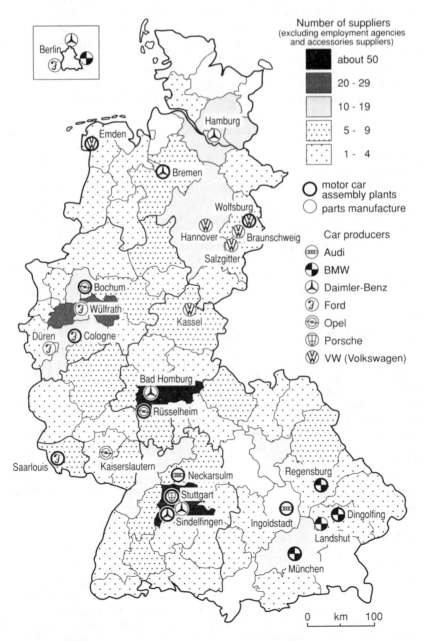

Figure 8.1 The spatial distribution of the car industry in West Germany by
Bundesanstalt für Länderkunde und Raumordnung (BFLR) regions

production. These days new plants such as BMW's Regensburg plant which was opened in 1986, and Daimler-Benz's planned factory at Rastatt, are few and far between. Until the present, moreover, the concentration of suppliers in the traditional industrial districts devoted to metal working in Baden-Württemberg and in the Bergische Land has continued, although in the last decades there have been fluctuations in the number of suppliers.

This fluctuation is particularly marked in the metal-working industries. In these sectors many car-industry suppliers have for a long time taken steps to ensure that they did not fall into a one-sided market dependence on the car firms. Further studies of the interrelationships between the car industry and its suppliers have shown that the structure of material linkages was not related to spatial proximity (see, for example, Grotz 1979) and was very variable in quantity and quality.

Figure 8.1 also shows that the West German vehicle manufacturers are to a large extent regional enterprises. This conclusion applies as much to a firm like VW, which is considered a mass producer, as to BMW, which is reputed today to be the prototypal supplier of upper-middle and high-class cars.

The turnover of the car industry exceeds that of any other sector of West German industry. In 1987, 57 per cent of its output was exported above all to other EC countries. Since the 1970s the car industry has grown considerably. The new ideas about production that are being introduced today are therefore not the response to a crisis: on the contrary, the car industry is making quite large profits. These ideas should be seen much more as strategic instruments to cope with an expected but distant crisis because a reduction in the volume of sales is anticipated, as are increasingly differentiated customer tastes, and greater competitive pressures from low-cost producers. Increases in a firm's market flexibility, which involves a limited standardisation of products along with a simultaneous ability to deliver quickly in accordance with the customer's wishes, and a reduction in production costs are, for traditional technologies and economics, contradictory objectives. In the German car industry, in something of a contrast to the Japanese, the number of models has increased quite substantially in the last decade. Whereas, for example, in 1976 BMW produced five models with eighty-seven variants, in 1987 it produced twenty-seven models and some 200 variants (Bertram and Schamp 1989).

Similar increases in the range of models are also recorded in the case of so-called mass producers like VW. The apparent dilemma between market flexibility and cost reduction is reduced with the help of new solutions which together are called new concepts of production:

(1) Through a modification of the construction of a car, some components from different variants are as far as is possible made similar to one another. In this way it is possible to achieve further economies of scale in the production of parts and to leave the manufacture of the variants until the last production stage of final assembly. Scale economies therefore remain of very great importance in a strategy of product differentiation. The difference from earlier mass production does not consist of a renunciation of scale economies, but of their displacement from the stage of final assembly to the prefabrication stage. This displacement can occur for

example with the use of the principle of modular construction. However this principle also allows the realisation of scale economies in final assembly through automation (as in the cases of the Golf and Omega).

(2) In spite of the increase in the number of small series, the use of very flexible machine systems in manufacturing makes it possible to reduce set-up times, to speed up the flow of materials, and perhaps also to reduce the stocks held in the plant. Included are the use of computer numerical control machines in the manufacture of parts, of robots in body spraying, and of automatic transfer lines and stock management systems. The German car industry is also in part the forerunner in the introduction of computer-controlled factories. In the 1970s when robots were not obtainable on the market, VW, for example, had to construct its own. Without doubt, however, these developments made the manufacture of cars ever more capital–intensive. In West Germany the ratio of the needs for fixed and circulating capital was said to be 4:1 (Weissbach and Weissbach 1987, p. 19) which is likewise higher than in Japan. As a consequence there is on the one hand a fall in the importance of labour costs, at least in certain phases of production, and on the other an increase in the inertia of production sites. I shall return to this argument later.

(3) Vehicle manufacturers can reduce their capital commitments by establishing new relations with their suppliers. In the 1980s this reorganisation was reflected in the sharp reduction in vertical production integration (*Fertigungstiefe*) in all German car makers, perhaps with the exception of Daimler-Benz (see Figure 8.1). Vertical production integration (*Fertigungstiefe*) can nevertheless be measured in various ways. Among them are money measures which record an increase in the relative value of the parts made by suppliers and a fall in the relative value of the parts made by the vehicle manufacturer itself: it occurs for example in the case of electronics. In spite of measurement difficulties it is clear that vehicle makers are anxious to pull out of certain production stages. The manufacturers increasingly concentrate their production capabilities on final assembly which has so far been only slightly automated. Nevertheless reduced vertical production integration (*Fertigungstiefe*) does not also mean a reduction in the activities of the car makers as is the case in what Scott (1988a, p. 176) calls vertical disintegration. In the case of car makers the contracting out of parts production coexists with strategies of vertical integration (*vertikale Integration*) which simply shift from the actual production of a car to the development of interests in the provision of services related to the use and production of cars (user and producer services). All large vehicle manufacturers dispose, for example, of their own motor vehicle credit agency, and in part of companies that lease, hire out and insure cars. In addition BMW and VW have acquired software houses for their own needs. These developments conform with a general trend in industries that supply goods which increasingly have services attached to them. However the new concepts of production make possible a considerable alleviation of the workload of vehicle manufacturers and allow them to take on new commitments in the areas in which services are produced.

These changes in production concepts can nevertheless have serious consequences for the spatial organisation of the car industry. They can affect on the one hand the location of a car manufacturer's own branch plants and on the other the location of suppliers. In both cases the transfer of tasks can create new networks of relations between locations. In the rest of this article I shall concentrate above all on the second set of problems, and I shall only refer to the first when it is directly related to the second. How likely is it, then, that a new spatial concentration of the suppliers to car manufacturers will follow from the introduction of new production concepts into the car industry?

Many authors assume that the greatest pressure for a change in the location of suppliers stems from vehicle manufacturers' introduction of just-in-time principles. Connected with rapid and flexible deliveries in accordance with just-in-time principles is the pre-assembly of components as well as a far-reaching assumption of quality-control functions and responsibilities for quality on the part of suppliers. In this case the car manufacturer can relieve itself from the management of stocks of semi-manufactures and from labour-intensive phases of production and high-cost production control functions. It is frequently supposed that a sound just-in-time relationship requires a supplier to locate near its customer. Included among the components that can at present be delivered in accordance with just-in-time principles are seats, exhaust systems and above all plastic parts such as bumpers and instrument panels. According to a forecast for 1995 the suppliers in these sectors can reckon on above average rates of growth of 7 to 10 per cent per year (*Handelsblatt* no. 193, 1988). The example of plastic parts is a good one for an investigation of the spatial consequences of these developments.

In recent years several new factories making plastic components for the car industry have been established. Figure 8.2 shows the new locations of several supplier firms. Obviously suppliers have located new establishments in the places where the production of a new model of car with new flexible production techniques was undertaken. It was the case with the Mercedes 190 in the Daimler plant at Bremen, the fifth series BMW in the Regensburg plant, and the new VW-Passat in the Emden plant. As a rule the new supplier plants produce for several neighbouring car makers. As a result they are often not located directly alongside a car plant. A further reason is the search for a local labour market in rural communities in which the supplier is the only large (in other words monopsonistic) employer of labour.

The relations between manufacturer and supplier can be described with reference to the example of a new branch plant for plastic parts established in 1987 in Neustadt an der Donau (see Bertram and Schamp 1989). Today this plant produces in the main shock absorbers which are delivered at four-hourly intervals to BMW which is located 80 kilometres away in Munich, and soon it will produce door fittings which are to be sent every four hours to Audi in Ingolstadt. The manufacturers require a zero reject rate. In other words the supplier must hold replacements for defective parts. Today shock absorbers are assembled parts which the supplier must provide with indicators and fittings and must deliver in several varieties of colour. At present the supplier can only cope with the risks of rapid and variable orders for specific shock absorbers by producing unfinished shock absorbers for stock. In this way the

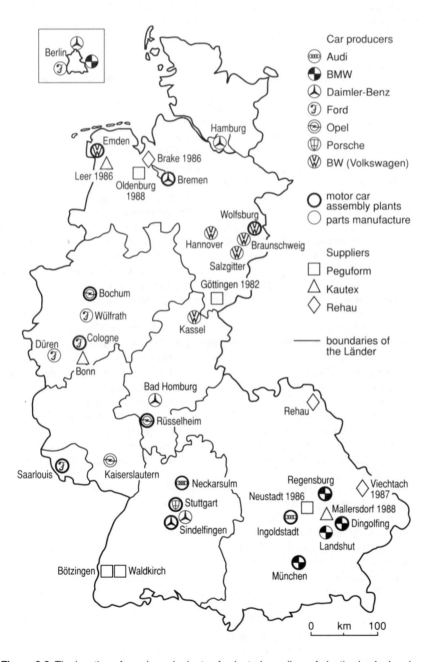

Figure 8.2 The location of new branch plants of selected suppliers of plastic shock absorbers

supplier can still take advantage of scale economies. The labour-intensive stages of production of assembly and spraying of many varieties in a short space of time must then be handled with the help of flexible work organisation.

How representative is this example in relation to what is said in general about the spatial organisation of the manufacture of motor vehicle parts and accessories? I would like to reply to that question with the aid of several different propositions:

(1) Just-in-time principles can in the strict sense only be applied to a few components. There are different definitions of 'just in time': I count for the time being only those deliveries of specified components which must be made during a specific hour on a specific day (that is a specific component that must be delivered between, say, 12 and 1 o'clock on Thursday 10 April) and which are synchronised with assembly operations, because it is above all these deliveries that may force the supplier to relocate. In this type of case, once an order is placed with the supplier, a component is delivered directly to the car maker's assembly line. The car manufacturers mostly consider the so-called type A parts as most appropriate for the use of this just-in-time principle. Type A parts are ones that vehicle makers need all the time but where there is a large number of variants, that have a high value, and are parts of which 100 per cent of deliveries must be reliable.

(2) Just-in-time principles do not in the least oblige a supplier to establish a new branch plant near the car manufacturer. If one confines oneself to the narrow definition of just in time, then the decision about a new location will be above all the result of a calculation that compares the requirements of rapid deliveries with the losses associated with the sacrifice of economies of scale and also with the need to write off existing productive investments. But if one extends the concept of just in time to cover, for example, deliveries that must be made on a particular day (that is deliveries of a specific component that must be made in a particular twenty-four-hour period), then examples show that with the help of a good developed motorway network deliveries can continue to be made over greater distances.

(3) New locations are established above all by supplier firms that are financially strong and that have adopted offensive strategies and are recent entrants into the West German components supply sector that is made up of medium-sized firms. Naturally it is much easier for these financially strong firms to break into the sector with those components that are new or are made from new materials: examples include components made today of plastic instead of metal as is the case with shock absorbers, and the components for the electronic equipment used in cars. The firm Peguform, for example, has in recent years established several new branch plants near to car manufacturers. This firm has of course been active in the plastics industry for a long time, but it first took an interest in the car industry in the 1980s. With the financial support of the BAT Industries Group to which Peguform belongs and the possibilities of cooperating across frontiers with other subsidiaries of the BAT group in France and Spain, a large firm actually made a new move into the market.

It follows therefore from the three points I have just made that the establishment of a new branch plant near suppliers must be analysed in the light of criteria that fall under three headings: the principle of just-in-time production, scale economies and market strategies.

(4) The settlement of new suppliers near to car plants is on the one hand quantitatively very insignificant and on the other probably only a transitory phenomenon. According to various publications there appeared to be a wave of new establishments in the German components supply sector around new car manufacturers' branch plants in the 1980s. However their number amounted in fact to only a fraction of the some 5000 supplier firms in West Germany. The establishment of about twenty suppliers around BMW's Regensburg plant was considered spectacular (see, for example, Lempa 1988), yet this plant has in all 1200 suppliers.

However the new locations, as shown in Figure 8.2, are probably only a result of the transitory problem of the coexistence of inflexible and flexible production structures in manufacturers who assemble motor cars in different places. In this case they are a sign of an upheaval which will disappear as and when flexible production structures are implemented in all car plants. An example of inflexible production structures is offered by VW's fully automated Hall 54 in which the Golf has been assembled since 1983: in this workshop at least 2000 vehicles must be assembled each day. An example of a modern flexible production structure is provided by the manual assembly of the new Passat in VW's Emden plant where each day at most 1000 vehicles can be assembled.

At the start of the 1980s large car manufacturers invested considerable sums in assembly lines in their main plants. These assembly lines worked on mass-production principles. Today the sales of cars assembled on these lines are still high. Examples include the Golf assembled in VW's Hall 54 and the Omega assembled in Opel's Hall 130. Whenever there was a model change in the age of inflexible mass production there was a need for a complete change in the assembly line. In the past therefore new models were always introduced into the main plant when the old model had reached the mature or saturation stage in its product life cycle. The production of old models was transferred to the car maker's branch plants where they could still be assembled in smaller numbers.

Vehicle manufacturers can pursue a strategy of this kind only when inflexible equipment can be used for as long as possible, and therefore when the product life cycles of models are long. However in the 1980s product life cycles were shortened. New models with new production methods were introduced when the sales of old models were still large and the old production facilities had still not been amortised. As a result the expensive but relatively inflexible assembly facilities in the main plants were used for as long as possible. In the case, therefore, of a radical technical change from inflexible to flexible manufacturing in car firms, new models were first made in branch plants where it was easier to depreciate old installations.

If, however, in the near future the old models, which are still assembled today in the main plants, are changed, then the moment at which new flexible production facilities can be introduced into the main plants will also have arrived. The flexibility of plants means more than the mere possibility of producing variable small batches at favourable costs. Even with a fundamental change of model, flexible plants can be preserved to a far greater extent than was the case in the recent past with inflexible plants. It is probable that in the future new models will again be first introduced in the main plant and will later be transferred to branch plants.

And whereas at present new locations of supplier industries are only the result of the introduction of new models into the flexible branch plants of certain car makers, in the future with the reintroduction of new models into the car manufacturers' main plants the old locations of the suppliers will be justified again.

(5) Vehicle makers also reduce their stocks obtained from the many suppliers who cannot be integrated into just-in-time networks in the narrow sense. As a result the makers demand deliveries of relatively small quantities at short notice on the orders of the assembly shops. However these new requirements of the car manufacturers have almost no consequences for the relocation of suppliers, but give rise to new forms of logistic and transport organisation between suppliers and car makers.

In the case of products that are not fit for just-in-time methods the car manufacturers at present create central warehouses which they have managed by independent carriers. (Examples include BMW at Eching near Munich, and VW at Peine.) From these central warehouses quantities of semi-manufactures that correspond with the needs of production are delivered to the assembly line. As a result there is a substantial increase in a car maker's transport needs. In the case of BMW, for example, the index of goods transported increased almost fourfold between 1978 and 1987. Where suppliers must make prompt deliveries of small quantities of their product on an irregular basis, and where they cannot be incorporated into just-in-time systems, the suppliers commission carriers with warehouses. Around the car producers' traditional production sites, one therefore at present finds a circle of storage facilities for suppliers. However a careful study of this aspect of the logistical system remains to be done.

If one therefore speaks of new locations associated with the car makers' adoption of new concepts of production, it is probable that one is referring in the main to the warehouses of independent carriers. The transfer of storage tasks and of logistical transport functions to carriers requires of the latter substantial capital expenditure. New efforts to develop standardised transport containers for small parts in order to reduce costly transshipment time likewise give rise to large expenditures on the part of carriers. As a result one can expect a selective process to operate among the carriers in favour of a few large undertakings which will be linked to the car makers via logistic concepts and long-lasting contracts.

If one only considers the new locations of suppliers in the German car industry, one will easily arrive at a false conclusion about the possibilities of a reconcentration of the industry. The arguments developed so far show that a few examples are unjustifiably taken as indicators for a whole industry and likewise as symptoms of a long-term trend towards a new locational order for productive activities. The thesis of a new spatial polarisation of production systems does not seem to hold true at least in the case of the German car industry.

A counter-thesis is near and can be developed in a few words : in the German car industry an increasing interregional and international division of labour is developing at the same time as a reduction in the density (*Ausdünnung*) of the map of local interdependencies between car makers and the system of suppliers. The reason why lies in the car makers' new strategies of single sourcing, on the one hand, which replaces several suppliers with one or two, and global sourcing, on the other, which substitutes global for regional linkages.

The car producers' new market strategies require a higher quality of delivered components from many suppliers. Under pressure from shorter product life cycles, the car makers also transfer important research and development functions to specific suppliers. Both these developments require a high level of trust of the car producers in their suppliers. If a supplier were to contribute just a few designs to a planned new model of car, simultaneous deliveries to several competing car firms could in the future be precluded. For components with a high research and development content, the car producers strive today for single sourcing: in other words for deliveries from only one and at most two suppliers. As a consequence there is at present strong competition involving innovation and prices between certain suppliers. Only firms that have large capital endowments and are research-intensive will emerge as winners from this competitive struggle. A process of selection therefore also takes place. The example of Ford shows just how strong this process is: in spite of the reduced vertical integration, since 1980 Ford has had to reduce its number of suppliers by 40 per cent (*Wirtschaftwoche,* no. 33, 12 August 1988, p. 80).

In the case of those parts which contain little firm-specific know-how, several different supplier firms can be used. Among these firms that tend traditionally to be small and medium in size there is an increase in price competition which can, for example, only be settled through a reduction in wage costs. The managers of the car companies at present get many suppliers to transfer production to certain low labour-cost countries whose labour forces have relatively high skills in spite of low wages. Today Britain and Spain belong to this group of countries. In addition the manufacturers take advantage of the new competition from suppliers in South East Asia. This strategy is called global sourcing.

The outcome of strategies of single and global sourcing is a reduction in the density (*Ausdünnung*) of German suppliers. Moreover the importance of the traditional metal-working regions may decline, on the one hand because in the future more plastic parts will be included in cars, and on the other because many metal parts are exposed to price competition as a result of global sourcing. The result therefore is not a stable new spatial concentration of production but further spatial instabilities in the network of interdependencies.

These instabilities will perhaps be extended to the whole of Europe with the creation of the Single European Market.

9 The determinants of the location of the semiconductor industry

Isabelle Geneau de Lamarlière

Very early in its development the electronic components industry was of great interest to those endeavouring to understand the determinants of the creation of new industrial spaces. In analyses of its location on a world scale, the preferred approach was almost exclusively the one based on the theory of the New International Division of Labour (NIDL). The identification in an industry of the future such as semiconductor fabrication of a locational structure that corresponded with the NIDL model should have provided substantial support for the construction of a post-Weberian location theory in which the labour factor played a leading role.

In the first section I shall examine the advantages and limitations of the application of the NIDL theory to the semiconductor industry. Afterwards I shall adopt a synthetic analysis of the determinants of industrial location that involves the identification of a network of constraints. Finally I shall attempt to use this approach to explain the location of Japanese semiconductor production.

9.1 The location of American firms and its theoretical interpretation

Several types of electronic components are classed under the heading 'semiconductors'. However manufacturing processes involve the same stages:

(1) the design and elaboration of the masks, where the circuits are conceived;
(2) the manufacture of 'wafers', slices of silicon on which several thousand chips are simultaneously engraved;
(3) the assembly of the semiconductors, cut from the wafers and
(4) the final testing of semiconductor devices, where the working of each circuit is checked before delivery to clients.

These four stages are characterised by the fact that they can be geographically separated, and it was American firms which were the first to disperse certain stages of production and develop strategies for production on a world scale.

9.1.1 The location of American merchant chip producers prior to the mid-1970s

After the Second World War, the majority of the discoveries concerning semiconductors were made in the United States. From the 1950s to the 1970s American firms accounted for about 80 per cent of world production. The industry had hardly started to develop when manufacturing was split up into different stages. This splitting up was accompanied by a relocation of activities within the United States, and their diffusion at a world level.

During the 1950s the production of the first semiconductors was concentrated in the north east of the United States, where the first electronics firms were to be found. At the end of the decade, some producers decided to set up in California, and to start making integrated circuits. The semiconductor industry then began to expand more quickly in this region than in the north east where the old firms were located (Scott 1987).

At about the same time, the principal American manufacturers started to invest in 100-per-cent owned subsidiary semiconductor operations in Europe. The areas the Americans penetrated were the most technologically advanced. During the 1960s the largest part of Europe's production of integrated circuits was accounted for by American subsidiaries (BIPE 1969).

Japan did not receive direct American investment in the production field because of the ban imposed on this type of investment until 1975. Only Texas Instruments managed to set up in Japan, through a 1968 partnership with a Japanese firm.

The relocation of the assembly stage in developing countries started in 1962, with Fairchild's investment in Hong Kong. American assembly units in Third World countries numbered five in 1965, fifty in 1970, and ninety in 1974. Devices assembled in these countries were shipped back to the United States to undergo final testing. The majority of these investments were made in South-East Asia (Scott 1987).

9.1.2 Attempts at a theoretical explanation

Few industries illustrated the relocation of production according to the labour factor as clearly as the semiconductor industry. Routine assembly processes, which made intensive use of relatively unskilled labour, were sent to peripheral areas in South-East Asia, while management and design units were kept in the United States. An analysis based on the notion of a new international division of labour seemed therefore to be the most appropriate.

9.1.2.1 The general framework

Within the framework of the NIDL model, strategies are essentially production-oriented: the manufacturing process is split into several distinct operations, which are carried out in different countries, to gain maximum profit from spatial inequalities in production costs, notably in labour costs (Michalet 1976). In this chapter I shall concern myself with an open conception of the NIDL, found in the work of Scott and Angel (1987a and b). The NIDL is, for them, less a static centre/periphery system than a 'complex patchwork' that undergoes constant change. Secondary regional articulations can exist within a world-wide NIDL, and some peripheral regions can develop and become centres themselves (Scott 1987).

9.1.2.2 Its application to the semiconductor industry

Even if the location of the other production stages was sometimes mentioned, the attempts of the NIDL model at explanation were essentially concentrated on the assembly stage. The shift of these activities towards Third World countries was explained by low hourly wages, or limited unionisation, particularly in South-East Asian countries, which, even in the 1980s, still accounted for nearly 90 per cent of the assembly work carried out abroad by American firms.

Within the South-East Asian sphere itself, a shift in location was apparent (Scott 1987). The first American assembly units were sent to Hong Kong, Korea, Singapore and Taiwan. During the 1970s and 1980s wages increased in these four countries. Then a movement into more sophisticated production processes occurred: the semiconductor factories in Hong Kong, Singapore or Korea became increasingly involved in manufacturing, and complex assembly and test operations were developed, as were subcontracting activities. Simple assembly processes were relocated in Malaysia, the Philippines, Indonesia and Thailand, where labour was cheaper. The parts assembled in these countries are then sent to Hong Kong or Singapore for final testing. A system of regional specialisation therefore appeared within Asia itself, and this specialisation is in fact what Scott called a secondary articulation of the world-wide NIDL.

9.1.2.3 Conclusions drawn from this work

Three types of generalisation were made on the basis of the study of American semiconductor assembly activities:

(1) The arguments were extended to industry as a whole: the development of an explanation of the location of American firms in this sector was expected to allow the construction of a 'post-Weberian' theory of industrial location (Scott 1987).
(2) The arguments were extended over time: the classical NIDL model could not explain the appearance of a centre within Asia after 1975. The amendments made, which highlighted the possible existence of secondary articulations in the world NIDL, allowed the validation of the general model and its application to locational decisions made after 1975.
(3) The arguments were extended to other regions: the identification of

subregional articulations allowed the application of the NIDL model to European and Asian companies. Scott and Angel, who expressed an intention of carrying out a study of the location of Japanese and European producers, wrote that they had no doubt that, whatever form they took, these investments would be structured by the same organisational dynamics as those analysed in the case of American assembly plants (Scott 1987, p. 24).

9.1.3 Criticisms of the application of the NIDL model to the case of semiconductors

The focus on the assembly process alone and the neglect of the location of other stages of production on the one hand and the confinement of attention to American firms — and among them to merchant chip producers — on the other was not really justified, especially if one concluded, on the basis of this limited field of study, that the locational structure of the semiconductor industry as a whole conformed with the NIDL scheme (compare with Sayer 1986).

In studies carried out on the basis of the NIDL model, very little attention was paid, for example, to American investments in Europe. These investments were seen as an anomaly, a distortion of the general model of the NIDL, caused by customs duties protecting the EC. But does not the decision to hold these customs barriers responsible for the discrepancy between theory and reality amount to an implicit recognition of constraints other than those linked to the labour factor, and would not a more logical analysis involve a deeper investigation into the nature and the meaning of these constraints?

The slowdown of the rate of investment in developing countries raises further difficulties. Until 1975 there was a clear correlation between the growth of the world market and the establishment of assembly units in Asia, but from around the mid-1970s the strength of this correlation declined (see Figure 9.1). Direct American investments in assembly operations in Asia gave way to some extent to local subcontracting which began to expand towards the middle of the 1970s. But as the location of other stages of manufacture and of Japanese and European producers of semiconductors had been ignored too often, the new importance of investments in industrialised countries was not fully appreciated.

The development of investments in industrialised countries was however of considerable importance. Table 9.1 was produced from a list of new investment projects in the manufacture and assembly of semiconductors for the period 1979-83 drawn up by the OECD. Europe topped the list of receiving countries and was followed by the United States and Japan. Developing countries came last.

The graph of investments in Europe (Figure 9.2) shows that a first wave of American investments started in 1952, peaked in 1960, and then dwindled slowly up to the beginning of the 1970s. General Instruments even closed its factory in Naples in 1973, because of strikes, and transferred it to Taiwan. But from the mid-1970s onwards a second wave of investments by US and

Figure 9.1 The growth of world sales of integrated circuits and
investments in assembly units in South-East Asia

Source: ERNST 1983.

Japanese firms in Europe and Japanese and European firms in the US
developed steadily.

American installations have developed over many years. At present some
group together certain design functions along with wafer fabrication, assembly
and test operations. In others, however, just the latter are represented.
European units in the United States include almost all the design and
manufacturing stages to which are sometimes added assembly and test
operations. The Japanese started by setting up just the assembly and test
stages, whether in the United States or Europe. It is only since 1986–87 that
they have added the wafer fabrication stage to their old units.

It was difficult to account for this shift towards industrialised countries with
the production-oriented NIDL theory, even if the development of automation
was considered, as it was less advantageous in terms of production costs than
the use of cheap labour in developing countries. A wider conceptual framework seems therefore necessary.

9.2 A synthetic analysis of location factors in the semiconductor industry.

For a long time two types of attitude towards the question of industrial
location factors have existed:

(1) a refusal to adopt a theoretical framework: lists of location factors were
drawn up, and

Table 9.1 New investments in semiconductor production and assembly facilities in 1979-83.*

Receiving country	United States	Canada	Japan	Europe	Developing countries (Mexico, Sri-Lanka, Taiwan, and Singapore)
Investing country					
United States	n/a	0	8	10	5
Canada	1	n/a	0	2	0
Japan	4	0	n/a	5	0
Europe	3	0	1	n/a	1
Developing countries (South Korea and the Philippines)	4	1	0	0	n/a
Total	12	1	9	17	6

* New investments and expansions. Acquisitions are excluded, as are domestic investments.

Source: adapted from data in OECD (1985, pages 136-8).

(2) the assertion that the transport factors highlighted by Weber had been replaced by constraints connected with the supply of labour and the related development of a 'post-Weberian' model of industrial location.

The limits of this latter approach, as applied to the semiconductor industry, have just been outlined. I shall now now consider the origins of these limits and the possibilities of overcoming them.

9.2.1 Objectives, needs and constraints in the location of firms

9.2.1.1 Objectives, needs and constraints in the Weberian and NIDL frameworks

One can find elements common to both the Weberian and the NIDL model which gave them a certain explanatory strength. We shall retain these elements, get rid of those limiting the explanatory power of these two theories, and enrich them with contributions from the new industrial economics and international economics.

(1) In both the Weberian framework and that of the NIDL, the objectives of

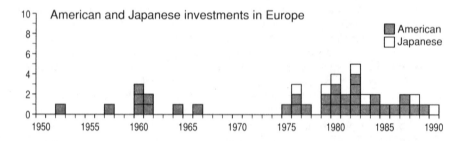

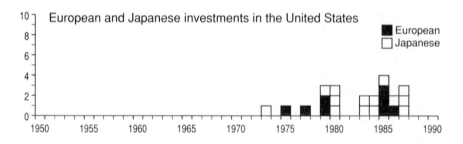

Figure 9.2 'Crossed' investments between industrialised countries in manufacturing, assembly and testing facilities

firms were examined. But they were limited to the maximisation of profit in the first case, and of surplus-value in the second.

(2) In both cases, the needs firms had to satisfy in order to accomplish their objectives were also carefully considered: Weber concerned himself with the need for markets, raw materials and labour. The NIDL model essentially considered the labour factor which is the source of surplus-value.

(3) In each case the constraints encountered in satisfying these needs were analysed. Weber handled the transport side, and the NIDL model the constraints that stem from spatial differences in the supply of labour.

9.2.1.2 Objectives, needs and constraints in the newly adopted framework.

(1) The objectives of firms in the new industrial economics go beyond the maximisation of profit alone. Firms attempt to optimise an objective function which can include as arguments profit expectations, the rate of growth, market shares, risks, and so on (Jacquemin 1985).

(2) Whatever their objectives, the company must satisfy certain needs to accomplish them. I shall concern myself with labour, capital, technology and markets.

(3) In seeking to satisfy these needs, the firm is subject to certain constraints. (i) The first constraint appears when the firm does not find in its country of origin the necessary production factors or markets. The consequences of these constraints on location have been investigated more fully in international economics in the work of Mucchielli on the 'discordance' between the specific advantages of companies and the comparative advantage of their country of origin (Mucchielli 1985).
(ii) But on its own this problem does not necessarily bring about relocation at an international level. In practice a firm can import the factors, or the technology, which it is unable to find in its home country, and export its products to satisfy its need for markets. A second constraint is therefore added in order to explain relocation: that of access to the factors or the markets that the firm does not find in its country of origin.

It is the combination of these two constraints of local non-availability of factors and difficulties of access to them which have an influence on industrial location on an international scale.

9.2.2 The operation of these constraints in the semiconductor industry.

9.2.2.1 The network of constraints.

In Figure 9.3 five constraining factors and their effects on the location of firms producing semiconductors are examined.

(1) An underdeveloped and expensive communication system slows down the movement of goods, makes control functions and contacts more difficult, and prevents the dispersal of activities.
(2) In order to relocate, one has to find in the new location people with a certain work discipline and basic skills.
(3) When one has product systems, composed of elements whose production can be carried out independently, the location of the manufacturing units that make these elements can also be independent of one another. However the need for precise and frequent monitoring due to the complexity of the finished product, and the need for strong interactions between different production stages or with clients impose strict constraints on location.
(4) The control of high-tech industries may seem to the state to be a prerequisite for the development of a country's economy, and a guarantee of relative national autonomy. This strategic factor gives rise to national policies which influence location, either because of the direct constraints imposed on national firms, or because of the strategies that foreign companies adopt to get around protectionist measures.
(5) The semiconductors produced by the large Japanese or European companies are nearly always produced by a division of an electronics firm. This division, which is often loss-making, is not necessarily required to be profitable in the short term. The semiconductor activities of these firms can be more freely located in places where they will have to meet other objectives.

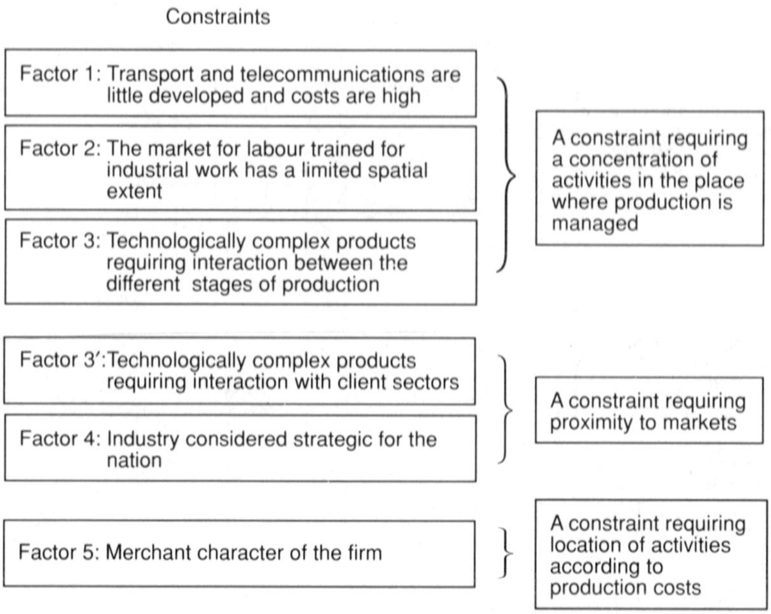

Constraints

Factor 1: Transport and telecommunications are little developed and costs are high	
Factor 2: The market for labour trained for industrial work has a limited spatial extent	A constraint requiring a concentration of activities in the place where production is managed
Factor 3: Technologically complex products requiring interaction between the different stages of production	

Factor 3′:Technologically complex products requiring interaction with client sectors	A constraint requiring proximity to markets
Factor 4: Industry considered strategic for the nation	

Factor 5: Merchant character of the firm	A constraint requiring location of activities according to production costs

Figure 9.3 The effects of constraints on location

But manufacturers are called merchant chip, or independent, producers when semiconductor operations represent the largest proportion of their turnover and when less than 10 per cent of their production is for their own use. Almost two-thirds of American semiconductor producers fall into this category. To survive the latter have to be profit-making in the short term, and for this reason have no choice other than to locate their activities where production costs are minimised. It is often this last and single constraint — profitability — which is considered in the NIDL theory. However, with reference to the American example, I shall show that one has to consider all the constraints in order to understand changes in location.

9.2.2.2 *The network of constraints and the location of American firms.*

(1) If one chooses three levels of constraint exercised by these different factors, the situation of the American industry after the Second World War is approximately as set out in Figure 9.4.

Firms which, at the time, were concentrated in the north east of the United States would have done better to set themselves up in other regions, where labour was cheaper, in order to satisfy the profitability criterion (Factor 5). But the strongest constraints were the ones connected with the weakness of the means of communication (Factor 1), the employment of north-eastern labour, with a long tradition of industrial work (Factor 2), control over the

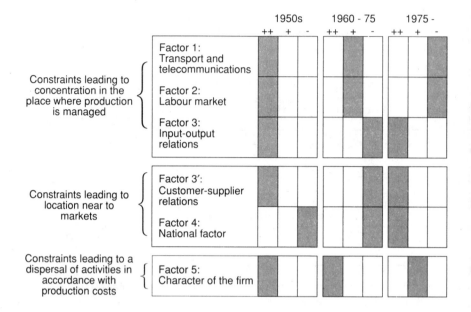

Figure 9.4 The network of constraints on American semiconductor firms

different production stages among which there were numerous interactions (Factor 3), and the need for frequent contacts with the armed forces which were the principal clients (Factor 3′). These constraints necessitated the concentration of these firms in the north-east, where the electronics firms which first invented semiconductors were to be found.

(2) The configuration of the network of constraints changed in the 1960s.

(i) With respect to communications, the constraints were made much slacker (Factor 1), as the quality of long-distance telephone links had improved and their cost had appreciably lessened. Computing was expanding and enabled the centralisation and analysis at management headquarters of all the data coming from the firm's manufacturing units. Numerous direct controls were unnecessary, and it became possible to relocate production activities over a wide area (Claval 1988).

(ii) The market for labour trained for industrial work had also widened (Factor 2). In some Third World countries, literacy and work discipline were developing. It became possible to find cheap labour capable of carrying out the tasks involved in assembling components.

(iii) At the beginning of the 1960s integrated circuits were only just appearing. The manufacture of discrete standardised semiconductors had been perfectly mastered. The technology involved was uncomplicated relative to that involved in the products which followed, and numerous interactions between the different stages of production were not necessary (Factor 3).

(iv) As the market was being supplied with standardised circuits, it was unnecessary to increase customer contact (Factor 3′).

(v) At the time the Americans largely dominated the world market which they were supplying. American state intervention, to protect the home market or market shares abroad, was almost non-existent. Japan refused to allow direct foreign investment, but, like Europe, remained open to American exports (Factor 4).

(vi) The only powerful binding constraint on American firms, which were almost all merchant chip producers, was the profitability of production (Factor 5). The situation that existed was in other words the typical one that favoured the development of an international division of labour.

Thus investments were spread far and wide. Research and design activities were concentrated in Silicon Valley, where they benefited from externalities. Manufacturing activities requiring skilled manual labour were kept in the United States. Unskilled assembly work was firstly relocated in areas mainly in the Third World and in particular in South-East Asia where wages were lower than in the United States. The assembled devices were then shipped back to the United States for testing, which required sophisticated equipment and skilled labour.

(3) After the production crisis of 1974–5 the network of constraints took on a new shape (Figure 9.4).

(i) The means of communication had further improved (Factor 1). As I shall show in the Japanese example, the appearance of satellite communications had a strong influence on the dispersion of design activities.

(ii) The market for labour with industrial skills had widened to include new zones and had improved in older ones (Factor 2). Engineers, technicians and skilled workers could be found in some South-East Asian countries. It therefore became possible to move the manufacturing and testing stages to Singapore, Hong Kong or Korea, and to extend the assembly area as far as Malaysia, the Philippines and Thailand.

(iii) The semiconductor itself underwent considerable changes. During the first half of the 1970s, a large proportion of the industry had moved from the old simple components to VLSI (very large-scale integration) circuits like memories or microprocessors, which carry out operations previously left to systems such as computers (Truel 1980a and b). As the complexity of the circuits increased, so did the need for interaction between different production stages (Factor 3). At this point it sometimes became preferable to automate the assembly process in order to keep it near the design and manufacturing units.

(iv) The increased complexity of semiconductors brought the industry closer to the manufacturers of systems. What is more, the demands of users for a wider and wider range of circuits resulted in the development of the Application Specific Integrated Circuits (ASIC), which are a cross between standardised and fully custom-built circuits. Gate-array circuits made up of a standardised set of simple components which are interconnected according to the specific needs of the client are a good example. At least for the design of these circuits, technical cooperation with the client is indispensable (Factor 3').

(v) There was a growing interdependence between the semiconductor industry and the industries making systems that use semiconductors, such as computers, telecommunications equipment, and so on.

The induction effects were such that control of the semiconductor industry became a matter of strategic importance for governments. The argument that the technology was vital justified extensive industrial or protectionist policies introduced by the authorities in most industrialised countries to encourage the development of indigenous production capabilities (Factor 4).

In spite of the very international character of the semiconductor industry, state interventionism was to a certain extent effective, and the national factor partly explains the current multiplication of crossed investments (an investment by a firm of country A in country B and vice versa) between industrialised countries: companies try to locate production in market areas in order to thwart the strategies states adopt to benefit/ advantage their national industries.

(vi) The development of an increasingly close synergy between the design of semiconductors and of systems, the increase in the costs of research and development, and the establishment of plant and equipment for increasingly complex production processes had led to structural changes. In the United States there was a tendency towards vertical integration, especially towards the downstream sectors that use semiconductor devices (Truel 1980a).

The American semiconductor industry is still characterised by the importance of merchant chip firms. But vertically integrated semiconductor divisions are more and more numerous. The short-term profitability constraint is still in force, but slacker (Factor 5). At the same time the requirement to disperse activities in order to take advantage of differences in comparative production costs have slackened.

In all, over the last few years, it is the constraints on proximity to markets that have been the most important, even if the short-term profitability constraint has always been in force for American companies, which continue to use their assembly units in developing countries. But developed countries are now the main destination of investments.

The American example clearly shows the reasons for the limited historical validity of the application of the NIDL theory to the location of the semiconductor industry, and the importance of changes in the role of different constraints.

9.3 An application to the location of the Japanese semiconductor industry.

(1) Figure 9.5 represents the location of Japanese semiconductor manufacturers. The locations of Japanese firms are very different from American ones:

production — including the assembly process — is mainly concentrated in Japan. A few investments were made in Third World countries between 1965 and 1975 but, from 1975, overseas investments were directed towards the United States and Europe.

(2) To explain these locational decisions I shall look again at the analysis set out at the beginning of section 9.2, in which the objectives, needs and constraints weighing on companies were distinguished. To do so, I shall situate myself within the universe of the new industrial economics in which structures are no longer intangible givens to which one has of necessity to adapt, but where governments and companies can have some effect on their environment (Porter 1980 and Jacquemin 1985).

9.3.1 The objectives of Japanese firms and the Japanese state.

(1) The Japanese government quickly grasped the strategic role of semiconductors. In the first instance, its aim was to get the electronics industry to move from the manufacture of electronic consumer goods to components. The semiconductors in question were still relatively uncomplicated. But by the second stage of the 1974 VLSI plan, the government set Japanese industry the goal of matching United States technological levels in order to be able to make the complex integrated circuits used in computing and telecommunications.

(2) In the United States the aims of companies are guided by financial indicators, profit rates, investment returns, and so on. The main objective of Japanese firms is to gain market shares and to displace their competitors. In the period prior to the establishment of a significant and solid market position, profitability is not of prime importance.

9.3.2 Needs and constraints.

(1) In terms of the specific needs of firms, and the comparative advantage of Japan, the situation in the mid-1970s was roughly the one set out in Figure 9.6. There were three important 'discordances': cheap labour, very advanced technological know-how and markets.

(2) The configuration of the general network of constraints in effect at the time for Japanese firms is shown in Figure 9.7.

9.3.2.1 The cheap labour 'discordance'

(1) The advantages of relatively low labour costs, which had previously favoured domestic locations, had progressively diminished. But the Japanese did not react to labour costs in the same way as the Americans, who had relocated labour-intensive processes in developing countries. The Japanese started to automate assembly operations, and then the other stages of production.

(2) To understand the reasons for this decison which turned out to be more

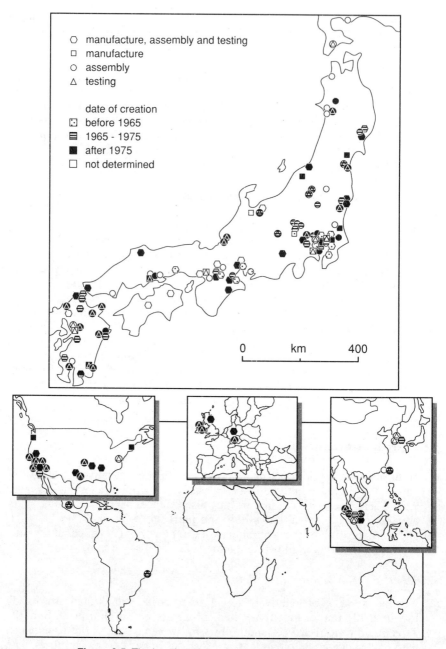

Figure 9.5 The location of Japanese semiconductor operations

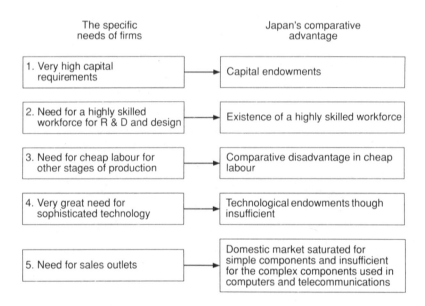

Figure 9.6 The specific needs of firms and the comparative advantage of Japan in the mid-1970s

costly than the relocation of labour-intensive operations, one has to refer back to the objectives of the companies and of the state on the one hand, and to the network of constraints on the other.

The problem at that time was to win market shares in VLSI semiconductors. The quality and reliability of circuits seemed to the Japanese to be the most important determinants of international competitiveness. Priority was therefore given to reducing the percentage of faulty devices, and not to labour costs. However the percentage of faulty products depends on the control of manufacturing processes and on the speed of 'feedbacks' from testing to the other stages of production. Automation and the retention of the different production stages in Japan made these checks easier.

The permissive factor was the structure of Japanese firms. Towards the middle of the 1970s, the average net sales, of all products, of the principal American semiconductor producers reached 950 million dollars, of which 71 per cent came from semiconductor sales (CNU 1983). In Japan these figures were respectively 6 billion dollars and 7 per cent. The size and the degree of integration of the great Japanese electronics producers allowed them to disregard the short-term profitability of their semiconductor division, and to opt for costly automation.

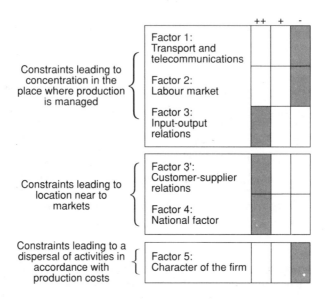

Figure 9.7 The network of constraints on Japanese semiconductor firms in the years following the 1974 VLSI plan

9.3.2.2 Technological 'discordance'.

This 'discordance' was important at the time of the VLSI plan, but access to technology was not as hard as it later became. One-third of the budget allocated to research and development under the VLSI project was dedicated to imports of the latest American equipment. The VLSI plan enabled this 'discordance' to be closed for many products, such as for memories, in which the Japanese became world leaders.

Today the constraint posed by access to technology has tightened because of the increasingly strategic character of the semiconductor industry. Often it is necessary to relocate, or to set up joint ventures, in order to gain access to the know-how of a more advanced country.

9.3.2.3 Market 'discordance'.

(1) Japan already met 70 per cent of its requirements for integrated circuits and almost all its requirements for discrete semiconductors before the launching of the VLSI plan. After it, the gap between production and domestic consumption never ceased to widen.
(2) At the end of the 1970s, a second constraint was added to the 'discordance' associated with the limited size of the domestic market: the increase in the difficulty of access to foreign markets through exports alone. The reason firstly was the strengthening of national protectionist measures — notably with regard to the export of Japanese memories — made worse by the

appreciation of the Yen. A second factor was the growing complexity and the systemisation of components, which required manufacturers to maintain increasingly close links with local clients.

Of the three 'discordances' the one associated with Japan's comparative disadvantage with respect to cheap labour was resolved by resorting to automation. To the other two of the availability of technology and markets must be added constraints on access to these resources: access to technology through the sole method of the import of patents, licences or machines was difficult, as was access to foreign markets just through the export of products. It was the coming together of these two constraints which explains Japanese relocation over the last few years, and their locational choices.

9.3.3 Current trends in the location of Japanese firms.

(1) As I have just shown, Japanese companies evolve in a universe that is more restricted by access to markets than to factors of production. The trend towards investments in developing countries was not, for this reason, comparable with the American case: in 1977 only 5 per cent in value of the discrete semiconductors produced by Japanese firms were assembled abroad, and only 3 per cent of integrated circuits (OECD 1985).

(2) To gain access to markets — as it is possible to separate the design process from the manufacturing stage — the design process alone, which is more service-intensive, can be located near the clients. Japanese firms use this method for ASIC circuits, where relations with the customer are very important. In several years the use of satellite communications completely overturned locational structures (Figure 9.8). The former enabled the Japanese to retain their trump card of high-quality automated production — located in their large units in Japan — while developing a real marketing strategy at their design centres located in the areas where their markets were found.

(3) But when it became harder to separate technically the different stages, or when protectionist measures against Japanese imports were strengthened, almost all of the production cycle had to be relocated in the market area. For these reasons, the Japanese started to invest in assembly and testing plants in the United States and in Europe from the mid-1970s. Around 1986–87, these initial plants were often completed by the addition of manufacturing units mainly to get around ever stricter protectionist measures.

Ever since 1987 when the EC announced its intention of carrying out investigations into Japanese dumping of memories, and 1989 when it took new measures concerning the entry into the Community of components which were already diffused on to wafers, and which were only assembled and tested in Europe, the Japanese Ministry of International Trade and Industry has been pushing Japanese companies to invest in Europe.

In 1987, NEC and Toshiba built manufacturing plants alongside earlier assembly and test facilities in Livingston and Brunswick. In 1988 OKI signed

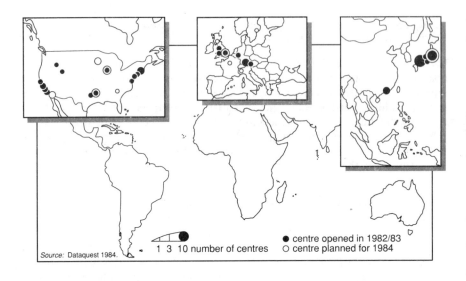

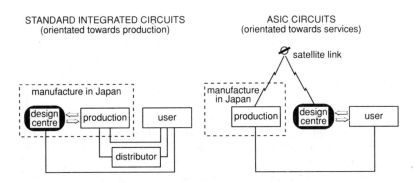

Figure 9.8 Japanese design centres for 'Gate-array' circuits in 1984

an agreement with SGS-Thomson to produce memories in the Franco-Italian company's factory in Nancy. In 1989 Fujitsu in turn added to its assembly and test activities in Europe a fabrication unit in Scotland.

One can note, in conclusion, that this focus on the objective of a growth of market shares has proved particularly successful for Japanese producers. In this way they have managed to penetrate the American market for memories, and have increased regularly and significantly their share of the world market, reducing the shares of the United States and Europe: Japan held a 27 per cent share of the world market for semiconductors in 1970, and 41 per cent in 1985 (Dataquest 1988). In 1986 NEC, Toshiba and Hitachi held the first three places among the world suppliers of semiconductors and six of the leading ten firms were Japanese.

Conclusions

(1) The location of the semiconductor industry has gone through several phases.

> (i) The first phase was dominated by the Americans. The overseas investments they carried out were mostly in developing countries and involved the assembly process. These locational choices were a response to production-related objectives: in part the NIDL theory could be applied to them.
> (ii) The second phase witnessed increased competition from Japan. It was characterised by a redirection of investments towards three large markets: the United States, Europe and Japan. This movement was a result more of commercial than production factors. It was harder to apply the model of the NIDL.

(2) Since the transport revolution which led to a reduction in the explanatory value of Weberian theory, frequent reference has been made in the literature on industrial location to 'footloose firms'. This ambiguous expression conceals the fact that firms develop in a world in which, even if communications have improved, the problems of access to production factors, technology and markets still have to be solved. The constraints have not disappeared at all. They have simply been changed or moved.

An analysis of the objectives of states and companies, of the needs of firms, and of the constraints on access to the factors or markets which are 'discordant' or lacking in the country of origin should enable one to explain, in a sufficiently general way, certain developments in the location of economic activities on an international scale.

Part Five: New technologies, new models of economic organisation, and the development of metropolitan systems

10 New models of production organisation and trends in spatial development

Pierre Veltz

The new industrial geography that is taking shape before our eyes, as yet in a vague way, is more a result of changes in the forms of production and exchange than of geographical movements caused by differences in the availability of resources and their prices. On this point observers agree: no longer is it just a matter of a spatial redistribution of activities within schemas of production and exchange that are stable at a global level (as in the case of the classical processes of the interregional and international divisions of labour which developed in the 1950s and 1960s and which, it should be added, are far from completely exhausted); no longer do production and exchange simply occur 'elsewhere'; instead production and exchange occur in space 'in a different way'.

From that starting point, however, the paths of analysis multiply. Some directly turn their attention away from the processes of division of labour and of cooperation within large organisations (firms or networks of firms) in order to focus on small and medium-size firms and local innovative environments, the new 'Schumpeterian' poles of innovation, in which new industrial and hence spatial developments are supposed to occur. To do so is, in my view, to forget that large multi-regional organisations are also the site of intense transformations, and that the mechanisms of 'polarisation' and the mechanisms that underlie the development of large national and international networks remain very closely related with one another.

In opposition to those who focus their attention on local micro-environments of this kind, others seek to reconstruct an integrated macroscopic perspective, combining in a single framework perspectives on the 'industrial model', macroeconomic structures, and the social and state structures of 'regulation' (wage relations, social relations, and so on). If the domain of the first approach is too limited, the objective of the second is perhaps too ambitious. After the Second World War the development of Western countries and in particular France was centred on models of growth that were extremely easy to identify. Micro-level changes in the organisation of work and production were particularly coherent and synchronised, resulting in very clear macro-level movements that were simultaneously economic, social and *spatial* (In France the bipolar model of industrial decentralisation was an almost immediate expression of the transformation of modes of work, the organisation of firms, and the overall 'Fordist regulation'.) However the *very nature* of current macroeconomic and macro-social changes — in particular, the erosion of the mechanisms of market stabilisation that allowed the spectacular development of Fordist mass production — evidently makes this relation between the micro and macro levels much more complex. Of course we are still not sufficiently distant from recent developments to identify the general direction in which the organisational experiments, which are being conducted in industry and services, mainly in order to adapt to the contraction and turbulence of markets, are leading. Nevertheless it is already clear that new organisational developments are creating a landscape that is much more *varied* than the landscapes created in the 1950s and 1960s, and that, as a result, the analytical short-cut between micro and macro levels, that the 'school of regulation' developed, is seriously threatened. It is, it seems to me, the major difficulty that current attempts to provide a global definition of 'post-Fordism and its space' come up against (Leborgne and Lipietz 1988).

In order to make progress one step therefore seems crucial: it is a deeper study of the micro-economic forms or, more exactly, of the new 'models of organisation' which are being experimented with in actual factories, workshops, offices, and in the networks in which products are invented, designed, made and sold. Of course, for spatial analysis, this micro-level point of view is very incomplete. Space cannot be reduced to superimposed spatial distributions of production organisations. Complex interactions permanently link the internal reshaping of these organisations with the major systems of resources (demographic resources, labour markets and technology markets) and also with the corresponding macro-level mechanisms of reproduction (Düll and Lutz 1989). But however insufficient it is, this micro-level analysis remains no less fundamental in the very fluid context in which we find ourselves.

In the first part of this chapter I shall therefore bring together some hypotheses concerning the changes that are taking place in the organisation of production and exchange and in particular in *large organisations* (large firms or networks of firms). My conviction is in fact that the latter continue to play a propulsive role in the reshaping of space. It is true that, in the course of the last two decades, the need for flexibility has often given new vigour and vitality to groups of industrial establishments that are closer to the artisanal world than to the structures of mass production, and that rely on geographical and social foundations that are specific to small areas and even to micro-milieux. It has happened just as readily in certain traditional sectors such as textiles in Italy as in certain leading-edge sectors. This phenomenon, which has been emphasised very strongly by certain economists (Piore and Sabel 1984) and geographers (Scott and Storper 1986), represents however only one aspect of current changes. The latter also include the continued attempts to expand, often at a global level, of the large organisations that emerged out of mass production and the efforts made within these organisations to adjust to a more unstable economic environment. The hypotheses set out will therefore concern above all large multi-establishment firms (and networks of firms): they are derived from the existing literature and from our research team's sectoral studies (of vehicles, electronics and banking in particular).

In the second section I shall briefly take up the problem of the analysis of inter-firm relations (integration and disintegration) which play a central role in the new economic geography.

I shall end, finally, with some ideas about the resulting spatial processess themselves and especially about remetropolitanisation. These spatial hypotheses come above all from research done in 1987 (Beckouche, Savy and Veltz 1987) and also from an inquiry into seventy-six French firms conducted by Bouvard and Calame (1988) which I have used extensively.

10.1 Networks and integration: key concepts of the new economics of production

As the various points that I shall mention are starting to generate a large literature, I shall proceed quickly, confining myself to the essential points and clarifying the spatial point of view. From the most obvious to the most deep-seated, I shall distinguish four major aspects of the transformations that are under way.

10.1.1 The transformation of structures of work

Whatever indicator is chosen (employment, value added or costs) the evidence shows that, in the cycle of production, the upstream phases (marketing, design of products and of plant, and operational management) and the downstream phases (distribution and sales) are constantly increasing in importance compared with the central phase of manufacture. Within the latter there is a spectacular decline in the activities of direct production relative to activities that are said to be 'indirect' such as maintenance. When one thinks of the 'car industry' one still thinks first and foremost of production workers in a factory: in fact their wages account today for just one-quarter of value added. In defence electronics the direct costs of manufacturing have fallen in ten years from 35 per cent to 10 per cent of value added. What is more, these trends hold just as much in firms and sectors that remain integrated as in firms and sectors in which the card of contracting out an essential part of their activities (including manufacturing) is played.

The rise of the 'industrial tertiary sector' — in its double form of (1) an internal tertiary sector which accounts, according to the country, for between two-thirds and three-quarters of the services consumed by firms, and (2) an external tertiary sector made up of marketed services provided to firms — is of course the sign of this change, as is the explosion of 'immaterial investments' (Documentation Française 1982). Two points deserve emphasis here. First, the geographical distributions of the internal and the external tertiary sectors are strongly correlated. (The regions in which the first is more numerous are also the regions in which the second is more developed (Valeyre 1985).) Second, the 'industrial' tertiary sector is a high-skill and high-productivity sector: in it nearly one employee in two is an executive (Audier, CEREQ 1981). The dichotomy between 'intermediate' services, which stand in a symbiotic relationship with industry, and low-productivity 'final' or 'isolated' services (services to households in particular) has a tendency to increase, and in particular is found in a very strong form at an international level (Berthelot 1988).

One of the most immediate consequences as far as space is concerned is that, in an economy like the French one, the recruitment of industrial employees becomes an *'intensive' much more than an 'extensive' process*. In Calame and Bouvard's survey a large proportion of company managers consider that the job market for executives and in particular for executives with technical skills has become the *main location factor*. This phenomemon gives a considerable advantage to large towns and especially to Paris (which in 1983 had 275 000 'high-level' tertiary sector jobs compared with 22 000 in Lyon, 8 000 in Strasbourg, and 3 500 in Montpellier: these figures indicate the disparity between the corresponding labour markets).

10.1.2 The 'systemic' model

The transformation of employment structures is of course connected with the increasing automation of production work. But automation in the strict sense (substitution of automatic equipment for human labour) is not the most important aspect of technological change. Likewise the major aspect is not, in my opinion, the flexible character of the new machines (although this characteristic is important). The essential element is the communicational component of the new techniques, the possibilities that they offer of interconnecting tasks, systems and organisations, and the powerful process of *integration* that results.

It is necessary to add immediately that this technical development receives a very strong stimulus from a more general and more fundamental tendency to review the functional divisions inherited from the classical Taylorist–Fordist model, and to develop transverse and horizontal relationships within organisations, in order to make them *more reactive*, more capable of responding to markets that are more variable and above all more unpredictable. Whereas the former principles of productivity were fundamentally additive (the movement from the 'local' to the 'global' level involving an adding up of the means and a hierarchical decomposition of objectives), the new watchword is: 'a sum of local optima does not make a global optimum'. It is necessary to integrate the cycle from design to distribution into an interdependent system. This principle is found just as readily in the great utopias of computer integration such as CIM (Computer Integrated Manufacturing) as in philosophies such as just-in-time management or 'project management'.

Finally these efforts to develop horizontal organisational structures within large firms lead of necessity to the development of forms of management whose characteristic is that they *extend beyond the firm upstream (to*

suppliers) as well as downstream (to distributors, and even clients) Here again
the emergence of logistic functions and the development of just-in-time
management constitute the most striking model. This development tends to
stabilise the networks of upstream and downstream relations of firms —
through 'partnership', a reduction in the number of subcontractors, and so on.
At the same time it increases not just the commercial, as in the past, but also
the technical control functions within the networks so constituted. In
particular in upstream JIT systems, cost control requires, in the medium term,
that stocks are not simply pushed back on to suppliers and therefore that the
latter use the same type of methods for organising production as the customer.
Moreover quality considerations require tighter control over the supplier's
process of manufacture itself. Processes of network integration of the same
kind also appear in the area of design and in the actual control of manufacturing processes (distributed CAD, and integrated CAD/CAM between a large
firm and a supplier).

As a whole these new organisational structures make up a landscape in
which it is no longer very clear where the 'boundaries' of a firm, which, in the
limit, is no more than a legal fiction, lie. What are and what will be the spatial
impacts of these processes? I shall consider them under two principal headings.

The first aspect involves the direct spatial effects of integration and of
technical 'networking'. These effects are potentially considerable. But they will
certainly not be mechanical. Will change occur in the direction of polarised
forms of concentration of subcontractors around major producers (the Toyota
City model)? It is not certain, and the investigation we carried out into the
heavy goods vehicle sector shows that in France this tendency still only applies
in a small minority of cases (Besson *et al.* 1988). In actual fact control over
waiting periods is more important in this case than the total length of these
periods, and the *control of time is more important than the costs of space.*
Whereas in section 10.1 I noted a major initial differential in favour of large
labour markets and metropolitan services, I arrive here, in spatial terms, at the
idea of a substantial comparative advantage for locations on major infrastructures. 'It is better to have suppliers that are reliable and distant but on
major infrastructures (above all motorways) than suppliers who are unreliable,
near and on second-rate networks.' This line of argument seems to be the main
one among industrialists. One can therefore imagine very closely integrated but
geographically spread-out systems of production distributed along major
transport axes (provided that the latter remain efficient, a condition which is
starting to pose problems in densely developed countries with congested
motorways such as West Germany).

The second aspect concerns the spatial expression of the new more
horizontal, more 'organic', more finely meshed, and less hierarchical organisation of large firms. In this case as well, it is difficult to come to a concrete
decision in favour of a single spatial schema. Calame and Bouvard's survey
suggests that a part of the current functions of headquarters and central service
departments could be diffused and 'distributed' (as in the case of distributed
computing), the shorter life cycle of products and the need for responsiveness
being points in favour of a physical rearticulation of sales functions and the
technical functions of design and manufacturing. Highly bipolarised models

would therefore give way to a more loosely woven network of small and medium-size multi-functional units, with the 'corporate culture' taking over from hierarchical structures in ensuring the cohesion of these diffused enterprises, in particular in the case of their executives. This argument must however be tempered in the light of the already mentioned central role of large metropolises which provide a critical mass of services and executives, of the need in mature markets for investments to reach a critical size, and also of the role of metropolises in the development of new markets. The entrepreneurs questioned by Calame and Bouvard thought that no new market, in France, could really develop outside of the capital, and that every regional enterprise of a certain size must, at least, have a large commercial office in Paris.

10.1.3 Time economies, the key factor in competition

The rise of the 'systemic' model is in the first place, as I have said, a consequence of the need for responsiveness. The temporal context of almost all sectors and markets has, as a matter of fact, been profoundly transformed. The life cycles of products have shortened, often dramatically. Above all the unpredictability of markets has undermined the concepts of planning and the models that rest on the idea of permanent methods of operational management that are strongly rooted in production organisations. Over and above the capacity to reconcile high productivity and product diversity ('static flexibility' on which analyses of 'flexible automation' are focused), it is 'dynamic flexibility' and adaptation to the uncertainties associated with movements in demand that are becoming the strategic factors (Cohendet *et al.* 1989). There is no point in substantially reducing production time and costs (through economies of scale for example) if delays in design and research remain prohibitive. But nor is there any point in reducing the times involved in all of these activities if one is not in time, and if the finished product arrives too late on the market.

This strategic role of time as a determinant of competitiveness combines finally with the fact that the *internal* time economies of integrated and reticulated technical systems are themselves very different, because they are non-additive, from those which applied in organisations of a classical kind. The unavailability locally of materials or labour can have disproportionate effects on the system as a whole because of the effects of propagation and amplification, which result in irregular production curves, and which put the management of these ups and downs at the heart of the regulation of all industrial activities. Conversely the interconnection of separate networks can produce effects that are positive, discontinuous (at the threshhold) and rapid.

Generalising the remark already made about logistics, one can therefore say that the integrated management of time is becoming the strategic factor in the search for competitive advantage and methods of regulation (Stalk 1988). This conclusion does not mean that space, globally domesticated, is ceasing to be a factor (as in the limiting case of permanent and instantaneous global financial markets) or even a secondary factor: it simply means that henceforth the impact of space will often operate through the medium of differential temporalities rather than differences in direct costs. (To give an illustration, the just-in-time system reinforces the relative advantages of the motorway compared with an ordinary road, even though the costs of transport are very similar).

The economies of networks centred on time are thus at the heart of the main mechanisms of hierarchisation and differentiation. The paradox that is constantly renewed is the following: while advances in the average accessibility of basic networks (transport, telecommunications and energy) in principle make space more and more homogeneous, the remaining differentials assume increasing importance. Henry Ford, who thought that electrical energy was going to make space unimportant, is constantly proved wrong: the narrower the differentials are, the more intense is competition with respect to these differentials.

10.1.4 The fusion of goods and services and the mutation of 'markets'

This last point, which is without doubt the most important, underpins most of the tendencies already mentioned. Traditional models of the economy make a very sharp distinction between the moment of production of a good (which occurs within a firm that is considered as having clearly defined boundaries), the moment of exchange, and the moment of use. This distinction is much less clear in the case of 'pure' services. However it also has a tendency to become more and more blurred in the case of industrial products. As Zarifian (1987) notes, the notion of the delivery of a service is becoming just as central for industry as for the service sector and is reaching a point at which one can wonder whether mediation through a physical good is a relevant distinction. A car is conceived from the outset as a set of services provided to the user; in addition it is sold with various services that make it a service-good.

Following in particular Bressand and Nicolaïdis (1988) one can distinguish several major aspects of these processes:

(1) the emergence of the idea of 'compacks' and the growing role of complex integrated ensembles of goods and services
(2) the key role of processes of aggregation and separation of products (goods and services) in competition: the range of products often becomes a continuum in which the capacity to extract an element (or to recombine elements that are not connected) constitutes the real strategic innovation on which competitive advantage and even the emergence of new firms or sectors depends (one sees it clearly in the world of 'value-added' services in telecommunications for example);
(3) the strong link between product innovation and process innovation which can go as far as fusion, especially if in 'process' one includes the downstream elements through which the good or service is put at the disposal of the final client and
(4) the renewal of the dialectic between mass production and customised production which no longer appear simply as alternatives for the producer and the consumer, but are increasingly combined in new areas of

'customised mass production'. Customised mass producton (which differs from the simple differentiation of listed mass-produced goods as in the case of 'flexible automation') results from the extension of value added chains up to the stage of consumption.

These developments, whose main source lies in the increase in competition and in the need to develop more detailed strategies to create, tap and differentiate consumer 'needs', are translated in organisational terms into developments which widely confirm what was said above about integration and reticulation as new central concepts of production. But whereas until now I have put special emphasis on inter-firm relations, this new insight highlights the growing interpenetration of the moments of production, exchange and consumption. The 'market' ascends higher and higher in the 'organisation' of production, and the latter descends further and further towards the market in the limit reaching the final consumer. There too the concept of a firm as a screen between the factors of production (combination of inputs) and a range of distinct and independent products for sale on the market becomes pro-blematic. The notion of a market itself, moreover, requires close re-examin-ation as, with the softening of the division between production and consump-tion, the neoclassical 'market place' gives way to a collection of networks in which a customer base is constructed and captured, and in which a continuous chain of creation of values and use-values is set in motion.

How finally should we perceive the spatial form of these changes? At this abstract level, even more than at the preceding levels, any direct inference is impossible. But the analysis that I have just outlined has some very important implications for the general discussion of the concepts of 'integration' or 'vertical disintegration' (as well as for the concepts of economies of scale, economies of scope, and transaction costs) whose role in economic geography is well known.

10.2 Integration and vertical disintegration and the paradigm of markets and organisations: a clarification of concepts

I shall not explain in detail the propositions of Anglo-Saxon economic geography about the new forms of the spatial division of labour, their relation with the concepts of economies of scope and Williamson's transaction cost model. (I refer, for example, to Scott 1986b and to Scott and Storper (1986)). These propositions are stimulating, and I agree with them on many points.

It seems to me however that some quite strong ambiguities remain, and that it is necessary to clarify certain points, such as the nature of what is called 'integration' and 'vertical disintegration'. Note first of all two aspects of these concepts which pose problems.

The first aspect, which has already been pointed out, is the importance given to the model of 'flexible vertical disintegration' (FVD). This model was inspired by the case of the 'Third Italy' and certain high-technology zones, and it was interpreted as the most efficient response to the global management of uncertainty in an interconnected system, as well as the way of minimising 'transaction costs' (thanks to the concentration of the basic units on well defined processes and products.) However it is clear that this model is only one of the particular empirical forms that the processes that I have described above can assume. These processes led me however to put more emphasis on the processes of 'integration' than on the processes of 'disintegration', and at least as much on organisations that are spatially disintegrated sometimes on a very large scale as on organisations that are highly concentrated. In fact it is clear that objectives concerning costs, flexibility, reliability, and product quality can be achieved *both* through processes of integration *and* through processes of disintegration, and that there is a permanent dilemma, which is resolved in practice in ways that vary a great deal, between the advantages of a *stabilisation* of inter-firm relations (as in the logic of 'partnership' connected with JIT management) and the advantages that stem from the existence of significant degrees of freedom within the networks that link manufacturers. It is also the case that a more disintegrated ownership structure (externalisation) can very easily coexist with strengthened technical integration. The question therefore arises as to the relation between the FVD model and the model that Leborgne and Lipietz (1988a) call, after Houssiaux, 'vertical near-integration' (VNI). The theoretical arguments that can be advanced in favour of the second model are in fact very close to those which justify the former. This claim squares moreover with the intuitive idea that the terms 'integration' and 'disintegration' are ambivalent. (Also similar is the way the setting up of a computer network allows *at one and the same time* a centralisation and a decentralisation of power).

A second question is the following. When Leborgne and Lipietz distinguish, with good reason, spatially disintegrated VNI and spatially integrated VNI, reference is only made in the main to a model in which the spatial separation of activities is functional and hierarchical, or neo-Taylorist (especially in the case of international specialisation). To my mind this view is a partial one which does not really take into account the possibilities of the 'networked firm'. For example it can be argued that in Europe today the car (or electronics) industry system works in accordance with the principle of spatially disintegrated VNI, except that the spatial distribution of activities does not correspond with the classical, hierarchical form. The 'global factory' and more and more the 'global research department' of firms and their suppliers are distributed across a greatly extended network of locations, which are no longer reduced to the classical bipolar forms involving centres of management at one pole and peripheries of workshops at the other (as in the French case in the period 1950–1970). There too it is clearly difficult to speak of integration or disintegration without specifying the nature of the links and of *the relations among units*.

Over and above these empirical remarks, it seems to me that a key point in the debate concerns the relevance of the 'transaction costs model', and of a description that continues to make a very strong distinction between the interior and the exterior of a firm, and to accept the idea that there is a strong dichotomy between 'organisation' and the 'market'. How relevant moreover is an analysis that focuses very strongly on the moment of exchange and of transaction, and that considers production itself as a 'black box'?

What I have said earlier in this chapter indicates in fact how problematic the concepts of the 'interior' and 'exterior' of the firm are becoming, how integration and networks weave their web not only among firms but *within a continuum that extends from 'organisation' to the 'market'* or from 'production' via 'transactions' to 'consumption'. If one goes back to a simple example like just-in-time and logistic integration, one sees clearly that the optimisation of exchanges and transactions provides only a very partial account of the process. What is central to JIT is in fact an industrial logic that entails a search for efficiency in the world of the *production operations* themselves, a search for efficiency which spreads from workshops to suppliers and to clients (Veltz 1988). I agree here with Bressand and Nicolaïdis (1988) when they maintain that 'networks' are not only a support for transactions, but more fundamental strategic structures that allow the incorporation of actors into chains in which the costs and the gains from integration are the essential economic factor. Similarly the model of 'vertical disintegration' cannot simply be described in terms of an optimisation of exchanges among more or less watertight production units: it is more accurately described, for example, by the concept of a 'value-adding partnership' (Johnston and Lawrence 1988) which puts the emphasis on the process of progressive and negotiated addition of value along 'chains' which cross from one part of economic space to another. This debate is not in the least rhetorical: it indicates that when one speaks of the 'economics of networks' one is not speaking of a second layer of intermediation among production spaces (as Gille 1988, for example, does) but rather of a global structuring of activities.

In practical terms it therefore seems to me that the progress we make in our knowledge of spatial processes will depend above all on our ability to open the black boxes of firms and of networks of firms to understand what is happening in the continuum that they are establishing among themselves and with the 'markets' that they construct and tap and not just in the somewhat unreal world of their 'external transactions'. It also means that the difficulties of economic geography at this point directly rejoin — how come that it should surprise us? — those of economics itself which for a century has overdeveloped the theory of exchange and markets, while leaving undeveloped the theory of production.

10.3 Some hypotheses about general tendencies in the development of the space economy: the network-metropolis

As I said at the beginning, it is impossible to 'deduce' directly from the analysis of changes within industrial organisations — no matter how well-defined and coherent they are — overall tendencies in the reorganisation of space. Micro-level phenomena like the ones I have mentioned are combined, in a constant dialectic, with macro-level constraints at various scales (labour markets, systems of technical resources, state regulations, the regulation of the economy as a whole, and so on) as well as with the powerful inertia of existing urban and spatial structures to produce specific spatial configurations. It is this fact in particular that explains why a country like France, which is characterised by the crushing domination of the Parisian pole, cannot have the same path of spatial development as Germany or Italy, even if there are strong similarities in the basic phenomena relating to the organisation of firms.

The general hypotheses that I shall briefly present to finish therefore require arguments that are more complex than the ones which have been outlined in this chapter. I put them forward here as *provisional* hypotheses, referring the reader to other studies (in particular Beckouche, Savy and Veltz 1987).

The basic trend, particularly in France, is, it seems, what I shall call the *transition from a polarisation among zones ('polarisation-zone') to a polarisation in the form of networks ('polarisation-réseau').*

As I have indicated, the critical importance of skilled labour markets, and of markets for services and technologies gives towns of a certain size, and above all, in the case of France, the urban region of Paris, a considerable advantage in the face of the new strategies of location. One can even hypothesise that for the first time in France industry in the broad sense is becoming a strictly *urban* phenomenon (whereas until now, with the exception of Paris, Lyon and a few other poles, it has been pushed away to the semi-rural fringes of the country). To that are added the specific effects of the 'economics of networks and of integration' that I have mentioned, and in particular the fundamental mechanisms of hierarchisation and differentiation that I have illustrated with the example of logistics.

In this manner the trends towards 'networking' and integration in industrial systems are creating a landscape in which 'geometric' spatial logics play a much less important role than topological processes in general and the connectedness and connectivity of networks (for definitions see Dupuy, 1985) in particular. More than through the processes, that have been fundamental up to now, of influence over interlocking concentric areas, the growth of poles depends on their capacity to connect up with the major flows and networks, to capture the rents associated with the intersections of networks, to constitute the nodes of networks, and so on.

In the specific case of France this argument leads us to the hypothesis that I shall summarise under the heading: '*the network-metropolis and the French desert*' (la métropole-réseau et le désert français). This hypothesis is itself linked to two considerations. The first is the increasing delinking, which can be demonstrated statistically and which can lead as far as strong divergences, of the economic growth of major towns from that of their hinterlands or regions. This delinking occurs both because the regional diffusion effects of urban economies are weak, and inversely because the traditional relations of economic control over, and appropriation of values from, these hinterlands are becoming of distinctly secondary importance for urban economies. The second is the increasing integration of the activities of the Parisian pole with the propulsive activities of second-rank towns. This integration is most evident in activities with a high technological content. (Classic examples are the electronics pole at Rennes or the aerospace pole at Toulouse which simply function as bipoles with Paris.) In essence, and in a way that contrasts sharply with the German case, the French space economy could therefore be heading towards a tendentially unified process of metropolitanisation, linking Paris and a few secondary poles into a network-metropolis. Within this network-metropolis processes of flexible vertical disintegration play a fundamental role, coexisting of course with industrial systems organised at a European and global level in accordance with the principle of spatially disintegrated 'vertical near-integration' (as in the cases of electronics and vehicles), and posing the agonising question as to the future of spaces that are not connected up with the major networks: the rural world, and small towns situated off the major routes whose destinies are linked with the declining course of 'Fordism'.

The reader will have noted that, in contrast to the analysis of the industrial transformations themselves, the 'spatial' hypotheses that I have just concisely outlined remain largely 'metaphorical'. The hypotheses must be tested and discussed *statistically*, and at the same time the *concepts* used must be specified.

11 French high-tech and space: a double cleavage

Pierre Beckouche

Paris is the thinking head of the national productive system. The idea is well known. Today it has reappeared (the option of DATAR) as the foundation of an organisation of production centred around urban networks. The expression urban network is however no longer used in the traditional administrative sense of the term, but in the sense of a division of functions in which a role for large provincial towns is affirmed and in which the position of Paris stems in the end more from its position as the head of the network than from a monopolistic position as the only centre.

11.1 A geographical method of analysis of high-tech

11.1.1 High tech: two related approaches

This model of Paris as the 'head of a national network' encounters two difficulties. The first is cognitive: our knowledge of the current national productive system does not provide us with sufficiently detailed information about the spatial organisation of high-tech production activities. In this chapter I shall attempt to add to this knowledge, at the same time distinguishing two often confused meanings of the over-used term 'high technology':

(1) Industrial *sectors*, or rather sectors of production (Planque 1986) where I do not confine myself to the usual classification of sectors. The reason why is that one cannot, as is now well known, simply equate high tech with the electronics industry — as in the case of the Trégor in Brittany, whose development was centred on electronics and in particular telecommunications activities, there are mono-industrial electronics zones which face

acute economic difficulties — plus the aerospace industry plus fine chemicals plus, etc.

(2) The *functions* of production. Technology occupies a growing role in *all* industrial sectors, and the transversal qualities of digital technologies make it very difficult to distinguish the boundaries of industries or sectors. High-tech activities are dependent then on a transversal approach.

The second difficulty, which goes beyond the subject I intend to consider, concerns the rapid changes in the strategies of territorial actors (large towns) and industrial actors (large firms) whose horizons have been internationalised. As a result difficulties stand in the way of the establishment of a well-defined national framework.

11.1.2 A method of sectoral and functional analysis

I shall therefore use an approach to the analysis of the French productive system which takes account at one and the same time of sectors and functions (for the details see Damette 1989).

11.1.2.1 *Sectors of activity*

Within industry, where of course statistical investigations make use of the most detailed classification available (the Institut National de la Statistique et des Etudes Economique's Nomenclature d'activité et de produit (NAP) 600), a distinction is made between:

(1) The 'high-tech' or 'technicien' activities ('activités techniciennes') which already have a high technological content (see Appendix C), and where the share of very skilled jobs (engineers, executives and technicians) is high. Included are the 'leading' sectors of French industry ('T1'): defence electronics, telecommunications, computers, automation equipment, aerospace, high-power electrical equipment, etc., and to a lesser extent the 'T2' sectors: basic chemicals, parachemicals, machine tools, industrial equipment, precision instruments and equipment, consumer electronics.
(2) The 'Q' activities ('Q' stands for 'ouvrier qualifié' in French) which are still characterised by the use of skilled workers: iron and steel, motor and commercial vehicles, rail equipment, linotype printing, general engineering, and even metal manufacturing in the global sense of the word.
(3) The 'S' activities ('S' stands for 'ouvrier specialisé' (OS)) which use a high proportion of unskilled workers: food processing, textiles, leather goods, shoes, furniture, etc.
(4) The construction of private vehicles and vehicle equipment forms a separate class due to the scale of its activity and the specific character of its spatial organisation (very large establishments and the extreme contrast between the employment profile of Paris and the provinces).

Outside of industry account was taken of *'periproductive' services*. The latter were divided into:

(1) Upstream periproductive services: services to firms, financial services, inter-industrial wholesale services, etc.
(2) Downstream periproductive services: non-industrial wholesale services.
(3) Transport and telecommunications.

'Upstream periproductive' services are a strategic sector for the productive sphere in the same way as the 'technicien' ('high-tech') sectors are.

11.1.2.2 Production functions

The only source that can be used to examine the whole of the French productive system (with data for industry and the periproductive services at least)[1] and which provides information about the functions of production is the INSEE's Enquête sur la structure des emplois (Valeyre 1985 and Bonamy 1986). Its distinctive classification makes it necessary to limit the functional approach to the following functions: (1) administration and management, (2) sales and marketing, (3) design and research, (4) manufacture, (5) warehousing, packing and transport, and (6) various services (simple maintenance, caretaking, and so on). In the case of design and research a wide functional meaning of high technology is used in this chapter (see the details of the content of this class in Appendix A).

11.1.3 The two spatial cleavages: Paris and the provinces, and North and South

These analytical distinctions make possible an account of the two handicaps of French high-tech activities[2] in a perspective which situates them in the productive system as a whole:

(1) The position of Paris in French high-tech activities verges on expropriation, even though everyday discussions of this subject are very disparate. It is necessary to measure and explain the concentration of activities in Paris, as, in its magnitude, the hierarchical segmentation of space is specific to the French case.
(2) The success of the theme of provincial technopoles, essentially in the South, poses, on the contrary, two related problems:
(i) the difficulties of the other large provincial towns, broadly in the northern half of the country, in setting in motion a similar dynamic, and
(ii) the small number of industrial activities on which the dynamism of technopoles is based. The dominance of the star sectors of French high tech (electronics in the broad sense, aerospace and to a lesser extent biotechnologies) resembles a national model with a high state-controlled content (telecommunications, defence, space) in which the provincial technopoles follow, at their level, in the tracks of the Paris region.

Moreover this success conceals a fundamental phenomenon which may well affect the whole system of technopoles: the internationalisation of these

Table 11.1 The share of national employees in activities with a high technological content in Ile-de-France in 1980 and 1987 (in percentages)

	1980	1987
Oil and natural gas	31.9	32.4
Parachemicals and pharmaceuticals	39.7	35.8
Electrical and electronic equipment	38.2	35.7[1]
Ships and aircraft	25.7	28.6
Market services to firms	41.7	41.6
Insurance	46.9	40.9
Finance	39.3	39.7
Total	24.1	24.1

[1] In defence electronics the share was 65 per cent.
Source: Lehoucq and Strauss 1988.

foundations, which until now have been essentially national, of French high technology, and an increase in the fragility of the Parisian head.

11.2 Paris: more than one-half of French high tech, and the theme of expropriation

11.2.1 The images of 'expropriation' by Paris

11.2.1.1 Paris, national pole of research . . . without industry?

Classical geographical analysis leads to a paradox. Geographers carefully measure the monopoly of Paris over public and private research. In the case of higher education and university research there is a view that there is a strong concentration of places in Paris but that it has been eroded by an undeniable process of decentralisation. But the share of the capital region in industrial jobs, including high-technology jobs, is moderate (about 30 per cent) and/or is declining (see Table 11.1).

We have therefore discontinuous indicators which are not very useful for an analysis of the productive *system*. The simple and still more frequent contrast between research, considered as a quaternary activity worthy of a great metropolis, and industry, which is destined to decline as in all the great metropolitan areas of the world (including Tokyo?), does not contribute to a systemic view.

11.2.1.2 The measurement of concentration

Recourse to several finer indicators gives the Paris region more than one-half of French high-tech jobs. In the productive sphere as a whole (industry plus periproductive services)[3] the Paris region[4] has 28 per cent of total employment but 46 per cent of design and research jobs compared with 18 per cent of manufacturing production jobs. We know in fact that in the years of growth the phase of what is called industrial decentralisation involved a powerful filtering process which not only reserved for Paris the advanced sectors (Saint Julien 1986), but also differentiated between functions of production and, last

Table 11.2 The share of national jobs in the functions of production in the productive sphere (in establishments with more than 10 employees) in the the Paris ZPIU (**Zone de peuplement industriel et urbain**) (in percentages)

Abstract functions	Design and research	45.5
	Administration and management	43.1
	Commerce and marketing	43.4
Functions of execution	Various services	32.8
	Warehousing and transport	21.1
	Manufacture	17.7
Total		28.4

Source: INSEE, Enquête sur la structure des emplois, 1985.

but not least, between socio-occupational categories (Cohen 1987). *Paris was thus assigned the 'abstract' functions*, the activities of engineers and of intermediate professions connected with the manipulation of monetary and informational signs upstream and downstream of production: design, research, management, marketing and commerce. On the other hand the functions of execution and of manual work nearer to physical matter were largely decentralised. In the striking contrast between the share of Paris in 'abstract' functions and the functions of execution, the most pronounced polaristion is found in design and research (see Table 11.2).

When one takes account of the level of skill of the jobs within this distribution, the plot thickens: 56 per cent of the executives and engineers in design and research functions are concentrated in Paris.[5] If one cares to take into account the fact that it is not just a matter of *researchers*, as the function of design and research is not confined to this single category of workers (see Appendix A), this figure is enormous. Indeed if one considers the *researchers* in the design and research departments of firms, the figure reaches 60 per cent, compared with 9 per cent in Rhône-Alpes and 7 per cent in Provence-Alpes-Côte d'Azur (Peyrache 1987), and if one considers defence electronics, engineering or the car industry, the proportion climbs to between two-thirds and three-quarters.[6] Moreover this proportion of 50 to 60 per cent corresponds with many other indicators (see Table 11.3).

11.2.1.3 The explanation of concentration

A concise explanation of this concentration lies in two fundamental factors:

(1) A dominant socio-political choice which, in the Paris region, has worsened the balance between a reduction in the size of the manual working class and the growth of jobs for engineers, executives and technicians.
(2) The fundamental role in national industry of the state which has promoted a small number of 'technicien' ('high-tech') sectors centred on sophisticated technologies which are organised in and directed from the Paris region.

The specific character of the functional profile of production activities in Paris is more exactly a *result* of these two historical factors, yet the current transformations in the organisation of production are focused on a redefinition of inter-function relations: the establishment of closer relations between

210   *Pierre Beckouche*

Table 11.3 Indicators of the position of Paris in the national productive system (in percentages of the national total in the Paris region)

	1982	1983	1988
Headquarters of firms of more than 500 employees		48.5	51.4
French value added associated with Paris enter-prises			58.0
Value of imports and exports*			69.0
Administrative and commercial executives of the firm	45.2		
Engineers and technical executives of the firm	45.2		
Number of students in grandes écoles and engineering schools			47.0

* The share of the activities of the services or departments of firms concerned with import and export operations in the Ile-de-France.
Sources: BIPE 1988 and Lehoucq and Strauss 1988.

Table 11.4 The (slow) decline in the share of Paris in research jobs in French industrial enterprises (national employment and percentages for each region of national total)*

Year	National Employment	Ile-de-France	Paris Basin†	Rhône-Alpes	South east and South west		
					Provence	Midi-Pyrénées	Aquitaine
1970		65.0	5.9	9.3	4.9	2.8	2.6
1974	28 700	63.0	6.8	8.7	5.8	2.6	3.2
1981	35 100	62.0	7.0	8.7	5.9	2.3	3.1
1984	41 500	60.4	7.0	8.9	5.9	3.2	3.3
1986	45 400	59.3	7.9	9.2	6.6	3.1	3.1

* The distribution in terms of expenditure is similar.
† The increase in the 'Paris Basin' is due to the Haute Normandie and Centre regions which are in fact geographical extensions of the Paris region.
Source: Ministère de la recherche (1988), La recherche-développement dans les entreprises.

design, marketing and manufacturing production, and the integration of production and sales (Veltz 1988 and Chapter 10, and Bressand 1989).

11.2.2 'Remetropolitanisation' or decentralisation?

11.2.2.1 The development of research employment and expenditure

Another source, that of the Ministre de la recherche et de la technologie on research and development in firms gives an idea of changes over time. The Ile-de-France contains 59 per cent of the national total of full-time equivalent researchers in national industrial firms, but the concentration of researchers has declined continuously (see Table 11.4).

The consideration of public research hardly makes any difference in spite of the decentralisation of centres of public research: in 1985 the Paris region received 58 per cent of the civil budget for public research. Strikingly in 1980 to 1985 this proportion increased.

Whether recent trends involve a slight reduction or, on the contrary, a renewed increase in polarisation — one should not close this question without a consideration of military research budgets — the share of Paris is remarkable.

11.2.2.2 The research and development of firms: a modification of the frontier between Paris and the provinces

Enquiries into firms do not suggest a decentralisation of design and research but a spatial rearrangement of the different *components* of this function. The part concerned with industrial development tends to move closer to manufacturing production sites even though one is reduced to hypotheses supported by examples that are considered significant a priori. In fact decisions vary sharply from one firm to another, and it is not unusual to find contrasting situations in different divisions of a single firm. If, for instance, one considers large groups in advanced sectors (which give an impetus to the trends), one sees that:

(1) In the Bull group the Massy establishment in the western suburbs of Paris does all the research (into hardware and software) and makes the preproduction models of the microcomputers made at Villeneuve d'Ascq near Lille. But the Angers factory is not confined to manufacturing: it is responsible for pre-production models of large and medium systems.
(2) The divisions of the Thomson group adopt very different arrangements. Some continue to separate geographically research and development on the one hand and manufacturing production on the other. In some provincial poles design activities are set up in the immediate vicinity of manufacturing operations (Brest, Bordeaux and Cagnes-sur-Mer near Nice), but these design activities are in narrow specialisms and/or incomplete with the essential research functions remaining in Paris. Only in semiconductors does one find in the provinces a base (Grenoble) where design functions have really developed at the expense of Paris, although in this case the division is between Grenoble, Dallas and Milan.
(3) The parent company Matra maintains a sharp division: research in Paris extends as far as the making of prototypes and development. All the same, one design activity has been completely decentralised to Toulouse: computing research in the space sector.
(4) Philips is attempting to promote centres of competence in manufacturing production and design. But the spatial distribution of fundamental research and of the strategic activities of the group is still very polarised (Paris, Eindhoven . . .), as the provincial 'centres of competence' at Caen, Evreux or Le Mans pose problems of accessibility (circulation of high-level executives) for which satisfactory solutions have not been found.

These variations indicate that the question of the functional and spatial caesura between design and research and manufacturing, which is especially

Table 11.5 The functional distribution of engineers and executives in a large French electronics group

	Distribution of engineers and executives in the Ile-de-France by function	Ile-de-France's share of French engineers and executives
'Industrial tertiary'		
Administration, management and directorate	9.0	85.0
Commercial	12.0	96.0
Purchases	1.0	66.0
Computing (especially for administrative purposes)	11.0	93.0
Research, applied research, and development	45.0	83.0
Manufacturing		
Production management (management, methods and organisation)	3.0	56.0
Manufacturing in the strict sense	3.0	63.0
Control (quality, trials and technical dossiers)	6.0	66.0
Installation (site, maintenance, and training)	9.0	80.0
Total	100.0	82.0

* The Ile-de-France accounts for only half of the company's manual workers.
Source: parent company, 1987.

pronounced in the French case, is far from finding a simple response, while it is an economic issue in its own right.

The case of the large electronics firm presented in Tables 11.5 and 11.6 allows us to recall the orders of magnitude: while more than 40 per cent of the engineers and executives in the establishments in the provinces are employed in research and design, these employees are very marginal when one compares their number with that of their counterparts in Paris. Moreover a consideration of the different components of research and design shows that the privileges of the provinces are still confined to development, with Paris reserving for itself the upstream phases (fundamental research and the design of the overall electronic system).

11.2.2.3 Functional integration: Paris first

In parallel with these developments, moreover, the different 'abstract' functions are increasingly integrated. This phenomenon affects the Paris region first of all and in particular its western part. Design and research move closer to marketing, maintenance and the ensemble of services to clients. The motivation for integration is

(1) upstream to rationalise supply by linking products and services through the setting up of teams (designers, technical sales specialists, sellers, and lawyers) that are modifiable and capable of responding quickly to demand in markets which are more and more competitive and international, and
(2) downstream to establish durable relations with the customer in order to

Table 11.6 The share of engineers and executives in research and development by type of task (in %)

	Distribution of engineers and executives in the Ile-de-France by function %	Distribution of engineers and executives in the provinces by function %	Ile-de-France's share of French engineers and executives %
Research and development as a whole	45.0	42.0	83.0
of which	2.0	1.0	89.0
advanced research			
global applied research or applied research into systems*	14.0	4.0	93.0
development	29.0	36.0	78.0

* A group made up of applied research requiring knowledge of a complete system, of the different technologies (electronics, radar, propulsion, guidance) involved in a system, and of the distribution of tasks between different services and divisions.
Source: parent company, 1987.

make the clientèle more captive[7] and to improve the relation between the design of products and their final uses.

This integration assumes the form of

(1) the gathering of these functions from several establishments scattered around the Paris region, as in the case of the industrial installations engineers SPIE Batignolles at Cergy-Pontoise or Matra at Vélizy. It is this kind of integration that is one of the foundations of the success of La Défense whose development was given a new impetus in the last few years. (Examples include the gathering together of the central functions and the customer services of Olivetti-Logabax, and of the central services of the different divisions of the Thomson group.) The decision made by SPIE Batignolles is significant: 3500 employees the majority of whom were engineers were concentrated at Cergy, but the autonomy of the divisions and the specialised subsidiaries in their areas of special competence (electrical equipment, pipes, civil engineering, etc.) were respected, with each having its own building. (There are twenty-three buildings on a 50-hectare site). As the base for the group's international activities, the site creates, through its modular organisation and the sophistication of its telematic facilities, the possibility of constructing multidisciplinary teams in order rapidly to put forward bids on world engineering markets.

(2) a networking of specialised and geographically distinct sites dedicated to 'abstract' functions in order to integrate their capabilities: Alcatel, or Bull with its establishments for applied and fundamental research at Clayes-sous-Bois, Massy, Louveciennes, Trappes, and Paris. In the case of Bull the motivation for integration is functional and, above all, sectoral: as the supply of computers is directed towards computer 'solutions' that combine software, microcomputers, minicomputers, and main frames, it is necessary

to put establishments with different specialisms (computer networks, microcomputers, minicomputers) into contact with one another.

(3) or, half-way between these two developments, a networking of establishments that are geographically quite close to one another in order to facilitate the transfer of personnel and, hence, of knowledge (SAGEM's system of four design centres situated close to one another between Cergy-Pontoise and Argenteuil).

Of course there are examples of integration that combine several of these forms as in the case if IBM: a concentration in the two towers of La Défense (4000 people)[8] of the directorate, management, marketing, and a part of sales on the one hand and the location of establishments devoted to sales functions along line A of the Réseau Express Régional. (It should be noted, however, that all of these sites — Argenteuil, Cergy, La Défense, Vélizy, Louveciennes, Trappes, and so on — are in the western part of the Paris region.)

In the light of these ideas the division between the 'abstract' functions located in Paris and the manufacturing functions located in the provinces seems greater, with enterprises overcoming the handicap of distance by decentralising several components of the abstract functions (non-strategic purchases, subcontracting, production management, and development as is shown in Table 11.6) and leaving the rest to the transport and telecommunications networks. An approach which treats the functions of design and research as separate and isolated functions therefore becomes of secondary importance in understanding spatial distributions. What emerges as the most important factor are the inter-functional (and also inter-sectoral) relations which distinguish the metropolitan economy of Paris.

The last point raises once again the question of the development of the provinces. In which towns in the provinces are there significant proportions and numbers of jobs in a key function such as design and research on the one hand, and does one find a significant metropolitan economy on the other?

11.3 The fragility of the economic and geographical base of French high-tech activities

11.3.1 The geography of French production: 'avoidance'

11.3.1.1 The non-technicien sectors are supported neither in Paris nor in the provincial metropolises

In France there are very sharp differences in the technological content of the monopolised and modernised sectors of industry, whether market-oriented or financed by the state, on the one hand, and the others in which the decision to pursue price-competitiveness encouraged the employment of unskilled workers (Lehoucq and Strauss 1988 and Appendices B and C). Metal working and other intermediate sectors were not, in contrast to the West German case, the object of a special effort. The contrast between the sectors with a high

Table 11.7 The share of the Paris ZPIU in national industrial employment by sectors and functions of production (in percentages)

Sector	Design and research	Sales and marketing	Administration and management	Various services	Storage and transport	Manufacture	All sectors
T1	54.0	66.0	58.0	48.0	32.0	29.0	44.6
T2	31.0	56.0	37.0	28.0	18.0	14.0	24.0
Vehicles	49.0	66.0	54.0	37.0	32.0	24.0	30.4
Non-'technicien' sectors							
Q1	15.0	38.0	22.0	19.0	11.0	12.0	14.4
Q2	14.0	31.0	20.0	6.0	6.0	5.0	8.0
S1	10.0	34.0	20.0	12.0	10.0	8.0	10.9
S2	13.0	27.0	18.0	16.0	8.0	6.0	8.8
Construction[1]	37.0	28.0	34.0	30.0	15.0	22.0	23.3

[1] Construction is not very well covered by the Enquête sur la structure des emplois (ESE) as does not cover establishments with fewer than 10 employees.
Source: INSEE Enquête sur la structure des emplois 1985.

Table 11.8 The share of the Paris ZPIU in upstream periproductive service jobs (in percentages)

	Sector total	of which design and research
Inter-industrial wholesale	30.0	50.0
Insurance and finance	43.0	60.0
Market services to firms	48.0	56.0
Research (private)	54.0	52.0

Source: INSEE Enquête sur la structure des emplois 1985.

proportion of engineers and the sectors dominated by manual workers was accordingly accentuated.

Geographically there are two illustrative situations: the 'technicien' sectors are Parisian, and the others are provincial (see Table 11.7). The metal-working sectors which typified the industry of Paris for a long time appear today spatially downgraded: in them Paris plays as small a role as it does in unskilled sectors. In relation to these situations the car industry occupies a position of its own, as it is at one and the same time a high-technology sector (polarised in Paris) and a sector founded on price-competitiveness and the search for economies in the wage costs of direct production workers (located in the provinces).

It follows that periproductive services, which are largely for the sectors that are most 'technicien'-oriented, are strongly concentrated in Paris: most of their design function jobs[10] are in Paris (see Table 11.8).

The overall results are summarised in Table 11.9. Industrial sectors 'T1' and vehicles are, like upstream periproductive services, directly polarised by Paris

Table 11.9 The share of the Paris ZPIU in employment in each sector (in percentages)

	Non-'technicien' industries	'Technicien' industries and vehicles	Upstream periproductive services
Abstract functions	23.0	44.0	46.0
Functions of execution	5.0	22.0	31.0

Source: INSEE Enquête sur la structure des emplois 1985.

and, to a much lesser extent, by the provincial metropolises. The 'T2' sectors also play an important role in provincial metropolises: jobs in the abstract functions in these sectors are strongly represented in these cities. The other sectors of production ('Q' and 'S'), which account moreover for 60 per cent of national industrial employment, are located to a very large extent outside of metropolitan areas even in the case of their research (which overall is very limited) and their other abstract functions. For these sectors the only form of metropolitanisation of some significance involves the location of sales functions in the Paris region. This vast collection of activities bypassed by modernisation and metropolitanisation is of crucial economic and territorial importance.

11.3.1.2 Northern France versus southern France: an interpretation

The geographical distribution of production in the provinces is a result of three related principles:

(1) The sectoral and functional filter of Paris is of course the first. This filter makes itself felt at the scale of the hexagon, and in particular within Paris's zone of regional influence which extends in many respects to the whole of the northern half of the country (see the map of the 'Paris complex' in Figure 11.1).

(2) Sectoral *'avoidance'*: modern high-technology activities, which are connected in large measure with the state, especially as a result of the importance of firms in which there are public shareholdings, largely avoid locations in France's traditional industrial areas in the north-east (Damette 1987).

(3) A contrast between the bases of the urban areas in the north and south of the country. When one examines design and research jobs in the French towns which make up the network of metropolises, one notices a striking paradox (see Figure 11.2):

(i) The towns of the north-east, Lille and Strasbourg, have a serious shortage of design and research jobs,[11] but are well endowed with the abstract functions of upstream periproductive services.

(ii) Conversely Grenoble,[12] Toulouse, and to a lesser extent Bordeaux are specialised in advanced industries that are largely controlled from Paris. The functional profile of these metropolises is radically different (except in the case of Grenoble) from that of their regional environment. Toulouse and Bordeaux have received 'grafts' of industries with a high design

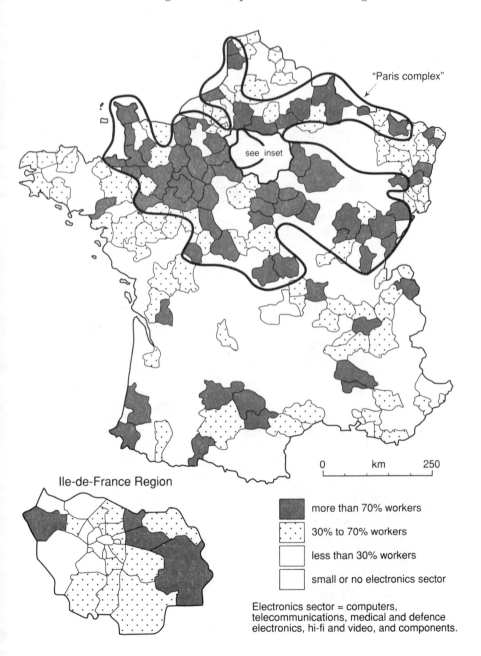

"Paris complex"

see inset

Ile-de-France Region

0   km   250

more than 70% workers

30% to 70% workers

less than 30% workers

small or no electronics sector

Electronics sector = computers,
telecommunications, medical and defence
electronics, hi-fi and video, and components.

Figure 11.1a Electronics-sector employment: manual workers

Source: ESE 1985

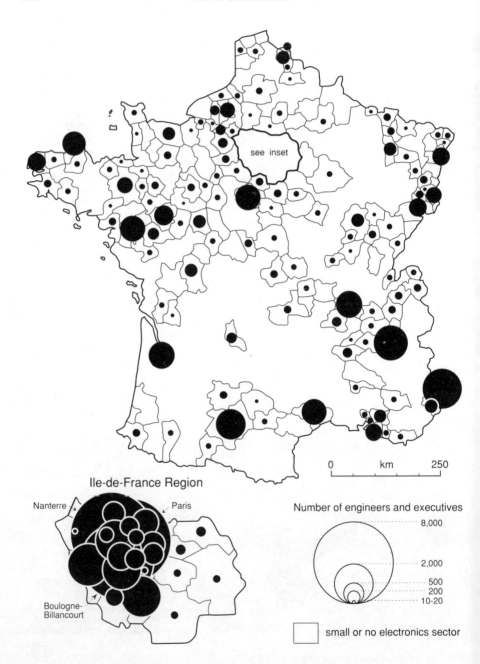

Figure 11.1b Electronics-sector employment: engineers and executives
Source: ESE 1985.

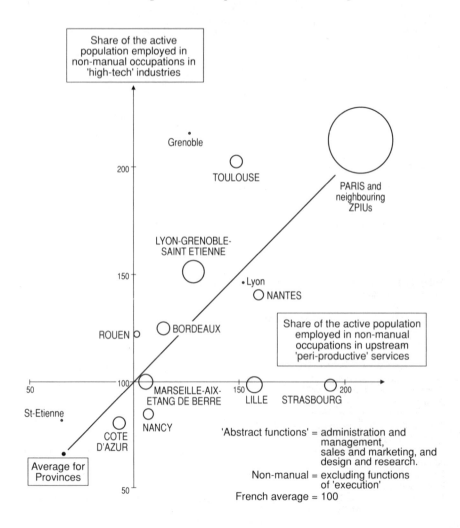

Figure 11.2 The 'abstract' functions of high-tech industries and upstream periproductive services by ZPIU

Source: ESE 1985

component out of proportion to their regional and urban capacities. One is almost tempted to say, emphasising this characteristic, that in the provinces the design function was located on the wrong side.

In Paris there is a reasonable balance between periproductive services and advanced industries, as there is, at their levels, in Lyon and Nantes. On the other hand the weakness of production activities in the Mediterranean regions

Table 11.10 The two cornerstones of Paris's high tech

	Employment in the Ile-de-France in 1985		Researchers* in the Ile-de-France in 1986		
	Number	Percentage of national total	Number	Percentage of national total	Percentage of researchers in the Ile-de-France
Electronics and computers	310 100	44.4	11 030	73.6	44.5
Aeronautical industries	119 400	44.6	3 980	58.9	16.1

* Full-time equivalent researchers.
Sources: GARP (Assedic) 1985 and Ministère de la recherche, La recherche-développement dans les entreprises 1988.

Table 11.11 The share of the aeronautical and electronics sectors in the financing of military research and development in 1986

	Research and development budget of which defence expenditure Million francs		Column 3	Column 4 see notes below	Column 5
				Percentages	
Aeronautical equipment	14140	5905*	63.0	42.0	5.0
Electronic equipment	14757	2786	30.0	19.0	17.0
All economic activities	71367	9422	100.0	13.0	

* Excluding subsidies to civil aviation.
Notes: Column 3: defence expenditure in sector as a percentage of total defence expenditure
Column 4: defence expenditure in sector as a percentage of research and development in the sector
Column 5: other public expenditure in sector as a percentage of research and development in the sector.
Source: Ministère de la recherche et de la technologie, Ministère de l'éducation nationale, and Conseil économique et social 1989.

downgrades the ZPIU Nice-Côte d'Azur and Marseille (even taking into account the Etang de Berre).

11.3.2 French high tech: headaches in perspective

In terms of industrial development Paris is falling back on a few very high-technology strongholds. Its specialisation is very narrow. In electronics, for example, Paris alone remains the main location for the four most advanced of the twelve segments of the filière: defence electronics, medical electronics, construction, and computer services (Beckouche 1988 and Veltz 1986). Even employment in the 'T2' sectors is in decline, while employment in the 'T1' sectors, which held up for a long time, has started to decrease. What remains of industry in Paris owes much to the military–industrial complex centred around the aeronautical and electronics industries. It is important to realise that at present 60 per cent of the researchers in industrial enterprises in the Paris region work in these two sectors (see Table 11.10). These two sectors are very dependent on defence expenditure (see Table 11.11 and recall that defence finances 35 per cent of national public research and development placing France behind the United States (70 per cent) and the United Kingdom (50 per cent), and well ahead of West Germany and Japan).

In the last two years the organisation of production in these two industries has started to change radically. At the root of these changes are the generalisation of international agreements, and the major external growth initiatives of large enterprises in these sectors that have occurred as defence budgets start to fall throughout the world. As long as internationalisation mainly takes the form of consortia, the Paris base can hold its ground. But from the moment mergers and the internationalisation of production undermine it, events may take a quite different turn. In difficulties French high-tech industries will then have to confront the problem of a transition from military to civil production.

Appendix A The function of design and research in the classification of occupations (Professions et catégories sociales) used in INSEE's Enquête sur la structure des emplois

INSEE Code	Occupation
Engineers and executives:	
3416 to 3417	Teachers in higher education
3422 and 3423	Researchers in public research
3435	Pharmacists
3443	Veterinarians
3820	Applied research and development engineers and technical executives in agriculture, fisheries, and forests
3821	Electrical and electronic engineers and technical executives
3822	Applied research and methods engineers and executives (mechanical engineering)
3823	Applied research, methods and control engineers and executives (building and civil engineering)
3824	Architects
3825 and 3827	Research and development engineers and executives (chemical, biological, metallurgical, materials, light industrial engineering)
3829	Other applied research engineers and executives
Technicians:	
4701	Applied research and development technicians in agriculture, fisheries, and forests
4711	Project draughtspersons (electrical and electronic engineering)
4712	Applied research draughtspersons (electrical and electronic engineering)
4714 and 4715	Research, applied research, test and installation technicians (electronic, electrical and electromechanical)
4721	Project draughtspersons (mechanical engineering)
4722	Applied research draughtspersons (mechanical engineering and boilermaking)
4723	Research, applied research, test, installation, quality control and maintenance technicians (mechanical engineering)
4731	Project draughtspersons (building and civil engineering)
4732 to 4735	Draughtspersons, surveyors, quantity surveyors (building and civil engineering)
4781	Methods assistants
4793	Laboratory technicians in public research and education

The INSEE classification does not allow a distinction to be made between research and development (codes 3825 and 3826), between methods (organisation, which can be distinguished, can be included with the function of manufacturing) and applied research (codes 3822 and 3823), and even sometimes between research and development and quality control or maintenance (code 4723). The definition of the function of design and research is therefore a wide one. Another deficiency of the classification is that the function to which computer scientists are assigned is not identified.

Source: adapted by GSP/STRATES from INSEE's *Professions et catégories sociales* used in INSEE *Enquête sur la structure des emplois.*

Appendix B The share of design and research functions in industrial employment (in percentages).

Group	Share	Examples of industries in group
High-level 'technicien' sectors (T1)	15.2	Defence electronics, pharmaceuticals, aerospace, computers . . .
'Technicien' sectors (T2)	6.4	Basic chemicals, industrial equipment, machine tools . . .
Private vehicles and vehicle equipment sectors	6.3	
Q1 sectors	5.0	Iron and steel, mechanical engineering, motor and commercial vehicles, shipbuilding . . .
Q2 sectors	2.0	Mining and materials
S1 sectors	2.4	Foundries, glass, forging, stamping, furniture . .
S2 sectors	1.1	Household equipment, textiles, shoes, food processing, toys . . .

Source: INSEE Enquête sur la structure des emplois 1985.

Appendix C Research and development by industrial sectors in 1986

Example sectors	Research and development (million francs)	Research and development as a percentage of turnover
Aircraft construction	14 140	21.0
Electronic equipment	14 757	13.3
Pharmaceuticals	60 40	11.9
Precision instruments and equipment	873	7.0
Textile industries	336	1.4
Agricultural and food processing industries	889	0.7

Source: Ministère de la recherche et de la technologie 1988.

Notes

1. INSEE's Enquête sur la structure des emplois (ESE) covers industry very adequately and, significantly, covers the service sectors considered. Only public research is poorly handled. It is therefore necessary to interpret 'research' as 'research within firms' (where the firms' capital may be public or private).
2. A third considerable obstacle is the poor quality of the relations between advanced training, university research and production activities. This aspect lies outside the scope of this chapter.
3. The ESE counted, outside of agriculture, 6 240 000 jobs. The Enquête surveys establishments with more than ten employees.
4. All the data from the ESE used in this chapter relate to Zones de peuplement industriel et urbain (ZPIU).
5. In the case of technicians in design and research the proportion is 40 per cent, and in the case of engineers and executives in administration and management and in sales and marketing it is 53 per cent.
6. In the same way one reaches a new level of geographical concentration when one distinguishes between different types of enterprise: internationalised industrial groups (large French groups and the subsidiaries of foreign groups) concentrate their abstract functions (especially design and research and sales and marketing) in the Paris region to a greater extent than other types of firm (Damette 1989).
7. In advanced sectors more than one-half of the orders are generated in the Paris region.
8. Excluding the 2000 people who work for the directorate of IBM-Europe in the Pascal tower.
9. In so far as these jobs can be distinguished in these activities in which it is more difficult to make the proposed functional distinctions than in the case of industrial sectors.
10. Recall that public research is excluded. The high potential of public research in Strasbourg is therefore not taken into account. This research is however not connected with the local industrial fabric.
11. Grenoble is included in the metropolitan network as it is a part of the tripolar metropolis Lyon-Saint Etienne-Grenoble.

12 Economic change and the development of new zones for economic activities in the Paris agglomeration in the 1980s

Jacques Malézieux

From the start of the 1980s and especially towards the end of the decade the agglomeration of Paris experienced a remarkable development of new zones for economic activities. The increase in the number of sites, the extension of their area, the speed with which they were occupied, the search for modern principles of architectural style and urban design, and the desire of their developers and occupants to create a strong public impression made the phenomenon spectacular.

The zones for economic activities proposed at the moment differ from older industrial zones organised and equipped mainly to attract production functions in their traditional sense. In contrast also with the equally numerous developments which exclusively contain office buildings or which just comprise warehouses, these new developments are characterised by the multiple uses to which they can be put. The zones themselves are called centres, parks, zones of economic activities, industrial estates or, in media language, club parks, science parks, enterprise villages, and so on. The major characteristics of location, organisation, design, setting and even styles of social interaction in these zones are selected in order to attract and retain enterprises that are seen to express current changes in the productive system. These changes are reinforced in metropolitan areas and have accelerated with the recent renewal of economic growth.

The recent questioning of institutions and policies has disrupted economic development planning and spatial planning. As a result the development of these new zones has been determined largely by supply-side factors. In this chapter I shall show that the dominance of suppliers is a source of sectoral and spatial malfunctioning whose seriousness is starting to be felt.

12.1 The principles of planning: a response to changes in the regional productive system at the start of the 1980s

The principles that govern the planning of new spaces for economic activities were defined by actors who sought to respond to the demands of firms which were involved in the recomposition of the regional productive system, all of whose characteristics were affected by an active process of destructuration and restructuration, and whose needs were not met by existing or planned industrial estates of the old kind.

12.1.1 The elements of change

The major changes in the nature, structure and conditions of operation of industrial activities can be summarised as follows:

(1) A specialisation in advanced sectors and industries in which first and foremost capital and information are combined in a search for a continuous valorisation of innovations. At the same time there is a continuous reduction in the material and an increase in the intellectual side of production, especially in information technologies, due to the interconnection of computing and telecommunications, new materials and biotechnologies.
(2) A transformation in the balance of functions with a reduction in the central productive functions of manufacturing in the strict sense and a strong increase in periproductive functions. The latter include (1) upstream, research and development, design, organisation and management, (2) downstream, standards compliance, adaptation to the needs of the client, distribution, maintenance, and training, including the training of clients, and (3) at the level of production the development of a system of subcontract relations of adequate quality and capacity. The separation of functions is reinforced as a result of tertiarisation within the secondary sector itself and external development which occurs as a result of the multiplication of producer service firms.
(3) The acceleration of processes of structural transformation is reflected in the multiplication of small specialised technical units that spin off from recently created small and medium-size firms or from large national and international industrial groups that adopt strategies of setting up subsidiaries.
(4) With the development of this more and more developed division of labour, there is a considerable increase in all kinds of exchanges, communications and movements between technical units at specific locations. These movements occur at larger and larger geographical scales and necessitate the definition and implementation of constantly improved logistic solutions. Exchanges of components and technological products increase, as do in particular the circulation of people, information and capital. At the root of these developments is constant progress in the application of computers to the handling, storage, transmission and diffusion of information. Little

by little the function of distribution becomes central, while the metropolis of Paris establishes itself as a platform for global logistic functions.

12.1.2 The definition of new planning objectives

These transformations are expressed first and foremost in the development of technical units that are small in size, specialised and flexible, that employ few workers but where the average skill level is relatively high, and that require small premises, but whose operation requires important communications facilities and the projection of a strong image as a firm.

Progressively a model was established empirically. It emphasised three major elements: industrial property, location, and infrastructure and services.

12.1.2.1 Industrial property

There has been an absolute and relative decline in number and size of operations involving the construction of units that are specific to a firm and that are developed for sale to house either a complex unit carrying out several of the dynamic new functions of the productive system or a simple unit set up to perform a function meeting special requirements: a prestigious head office or management centre, warehouses with specific characteristics, laboratories with particular requirements.

Developments of this kind have given way to the construction of multi-purpose premises for letting in order to meet the constantly refined principle of supplying:

(1) premises that are divided into units ('lots') of from 200 to 5000 or 6000 square metres, that are modular and extendable, and that have different uses: workshops, stores, laboratories, white rooms, and offices with additional internal facilities especially for communication;

(2) programmes made up not of one but of several buildings constructed on demand in which either each individual construction project is identical in every respect (identical buildings, identical decor, identical organisation, etc.) or alternatively a certain diversity is sought at the same time as certain distinctive signs, types of decor or logos are repeated to aid identification of the constructor;

(3) developments with a modern appearance created through the use of refined shapes and a decor that is simple but that involves great care mainly in the materials used; and

(4) public-image-conscious developments in which a systematic attempt is made to increase the prestige of the place and its designer, of the programme and the developer, and of the buildings and the enterprises that occupy them.

12.1.2.2 The location

The locations that are selected can be defined as 'communication nodes' or, in other words, as the places that are most accessible with respect to all the networks of communication and exchange including the means of circulation of public images.

The fundamental element is nearness to a radial or orbital motorway. In clear rank order it is followed by the closeness of

(1) a rail service allowing people to travel quickly: métro, suburban lines, and especially the Réseau Express Régional (which is important for clients rather than employees),
(2) the sphere of influence of a pole of activities: the business centre at La Défense, the scientific and technical complex on the Saclay plateau, and the network trans-shipment centres at Garonor, Rungis, and so on, and
(3) an airport, especially an international one.

The renewal of the development of large zones for economic activities (of several tens or even hundreds of hectares) first affected the zones designated for these uses in the Schéma directeur d'aménagement et d'urbanisme de l'Ile de France (SDAURIF): zones for economic activities in the second or outer 'couronne' and the New Towns. Subsequently, however, it also affected the first or inner 'couronne' with increasing intensity, especially in the west, in line with the high level of office development.

12.1.2.3 Facilities and services

The more extensive and the more spatially and functionally distinct from the other elements of the urban system that a development is, the more the facilities it contains must be complete and the more attention must be paid to them. A distinction therefore arises between:

(1) a centre of activities situated in a diversified urban area in which the facilities and services are confined to somewhat superficial decor and landscape design considerations and the establishment of a restaurant or even a hotel (of which the Zone d'aménagement concerté Klèber at Colombes is an example), and
(2) a very large peripheral industrial park like Paris-Nord II in which the facilities and services include, first of all, landscape design with a modification of the relief, the creation of stretches of water, the creation of lawns and wooded areas, and the search for an integration of architectural and urban design. Secondly the progressive completion of a system of services is sought, associating the developers of restaurants, hotels, meeting rooms, a post office, banks, and so on with the project, and envisaging the addition of training centres, nurseries for new firms, various sport facilities, etc. In the third place an animation of the zone is actively sought through an association agreement with the developers of an international exhibition centre and a dynamic commercial centre with a large floor area devoted to the sale of household equipment.

In the first years of the decade the planning of new spaces for economic activities was characterised by the modesty of the commitments as much of the planners as of the developers: developments of a limited size were progressively carried out without particular fuss in the best locations identified in the structure plans/programmes that had already been approved. These developments were a response to the demands, still hesitant, of firms and were inspired by American and English examples. Demand determined supply.

12.2 The modes of planning: the supply-side logic of an industrial property development system

In the middle of the 1980s a change occurred as a result of the convergence of many factors. There was a substantial increase in the demand for properties from firms: tertiarisation, the growth of financial activities, and the internationalisation of the productive system assumed a prominent role that none could doubt. At the heart of these developments stood the role of the metropolis as the privileged and inevitable point of articulation of regional-, national-, European- and global-scale activities. The renewal of economic growth was associated with a new wave of productive investments and provided grounds for an interest in property investments.

The agglomeration was faced with an unsuspected opportunity. In opposition to the policies previously pursued, the state, the region and the municipalities encouraged the development of economic activities in the metropolis. The state did so in order to reinforce its international role, while the regional and local authorities did so in order to equilibrate its growth and development.

All of these factors favoured the development of a real filière of production whose supply of properties dominated a competitive market in which, with the intensification of competition, high status was to become the key element. This filière combined, in a single process of development, planners and their limited partners, developers whose influence became greatest, and firms able to profit from the opportunities that were created. The filière determined the modes of planning in accordance with its own interests.

12.2.1 The planners or initiators

With the implementation of the laws on administrative decentralisation (1982–3), the planners saw their numbers increase substantially and came to play a decisive role in the increase in demand and supply.

Major planning agencies like the Syndicat d'agglomération des villes nouvelles (SAN) and the Agence foncière et technique de la région Parisienne (AFTRP) continued with the implementation of the developments envisaged in the structure plan (SDAURIF).

Many local authorities got involved directly, either alone or in structures for intercommunal collaboration, or indirectly, through the medium of Sociétés d'économie mixte et d'aménagement (SEM) or other forms of delegation or association, in actions likely to aid their economic development. The intervention of municipalites was very varied, but it tended to become more general and more intensive: its scope could be remarkable especially in the planning of the spaces for activities which were developed to replace old industrial areas that had been abandoned or destabilised, or which were located on available sites whose accessibility was good.'

Public administrations themselves attempted to increase the value both of their activities and of their landholdings through the implementation of different programmes. The freight division of the Société nationale des chemins de fer (SNCF) and the Aéroport de Paris are significant examples.

The increase in the number of sites offered for development and the extension of existing ones increased competition between different parts of the agglomeration, between the inner and outer 'couronne', and between the ZACs and the industrial estates of New Towns. In the end competition occurred on the same site: near Roissy, for example, between the developments carried out by the Agence foncière et technique de la région Parisienne (AFTRP) which was a public agency whose role was to acquire and prepare land for development, the Aéroport de Paris (ADP) whose task was to manage and develop the airport, and the municipality of Tremblay les Gonesse.

To develop estates the planners enter associations with property developers who make up the heart of a rapidly growing property development system in which finance, design, implementation, marketing and management are very closely related.

12.2.2 The investors

In the market for industrial property in general, which includes offices and warehouses, there is a high rate of profit due to its rapid growth. Investment increased from FF13 billion in 1983 to FF32 billion in 1987, with a large part occurring in the Paris agglomeration. In addition the number of investors increased. Included among the investors are banks and specialised financial institutions, large French and international banking groups anxious to diversify, institutional investors (pension funds, insurance companies and mutual benefit companies) who are required to invest a part of their funds in property, and collective investment organisations. (In 1987 more than 700 institutions were investing capital they had received in portfolios that included industrial property: Société d'investissement dans le commerce et l'industrie (SICOMI), Société civile de placement immobilier (SCPI), Société d'investissement immobilier (SII), and so on.)

This exceptional supply of capital stimulated the development of products of a high quality that were expensive but that ensured a high rate of return. Investment criteria tend to lead to a constant increase in rental values which are justified by reference to the sophistication and the presentation of the facilities and services. The properties called 'high-tech' due to their high status can provide incomes as high as offices.

12.2.3 The property developers

The explosive expansion of the market led to a remarkable growth of enterprises which diversified their services. These enterprises either intervened in a very specialised way or integrated, according to the development, all the activities from finance to management. Small local developers, and large national and international (English, American and, since a short while ago, Japanese) groups, which have been involved in this niche market for a long time, or which have recently moved into it as a result of the higher rate of profit it offers compared with residential and leisure developments, compete very fiercely.

Competitive success depends on the quality of the relations with the planners, limited partners and the investors as well as on the quality of the products and services provided. An essential determinant of the latter is management skills as more than 50 per cent of the premises for economic activities are let rather than sold. Some property development companies have thus become property advisers for industrial firms offering a comprehensive service that includes the identification of their needs, of the location and of the characteristics of projects, and the financing, implementation and management of developments whose numbers and/or size are destined to increase as a result of the ever more flexible character of the production system.

This industrial property development filière in general and the filière concerned with the development of spaces for economic activities in particular have experienced a very fast rate of growth. Continued growth depends on a constant extension of the market. It becomes necessary not just to meet the needs of firms but to anticipate and even to create them. Supply shapes demand in two ways: the architectural and urban design of these developments are refined, and their technological facilities and services are constantly improved.

The rapid increase in financial costs in the whole of the agglomeration and in particular in areas of growth accentuates the speculative character of the industrial property market, and developers are pulled in the direction of increased sophistication and even of luxuriousness, if not for real at least at the level of appearances.

All the components of planning are involved. The landscaping of parks of economic activities is improved: plantations of tall trees, jets of water and waterfalls are quite common. The share of offices increases in various forms: within premises for economic activities, in specialised buildings and, in extreme cases, in a prestige building for headquarters or international management functions.

Above all the reference to technopoles or at least to high technology is generalised: premises, groups of buildings and parks become 'high tech' as a result of the decor in just the same way as buildings become intelligent as a result of improved cabling and the prospect of links with future teleports.

All the actors participate in this process in order to get a share of the excess profits of the sites that prove the most attractive: municipalities, planners, developers, and enterprises form associations in order to promote the public image which will result in the highest possible returns.

Table 12.1 Industrial properties started in 1983–87 ('000 sq. m.)

	Total	Offices	Industrial premises	Warehouses
Paris	620	400	210	10
Seine et Marne	980	260	310	410
Yvelines	960	530	220	210
Essonne	860	340	200	320
Hauts de Seine	2 490	1 900	330	260
Seine Saint Denis	1 110	450	250	410
Val de Marne	1 080	500	130	450
Val d'Oise	870	360	120	390
Total	8 970	4 740	1 770	2 460

Source: Unpublished Direction régionale de l'équipement data (Rousset-Deschamps 1988).

12.3 The sectoral and spatial consequences of the domination of the supply side

The effects on changes in the productive system are evident. The character of industrial properties and especially their cost, even if the growing practice of renting modifies their incidence, contribute to the development of peri-productive functions and the increase in tertiarisation. The quest to attract the activities that require the most skilled workers and perform the most advanced functions is accentuated. It is the large groups and in particular foreign ones that are very active in the search for the best locations between and within the different European metropolises, that are the active agents in the development of this phenomenon.

Sectoral segregation occurs: the plans for new spaces for economic activities do not envisage the establishment of small and medium-sized firms involved in traditional sectors (like metal manufacture, metal stamping, surface treatment of metals, and motor vehicle subcontract work) which have only limited financial resources for the organisation of production and work space, or whose development would pose environmental problems. Any locational change, caused by factors that are internal or external to the firm, is a source of serious problems which could accelerate either the transfer of the establishment from the centre or the inner 'couronne' to the edge of the region or its disappearance.

Geographically the influence is even clearer. The supply of spaces for economic, activities like the supply of industrial properties in general, has expanded sharply with an increase in the number of sites. It is in the inner suburbs that recent growth has been most pronounced (see Table 12.1 and Figure 12.1), as most enterprises wanted a central location and the local authorities in these areas were most active. The exceptional attractiveness of the west is confirmed, naturally, for offices but also for developments that included mixed properties and what were called high-technology properties. However this phenomenon occurred throughout the départements of the inner 'couronne'. The concentration of developments in Boulogne, Courbevoie, Nanterre, and Issy les Moulineaux increased, but communes like Pantin and

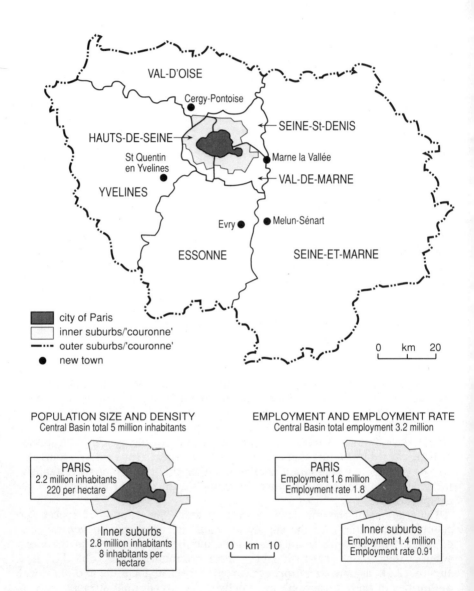

Figure 12.1 The Central Basin and the Ile-de-France region

Montreuil joined in undaunted. Colombes and Fontenay sous Bois took advantage of their potential at the intersection of the orbital A86 motorway, at present under construction, and rail networks, Clichy, Saint Ouen and Saint Denis attempted to valorise their land along the Seine, Ivry reclaimed its derelict industrial land . . .

All these developments in the inner suburbs were in competition with the estates in the outer 'couronne', whether these estates were the zones for economic activities in the New Towns or sites developed near major transport interconnections or scientific and technical centres. The increase in competition resulted in an increase in the quality of the architecture and the decor in the developments at Cergy-Saint Christophe, at Bois-Briard at Evry, at the parc aux Vignes or the Cité Descartes at Marne la Vallée, at Massy and at Paris-Nord II.

The launching of ambitious programmes like the one at Goussainville reconfirmed this phenomenon. At present the Goussainville development involves a 60-hectare site in the immediate vicinity of the airport of Roissy, with a future high-speed railway station, and teleport, with good access to the motorway to the Nord and to the Fancilienne (the Ile de France's orbital motorway at present under construction at a distance of about 20 kilometres from Paris), and with RER connections.

Conclusion

The dynamism of the development of new spaces for economic activities in the Paris agglomeration is a result not only of the demands of enterprises but above all of the convergence of the actions of local authorities and an active filière of production: the industrial properties filière. Quantitative increases and qualitative improvements in industrial properties are confirmed. But two fundamental problems arise.

The first concerns the market. An excess of supply over demand is a real threat which is starting to affect the zones which are least well endowed due to their location or their facilities which depend on their age. As the life cycle of products has a tendency to shorten, there is a risk that problems concerning the economic efficiency of numerous developments will arise more and more rapidly.

The second concerns the organisation of space. Just as in the case of office developments, the multiplication of spaces for economic activities, particularly in the inner 'couronne', results in multiple disequilibria and disrupts the functioning of an agglomeration whose organisation was conceived in a different way: there is a risk of a long-term saturation of transport networks, whose traffic capacities are traditionally too small from the moment they are designed, and of a major alteration in the economic efficiency of the agglomeration as a whole.

The announcement at the start of 1989 of a revision of the Schéma directeur de la région d'Ile de France was made too late to allow the establishment of a coherent regional plan capable of reconciling the interests of the state, the region, the départements and the communes because each of these actors had already proceeded a long way in the pursuit of individualistic strategies that correspond with their own particular interests.

13 The rise of a technological complex: some comments on the Phoenix case*

Claude Manzagol

Alongside recent changes in the face of capitalism and a major technological revolution, a new locational structure of production has started to develop. Certain older industrial regions have been recolonized, while new areas have emerged as nodes of a new configuration that has taken root. These 'technopoles' are outstanding concentrations of science-based activities. According to Castells (1985), they possess all or some of the five characteristics that the processes of production and management in high-tech manufacturing require: production of knowledge (universities and research units), an influx of public (especially defence) spending, a good business climate, the existence of venture capital, and an excellent communications network to facilitate exploitation of a hierarchical division of labour across space. However a set of locational factors is hardly a model. Nevertheless this mix has gained a magic reputation because of the Silicon Valley and Route 128 experiences which have captured the public imagination. States and countries have rushed to join the race for high-tech activities, have attempted to construct an organisational framework for development, have built science parks with university–business interfaces, and have tried to engender synergy from the juxtaposition of private firms, public agencies, and educational and research institutions.

But the development of Silicon Valley and Route 128 was related to a particular historical context, and replication of these experiences seems unlikely. There is no single prototype: if new industrial spaces share many environmental amenities, they do not follow the same path of growth. If the mechanisms of the global process can be comprehended in terms of the organisation of production and the social division of labour (Scott and Storper 1987), the diversity of technological complexes can be interpreted as the

*This research was supported by the Social Sciences and Humanities Research Council of Canada under grant number 410-88-0594.

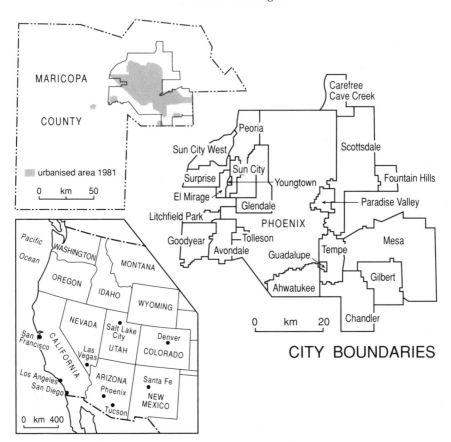

Figure 13.1 The Phoenix area

outcome of various socio-technical combinations. The Phoenix area (Maricopa County, Arizona) typifies one of these combinations of industrial organisation and labour market (Figure 13.1).

13.1 The growth pattern

A meteoric fifty-year rise brought a small regional centre to the highest echelons of the American urban system. Currently ranked nineteenth with 2 million inhabitants, metropolitan Phoenix is still climbing the urban hierarchy, and invariably appears in INC's list of the ten cities with the fastest rates of growth and job generation.

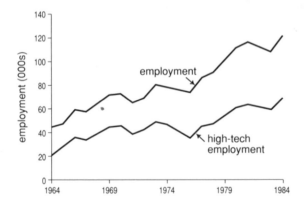

Figure 13.2 Employment in manufacturing industry in Maricopa County 1964-85

13.1.1 Humble beginnings

Until the Second World War, Phoenix's functions were restricted to the regional level: banking and wholesale trade for Arizona' economy based on the four 'Cs' (cotton, copper, cattle, and citrus fruits). A few tourists looking for striking landscapes, and people in search of a healthy climate made only a marginal impact. The Second World War brought army and air force bases (Luke, Williams, for example) as well as the first aluminum and aircraft plants in a strategic move generously funded by the federal government. The year 1949 was a turning point when Motorola's vice-president, Daniel Noble, chose Phoenix as a site for the new firm's electronics laboratory.

13.1.2 The emerging technopole

Since then, Phoenix has experienced high rates of population growth. After a fourfold increase during the 1950s, Phoenix's population grew from 1 million in 1960 to 2 million in 1988, and is expected to reach the 3-million mark before the turn of the century. This demographic expansion was the result of industrial growth. Manufacturing jobs increased tenfold in fifty years. The hard core of the manufacturing complex is the high-technology sector. This sector is defined as an aggregation of industrial categories employing high proportions of engineers, scientists and technicians (Glasmeier 1985) and is responsible for 56 per cent of 143,000 manufacturing jobs (Figure 13.2). The high-tech ratio exceeds the 16 per cent national average by far.

Five major features must be underlined:

(1) The growth process was triggered by Motorola's decision to expand its facilities in Arizona. Also, in the mid-1950s, General Electric (GE) began building computers in Phoenix, and Sperry Corporation opened an

Table 13.1 The leading high-tech firms in Maricopa County in 1987

Company	Year of establishment	Employment
Motorola Incorporated	1955	20 000
Garret Corporation	1951	8 300
Honeywell Incorporated	1979	6 000
McDonnell Douglas	1983	5 000
Sperry Corporation	1956	3 700
ITT Courrier	1969	2 500
Intel	1978	2 200
GTE	1960	1 650
Goodyear Aerospace	1941	1 500
Digital Equipment	1974	1 000
Total for 11 companies		51 850
High-tech total		75 000

aerospace factory. GE's and Sperry's assets have since changed hands, but Motorola is still the leading firm in the area with more than twenty facilities and 22,000 workers gravitating around research units and divisional headquarters (semiconductors and governmental electronics).

(2) The firms which followed these pathsetters were divisions or branches of large corporations: Honeywell, McDonnell Douglas, Digital Equipment, Intel, and so on. But they are 'technical branch plants' which, unlike standard branch plants that focus on production, are 'sites where both research and development and production are carried out' (Glasmeier 1985).

(3) Large firms play a leading role in Phoenix. The ten biggest firms account for more than 67 per cent of the 75,000 high-tech jobs (Table 13.1).

(4) Most of these firms have expanded or migrated from the Manufacturing Belt (Honeywell from Mineapolis, Genrad from Connecticut, etc.) and more recently from California (Intel from Santa Clara, McDonnell Douglas research unit from Culver, and so on). The first Japanese firm to arrive was Fujitsu, which took over from GTE.

(5) High-tech production in Maricopa County is actually concentrated on a few sectors like semiconductors, aircraft parts, communications equipment, and computers (Table 13.2).

13.1.3 A broader economic base

Despite its strength and vitality, manufacturing industry is hardly the sole engine of the region's phenomenal growth. Silicon Desert is also the Valley of the Sun attracting tourists, retired people and headquarters (Table 13.3).

(1) Approximately 200,000 'snowbirds' spend an average of four months a year in the Valley. Phoenix is also a leading conference centre.

(2) Some 250,000 retired people live in Maricopa County, especially in

Table 13.2 Manufacturing employment in Maricopa County in 1984

SIC code	Sector	Employment	Plants
20	Food and kindred production	4 660	113
22	Textiles	82	5
23	Clothing	3 409	91
24	Wood	4 103	133
25	Furniture	2 168	48
26	Paper	866	27
27	Printing	8 864	445
28	Chemicals	3 196	84
29	Coal and petroleum	222	12
30	Rubber and plastics	2 722	105
31	Leather and shoes	72	8
32	Stone, clay and glass products	4 461	124
33	Primary metals	3 858	33
34	Fabrication of metal products	5 909	262
35	Machinery except electrical	15 438	380
36	Electrical and electronic equipment	39 898	195
37	Transport equipment	10 923	78
38	Instruments	4 264	57
39	Miscellaneous manufacturing	2 192	137
		117 307	2337
35	Machinery except electrical	15 438	380
357	Office and computing machinery	8 562	34
36	Electrical and electronic equipment	39 898	195
366	Communications equipment	16 165	38
367	Electronic components	22 427	102
3674	Semiconductors and related devices	17 728	23
37	Transport equipment	10 923	78
372	Aircraft and parts	8 910	19
376	Missiles and space vehic.	980	4
38	Instruments	4 264	57
	High-tech core	70 523	710

retirement communities, such as Young Town, Sun City and the developing Sun City West. Elderly citizens are attracted by the climate, leisure-time opportunities, and the nationwide reputation of Phoenix as a hospital centre. The health sector employs 50,000 workers, of whom 1,500 work in a Scottsdale branch of the famous Mayo Clinic.

(3) The climate and a prosperous economy, as well as Phoenix's role as a communications hub, appeal to large corporations. Ramada Inns, Greyhound, America West Airlines ... established their national headquarters in the Valley, which is also the seat of many regional headquarters (Exxon, American Express, and so on).

Such a mix of compatible activities is now a classic pattern in California, Florida, Colorado, etc. Juxtaposition of various high-level activities generates agglomeration economies, increases the need for new infrastructures and spurs further growth. With 78,000 workers and 10 per cent of employment, the construction and real-estate sectors represent twice the American average.

Table 13.3 The employment structure of Maricopa County in 1984

Sector	Employment	Percentage of total
Construction	63 000	8.8
Manufacturing industry	128 000	17.9
Transport and communications	34 900	4.9
Wholesale trade	42 800	6.0
Retail trade	140 400	19.6
Finance, insurance and real estate	52 500	7.3
Services	178 000	24.9
Medical services	46 200	6.5
Legal services	6 500	0.9
Education	6 500	0.9
Social services	8 700	1.2
Non-profit organisations	8 500	1.2
Total	716 000	100.0

13.2 An original socio-technical combination

This general survey clearly shows that Silicon Desert is no Silicon Valley. It lacks its magnitude and complexity. However, the pace and nature of the growth of this technological complex are significant. Silicon Desert's geographical interest does not lie in anecdotes about its development or in its peculiarities, but in its capacity to cast light on the logic of the development of new growth centers.

The major shift in the structure of the space-economy is a clear sign that the Fordist mass-production model is no longer hegemonic. A new model, whose three pillars are a new industrial paradigm, regime of accumulation and mode of regulation, is now emerging. But its status is not quite clear and has to be defined. New industrial spaces vary in form and content. In order to comprehend the spatial logic of new industrial spaces, Scott and Storper (1987) have suggested focusing on industrial organisation and labour markets. In Orange County, Scott (1987) described a developmental logic based on a vertical disintegration of production conceived as a mode of optimisation of economic transactions in a segmented labour market. One can assume that different interdependent combinations of industrial organisation and labour market are associated with different types of industrial spaces. Maricopa County features one of them.

13.2.1 Labour market characteristics

The area's labour market characteristics can be summarised as follows:

13.2.1.1 Market dynamics

Maricopa County gained 60,000 residents in 1987, 40 per cent by natural increase. There were 34,000 net migrants, and a very substantial turnover of

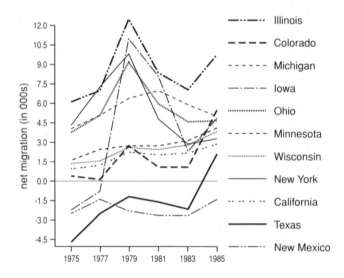

Figure 13.3 Arizona's net migration 1975-85

Source: Morrisson Institute.

people (134,000 inmigrants and 96,000 outmigrants). Maricopa County has a large net population gain primarily due to large-scale migration from the Northeast and the Midwest (Figure 13.3). Between 1975 and 1980, Arizona suffered net outmigration to California and Texas, but the trend has now reversed. Abundant jobs combined with a moderate cost of living, which is 25 per cent less than in San Francisco, result in very competitive wages and salaries and advantageous labour costs.

13.2.1.2 A flexible labour market

Arizona is a right-to-work state. Unions are practically absent from the manufacturing sector. An absence of unions is a major component of what American firms call 'a good business climate', while the level and structure of taxes are significant further contributors. Workers consider lay-offs and recalls routine events. That kind of employment relation gives firms the kind of flexibility they are looking for.

13.2.1.3 A moderate segmentation of the labour market

Because of weak unionisation, the labour market is not deeply fragmented. Moreover, minorities do not play a major role in manufacturing as they do in California. Blacks make up 2 per cent of the population. Hispanics account for 10 per cent, but are less numerous in the manufacturing sector. Women however, represent 38 per cent of the workforce.

13.2.1.4 Education and research

The percentage of people who have a college education provides a crude but significant measure of skills. Phoenix's rate (19.7 per cent) is well under Austin's (28 per cent), Raleigh-Durham's (26.6 per cent) and Santa Clara's (26.2 per cent), but it is in the same class as Dallas (20.4 per cent) and San Diego (20.9 per cent), and it is far ahead of New York (17.9 per cent) or Cleveland (15.9 per cent). As in the case of Orange County, the university was not an initial factor of growth: Arizona State University's (ASU) increasing role did not precede the rise of the technological complex, but followed it. In terms of the size of its student population ASU is the sixth biggest university in the United States. But its role at graduate studies' level is far from brilliant. Motorola's first manager in Phoenix, Daniel Noble, played a prominent part in the creation of the College for Engineering and Applied Sciences and the Centre for Engineering Excellence which still cannot match the firms' demand. More than 12,000 managers and engineers were transferred to Phoenix by their own companies in 1987. To a certain extent, its geographical location protects Phoenix from the extreme turbulence which characterises Silicon Valley's labour market.

13.2.2 Features of Phoenix's industrial organisation

In the beginning, Phoenix and Orange County were dominated by large firms. But there has been a major divergence in the development of these two areas: in Phoenix large firms have remained prominent because of their market-oriented production and the way they exploit the labour market.

13.2.2.1 Market-oriented production

Motorola started its research facility in 1949. But car radio transistors made its first plant, built in 1955, a big success. After the Phoenix laboratory mastered integrated circuit technology, Motorola became a world leader in research into and production of semiconductors, selling its silicon devices on the world market. The same strategy prevailed when microprocessors appeared. Motorola sells its 68000 series to Apple and Radio Shack among other companies. In order to maintain its leading position, Motorola manufactures a broad range of proprietary chips and custom products, but commodity memory chips, supplied in large volumes, form the bulk of its output. Mass production of standardised products made extensive use of an international division of labour and the location of the more labour intensive operations in developing countries feasible. Chip design and wafer manufacture occur in Phoenix. Assembly and testing take place in plants located in Seoul, Kuala Lumpur and Guadalajara. As Glasmeier (1985) put it, 'the product largely determines the type and scale of linkages'. Mass production and a weak segmentation of the local labour market led to a socio-technical combination which is very different from Orange County's or Silicon Valley's, where many small-batch producers can be found. There are very few subcontractors in Maricopa County. For instance, Motorola manufactures its own printed circuit boards. Vertical disintegration did not occur, while the reagglomeration of the production process with the establishment in 1985 of the fully automated Chandler assembly plant confirmed Motorola's neo-Taylorist orientation.

Phoenix Intel followed the same path. Its automotive product division was transferred to Chandler in 1980. There, controllers are manufactured. Controllers are used particularly in anti-locking brake systems. The EPROM manufactured by Intel is programmed by the car-maker itself. It is a mass-production item which does not require proximity and constant links with customers (Ford, Nissan, Bosch, etc.).

13.2.2.2 National subcontracting networks

Computer and communications equipment production is also dominated by large firms, like Honeywell and Motorola, that privilege their own supply network. The local multiplier effect is rather limited. The same pattern prevails in the military sector: avionics with McDonnell-Douglas and Garrett, communications equipment and guidance devices for missiles and satellites, and so on. Motorola's Governmental Electronics division employs over 8000 workers. This military sector provides at least 30 per cent of high-tech jobs. Contracts are granted to national consortia in which Phoenix firms are partners. Because of the scale of these markets, suppliers and customers are from out of state. Arizona's Economic Security Department found that local manufacturers buy less than 15 per cent of their supplies within Arizona.

13.2.2.3 Small is not beautiful

The weakness of industrial linkages can be seen from the spectrum of firm sizes. Vertical disintegration which was described by Scott in Orange County produced a rapid decrease of the average size of plants and a swarming of small and medium-size plants. In Phoenix, eleven firms account for 72 per cent of high-tech jobs, and firms with less than 100 workers are few in number. Moreover, because of the absence of unions, large firms had no incentive to subcontract work to low-wage secondary labour market firms, as they did in California where segmented labour markets prevailed.

13.2.2.4 The lack of spin-offs

Very few spin-off ventures stemmed from large firms or university research laboratories. Market-oriented production and consolidated purchasing practices provided very few niche markets. The character and scale of defence production did not favour local upstream and downstream relations. Large Phoenix firms adopted a rather conservative approach and did not encourage either 'intrapreneurship' or spin-offs. It was not until 1972 that Motorola created a 'new venture' program, and it was not very fruitful. Until recently, Arizona State University did not reach the quality threshold beyond which numerous 'acorns' can be expected. During the first years of existence of ASU's research park attempts were made to attract prestigious firms and there were some successes with the establishment of ICI and VLSI Technology. Venture capital for start-ups is, however, scarce in a valley flowing with money. Arizona's banks are used to dealing with farmers and mining companies and are not well prepared to cope with the uncertain prospects of new microelectronics start-ups. Besides, high and quick returns from real estate attract investors. Land speculation is booming. Real-estate transactions amounted to $10 billion in 1987, and the Japanese are now active participants in this market ($1.8 billion).

The intertwining of a certain type of industrial organisation with the local labour market sets up a developmental logic and a model of spatial organisation which are very like what Leborgne and Lipietz (1988 and Chapter 2) called 'spatially disintegrated vertical near-integration'. This socio-technical combination is of a neo-Taylorist sort and outperforms the Fordist model because of its flexibility.

13.3 Options for the future

At this point the question arises as to whether or not such a model of development has its own limitations. In the context of global competition, a sustained wave of growth is not enough. Technopoles must constantly improve the qualitative content of their growth in order to maintain their leadership, and this improvement means more research and development. Yet Phoenix recently failed to attract two major research laboratories. In 1984, Microelectronics and Computer Technology Corporation — a consortium of 12 large firms set up to work on a fifth-generation computer — rejected Phoenix's offer and located in Austin. Phoenix was also rebuked in its bid to lure the Semiconductor Manufacturing Technology Corporation (Sematech) — another consortium devoted to new chip-making processes — which also chose Austin. Both research groups were backed by federal funding and each brought with them approximately 1000 high-level scientists. While the causes of this double failure are multiple and complex, it nevertheless seems that the city image and the quality of the environment, as well as Phoenix's poor capacity for collective action, played the major part. Phoenix's growth received a strong impetus from frontier values which are now a handicap for the blossoming of the technopole.

13.3.1 Frontier values

The frontier was a fading reality at the end of the last century, but the myth lived on. Wild life and adventure are now minor dimensions of the myth, but the West remains the land where the American dream seems within reach: a land full of opportunities and a *laissez-faire* context, where determined individuals believe they can be duly rewarded for their efforts. For many people, it is a return to fundamental capitalist values. These values please the business community and Phoenix always gets high marks from business consultant firms like Grant and Fantus. But these persisting values also create a type of city and urban society which could be far less positive for further development.

13.3.2 A disorganised urban structure

City growth went along with stunning land consumption. The metropolitan area occupies over 4000 square kilometres. Because of the generalised leap-frogging process, 60 per cent of the metropolitain territory (and 56 per cent of the land inside Phoenix) is still empty. The two main hotels and the convention centre in the city centre tower over vacant lots and derelict buildings. The real CBD with offices and fashionable shopping malls was built two miles north of the centre.

Developers imposed their own rules, by planning their development projects and leaving the community with the burden of infrastructure provision. In 1986, they succeeded in preventing the adoption of a bill making the use of recycled water for artificial lakes compulsory.

Deep concern for the environment is new to Arizona. For decades, toxic wastes from manufacturing plants like Motorola's have polluted ground water. The Rio Salado's dry bed has become a dump that will be very expensive to clean up. The enormous use of private cars on an ever extending road network coupled with the limited importance and efficiency of public transport cause worrying air pollution.

13.3.3 The weakness of public investment and facilities

Even though expenditure on social services is partially funded by the federal government, it is lower than in any other large American city ($563 per capita). Cultural spending is ridiculously low ($8 per capita), and philanthropic foundations are non-existent in the area: 'first generation wealth is selfish wealth'. The number of golf links (111 in the Valley) cannot compensate for the low quality of education at the primary and secondary levels. First-rate education is a major concern of managers and scientists. But reforms either were not undertaken or failed because of inadequate funding. Local government revenues depend heavily on sales taxes, and in Arizona property transactions, which are considerable, are paradoxically tax-free. Local businessmen are not keen to lure newcomers with public money. Besides, Arizona's constitution practically forbids state authorities from giving incentives such as interest-free loans, capital grants, tax concessions, etc. It is easy to understand why Austin's proposals were more appealing to Sematech: Austin University offered facilities in its research park, and the city of Austin contributed $62 million.

13.3.4 A fragmented society

Meteoric growth created a highly mobile and rootless society. Approximately one-third of the adults in Phoenix have lived there for less than five years, and more than 50 per cent of tenants move every year. Phoenix is to a large extent a 'city of strangers'. The lack of networks and structures of socialisation is reflected in high rates of divorce, suicide, alcoholism and crime. The metropolis and its neighbourhoods have a weak identity: for a majority of people, the city is mainly a residential development with its fence, its pool, its security guard and magnetic card; mental maps are hazy. The absence of mediators like unions add to the fragmentation. Low interest in public issues is demonstrated by the apathy of voters.

13.3.5 In search of consensus

While the mosaic-like structure of local government, the 'shattered mirror', is the rule in urban America, the proliferation of local entities adds to the general disorganization of a rapidly growing and sprawling metropolis like Maricopa County. Cities such as Mesa and Chandler have existed for decades as independent entities and resent being overshadowed by the central city. Periodically, Mesa demands its own county and the East Valley Partnership is a sign, among others, of these centrifugal forces. There is no consensus between the different cities on major issues such as land use, transport, environment, and growth policy. The Maricopa Association of Governments makes wise assessments and proposals, but has no power to implement them. Special interest groups like the Group of 40 can therefore exert a hidden but decisive influence.

Phoenix's failure to attract the two major research consortia helped to sensitise people to the necessity of a global strategy. The need for a strong image, a clear purpose and vigorous leadership are now perceived as indispensable conditions for Phoenix to acquire a sharper edge in the competition among technopoles. A first step in this direction was the 1985 referendum on tax increases for the upgrading of the transport network. Organisations such as the Phoenix Economic Growth Corporation and the Phoenix Community Alliance have undertaken the task of vigorously promoting the city's interests. Finally, the improvement of the urban environment is under way with the implementation of an 'urban village' concept.

13.4 Conclusion

The Phoenix metropolitan area is a technopole searching for maturity. Like most growing technological complexes in America, Phoenix differs significantly from its European counterparts in four ways:

(1) a faster rate of growth,
(2) a closer spatial association between research and development and maufacturing activities,
(3) a lesser involvement of public authorities in subsidising and planning the development of the technopole, and
(4) a spontaneous and somewhat erratic process of urban development.

Among new technological complexes, Phoenix shows a distinctive growth pattern. Because of its socio-technical combination, Phoenix has a developmental logic very near what Leborgne and Lipietz called spatially disintegrated vertical near-integration. Further research must focus on how this particular kind of territorial complex is linked to complexes based on different socio-technical combinations involving, for example, vertically disintegrated and network production.

14 Cities in transformation: the case of West Germany

Stefan Krätke

Many urban researchers proceed from the assumption that we are at present in a phase of social 'transformation' in which urban systems are split up into differing developmental types and regional inequality assumes new forms. In this chapter I shall critically portray some recent contributions to political-economic urban research (the 'regulation' and 'global city' approaches) and I shall sketch out the spatial restructuring processes at work in the West German urban system.

In the current phase of social development, there is an intensification of spatial restructuring processes which may initiate a transformation in regional and urban development: amongst other things there is a shift in the centres of industry and growth on a world scale and also a differentiation of types of urban development in highly developed capitalist countries. Centres that in the past were foci of industrial production, economic growth and relatively stable employment are characterised by disinvestment and industrial decline ('deindustrialisation'). The cities affected are confronted with continuously high unemployment rates, declining populations and abandoned industrial areas. At the same time other urban regions profit from a spatially selective concentration of investment and growth. Some privileged urban regions develop into central locations for high-tech production. The emergence of producer services and the further expansion and increasing independence of the finance capital sector contribute to a 'revival' and to the prosperity of large-city business centres. These developments culminate in the establishment of 'high-tech centres' and 'global cities'. In parallel with these general tendencies, a process of spatial restructuring is taking place which is accompanied by new manifestations of spatial inequality: the increasing internationalisation and flexibilisation of production and capital valorisation and further advances in the functional fragmentation of large capitalist concerns lead to an increase in the spatial mobility of capital and a high degree of flexibility in the choice of location. Tied to these developments is the selective concentration of investment and growth in a few privileged areas. What results is a polarisation of urban development, the 'deindustrialisation' of previously prosperous industrial regions, and the rise of 'peripheral' regions as new centres of production growth. The increased mobility of capital and the impending 'devaluation' of existing industrial centres leads to an intensification of competition amongst localities. In conjunction with the increased market orientation and deregulation of governmental control mechanisms, competition between cities makes local politics more capitalistic and flexible in character, so that local politics makes a decisive contribution to the promotion and implementation of the new production and consumption models of contemporary capitalism. Thus tendencies towards a polarisation and hierarchisation of consumption patterns in society as a whole can be especially effective at the local level. A pronounced polarisation of the labour market and a heterogenisation of social–spatial reproduction conditions take place above all in 'high-tech centres' and 'global cities'. The establishment of new consumption models, mediated through spatial reorganisation processes (such as gentrification, or the structural-aesthetic revaluation of urban areas and the construction of new consumption and cultural centres) is being pushed forward especially in these large cities and is supported by new regulatory forms for planning policy. The increasing small-scale segregation processes in the capitalist city correspond with the tendency towards an increasing heterogenisation of social structures and a fragmentation of social life contexts. The connection between social and spatial restructuring processes can thus be shown at many points.

In the face of these radical contemporary changes in the development of capitalist societies, theoretical approaches to spatial restructuring have aroused great interest, as the development of regional and urban areas plays an active role in processes of social reorganisation. However, one cannot rule out the possibility of a temporal disparity between spatial and economic and social restructuring: it is possible that only a part or only some elements of ascertainable tendencies in the transformation of regional and urban structures are determined by contemporary processes of socioeconomic reorganisation in capitalist societies; these tendencies may also be in part an expression of long-term spatial development processes. This possible temporal disparity between spatial restructuring processes and those in a society as a whole should be kept in mind when analysing current developments.

There is a unanimous view that capitalist societies are in a historic phase of radical change. There is, however, no unified framework of reference and no unified set of criteria to distinguish between different historical phases or formations of capitalist social development, although many of the more recent contributions are more or less explicitly based on the so-called 'regulation approach'.

14.1 Spatial restructuring processes in a phase of social transformation

The most sweeping hypothesis concerning the connection between the social formation and the spatial structure is that each historical formation of capitalism simultaneously creates its own regional structure (Esser and Hirsch 1987). The relative rigidity of existing spatial structures and the fact that existing spatial centres can outlive particular social formations preclude this result, as is shown in many contributions to the history of locational and spatial development in West Germany (von Borries 1969). The relative rigidity of spatial structures arises from spatial impediments to mobility and the inflexibility of physical facilities, as well as from the continued attractiveness of established spatial centres.

Moulaert and Swyngedouw assume that each historical accumulation regime corresponds with a specific pattern of spatial organisation and that the current restructuring process can be understood as a way of using spatial rearrangements to overcome the 'crisis of the Fordist formation' (Moulaert and Swyngedouw 1987). The emerging 'flexible accumulation regime' also opens up new regions as potential production areas. All in all, the 'flexible production system' and its method of regulation reproduce interregional inequalities or spatial disparities, though in a new and more complex manner. According to Moulaert and Swyngedouw, the formation of spatial complexes (clusters) of high-tech factories, frequently in areas without an industrial tradition, is one of the main new tendencies of spatial development. The regions and cities in a process of decline and the 'older' industries that are closed down are associated with the 'old' (Fordist) accumulation regime, while 'space is created' for new socioeconomic, technological and industrial structures in newly developed or rehabilitated areas. The traditional urban hierarchy is also being transformed through the growth of flexible production complexes: smaller and more remote (peripheral) cities, which hardly had an industrial base up to now, are able to attract a substantial part of the new growth potential.

14.2 New spatial centres of growth: 'high-tech centres' and flexible production complexes

According to Moulaert and Swyngedouw, the restructuring of urban production areas corresponds to changes in industrial organisation. The efforts of companies to achieve increased flexibility tends to favour the 'vertical disintegration' of production organisation (Moulaert and Swyngedouw 1987; Leborgne and Lipietz 1988). In contrast to the (Fordist) organisational model of 'vertical integration', in which the entire production process is organised by one large concern, 'vertical disintegration' means that the 'main' concern only controls the end products and the key technologies. Activities without strategic importance and component production are organised as a 'subcontracting system'. High-tech production complexes in particular are structured as a network of formally independent companies and are generally made up of a few dominant main firms and many more-or-less dependent suppliers and subcontractors. 'Vertical disintegration', however, requires close relations ('quasi-integration') between the customer and the subcontractor, and an efficient, rapid and continual exchange of information. As a result the organisation of flexible production systems requires spatial proximity and furthers agglomeration in high-tech production centres (Scott 1988a).

Although the establishment of new production structures is based on the use of new technologies (such as CAM and CIM systems), new production concepts and management strategies are much more significant for forming a 'flexible accumulation regime' than the use of new technologies. It is for this reason that it would be misleading to speak of the emergence of 'high-tech capitalism'. New production concepts and management strategies are being implemented across industries. Included in these concepts are (1) 'world-wide sourcing', which involves the transnational organisation of supply linkages and certain production processes (especially for standardisable components and parts), (2) the flexibilisation and deregulation of work and employment relations, and (3) the introduction of the 'just-in-time' principle for making supply interconnections more flexible in the context of new models of industrial organisation involving an expanded system of subcontractors. The new production concepts and management strategies are found both in classic 'Fordist' industries like automobile production (as, for example, in the 'world car' concept) and in typical high-tech industries like computer production. While 'world-wide sourcing' furthers the emergence of specialised production areas and thus tends to promote a territorial disintegration of production, the 'just-in-time' principle acts as a stimulus to the territorial integration of production processes in new flexible production complexes (Leborgne and Lipietz 1988). Thus the spatial effects of the implementation of new production concepts cannot be clearly determined, especially in the framework of national or regional economic areas.

The introduction of new production concepts in classical 'Fordist' industries, for example, need hardly be apparent in the old 'Fordist' industrial agglomerations, as it frequently only creates new production areas overseas. The global achievement of a flexible accumulation regime can thus mean that no flexible production units emerge in old industrial agglomerations. Instead traditional (rigid) Fordist production organisation and technology are retained, and a flexibilisation and deregulation of wage labour relations takes place (Hudson 1989). In this case the establishment of a post-Fordist accumulation regime means, above all, an increase in the flexibility of capital. A post-Fordist model can encompass the maintenance of 'Fordist' production forms in selected economic spaces as well as the the reorganisation of production in the form of flexible systems. New production concepts and management strategies can involve both a progressive Taylorisation of space, in the sense of marked inter- and intra-regional specialisation (Leborgne and Lipietz 1988b), which does not represent a genuine 'post-Fordist' tendency for spatial development, as well as the formation of new territorially integrated production systems.

The emergence of new 'flexible production complexes' is likewise not limited to high-tech industries, but is perhaps most visible in these sectors. The spatial effects or the patterns of site distribution for flexible production systems cannot, however, be clearly determined: these production forms can be integrated into the traditional locational structure as well as create new areas for production. Moulaert and Swyngedouw point out that high-tech industries are frequently concentrated near large urban areas or in the peripheries of agglomeration centres. Scott, on the other hand, emphasises the strong agglomeration effects which large urban labour markets exert on the leading sectors of flexible production. These agglomeration advantages stem from the fact that the possibilities for a 'flexibilisation' of the use of workers also increase with the size of a local labour market: the new production models make use in particular of part-time employment and 'precarious' employment relations as well as of 'marginalised' (and generally non-union) workers and especially of foreign workers and women (Scott 1988). Thus new flexible production complexes have been established in very different types of area. These locations include (1) the peripheries or suburban expansion areas of existing metropolitan regions (where one primarily finds high-tech industries), (2) the gravitational field of existing office and business centres within the cities (where one mainly finds companies in high-tech production and process development and the new 'service sectors' made up of highly developed producer services), (3) previously undeveloped peripheral areas (where one primarily discovers high-tech industries as in the case of new 'technocentres' or industrial districts like California's 'Silicon Valley'), and (4) traditional regions which had been characterised by craft industries (where one mainly finds 'design-intensive' production). In the last two cases, flexible production is able to generate new production centres, which could develop into stable 'poles of growth' by means of self-intensifying agglomeration effects. It was above all in the United States (as in the case of the so-called 'sun belt') that the formation of new areas for industrial production outside of established urban regions emerged. In the first two cases, however, the new flexible production complexes remain clearly within the existing 'Fordist' spatial structures. Site selection for these high-tech and new service industries which establish themselves within existing urban regions is based on the attraction of existing urban centres and the agglomeration effects already in force there. 'High-tech centres' arise when the potential for new growth — in the form of flexible production complexes (for product and process development and the production of new technologies) — is concentrated, in a spatially selective way, in particular existing urban regions. The hypothesis that new spaces for industrial production appear at the same time as a new accumulation regime emerges, because modern flexible production systems tend to avoid the old spatial centres of the accumulation process, will have to refer less to intra-national than to intra-regional spatial structures and will have to involve a more differentiated analysis: 'new areas for industrial production' frequently emerge as enclaves within older industrial regions. Among these enclaves one can find both 'revitalised' inner-city production districts, in which flexible production complexes settle, and suburban production districts of cities in which new high-tech industrial complexes are established.

The importance of flexible production systems or complexes for the development of the locational structure of West Germany can be illustrated using the example of 'high-tech industries'. In the course of this account, it must be kept in mind that the corporations dealing in information and communications technologies only represent a particular (but possibly 'driving') force in the creation of flexible production systems and in the introduction (which cuts across industries) of new production concepts. The locational development of high-tech industries has only a limited importance for the restructuring of the spatial structure as a whole. The heterogeneity of the industries that make up this sector should also be noted: it encompasses the production of customised and standardised semiconductor devices, 'assembly firms' which make products from finished components, the producers of software, and firms whose 'product' is chiefly production-related services (as in the case of specific programming work).

In West Germany, the main tendency seems to be the selective incorporation of the potential for high-tech growth into existing centres for industrial sites (like the urban regions of Munich and Hamburg) instead of the formation of new high-tech complexes in peripheral regions. The spatial distribution of companies involved in information and communications technologies, which would have to function as the catalysts and crystalisation centres for the establishment of high-tech production structures, shows

a clearly unequal distribution between the western and eastern parts of the Federal Republic: whereas along the course of the Rhine from Düsseldorf to Freiburg (including the areas around Frankfurt/Rhine-Main and Stuttgart) the number of companies is almost continuously high, in the eastern parts of the country 'islands' (Hamburg, Hannover, Munich) predominate. These 'islands' are an expression of a much stronger concentration of company establishments in few locations. The concentration in Bavaria is very apparent. In addition to a large number of concerns in Munich and some of its surrounding districts, smaller concentrations are found in the Nuremberg area and in the cities of Augsburg, Coburg and Würzburg . . . Similar concentrations in a few districts can be noted in Lower Saxony (Hannover and its surroundings) and Hesse (Frankfurt and its surrounding districts). The course of the Rhine, and above all the districts around Düsseldorf and Cologne, form the focus in North Rhine-Westphalia . . . Baden-Württemberg did have three focal points (Stuttgart, Karlsruhe, and Villingen-Schwenningen), but there are also information technology companies in countless rural districts. This distribution appears to be a peculiarity of Baden-Württemberg, as it breaks off directly on the Bavarian border. (Grabow and Henckel 1986, p. 2 ff.)

New production areas in the sense of high-tech production locations in 'peripheral' regions have apparently developed in Baden-Württemberg: high-tech production is scattered over the entire state. This distribution of sites corresponds with the traditional production structures found in Baden-Württemberg where there are many specialised small and medium-size companies. These production structures appear to resemble those found in the areas of 'flexible specialisation' in the 'Third Italy'.

In West Germany, the companies in information and communications technologies are concentrated to a high degree in large urban centres: in 1986, 75 per cent of all main locations of these concerns were found in 'administratively independent cities with more than 100,000 inhabitants and the very densely populated districts surrounding large urban areas' (see Figure 14.1).

Within the urban regions there is a 'decentralised' distribution of locations:

The highest concentrations of firms, measured in terms of the number of employees in a district or an administratively independent city, are not in the central cities, but in the areas that surround large urban centres, such as, for example, the administrative districts around Munich and Starnberg and the areas surrounding Frankfurt. (Grabow and Henckel 1986, p. 3)

Munich is the undisputed leader in the number of high-tech companies; in 1986

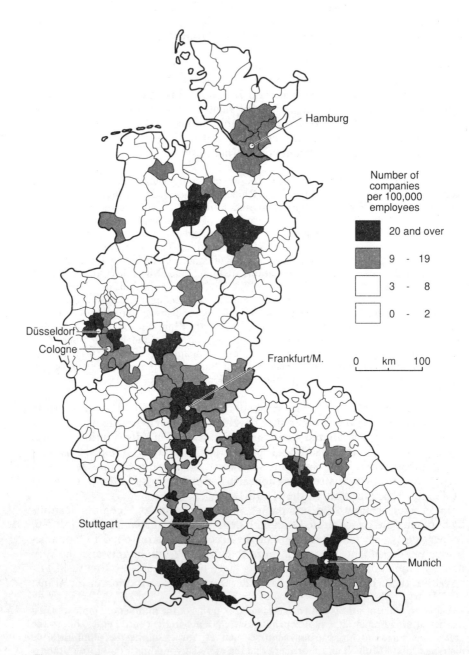

Figure 14.1 Regional distribution of high-tech information-technology companies in 1986

the cities after Munich were, in order, Hamburg, Frankfurt, Düsseldorf, Hannover, Berlin, Stuttgart and Cologne (Grabow and Henkel 1986). The general concentration of high-tech companies in large agglomeration areas, their core cities and densely populated surrounding districts indicates, according to Henckel and Nopper (1985), that the increasing degree of freedom in site selection connected with the use of modern information technology has primarily been exercised in favour of urban areas, so that high-tech production acts spatially as a 'trend intensifier' reinforcing a continuous long-term suburbanisation process.

The long-term tendencies in the development of regional employment structures in West Germany can be described on the one hand as an incessant suburbanisation process within urban areas, and on the other hand as a process of restructuring between existing agglomerations. In the restructuring between agglomerations the Ruhr region has proved to be the big loser: it is the region with the largest decline in the share of employees. All northern agglomerations were confronted with job loss, above all after 1976. The 'winners' in the restructuring process were all, when seen geographically, south of the line formed by the River Main. In particular the agglomerations of Munich, Stuttgart, and Frankfurt-Rhine-Main increased their share of employment.

The spatial restructuring processes in West Germany appear to consist, therefore, of interregional shifts in position and intra-regional redistributions within a relatively stable spatial structure of location centres. Modifications in the urban hierarchy are above all indicative of the effects of an irregular distribution of high-tech growth potentials between the large urban agglomerations which already had prominent positions in the urban hierarchy.

With industrialisation, regional growth centres shifted within the existing urban system as a result of long-term changes in sectoral structure and the establishment of new leading sectors and growth industries:

The Ruhr region, for example, received its characteristic shape in the spatial interaction of coal deposits, mine locations, and iron and steel works, and the essential features of its regional structure have not changed significantly since the beginning of the 20th century. After the Second World War, growth was determined by the expansion of processing industries, and specialised capital goods industries in particular. With their expansion urban areas like Stuttgart, Munich and Nuremberg grew . . . The former leading sectors, mining (energy) and iron and steel production, on the other hand, had to concede leadership to different industries in other regions. What resulted was therefore a process of economic stagnation in the Ruhr Region and in Saarland, which were both first generation urban areas. (Gatzweiler 1985, pp. 221 ff.)

Although the shift in the focal points of regional growth is determined primarily by sectoral restructuring processes, the growth-related regional 'north–south gap' was not due primarily to location-specific factors. The south profited rather from relocations of companies (like AEG and Siemens) necessitated by the war and a methodical, government-regulated resettling of armaments complexes and high-tech companies, which are among the most rapidly growing 'leading sectors' today. The raw-material-based and heavy industries (coal, steel and shipbuilding) and also, in recent years, the sectors producing standardised consumption goods (such as household appliances and simple consumer electronic products), where the market is increasingly saturated or there are competing products from 'low-wage' countries, have been among the 'shrinking sectors'. The contemporary foundations of (export-oriented) West German industrial production are vehicle production, the electrical industry, machine building, and the chemical industry (Sinz 1984), that is, industries of the 'Fordist' age. The actual growth sectors of West German industry are at present (1) high-tech products, (2) 'precision products' exhibiting a high degree of engineering work, long testing phases, and a large amount of maintenance, and (3) 'special production', in which machines, apparatuses, complete production installations or technological infrastructures are produced in response to special orders or in small series (Sinz 1984). The current tendency for a large part of high-tech production to be established in the southern part of the Federal Republic can be explained by the suction effect of the high-tech industry which is already there ('Munichon Valley' effect) (Heuer 1985).

14.3 'Global cities': cities as command centres for internationalised production and capital valorisation

The 'global city' concept represents an approach which avoids overvaluing the production function of cities: this theoretical aproach proceeds from the assumption that a very close relationship exists between the world-wide network of capitalist companies and the world-wide network of cities. The cities should be seen as the 'primary geographical centres' of a transnationally organised capitalist economy (Feagin and Smith 1987). The global city concept emphasises the existence of a functional hierarchy of cities in the framework of the capitalist world economy and recognises the supralocal functions of cities as a basis for the establishment and modification of the urban hierarchy. The most important large cities are those with high-ranking, transnational command functions, that is, the places where the world-wide network of capitalist companies finds its 'physical' spatial anchoring points (Smith and Feagin 1987). According to this view, restructuring processes in the urban hierarchy can be explained by changes in the international division of labour. What is new about the current international division of labour is the fact that it is no longer characterised by capitalist companies with 'national identities' which engage in world-wide trade in their products. The determinants of the contemporary international division of labour are corporations which are organised transnationally, which operate in countless countries at the same time, and which, in so far as they have a world-wide network of their own company departments at their disposal, frequently realise their world-wide transactions within their own organisations.

The 'global city' concept traces the hierarchisation of the (world-wide) urban system back to the unequal distribution of (supralocal) command functions over production and capital valorisation processes (Smith and Feagin 1987): the rank order of cities is in the end constituted by the distribution of the headquarters of the 500–1000 largest multinational corporations, as the command centres of multinationals have decisive 'multiplier effects' on the urban economies in which they are located.

The intra-national site distribution of the head offices of the largest industrial corporations located in West Germany has been investigated by Bade (1983) and Nuhn and Sinz (1988). Almost 80 per cent of the 500 largest companies in West Germany had already located their headquarters in one of the eleven agglomerations; and the larger the company, the more likely it was for its headquarters to be located in one of the five central agglomerations (Hamburg, Rhine-Ruhr (Düsseldorf and Essen), Rhine-Main (Frankfurt), Stuttgart, and Munich) (Bade 1983). There is therefore a very high degree of centralisation of the management and control functions of industrial capital. According to Bade, however, 'the frequently assumed type of spatial division of labour — with headquarters in and production plants outside of urban areas — appears not to be accurate as most of the plants of large corporations can also be found in urban areas' (Bade 1983, p. 315). The locational concentration in agglomeration areas has intensified in the course of time. The degree of spatial centralisation of corporate headquarters in a few 'headquarters cities' differs from one country to another: in West Germany, for example, in contrast to Great Britain and France,

the headquarters functions are spatially distributed more widely. In 1982, the 5 most important locations — Hamburg, Frankfurt, Düsseldorf, Munich, and Essen — contained 189 main administrations. This figure corresponded to 38 per cent of the firms included in the analysis ... For the London and Paris areas, on the other hand, concentrations between 65 and 85 per cent were found . . . The hierarchy of locations, with reference to headquarters' functions, has remained relatively constant in the last three decades. (Nuhn and Sinz 1988)

The urban hierarchy is certainly not just determined by the distribution of the headquarters of the largest industrial corporations. Command functions in the capitalist world economy are exerted by international banks and the entire 'finance capital sector'. Influential decisions are made by banks just as much as by large industrial corporations. (Indeed the concept of 'finance capital' encompasses the close interconnection of these two areas). Other command functions are carried out by increasingly internationalised 'commercial capital' organisations (Thrift 1987), which act as intermediaries in the global circulation of money and commodity capital. Organisations concerned with currency exchange and futures markets for commodities, increasingly international real-estate functions (especially in the area of large office complexes), the supplying of loans and dealing in company shares, insurance and first-rate corporate services are all included in this group. According to Thrift, most of the large urban financial centres were still primarily oriented towards their respective national markets until the end of the 1960s. The exceptions were London, New York and Paris, which had long been established as international financial centres. Since the beginning of the 1970s, one can note an increasing internationalisation of commercial capital's transactions and of organisational forms in the entire finance capital sector. This development has led to the establishment of a world-wide network of international financial centres, in which most of the larger companies maintain offices, and thus to further advances in the internationalisation of the use of capital. Since the 1970s, therefore, a world-wide hierarchy of urban financial centres has formed, whose operations have become largely independent of their respective national economic contexts.

A hierarchisation of the urban system implies the dominance of some cities over others. The forms of dominance are multi-dimensional: dominance can be structurally and infrastructurally reinforced where a city forms a centre of a trade, transport and communications network (as in the case of Paris), it can also appear as social and cultural dominance when a city becomes the leading centre of cultural 'innovations', and it can appear as dominance over complexes of production and financial activities. The dominance of a city over capital valorisation processes in other cities is scarcely visible, and can only be symbolically demonstrated in a few cases through the size and layout of the office blocks constructed for leading companies. It is, however, the decisive form taken by the hierarchisation of the urban system in capitalist societies. There are other forms of urban 'hierarchies' which do not signify dominance, like the ranking of cities according to their population and employment.

The possibilities of dominance over capital valorisation processes is dependent on the structure of a city's corporate sector: the city which can attract a concentration of enough financial power and headquarters of important corporations so that the decisions of these urban administration centres can determine the decline or prosperity of the corporate sector of other cities is accorded a position of power and leadership. For this domination to exist, a coordinated 'exercise of power' is not required.

The dominance relation between cities is not only dependent on the number of finance centres and corporate headquarters concentrated in the city, but primarily on their actual administrative and control capacities. It is for this reason that it is not just the progressive concentration of financial centres and corporate headquarters in selected cities that is intensifying the hierarchisation of the urban system in the current phase of social transformation. What is more important is the centralisation of capital, and the observed increase in corporate buy-outs and takeovers (Hickel 1988). The centralisation of capital accelerates when more and more corporate buy-outs take the place of tangible investments in new productive activities. According to Zinn, the (world-wide) process of centralisation of capital represents the continuation of a very long-term trend, but, due to the specific political-economic circumstances that have developed in the 1970s and 1980s, there has been an acceleration in the rate of centralisation and the old 'law' of capital centralisation has assumed qualitatively new characteristics. In particular with deregulation, including more relaxed anti-trust laws, the opportunities for using 'superfluous' money capital to buy up companies have increased (Zinn 1989). Logan and Molotch used the example of the United States to show that the hierarchy of US cities finds its counterpart in a largely similar ranking of corporate buy-outs (Logan and Molotch 1987). The 'headquarters cities' are also the seats of the companies which are buying up the greatest number of other companies. Corporate buy-outs have become elements of investment strategies that are purely financial. (It is this financial aspect that gives the centralisation process new qualitative features.) In some cases these investments are made with the intention of squeezing the acquired company dry as quickly as possible, and using the inflated short-term profits that result as a means of selling it again at a profit. Despite their partially destructive consequences, corporate buy-outs consolidate and strengthen the 'dominance' of existing urban control centres because the leading banks and large corporations, which appear as the purchasers of smaller companies, are concentrated in these cities. The acquisitions themselves are arranged and mediated by producer service industries. The growth of these service industries in dominant cities can thus be regarded as the formation of an increasingly large and more differentiated apparatus for expanding economic control over other cities (Logan and Molotch 1987).

As centres of capital valorisation, value production, and the acquisition of the value produced in more or less far removed production sites, large cities play two major roles. On the one hand large cities are the 'primary' spatial units within which economic and social restructuring occurs. On the other the development of central city management, finance and service functions determines the development of their regions and interregional differences in economic growth.

What is more, the hypothesis of a deregionalisation of the urban hierarchy can be supported on the basis of the 'global city' concept: the rank and economic potential of a capitalist city are based less and less on its function as a central location for the surrounding region, and more and more on its transregional command functions. The centres of the capitalist urban system are spatially anchored command centres for the control of production and valorisation processes which increasingly are organised and structured transnationally. In the course of the internationalisation of capital valorisation processes, the development of such cities is more than ever before determined by decisions which are made in other distant cities. For cities like London or Frankfurt, their relations and competition with cities like New York and Tokyo are much more important than their relations with their surrounding regions or national territories (Mayer 1988a).

The establishment of 'global cities' which further a deregionalisation of the urban system is sometimes interpreted as a consequence of an advancing functional differentiation within the service sector and the selective locational distribution of different service functions (Sassen-Koob 1984; Brake 1988). In this argument a distinction is made between 'direct producer' services, which include above all product and process development services, and 'indirect producer' services, which mainly comprise finance, marketing and management consultancy. The location of direct producer services is dependent on the spatial distribution of the 'users' of new products and processes, and hence above all of centres of high-tech production. On this basis the high-tech centre is constituted as an urban developmental type, represented in West Germany, for example, by Stuttgart and Munich. On the other hand, indirect producer services depend very little on locational links with a particular regional production structure. They depend instead on transregional or international business connections and capital flows. Their locational concerns are with the centrality of a place within the world-wide network of finance, control and competitive relationships and their location follows the agglomeration advantages offered by existing urban financial and command centres. These considerations result in the identification of an urban developmental type referred to as a 'global city'. 'Global cities' can be characterised as locational centres for national and international economic activities which develop independently of their immediate local and regional environments. The prosperity and decline of local production activities is largely irrelevant for these centres for finance capital, headquarters of high-ranking corporations and specialised services. In the global city, the local area is primarily used as a 'space reserve' for the expansion of office and business centres and for gentrification projects. The best West-German examples of this urban developmental type are Frankfurt-on-Main and Hamburg.

As early as 1970, Lefebvre (1970, p. 212) presented the theory that the share of surplus-value created and realised by industry would decrease, whereas the share realised in the finance sector, in speculation and in the real-estate sector would grow. This 'secondary circuit of capital' would increasingly 'outstrip' the primary circuit and, at the same time, initiate an 'urban revolution' (a far-reaching restructuring of spatial relations). This broad version of the theory of a 'secondary circuit of capital' is much more meaningful for the current development of capitalist societies — where the increasing independence of the monetary sector and the separation of the financial sphere from the real production sphere are at the centre of attention — than Harvey's more limited version (Harvey 1985), which refers primarily to the construction sector. At the level of international economic relations, the establishment of 'floating exchange rates' in the early 1970s brought about an explosive growth in financial transactions, permanently increased the mobility of money capital between investment spheres, and set off a considerable expansion of the world money market (Hübner 1988). Since the late 1970s the world money market has become an independent sphere for the valorisation of money capital. An 'uncoupling of the monetary from real spheres of the world economy' (Hübner 1988) has developed. According to Hübner, the enormous increase in the importance of this 'secondary circuit of capital' made up of international financial investments and transactions can be considered a result of a secular overaccumulation crisis in developed capitalist countries: 'The growth of the world money market since the 1970s can be interpreted . . . as a reflex of the build-up in the real economic accumulation process of excess liquidity, which, in the prevailing conditions of valorisation, is not productively invested' (Hübner 1988, p. 58).

With the independence of the world money market, there has been a structural increase in interest payments in relation to the surplus value fund. The real production sector has adjusted itself to these valorisation structures in that a relatively large share of the profits attained are used to finance investments, and interest payments make up an ever larger share of the cash flow. The consequence of this transformation of capitalist valorisation structures is a modest development of accumulation and growth and the persistence of a stagnation spiral. (Hübner 1988, p. 62)

The fact that the independence of the sphere of valorisation of money capital develops with the direct participation of the real productive sector can be described with the help of the formula which identifies an 'uncoupling of production from capital valorisation'.

A structural change in accumulation strategy has frequently been shown for the corporate sector in the Federal Republic (Welzk 1987; Hickel 1988). The trend is for the share of profits used for capital investment to go down, and a clear restructuring of the sources of corporate wealth in favour of financial investments can be detected.

[Today] large German companies invest much more capital on the money markets than they get themselves. In 1974, the corporate capital of industrial joint-stock companies reached one-third of their debt burden. In 1984, on the other hand, this money capital was already some 60 per cent more than their total loans and bond issues . . . The extreme case of money hoarding is offered by the House of Siemens . . . The money market investments of this one industrial corporation are more than half as large again as the combined capital, including reserves, of all of the big German banks. The firm has long been jokingly referred to as a banking house with an affiliated electronics department. It does seem absurd when an electronics firm . . . builds up a larger interest surplus than the Dresdener Bank AG. (Welzk 1986, pp. 82 and 85)

The tangible fixed assets of the West German industrial joint-stock companies was 16 per cent higher in 1984 than in 1973, yet in the same period their financial investments grew by some 84 per cent (Welzk 1986). In addition to the growing capital investments of industrial corporations on foreign and domestic finance markets 'it can be shown that the process of capital formation is being detached from the place of industrial production' (Hickel 1988, p. 72), and that similarly directed transformation processes are taking place in the corporate sector, as larger concerns are splitting up production and finance into legally independent corporate divisions.

The increasing importance of the finance capital sphere (and command centres) of large corporations will, from the viewpoint of spatial restructuring tendencies, increase the influence of the financial and command functions in large cities over urban economies and spatial organisation — with possibly devastating consequences for spatial structures within the cities. Overall the formation of 'global cities' makes clear how the 'uncoupling of production and capital valorisation' that is accompanying general restructuring processes in capitalist economic relations is receiving a concrete spatial manifestation in the urban system. The increasing independence of finance capital valorisation mechanisms and financial investments from 'real' production activities corresponds at the level of the urban system with the spatially selective formation of international financial and administrative centres, which are increasingly independent of the production relations of the traditional urban economy.

14.4 The change in urban hierarchies and spatial structures as processes of heterogenisation and polarisation

Because the directions of spatial restructuring are contradictory and cannot be clearly determined, one is led to a subtly differentiated conclusion: the central element of the 'new' economic geography is made up of many of the old

'Fordist' urban centres together with some new areas specialising in high-tech production and accompanying producer services; many traditional industrial regions are also included in the 'post-Fordist' division of labour. A new flexible accumulation regime would reproduce the old 'Fordist' spatial division of labour and the existing urban hierarchy, and on this basis would develop a more differentiated and more strongly accentuated hierarchy of centre–periphery relationships (Moulaert and Swyngedouw 1987, p. 27). The position of Esser and Hirsch (1987), that the economic and social restructuring processes involved in the transformation to a 'post-Fordist' model of capitalist social development are connected with significant 'spatial heterogenisation processes', points in the same direction. Established urban financial and administrative centres (still) prosper within the framework of the urban hierarchy, whereas in many traditional industrial cities stagnation and decline are setting in. In the process there is a polarisation between cities characterised by different types of development and a further accentuation of urban hierarchies.

If a polarisation between cities and urban regions represents the main tendency of current spatial development, spatial analyses should go beyond the traditional centre–periphery perspective, because

with respect to these relations a new development has emerged since the transformation in the world economy in the mid-1970s: the disparity between urbanised and peripheral areas is being eclipsed by an increasingly clear inequality in the development of the centres themselves. In the period from 1976 to 1983, when total employment in the West German economy increased by 1 per cent, not all agglomerations took part in this growth: the urban areas south of the line formed by the River Main (Rhine-Main, Rhine-Neckar, Karlsruhe, Stuttgart, Munich and Nuremberg) had above average increases in jobs, whereas the agglomerations lying north of the Main (Bremen, Hamburg, Hannover, and the Ruhr region as well as the areas along the Rhine north of Cologne) showed employment losses. This drifting apart of the agglomerations is the new feature of current spatial development in the Federal Republic (Häußermann and Siebel 1988, p. 79ff.)

With spatial disparities in employment, the unemployment rates in the large cities of the Federal Republic also drifted apart between 1980 and 1986: the range of unemployment rates almost tripled in this period. In 1986, the highest unemployment rates were found in the cities of the Ruhr region, Cologne, Bremen, Hamburg, and Hannover, and the lowest in Stuttgart, Munich and Frankfurt (Autzen and Becker 1988).

Spatial differences in employment change are the main indicators that urban researchers in the Federal Republic use to demonstrate polarisation processes between cities or urban regions. However, emphasising employment figures is not appropriate for an analysis of the 're-hierarchisation' of the urban system: if the capitalist city is increasingly becoming a place where command functions are concentrated and capital valorisation processes are spatially centralised, and if the urban system is being differentiated and split up on these very lines (among others), then an individual city can secure and retain a 'high rank' in the urban hierarchy even with relatively large employment losses. (The city of Hamburg is a good example of this constellation.) The capitalist city prospers in line with its economic power judged by the standards of capital valorisation, value production and value appropriation, and in these areas employment growth is of secondary importance. The reason why is, as I pointed out in the last section, that there is an increasing uncoupling of capital accumulation and 'productive' investments as well as of the development of investments and employment. For example, many cities in West Germany are confronted not only with the loss of jobs in production activities, but also with the stagnation of employment or even job losses in banks, insurance companies and commercial organisations (Sinz 1984). In no way, however, did these developments mean that the economic importance, value production and value appropriation of the corporations in this city had fallen. Declining employment figures are consistent with increased prosperity measured in terms of valorisation for the corporate actors involved in urban development processes. Corporate administrations, banks and insurance companies could, for example, invest to meet a pent-up demand for new office space. However, the erection in large cities of palatial new offices for the companies which are the main contributors to the loss of jobs in the production and service areas makes the drifting apart of capital investment and employment especially obvious.

A polarised development of the 'economic power' of cities or urban regions can be demonstrated with the help of a regional breakdown of West Germany's national product. The 'gross national product' of a city or region is considered to be the central monetary indicator of its economic potential. Estimates for 1974 and 1984 of the gross national product (GNP) of 75 environmental planning regions in West Germany clearly show a polarisation of the economic potential of urban regions (see Figures 14.2 and 14.3). Between 1974 and 1984, the differences in the economic power of urban regions increased: in terms of the deviations of their per capita gross national product from the national average, the majority of these regions moved closer together, while the urban regions with values which were considerably above average distanced themselves further from the 'rest'. In the same 1974–84 period the range of values in West German urban regions more than doubled.

However, the data on per capita gross national product for the West German regions do not indicate a uniform 'North–South gap': in 1984, nine of the twenty (urban) regions with the largest absolute levels of national product per head (measured in DM per capita) were located north of the line formed by the River Main (see Figure 14.3). Among these were several regions which in employment terms were in a process of decline. The development of the economic power of urban regions like Hamburg, Cologne, Bochum and Essen does not correspond at all to the development of their employment situation. In addition to Frankfurt and Munich, Hamburg and Düsseldorf are also among the urban regions with the highest absolute economic power. Most of the urban regions with an 'average' per capita national product lie south of the Main line (Stuttgart, Nuremberg, Ingolstadt, Karlsruhe, Mannheim, and Ludwigshafen). Between 1974 and 1984, several regions with below-average economic power improved their relative positions, but without attaining an economic potential comparable to that of the leading large cities. Many cities lying outside the traditional urban agglomerations are found in this group (such as Augsburg, Freiburg, Osnabrück, and Oldenburg).

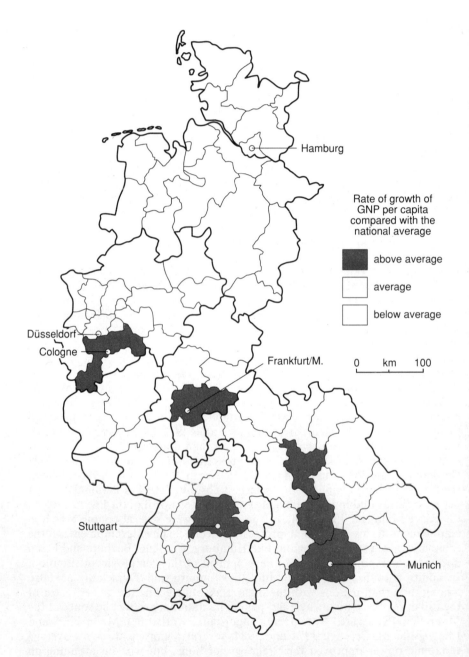

Figure 14.2 Economic growth of West German urban regions, 1974-84

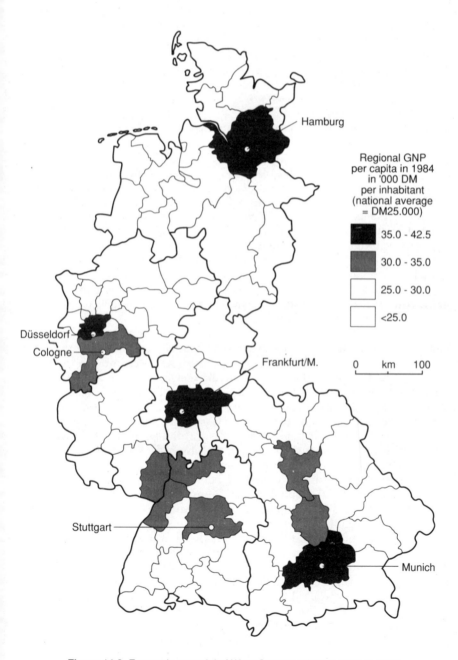

Figure 14.3 Economic potential of West German urban regions in 1984

A 'North–South gap' appears when one considers the growth rather than the level of development of the different regions (see Figure 14.2). In 1974 there were ten regions north of the Main line and ten south of it with above-average per capita national products. In 1974–84 the position of all the regions in the North except Cologne worsened, with six dropping below the national average, while the position of southern regions improved.

The processes of heterogenisation or polarisation of the spatial structure (Esser and Hirsch 1987) are also reproduced within the cities: among the intra-urban restructuring processes are the upgrading and 'cultural revival' of the inner cities, as well as the structural renewal, economic revitalisation and 'gentrification' of living quarters near the city. These zones are tailored above all to the needs of the highly qualified workers of the (expanding) urban 'management centres' and 'industries of the future'. At the same time, a polarisation of social space develops between inner-city zones of high-tech activities, financial power, exclusive consumption and cultural centres and those spatial zones which function as survival spaces or reservations for impoverished and socially marginalised groups and for ethnic minorities. In the opinion of committed urban researchers, the heterogenisation of urban spatial structures is leading to the development of a multiply divided city: within each city there are internal divisions into a 'nationally and internatio-nally competitive city of the integrated and wealthy and a city of the marginalised and poor' (Häußermann and Siebel 1987).

The current processes of urban socio-spatial heterogenisation should be understood as modifications of pre-existing spatial hierarchies and functional differentiations within cities. What are decisive, however, are not the spatial divisions and functional differentiations themselves so much as their histori-cally specific manifestations in the current phase of capitalist social develop-ment. Among the latter are (1) the duplication of socio-spatial differentiations and the increase in small-scale segregation processes in the capitalist city (Krätke and Schmoll 1987; Marcuse 1989), (2) the increasing polarisation of those employed in the urban economy (Sassen-Koob 1984), and (3) the intensive gentrification of residential quarters within the city, the re-establish-ment of spaces for consumption and the reappropriation of the inner city as a place of residence for the 'ruling classes' of modern capitalist societies.

Processes of spatial and employment polarisation go hand in hand with one another: the expanding finance and command functions in the city, and high-tech complexes and the specialised services that go with them, not only attract highly qualified workers but also create an expanded field for the exploitation of low-paid labour (Sassen-Koob 1984). Thus in West German cities 'low-level' producer services (like office cleaning and messenger services) are expanding, as are services for privileged and affluent city workers. As a result there is an expansion of insecure, flexible and low-paid jobs.

The intensification of gentrification processes — mediated by intensified competition among cities to attract 'higher' classes of consumers and workers — is a very important feature of current spatial restructuring processes in the large and 'global cities' that are prospering. Indeed processes of land use change and increases in the standards of urban 'residential functions' are as (if not more) important than changes in the use of residential dwellings near the city to meet the expanding space requirements of banks, company headquarters and producer services. These forms of urban restructuring are a consequence and elements of far-reaching socioeconomic transformation processes (Smith 1987), which also create 'new areas for consumption'. The creation of new areas for changed and re-hierarchised consumption patterns is part of the establishment of a new accumulation regime, and is by no means limited to rebuilding residences.

In the course of urban spatial development, the more extensive functional differentiation of the 'Fordist' city structure is superseded or reshaped by smaller-scale differentiations (Krätke and Schmoll 1987). The reason why is, for example, that gentrification processes are spatially selective: in other words, they do not involve all of the residential areas near the inner city. Socioeconomic heterogenisation processes as a whole result in an increase in small-scale segregation within the cities. The developing urban structures can be best characterised as a 'quartered city' (Marcuse 1989) with socio-spatial differentiations that are increasingly accentuated and numerous.

Within cities, processes of spatial restructuring are mediated through real-estate valorisation and land-rent mechanisms, so that a hierarchisation of the urban system must also be expressed in a polarised development of urban property markets and land-rent potentials. The existence and extent of this hierarchisation can be empirically investigated by determining whether and to what extent there have been increases in land-rent and land-use differences between cities.

In the case of office and business uses, the land-rent difference between cities in the North and South of West Germany diminished between 1971 and 1988, while the difference between large cities (with more than 500 000 inhabitants) and 'smaller' cities (with 100 000 to 500 000 inhabitants) grew considerably. If the land-rent level for these uses is an indicator for the prosperity of urban office and business centres, then one can conclude that the largest cities in West Germany have further improved their position as economic command and control centres independently of their regional situation. In the case of rented housing, on the other hand, the land-rent differences between cities in the North and South have clearly increased, with the cities in the South clearly showing higher land rents, while the differences between cities of different sizes have remained approximately the same. A clear increase in the North–South difference in the price of sites for owner occupation can also be noted.

A 're-hierarchisation' of the urban system in West Germany can, in fact, be observed when the rank order of ten of the largest cities is compared using the criteria of the land rent level for different types of urban land use (see Figure 14.4). In the diagrams the order of the bars corresponds with the rank order of the cities in 1988. The more the 1971 profile deviates from that for 1988, the more pronounced were the shifts in rank for the land use concerned.

In the current phase of social development there is not only a re-hierarchisation but also a heterogenisation of the West German urban system. A heterogenisation of the urban property market can be proved when the deviations in the land price levels between cities grow. In 1971–88 such a heterogenisation of urban property markets emerged for the best locations for office and business uses. In the case of rented housing land there was a levelling

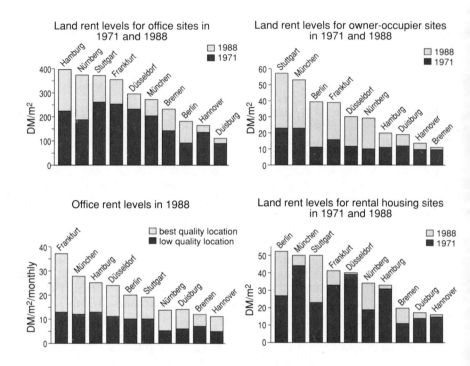

Figure 14.4 West German urban hierarchy

of urban land-price differences. A marked heterogenisation appears in the property market for owner-occupied homes and industrial uses: the land-price deviations between cities increased considerably after 1971. Absolute changes in land price deviations and increases in the heterogeneity of the urban system were most pronounced in the case of the central office and business uses, which house the economic, financial, command and control functions.

The internationalisation of capital and the 'de-regionalisation' of the capitalist city have increased the differences between cities and, in the process, led to a rise in the rent yield of the entire urban system. At the present time the ground-rent levels in a city are determined less by local site differences or the prosperity of local firms and economic relations in the region. Instead there is a growing dependence of cities on firms operating at a supra-regional level, large multinational companies and finance institutions. At the same time, there is a growing dependence on other cities (in far-away regions) which house the command and control centres of the leading companies. Under these conditions, the urban ground-rent level is to a large extent no longer based on local differences (within the urban area and the surrounding region), but is determined at a supra-regional or international level: large international corporations, for example, have a much greater ability to pay rent than those companies which only operate on the local or regional level, and can therefore always 'outbid' the latter in the competition for sites whether it be for land for headquarters buildings or for manufacturing plants. The space requirements of the activities (especially the corporate headquarters) of companies whose economic power and ability to pay rent are determined at the supra-regional or international level increase the monopoly rent yield of the preferred cities and accentuate the hierarchisation of property markets in the entire urban system. The rent level of the 'preferred' cities can develop largely independently of the qualities of local sites. These tendencies are further reinforced by the activities of international real-estate agencies which differentiate and manipulate the monopoly prices for office complexes and business properties in central cities. With the hierarchisation of consumption models and the differentiation of 'new areas for consumption' into ever smaller elements (such as exclusive shopping areas and islands of gentrification), monopolistic price differentials in urban property markets can, furthermore, be actively created. The reason why is that the 'prestige' or symbolic meaning of the space these uses occupy is of great importance. High-prestige islands can be created in the city through strategies of architectural renovation and active marketing which give rise to monopoly rents that are out of all proportion to the material locational advantages of a piece of land.

14.5 Closing observations

The development of spatial structures and urban hierarchies is determined by diverse factors and contradictory processes so that no clear statements about 'the' spatial patterns of a new 'flexible accumulation regime' can be made. Spatial development is, on the one hand, still characterised by 'Fordist' principles: further functional fragmentation within large capitalist corporations can be regarded as an intensification of Fordist organisational forms (Massey 1984), as can the accentuation of the spatial separation of production and management functions. The 'Taylorisation of space' that results was already highly developed under the conditions of a Fordist accumulation regime, while the flexible use of different sites is no new phenomenon. The possibilities for increased freedom in choice of location have given the locational diversification of corporate investments a transnational dimension. At the same time, the shift of standardisable production functions to 'peripheral' locations, which was already common in the Fordist accumulation regime, and the concentration of financial, command and control functions as well as producer services in metropolitan centres are continuing further.

This basic pattern of spatial development, which has long been decisive and continues to be effective in the current phase of transformation, is supplemented by new elements: the increasing internationalisation of the entire finance capital sector is leading to the formation of an expanded hierarchy of urban financial centres with interconnected global corporate sectors whose business activities and transactions are becoming more and more independent of their respective national economic contexts. The introduction of new production concepts founded on new technologies and more flexible organisational relations results in 'new' agglomeration effects, as the interconnected firms tend to create spatially concentrated production complexes. To the extent that new flexible production complexes are established in previously 'peripheral' cities and regions, new spatial growth centres of production can arise and modify the traditional locational structure.

The trend towards a pronounced functional spatial division of labour and locational differentiation continues and increases the growth of business and office centres in a few privileged cities. The pronounced polarisation between urban developmental types and the re-hierarchisation of the urban system connected with it can be seen as the most significant change in the direction of spatial development in the current phase of social transformation. Underlying them is the current increase in the mobility of capital which leads to a de-regionalisation of the urban system and supports the spatially selective concentration of growth potentials. This change in direction creates and strengthens new forms of socio-spatial inequality, above all in cities that are prospering. The development of the city into an internationally competitive centre of finance and corporate headquarters and a consumer and cultural centre for the dominant classes of modern capitalist societies which culminates in the development of 'high-tech centres' and 'global cities' has two consequences. The first is a pronounced polarisation of the labour market, which also occurs within urban office and business centres, with the increase in highly paid skilled and management employees and the simultaneous expansion of low-paid, flexible and insecure employment relations. The second is the polarisation and heterogenisation of the socio-spatial structure of the capitalist city through intensified gentrification processes in residential areas and an increase in small-scale differentiated segregation processes. The actual working out of these spatial restructuring processes is furthered not least by competition between cities which the mobility of capital, increased by the flexibilisation and internationalisation of production and valorisation processes, serves to increase. At the same time socioeconomic reorganisation processes in cities are reinforced by the switch from 'redistributive' to 'entrepreneurial' urban policies (Mayer 1987). In these ways the capitalist city emerges as the geographical focus of global processes of social restructuring.

Part Six: Conclusion and further directions

15 New industrial spaces: realities, theories and doctrines

Paul Claval

15.1 A Long-neglected field

15.1.1 Location? A problem that businessmen cannot isolate from their other practices

The Western World was industrialised in the nineteenth century without the location of these new activities giving rise to any systematic thought on the part of the theorists who were trying to understand the society of the period, or of the men who originally introduced these revolutionary methods of production. One is struck by the lack of any explanation offered by the geography or economics textbooks of that time: the cotton industry thrived in Lancashire, in Normandy or in the Vosges as these were humid regions where the thread was less brittle! (The role of hygrometry as a location factor for the cotton industry was still mentioned in Prévot 1979.) To what can one ascribe these worrying pseudo-explanations? To what the industrialists said themselves. Location was not, for them, a real problem in the sense that it did not appear to be separate or separable from a whole series of other considerations: costs and prices, available workforce, and warehousing and distribution facilities. They did not reason in terms of geometry. They integrated themselves into the social and economic fabric, gained from it, manipulated it, and changed it. The geographical dimension never seemed to be an element separable from other factors to be considered.

The situation has not changed substantially: it is still difficult to get businessmen to talk about their preferred locations and the reasons for their choice. As in the past, they are unable to abstract them from the global context they are used to considering (Luttrell 1962). When they do, what they identify depends on the local factors that favour their company. In a nineteenth-century perspective, the individual who succeeded did so thanks to his ability to draw on what the environment originally had to offer: hence the importance given to natural resources, mostly coal and minerals, and, where these factors were not relevant, to the specificities of climate, the pureness of the water, or the working population's attitude to work.

The intellectual climate is different today. Businessmen know that success crowns the efforts of the enterprising. When asked to speak of their locations, they think of what gain, in the development of new products, is to be had from innovative social milieux. They remain incapable of synthesising the totality of the processes which dictated, or dictate their decisions, and of picking out their spatial components.

15.1.2 The lack of curiosity of politicians

Industrial growth was hailed as a godsend by most political leaders in the great age of liberalism. The state did all in its power to promote it : it created a legal framework for limited companies, speeded up the development of financial and monetary markets, protected patents, and helped companies to fulfil their potential by setting up a favourable fiscal system. But the state did not allow itself to intervene directly in the organisation of space, other than by instigating or encouraging the setting up of transport and communications infrastructures that are indispensable to business.

Politicians did not therefore concern themselves with why activities were set up in one place rather than another: they were happy, when they were a mayor or member of parliament, with anything which enriched their voters, but they were not interested in taking charge of processes which were beyond their control. Some were more open to discussion with businessmen than others, and took more notice of their suggestions. Thus they learned how better to organise the milieux where manfacturing was carried out, or where decisions were taken.

For the politician, the idea that industrial success stemmed from the natural aptitudes of a country was firmly entrenched: it justified the place that the country (or a town, county or region) had taken in the division of labour, and avoided asking questions about its rationality or its social consequences. That a country should have no coal was regrettable of course, but it was not the politicians' fault, and they could not be held responsible for the inequalities that resulted. The argument for specialisation in those activities for which one was naturally more gifted was fine for those in power. They did nothing to change these attitudes.

15.1.3 A discontinued theoretical effort

One can understand, within such a context, the slow pace of theoretical reflection on industrial location. The economists reasoned in terms of cost. Essentially they reduced the problem of optimal industrial location to that of determining the point at which transport costs were minimised: when the other components of cost, and labour costs in particular, do not vary, it is there that highest profits are to be made. From Launhardt to Alfred Weber, one can see the development of this line of reasoning.

Alfred Marshall (1890) was a theorist, but he had a sense of concrete realities: he was struck by the concentration of certain branches of industry in very specialised districts. Thus he introduced a new perspective by showing that one cannot reduce industry to one isolated company, and proposed, through the idea of external economies, a means of analysing local links formally, and including them in a spatial analysis. External economies of scale, whose role in the original formation of industrial districts he showed, meant that scant attention was paid to the availability of adequate information as a source of local advantages.

Alfred Weber (1909) drew on this idea of externalities, but without realising that it should logically lead him to supplement the analysis of transport costs with an analysis of the firm's expenditure on information: thus the basis of the classical theory of location was biased from the outset.

15.2 New intellectual preoccupations and planning concerns

15.2.1 The emergence of the need for intervention

The industrial geography of the nineteenth century and the beginning of the twentieth resulted essentially from the activities of firms and the working of markets. The state was not interested in dictating the distribution of these activities. It merely created a framework conducive to the expansion of firms. If the measures taken by the state helped to increase the economic differentiation of national space, it was not from a conscious choice or out of a desire to plan/organise space.

Some industrial regions started to get into difficulties after the First World War: the new structure of costs, linked to an increase in wages, put an end to whole sections of British industry. However, new activities developed, but elsewhere, around London and in the Midlands. Does it make sense to leave hundreds of thousands of workers in the North and the West unemployed, or to encourage them to move to the South, which already suffers from congestion? Would it not be better to attract these jobs to the depressed areas? In this manner the idea of direct state intervention in industrial location emerged in England during the 1930s. In the United States, the idea developed at the same time, but in a different context. To save the interior valleys of the Appalachian mountains from poverty, would not a more rational management of their resources be appropriate, equipping their rivers with dams to regulate the flow, and using the electricity produced as a basis for the development of industrial activities until then under-represented in Tennessee?

After the war, awareness grew of the injustices that unequal development brings. States could not remain indifferent to the misery of certain of their regions, or to the economic and demographic decline which had hit them (Gravier 1949). How does one arrive at a better distribution of activities and labour? Politicians are always searching for planning principles. When they find them, they are ready to make use of them to better the situation. Henceforth, industrial geography was not purely the result of mechanisms created on a national scale by the state. It reflected policies of active intervention, and the principles they inspired.

The British example is seductive: why not take advantage of general industrial dynamism? National economies are given a considerable boost by the propulsive force of industry. One only has to influence the choice of new locations to redesign space. Britain in the 1950s provided the two recipes for carrying out such operations: its governments showed that one can use the granting of planning permission to call a halt to expansion in regions where development is no longer necessary, and also set up systems to provide fiscal incentives and differentiated assistance in an attempt to persuade industrialists to locate their companies where regional development objectives were met. It was possible to make further improvements in the control of location in countries where credit restrictions were in force: it was the case in France.

For the last thirty-five years in most West European countries, sixty in Britain, and twenty or so in Japan, industrial location has therefore been carried out within a new framework (Gottman 1952). It was not enough, in order to understand the geography of economic activities, to be a good analyst or a good theorist of the mechanisms which affect the firm or industrial sectors. One had to understand the principles which first appealed to political movements, clarify the modalities of their implementation and measure their efficiency. Until then this aspect of the analysis of new industrial spaces had been neglected.

15.2.2 The first principles

The first systematic attempts to influence industrial location were not the result of any wish to control or influence the structure of industry. They stemmed from the desire to bring about a more equal distribution of activities. The activities which appear to be the easiest to relocate at will are those involved in the transformation of goods. Obviously it is not possible to alter the distribution of what Colin Clark called the primary sector: agriculture and mining are tied to the location of natural resources. Awareness of the specificities and criteria governing the location of tertiary activities is only just emerging. It was therefore at the level of manufacturing that one had to start. From that period onwards energy was available everywhere thanks to oil and electricity. For light manufacturing, transport costs were also limited, so that the accessibility of the market was no longer as strict a determinant of success as in the past. It was on this body of ideas that the regional development policies of the 1950s were founded.

However, the dangers of sprinkling investments around did not escape anyone. There was a risk that a disordered multiplication of sites would result in a loss of the benefits of the multiplier effects so necessary to the long-term success of any interventionist policy. The accepted principles therefore considered the action of the state as temporary: it was just a question of taking corrective measures. Once the new healthy spatial structures they had helped to create were in place, the state would no longer be needed. The play of market forces would once again be sufficient.

15.2.3 The quest for efficient principles and advances in theory

By the end of the 1950s, the desire to construct more coherent national and regional development policies led to theoretical reflection and quite often to further theoretical advances. In France, the new trends were born of a need for rigorous proof of an image, that of the pole. Two leads were investigated simultaneously. The first highlighted the role played by larger urban areas, metropolises, and sought to use the multiplier effects they allowed to create a more balanced regional structure: hence the idea of the counter-balancing metropolises or 'métropoles d'équilibre' (Hautreux and Rochefort 1965). Is it a real theory? No, it is more a principle relying on a doubtful interpretation of the theory of central places.

The second trend is linked to industrial structures. In the company of François Perroux (1955, pp. 142–4 and 1961) one willingly stresses the role of the large firm as the propulsive force of polarisation. Do we not often see a whole swarm of subcontractors develop around dynamic companies? Is this not how some of the major industrial centres of the nineteenth century were born?

Progress in regional analysis helped to understand the mechanics of these induction effects, but also pointed out their limits. There are areas where increasing the number of companies within the same sector does not intensify their interaction: in the south-east of France, chemical factories buy and sell practically nothing from or to other regional establishments (Cartalas 1970). As for the propulsive firm, there are cases where they actually impoverish the industrial structure instead of enriching it, as is shown, for example, by Goetz-Girey (1960) for the Belfort-Montbéliard region. These refutations do not prevent the theory of a polarised expansion induced by a powerful propulsive firm from going a long way: the operations in Annaba in Algeria or Fos in France were conceived in the name of industries whose development creates other industries.

In these cases, theoretical thought went alongside, rather than stimulated, the formulation of principles.

15.2.4 The emergence of Marxist themes

For liberal economists and for most regional planners of the 1950s and 1960s, the interest shown in industry was not based on the idea that this sector constituted the heart of the modern economic process. Agriculture or services were analysed with the same care. If they were not used to carry out the development policies identified at the time, it was simply that one was not sure what strategies they allowed. As soon as the idea became apparent that the location of office activities was as flexible as that of industry, new ways of promoting the expansion of outlying areas and their towns were thought up. This change occurred between 1965 and 1970.

The Marxists, who were very active on the intellectual scene throughout this period, thought differently: industry was for them the cornerstone of modern society. The tertiary sector was considered a necessary evil to which the liberal economies had attached an undeserved importance.

For the Marxists, therefore, working on society, transforming it, and developing it, relied upon an understanding of the mechanisms at work in the industrial world, and implied their control. The means at their disposal for analysing the industrial tissue of a country were unfortunately far from perfect. They were fascinated by the composition of capital of these firms, and of the mergers which periodically took place (George, Guglielmo, Kayser and Lacoste 1964). Throughout the 1950s and 1960s, they did not contribute much to the understanding of the spatial organisation of industrial activities within national economies: they published regional monographs which were not substantially different from those produced by researchers inspired by liberalism. In the field of industrial relations between nations, they played a more important role: they were the first to understand the significance of new industrial investments in the Third World.

15.2.5 Little-used empirical analyses

Throughout this period, geographers and historians readily worked on industrial problems. Thanks to regional studies, or to monographs on firms or sectors of industry prepared by one or other of them, it became possible to follow the formation of the industrial districts (see, for example, Perrin 1938) which economists from Marshall onwards had pointed out, but without analysing them in any detail.

Dynamic industrial areas often mushroomed in regions which had experienced considerable pre-industrial development. They were found in areas where in the past workshops were scattered over the countryside, around centres where 'manufacturers' organised the work, bought the raw materials and marketed the finished articles. Other districts emerged during the Industrial Revolution. In a context where transport was still costly, knowledge about other places was limited and technical know-how was hard to transmit — it was preferable to use on-the-spot suppliers to meet one's needs rather than distant subcontractors. Thus weaving brought about the emergence upstream of spinning mills, and downstream of a chemical industry which was so necessary to improve the appearance of its products. The textile industry brought increasingly sophisticated machines into service. It was in their interest to find locally the engineering firms capable of designing, modifying and maintaining suitable machinery.

The industrial complexes (Chardonnet 1953) which were analysed in this manner were only exceptionally linked to a large propulsive firm. When the latter was present at a given moment in time, it was often because of a concentration of smaller firms which had played an essential part in the expansion of regional activities.

Geographers and economists were more inclined to stick to contemporary realities, even if they admitted a certain 'significance' of what took place in the nineteenth century and before. They willingly pointed out the diversity of contacts which flourished within some mechanical engineering regions or in certain textile areas. They also demonstrated that sometimes there was a simple juxtaposition of firms which remained independent of and had no business relations with one another.

These findings were ignored by the dominant theory: they were hard to make use of in the sense that there was a lack of a suitable framework for theorising them, and no one willing to undertake it. They were of little use to those who were trying to understand development in order to establish doctrines/principles to inform interventionist policies: what was to be gained from studies which presented the facts but which made no effort to hierarchise them or to uncover the causal structures which linked them?

15.2.6 The macro-geographic approach

There was a field where much research was done, and where the efforts made in conceptualisation were considerable, but in which planners showed no interest: that of macro-geographical studies (Claval 1968). They said the same things as the work on polarisation but on another scale: expansion is not spread equally over space — it is only beneficial to certain points (as underlined by the polarisation experts) and to certain areas. These areas are generally in a central position relative to the markets served.

Interpretation of these tendencies often rests on liberal economic theory. Companies drawn to a particular market by favourable transport costs choose the central zones. The phenomenon is even more pronounced in that they can then gain from stronger economies of scale. Between firms which set themselves up in this way, external economies appear. The latter reinforce the advantages of these areas. Thus the process has a cumulative effect. Only the appearance of diseconomies is capable of stopping it.

As soon as one abandons the hypothesis of an absence of technical progress — that is of economies of scale and external economies — on which the classic models of the location of companies within national or international space implicitly rest, then unequal development is inevitable.

The Marxists discovered the centre/periphery schema in 1960 — or rediscovered it inasmuch as one finds outlines of it in Marx, Lenin and Rosa Luxemburg. For them, the advantage of the centre stemmed from primitive accumulation. Nothing threatened it. When, at the beginning of the 1960s, the industrialisation of certain Third World countries began, the Marxists strove to show that it was nothing but a new type of unequal growth.

Macro-geography is not intended to attract the planners. Their major concern is, then, to achieve greater equality in the distribution of production capacities, and in incomes. What can one do with a theory which tells you your efforts are in vain? Ignore it: that's what they usually do.

15.3 The crisis and the renewal of principles and theories

15.3.1 The obsolescence of classic planning formulas

The process of industrial expansion which characterised the thirty glorious years (from 1945 to 1975) lost impetus by the mid-1960s. The oil crisis brought about an awareness of the gravity of the situation. To meet the new deficit in foreign trade, most industrialised countries wanted to increase their exports of manufactured goods. Increases were not possible in all sectors because of competition from new producers whose agressiveness and whose possibilities were suddenly discovered: textiles, the clothing industry, the simplest engineering industries, part of the domestic electrical appliance trade, and down-market electronics were all affected by the beginning of the 1970s.

In the majority of developed countries, industrial growth was no longer spontaneous. Planning formulas in use until then gave the impression of a large engine which worked on its own. All that was required was to channel some of its energy to depressed areas. The nature of the problem changed: what came to count was the recreation of the lost conditions of economic dynamism. It was no longer a question of driving an engine with a powerful tiger in its tank with the brake on, but more of finding a means of replacing the weakening tiger with several cougars or cats of lesser calibre!

In these new circumstances, the public authorities were once again on the look-out for doctrines/principles: firms on which they had had a hold until then were increasingly escaping their influence. From the second half of the nineteenth century, the transport revolution had permitted such a widening of markets that most had grown to a world scale, but manufacturing had remained the monopoly of a few countries, and firms were reluctant to internationalise their production activities because of the imperfect character of knowledge about other places ('transparence de l'espace'). The latter was a result of two factors (Claval 1989):

(1) the difficulties of transmitting the technical knowledge, indispensable for industrial production, out of the areas where it was developed, and
(2) the tendency for branches partially to escape the control of senior management as soon as they were too far removed from the head office and the directors to be subject to frequent inspection.

Conditions had changed in the course of the 1950s and 1960s. For many factories, know-how had become scientific. It was no longer passed on by direct imitation on the job. It could easily be taught in schools because of the spread of learning in the Third World. Modern means of telecommunication and air transport had changed the organisation of companies: it was now possible to have establishments on the other side of the world and be up-to-date with what was happening there. Executives could visit them easily. Distance was no longer synonymous with rupture. There was no longer a need for a quibbling management and a heavy bureaucracy! No more were branches merely places where one carried out as faithfully as possible the decisions of senior management: they were expected to show initiative, and to contribute to the dynamics of the firm as a whole.

In these conditions, companies felt liberated from the limitations which held them semi-prisoner in a particular national space. The suppression of the traditional constraints on movement and the distribution of information enabled them to reach out to the four corners of the globe and to gain maximum benefits from the division of labour: they could set up their commercial departments at the nerve-centres of distribution networks and their production operations in the countries where wages were low.

States are now having to deal with volatile companies. Instead of being able to impose their will on them, they now have to impress and win over difficult partners. The latter excel at playing one state off against another to obtain loans, allowances and better conditions for the employment of the workforce. Within nations, local governments join the process of competitive bidding for industrial investments: without them, how is one to increase employment, and ensure, in a country like France where local taxation relies heavily on businesses, prosperous communal finances?

15.3.2 New theoretical trends

There is at present a revival in the popularity of research on industrial location. The new geography led to the rediscovery of the models of Alfred Weber, but the latter barely allowed one to understand the organisation of large establishments, or of industrial districts and complexes. Conditions are changing: the concern is to get a real picture of the life of a company and to measure the strength of the various links involved in the transport of goods and of information. Systematic approaches to complex situations produce surprising results and do not involve recourse to textbook examples which are easy to conceptualise but which give a poor account of most concrete situations.

Marxist research is also diversifying. It is benefiting from the theme of the new international division of labour. This theme enables it to explain the movement of activities away from old industrial regions to developing countries, or at least to some of them. To understand what is happening within national spaces/territories, one must go further. It was to this end that the Marshallian analysis of industrial districts was rediscovered. On it is based the entire theory of flexibility elaborated by Allen Scott (Scott 1988a). As long as it is combined with a global analysis of the structures of relations and of information fields, this line of thought allows one at last to account for a part of what happened during the Industrial Revolution, and since the emergence of the modern adjustment crisis.

The alternative theoretical approaches put more emphasis on the role of information in the new forms of structuring of space. It is greatly to their credit that the forces underlying the metropolitanisation of the world economy are understood. Until now, they had not provided such good accounts of what was happening within industrial regions.

The theory of industrial districts allows one to incorporate, as Allen Scott (1988c) showed so well, some of the results of the empirical analyses of geographers and historians, as well as the contributions of sociologists fascinated by the expansion of dynamic industrial activities in regions which seem to have remained very rural.

May one take it that this wave of theoretical thought covers all aspects of the new industrial landscapes? No. Nothing demonstrates this fact better than the gap left by the collapse of the old centre/periphery model: one of its attractions was that it offered an interpretation of macro-geographical imbalances. It did not account for recent changes: had it continued to be valid one would have expected to see activities concentrate in Europe's most developed axis which extends from the London Basin to Northern Italy. Today there are a greater number of crisis regions in that belt than flourishing areas. The same patchwork pattern is repeated throughout the peripheral areas of Europe. To explain this situation, one has to start with the idea that the space that is shaped by the new means of fast transport, and telecommunications, is not continuous, but is made up of a collection of discontinuous elements: the centre is split between several places which have good links with global networks, and the new peripheries are arranged around each of these centres.

Perspectives such as these show that the theory of industrial districts (Becattini 1987) is only able to account for a part of contemporary reality. To go further, one has to widen one's analytical perspective and not isolate industrial location from the context in which it develops. The theoretical deficiencies are all the more difficult because politicians need to act, and are prepared to consider any new departure that can inform political action.

15.3.3 New doctrinal perspectives

Politicians did not take long to understand that the formulas on which they had based their regional action in the 1950s and 1960s had had their day. In many sectors, large firms had experienced difficulties, and were hit harder than others by employment legislation. In the race to innovate and be competitive, they did not always appear the most successful. Small and medium-size firms, or at least some of them, came out better. Their freedom to choose a geographical location is, however, more restricted than that of large firms. The relocation of some productive activities, and their international dispersal, according to the advantages to be gained in different places from the cheapness of labour, of energy or of whatever other factor, requires a size that they have not yet attained. The state therefore has more hold over relatively modest businesses than over larger ones. The problem is to create them where they do not yet exist, and to make them increase in number and grow where they are already in existence.

In a conjuncture in which action was not only necessary but urgent, politicians made a success of a theory of polarisation which was a theory in name only: they were ready to accept any set of underlying ideas as long as it seemed to justify their choices and got them out of the embarrassing situation of having the means, but not knowing how to use them.

Panaceas have changed their name. Today they have two faces. One is the technopole, and the other is development from below, which seems to get some support from the analyses of industrial districts. In the first case it is the relations between research and innovation which is brought to the fore by several examples: Silicon Valley (see Saxenian 1985) or Routes 128 and 428 around Boston — to which one can add the M4 corridor in Britain. The model of dynamic industrial districts is based on the well-known cases of the Third Italy, and on examples from East Central and Western France, Catalonia, certain parts of Switzerland, South Germany, and the Scandinavian countries.

The studies devoted to these regions are fascinating, but the need for intervention is such that principles of action are deduced without weighing up all the elements of the problem. One is perhaps too quick to condemn the large company, which often has no equal in the organisation of the international division of labour. One expects too much from the effects of synergy, because of the lack of comprehension of the mechanisms involved.

The interaction between research and the need to act is undoubtedly an obstacle to the maturation of theory.

15.4 Conclusion

The industrial geography that we perceive today is very different from that which geographers, economists and historians analysed at the end of the nineteenth and the beginning of the twentieth centuries. Inasmuch as the state stood back from directly influencing the choice of location and was happy just to exercise partial control over market organisation, the distributions could be analysed in the same way as natural distributions. They were the result of mechanisms that were different of course from those at work in nature, but which, in common with the latter, did not correspond to any prior global design.

The current situation is very different: the distributions lie within areas which planning has altered, or tried to alter, for at least a generation, and more often nearer two. One of the fundamental problems posed today is that of weighing up the results of these interventions.

An awareness of the limitations of the policies in vogue in the 1950s and 1960s is emerging: expansion was halted in areas where new investments were disallowed, but the relocation of firms did not happen as was intended. In France, for example, the West, Centre and South, in spite of having benefited from the highest levels of aid, were hardly considered attractive before the middle of the 1960s. From then on, decentralised factories went further afield, often into the zones into which attempts were made to attract them, but only within a radius of forty-five to sixty minutes around the main airports. In the end transport and communications facilities were the deciding factor, not the incentives offered.

We have not really tried up to now to measure the impact of the policies in vogue in the last ten years. Has the money spent freely to promote technopoles been put to good use? Have we really succeeded in creating industrial districts capable, after a short space of time, of self-sustained development? It is about time to start to ask oneself these questions. They are essential for appreciating the gains that policies can make from research — and for appreciating the danger that comes from using ill-founded theories to justify the principles of intervention.

16 Neo-Fordism or post-Fordism? Some conclusions and further remarks

Mick Dunford and Georges Benko

The 1970s and 1980s represent, in the eyes of most of the contributors to this collection, a phase of crisis and a turning point in economic and social development. With the defeat of fascism at the end of the Second World War two broad paths of development survived. One was Stalinism whose sphere of influence was extended from the Soviet Union into Eastern Europe and which came to shape economic and social change in areas that were historically underdeveloped and devastated by the war. The other was Fordism or the 'American way' which offered a way out of the crisis that had convulsed the capitalist world in the 1930s and which was to underpin the integration of the more advanced western half of Europe into a hierarchical order under the leadership of the United States. Between these two worlds there was an immense imbalance, as, at the end of the war, the United States on its own accounted for three-quarters of the world's invested capital and two-thirds of its industrial capacity (Horowitz 1967, p.74). In the 1970s and 1980s these models of development came up against limits of their own. In the social-democratic countries of the West there was an economic crisis as Fordism itself broke down. In 1989 in Eastern Europe, after it had failed to switch to a model of intensive development and after a decade or more of stagnation in which the costs of an arms race proved unsustainable, communism disintegrated. It was the crisis in the West that led to one of the central questions posed in this collection: what comes after Fordism, and what implications do the new paths of economic and social development that one can discern have for the development of cities and regions? The answers, however, also have implications for the ex-communist world.

In this conclusion we intend to suggest how the views expressed in earlier chapters challenge and go beyond some of the debates of the last decade. In essence there are five sets of issues that we shall consider.

(1) What is the character and what are the implications of the new technologies? This question is important because differences in the answers to it underlie two different interpretations of Fordism, its crisis and what follows it. One identifies Fordism with mass production and sees in the new technologies the means for an alternative productive order (called flexible specialisation), while the other identifies Fordism as a model of development and views alternatives as multi-faceted and differentiated. In this collection it is agreed that the new technologies are flexible. It is also argued however that innovations of the computer and communications revolution are integrative in character.

(2) What implications do the new technologies have for industrial organisation? In particular if the new technologies are flexible, does it follow that mass production and the oligopolistic groups that dominated the mass production industries will decline in relative importance as the advocates of flexible specialisation sometimes suggest? The answer given is, as we shall suggest in section 16.2, that flexible specialisation will indeed prove successful but only in certain very specific conditions. In many sectors, mass producers can take advantage of flexible production techniques and oligopolistic groups will dominate the scene.

The second characteristic of the new technologies (their integrative role which is also examined in section 16.2) also has major implications for industrial organisation. In this case however the emphasis is not on an extension of market relations among firms but the development of planned and well-organised networks, infrastructures and logistic functions.

(3) What are the implications of the new technologies and the alternative models of industrial organisation identified for spatial development? In section 16.3 we suggest that in recent years several authors have identified new industrial spaces with more flexible technologies and social relations. In this collection there is an insistence on the varied and differentiated character of new industrial spaces. The Italian industrial districts, which have offered exemplars of flexible specialisation, are acknowledged as a particular rather than a general model: the model is applicable in certain sectors, in certain circumstances, and is subject to change. Technopoles on the other hand are interpreted as products of the articulation of the strategies of large industrial and financial groups and public sector establishments on the one hand and networks of small and medium-size enterprises on the other. What these studies of new industrial spaces have overlooked however are the consequences of the internal reorganisation of the mass production system itself.

(4) The development of integrative functions and changes in the relationships among productive and non-productive functions have further spatial implications that have received far too little attention in recent years. Several contributors show how these developments are associated with the growth of global cities and new kinds of polarisation and hierarchisation of economic space. In section 16.4 we shall summarise this second set of conclusions about the spatial consequences of technical and organisational change.

(5) These variations in the implications of new technologies, in modes of

industrial organisation and in the logic of spatial development lead finally to the debate as to what follows Fordism. Is there a new logic of uneven development connected with the strategies of groups? Are dualism and polarisation inevitable? Why are some social and economic adaptations to the crisis of Fordism more successful than others. In the last section of this chapter these questions will be addressed in a discussion of the contribution of this volume to the debate about neo-Fordism and post-Fordism.

16.1 The character and crisis of Fordism

Not all agree about the significance of Fordism, while those who do do not always agree about what it was. Two approaches can be distinguished: one is associated with the work of Piore and Sabel on the rise of flexible specialisation, and the other with French theories of regulation.

To Piore and Sabel (1984) Fordism was an industrial model: mass production of standardised goods with dedicated machines and unskilled workers. The applicability of this model was, however, far from universal: while Fordist sectors made up the leading-edge of advanced economies, sectors and enterprises organised in accordance with different principles were more numerous. Indeed it was on adjustments in these non-Fordist sectors that the flexibility of economic reproduction depended. Over time, however, small and medium-size craft enterprises were squeezed, and as a result advanced economies were made more inflexible. In the view of Piore and Sabel, however, the eventual breakdown of mass production was a result of demand-side factors. The demand for mass-produced goods stagnated, as markets in advanced countries were saturated, while consumers (in the main the new upper-middle classes) sought goods that were more diversified and had a higher design content.

In theories of regulation, on the other hand, Fordism was (1) a regime of (intensive) accumulation and a related industrial model, and (2) a mode of (monopolistic) regulation. (Authors such as Piore and Sabel (1984) do maintain that Fordism was dependent on a framework of institutional regulation made up at the microscopic level of the shop-floor, at the microeconomic level of the corporation, at the macroeconomic level of industrial unions, the wage-determination system and the Keynesian state, and at the international level of organisations regulating trade and the monetary framework, but use a narrower definition of Fordism.) At the same time, however, the crisis of Fordism is also given a different interpretation. In the regulation approach it is seen as a product of two factors: (1) a supply-side crisis, reflected in differential reductions in the rate of profit, and rooted not in the conditions of market demand but in the system of value production, and (2) a demand side crisis, which resulted from the internationalisation of production (as a result of the search for economies of scale) and the delinking of domestic wages and the demand for a nation's output, and which assumed major significance in the recessions that monetarist strategies induced (see Coriat, Leborgne and Lipietz, and Benko and Dunford). The saturation of markets was relative. However stagnation and economic instabilities did follow and were at the root of the search for more flexible structures. In this second tradition therefore the market conditions which the advocates of flexible specialisation see as the cause of the crisis of mass production were more a result. In this collection it is this second view that predominates.

16.2 New technologies, new industries and new principles of work organisation

In the West the 1970s and 1980s were also the years of a new technological revolution. Involved were a sequence of major product and process innovations with the most far-reaching effects. There was an accelerated development of new technologies, processes and products and, in particular, a rapid development and convergence of electronics, computing and telecommunications. Where these developments involved persistent differentials in output and productivity growth rates across sectors, the shares of different industries in output and employment changed. The consequence was a process of structural change linked to deindustrialisation on the one hand and the rise of new growth ensembles on the other. In addition there was a transformation of the structure of employment within sectors.

At the same time there were major process innovations associated with the use of new information technologies in the production and distribution of goods and services. As Coriat indicated, one can identify a *new technological trajectory* (programmable automation) centred on two principles. One was the principle of integration and real-time control which offers new ways of achieving productivity gains through an optimisation of the sequence of operations and a conversion of '*dead time in production into time that is actually productive*, whether the dead time relates to workers, the rate of use of machines, or the time in which raw materials and semi-finished goods are stored'. This principle depends on communication and coordination. The other was the principle of production *flexibility*. Through the use of machines that, under computer control, can produce a variety of different parts or products, adaptation to the unstable, volatile and differentiated character of market demand is facilitated, and the life cycle of a machine is deconnected from the life cycle of a product.

16.2.1 New technologies, flexible specialisation and flexible mass production

The question of the impact of structural change and in particular of integrated-flexible automation on industrial organisation and the industrial geography of advanced countries is one of the main issues addressed in this collection.

To some extent the agenda was set by the ideas of Piore and Sabel (see Sabel 1982, pp. 209–19 and 220–27, and Piore and Sabel 1984, pp. 28–35). With, they argued, changes in the composition and stability of demand, smaller and more flexible specialised enterprises that provided more diversified and innovative goods and services and that employed skilled craft workers started to gain the upper hand. Involved was therefore a supply-side response in the shape of skilled work and flexible machines, and a demand-side response in the shape of customised products and changes in product mix. In Italy, West Germany and Scandinavia dynamic and successful specialised industrial districts and regional economies made up of networks of such small and medium-size enterprises and supporting local collective services and community networks were identified. The success of these areas offered, in their view, the prospect of the end of mass production, the emergence of a new model of development called 'flexible specialisation', a reconsolidation of regional economies as integrated units of production, and the creation of a new post-Fordist world. Indeed if development does finally proceed along this path, argued Piore and Sabel, the 1970s and 1980s will be seen in retrospect as a major turning point in the historical process of industrialisation: in the nineteenth century craft production was destroyed by mass production, while the 1980s may represent a second industrial divide in which industrial societies started to abandon mass production and return to nineteenth-century craft methods.

Several of the contributors to this volume directly question this view. The approach of Coriat is to analyse the *modus operandi* of the new technologies. To succeed flexible specialisation requires that economies of scope are greater than economies of scale. This condition will hold when overall demand is static, and when demand is irregular, or products are subject to rapid obsolescence. In these conditions an enterprise that can change almost instantaneously from one product to another will have the edge over one that seeks to achieve scale economies, and in the conditions of monopolistic competition that characterise these sectors the more dynamic flexible firms can actively pursue strategies of product differentiation so as to maximise monopoly rents. Strategies of flexible specialisation offer therefore not a new macroeconomic model of development but a principle that will succeed in the case of certain conditions of demand and competition. The model is in fact one that is most appropriate in particular sectors (clothes, knitwear, textiles, ceramics, and shoes where fashion and/or seasonal factors lead to rapid product changes), in particular conditions of income distribution, and in economic conjunctures when instabilities predominate. What is more its orientation towards elite markets and its monopolistic character qualify the ideal properties its advocates attribute to it.

Coriat pointed to the existence of an alternative adaptation to the new technologies. Dynamic flexibility involves the search for economies of scale and scope. The development of strategies of product renewal or product succession (from, for example, compact discs to compact video discs) allows a dynamic reuse of equipment that reduces the risks of volume production, allows the adoption of strategies of cost reduction through the search for scale economies, and involves the development and extension of oligopolistic mass markets. In these sectors moreover the volume of research and development costs is often immense so that the valorisation of these initial outlays requires very high sales volumes: in other words research and development activities are characterised by major economies of scale as the creation of the first product involves a very large fixed cost. At the same time modularisation allows the survival of traditional mass production: modules or components are mass produced, while differentiated final products are assembled in flexible production islands. In short volume producers can take advantage of flexible technologies and, in certain sectors and conditions of demand, will have the competitive edge.

What combination of these strategies will emerge will depend to a significant extent on the macroeconomic framework. The arguments of Coriat and also of Martinelli and Schoenberger and Schamp suggest, however, that the adaptations to new technologies that will predominate, if growth occurs, will give a major role to large oligopolistic groups and to new and old models of mass production. This conclusion has, as we shall see, major implications for the development of industrial space.

16.2.2 Integration and networks

The communicative and integrative character of new technologies is a second factor emphasised in this collection. As a result of these integrative functions there have been two important developments. One is the transformation of job structures in the industrial sector. In production, direct production jobs have fallen relative to maintenance, while in the industrial sector 'periproductive' jobs in marketing, design, sales and distribution have increased relative to production jobs (see Veltz and also Krätke and Malézieux). The growth of internal industrial sector services (which amount to some two-thirds to three-quarters of the services a firm uses) and of marketed services, the high skill content of these jobs, and the concentration of these activities in major cities are major factors in the polarisation of economic activities. If development is to be evened out, it is these developments that need to be addressed.

These changes in the structure of jobs are connected not just with differential productivities but also with the increased role of integrative and management functions. Integration is of two kinds. In the first place horizontal integration occurs among the different research and development, design, production, and commercial functions.The development of horizontal and less hierarchical relations in large organisations creates possibilities for the disaggregation of some headquarters functions and some central services and the development of small and medium multi-functional units. The decentralisation of these units would depend however on a wider distribution of centres with a critical mass of skilled workers and services and of networks for the integration of decentralised units.

Second integration occurs along product chains:

silicon » semiconductors » computers » factory control systems »
machine tools » cars.

Involved is the development of logistic systems that integrate means of telecommunication with means of physical transport and that cut across the boundaries of firms. Integration occurs upstream with suppliers and downstream with customers and clients and involves the development of stable networks of organised relations that require coordination and cooperation over methods of production, quality control, stock management and the development of management information systems. What results is a new world in which the boundaries of firms are less clear, in which values are created along networks, and in which the global optimum for the value-adding network is not a sum of individual optima. In these circumstances partnership and co-operation are substituted for competition, and planning is extended from intra-firm to inter-firm relations.

16.2.3 New technologies and industrial organisation

The initial account of flexible specialisation highlighted the role of networks of specialised small and medium-size firms and of a set of support structures (vocational schools, research institutes, marketing organisations and so on) concentrated in a small area. In the 1970s and early 1980s these ideas had some empirical support as there were significant changes in the social division of labour, in the size distribution of firms, and in the sources of economic growth. In particular large firms found themselves in economic difficulties. At the same time there was an increase in the rate of new firm formation, and small and medium-size firms accounted for a larger share of employment growth. (In output terms, however, the performance of small and medium-size firms was less remarkable, and their survival rate was low).

The initial ideas of Piore and Sabel are similar to the ones that Scott has put forward. In several recent articles and books Scott has introduced the Coase-Williamson analyses of the role of transaction costs, of economies of scale and scope, and of the relative advantages of vertical integration and disintegration into spatial analysis. Scott identified tendencies towards an extension of the social (at the expense of the technical) division of labour, an increase in the number of small and medium-size industrial establishments connected via market transactions, an increase in the role of external economies, and a marked agglomeration of production in localised territorial complexes and 'new industrial spaces'. In these areas 'vertical disintegration encourages agglomeration, and agglomeration encourages vertical disintegration' (Scott 1986b, p.224).

In this volume Leborgne and Lipietz offer a more open account identifying vertical integration, vertical near-integration (vertical near-disintegration) and vertical disintegration as alternative paths. In their more qualified view, however, industrial organisation will evolve in favour of specialised enterprises and near-integration. Near-integration can assume several forms from vertical subcontract relations to horizontal partnerships and strategic alliances, with intermediate oblique variants of near-integration (see Figure 16.1). In each case the network of relations among firms can be either territorially dense, as Sabel and Scott anticipate, or territorially disintegrated.

These analytical and empirical arguments suggest reduced vertical integration. In the 1980s, however, there has been an almost unparalleled concentration and centralisation of capital: mergers, takeovers, strategic alliances, and joint ventures have mushroomed, and the influence of international financial institutions, multinational firms and transnational finance capital has grown. As Martinelli and Schoenberger point out (1) concentration and centralisation concern mature (oil, chemicals and food) and newer sectors (electronics,

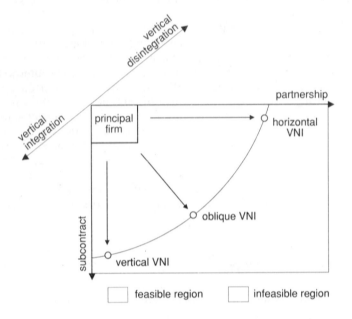

Figure 16.1 Strategies of integration

Source: Leborgne and Lipictz 1990

telecommunications and business services), (2) there is some evidence of a prevalence of intra-sectoral concentration, and (3) acquisitions are carried out not only by large multinational groups but also by smaller national or local firms whose goal is to strengthen their market positions.

What is more, there are production strategies in which scale continues to play a significant role. Sorge and Streeck (1988), for example, have identified four 'production strategies' centred around distinctions between high- and low-volume production on the one hand and standardised price-sensitive and differentiated quality-sensitive production on the other. This classification yields (1) specialised component production, (2) craft production, (3) mass production, and (4) diversified volume production. Volume production involves therefore not just standardised mass production but also diversified quality production.

In these circumstances, and in the light of studies of the development of large groups, Sabel has argued that there is an increasing resemblance and convergence of multinational companies with the autonomous small and medium-size firm model: multinationals are decentralising into looser federations of independent operating units responsible for particular product lines, hierarchies are becoming more blurred, and deep-seated uncertainty about market demand stimulates cooperation and collaboration with subcontractors and the creation of localised production networks. (As, moreover, industrial districts develop common services, the small firm model converges, Sabel argues, with the new large firm model.)

However the initial identification of flexible specialisation with small and independent craft producers was so close that its application to volume production does seem questionable (see Sorge and Streeck 1988). In any case several of the contributors to this volume disagree with Sabel's interpretation of the development of large firms. On the one hand, it is argued, there are significant sectoral differences in industrial organisation. On the other, tendencies towards a vertical disintegration of production, agreements over research and development, and agreements among large and small or among small firms are not inconsistent with a concentration of financial control and market domination (see in particular Martinelli and Schoenberger). In short there is evidence that large firms have started to come out of the corner.

At this point another question arises: what are the implications of the structural changes of the last decade or so for the map of economic development?

16.3 New industrial spaces

In the literature on new industrial spaces several varieties of new growth centre are identified. (1) Areas centred on revitalised craft industries. (2) Complexes of high-technology industries: in the last five years there has been a rapid growth of research into areas such as Silicon Valley, Orange County and Route 128 in the United States, while in Europe similar studies exist of high-technology industrial complexes and of the French technopoles. In these sectors it has been argued one can often identify dense geographical agglomerations of rapidly growing firms. (3) Metropolises with concentrations of producer services: in many countries some of the fastest rates of growth of employment are in financial, management and legal services which exhibit strong agglomeration tendencies. With these new developments the map of regional economic development was profoundly changed: the relative success of different regional economies depended on their success as centres of these new growth sectors, and on their economic organisation which conditioned their speed of adjustment to market trends. Yet in the light of the arguments outlined in the last two sections these cases need separate consideration.

16.3.1 Craft industries and the Three Italies

The phenomenon that has received more attention than most is the development of agglomerations of small- and medium-size specialised firms in semi-rural and small-town environments in central and north-east Italy (the Third Italy). The start of the renewal of small firms especially in the engineering industry was a result of the putting out and decentralisation of work from large and medium-size firms after the industrial unrest of the late 1960s and early 1970s (see Garofoli who considers this phase important as it led to a diffusion of knowledge about production and marketing and to the establishment of new firms).

The subsequent development of small firm systems was connected however with specific economic conditions: a slowdown in the growth of markets for mass-produced goods, which opened up a space in which companies making higher-quality specialised products with a high design content could expand, and instabilities which gave integrated networks of highly specialised and adaptable small firms without major overheads advantages over large firms.

In the view of Garofoli most of the redistribution of economic activities that followed was not a product of productive decentralisation. The phenomenon was most pronounced in traditional consumer-good industries. In these sectors the development of independent, specialised, innovative and design-intensive small craft enterprises was rapid, extending the social division of labour. New technologies and new management methods helped reduce the relative costs of small-scale production, although, in the view of Martinelli and Schoenberger, new technologies are confined to the larger firms or firms directly connected with the market. Information networks connected input and output markets, and complex and shifting networks of inter-firm relations were established. Individual industries are concentrated in particular localities: knitwear in Carpi, textiles in Prato, ceramics in Sassuolo, shoes and musical instruments in Marche and so on. The development of these industrial areas depended not just on inter-firm relations but also on relations with the local environment and on the support of local government and local institutions: local financial institutions, vocational schools, research institutes and *consorzi* that provide a whole range of services to local enterprises, as well as the development of specialised merchants (such as the *impannatori* of Prato) responsible for the sale of the zone's products on national and international markets. The model of development is therefore not, as Garofoli insists, a market model but one that rests on a mix of competition and collaboration and in which services, knowledge and orders (via subcontracting or the leasing of production facilities) are shared.

Garofoli (1983b) has suggested a useful classification of these areas. (1) Areas of specialised production are zones in which there are many producers of the same product, and where there is little cooperation and a high level of inter-firm competition. These zones which developed either via the transformation of craft producers into industrial producers or via the arrival of external firms developed due to favourable labour market conditions. (2) What he calls local productive systems are characterised by closer inter-firm relations and a longer industrial tradition, and are a product of a more diffused model of development. (3) System areas, which are similar to what Becattini (after Alfred Marshall) calls 'industrial districts', are more complex territorial systems with a close integration of firms in different interconnected sectors.

These zones have a distinctive social structure with large numbers of small entrepreneurs, skilled male craft workers, and working wives and families, and local subcultures and social traditions associated with mutual trust and consensus and that allow, as Becattini indicates, collaboration and the exchange of ideas in face-to-face encounters. In these areas agriculture and in particular the *mezzadria* were important, extended families predominated and cities were small. Agricultural structures provided low-cost residential accommodation, premises for manufacturing operations, and capital through the sale of farmland for urban development. The value systems associated with the *mezzadria* were important factors in the emergence of ideologies and world views of the individuals who set up as entrepreneurs and self-employed artisans (Paci 1979). The resources at the disposition of extended households allowed them to meet their subsistence needs through complex allocations of roles among household members (Vinay 1987). In some places wage costs are low, and the evasion of tax and social security contributions is widespread. (Wage and employment flexibility are considered in the final section.)

With the growth of these industrial areas and the crises of central areas the map of Italian economic development was changed: the role of older poles declined, growth occurred in non-metropolitan areas, counterurbanisation processes were set in motion and development was more diffuse. In the view of Garofoli it was endogenous in character in the sense that it was not a consequence of an interregional mobility of investments and that it depended (increasingly) on local resources. Several other contributors who draw in the main on different national experiences would see these phenomena as more conjunctural and short-lived.

Garofoli does insist, however, on the specificity of the Italian model and the variability of the specific forms it assumed in different regions, and he would resist its conflation with the models of development found in other new industrial spaces. In a similar way Becattini sees the Marshallian industrial district (MID) as a mode of economic organisation that is different from the vertically integrated corporation and the network firm with which it has to compete if it is to survive. What he argues is that the survival of the MID in the face of competition from these modes of organisation that are better financed and that make rational use of scientific and technical knowledge lies in its creativity. Its creative character, he continues, is rooted in the existence of different competences, in the role of the *impannatore* in particular in stimulating interaction between these competences, and in the unusual connections that are consequently made between solutions to seemingly different practical problems encountered in different areas of economic life. To Becattini the fact that the MID is a creative milieu means that it offers an efficient mix of institutions. With a remoulded education system aimed at the expansion of human creative potential and a commitment to the development of creative human work it offers, in his view, an ideal social order.

One of the characteristics of Becattini's ideal world is the absence of dominant firms. Schoenberger and Martinelli argue that the dynamics of these zones involve a renewed process of concentration not so much at the level of production as upstream in the sourcing of materials and finance and downstream in marketing. The reasons for reconcentration are rooted in increased competition from low-cost producers and other developed economies and the quest for scale economies in finance, design, marketing and distribution (see also Amin and Robins 1990). Inter-firm relations concern not just the organisation of production but also the distribution of surplus value between the participating firms and the exercise of control: while production remains disintegrated, the division of profits can move in favour of the enterprises that assume a dominant role by virtue of their activities as financiers, marketing organisations, designers, and co-ordinators of production.

There are, moreover, reasons for doubting whether small firms in the Third Italy are really small. As Brusco (1986) notes, some of the firms which are the foundation of the industrial districts 'are small only in name' because they subcontract many stages of production to other firms or homeworkers. While the value added by these firms is low, the value of their sales is often considerable, and some are large in a financial and commercial sense.

One of the most striking cases is Benetton. To writers on industrial districts such as Garofoli, however, Benetton is an example of a flexible (multinational) firm which dominates its subcontractors and whose goal is to bypass the districts. Benetton operates with extensive subcontract networks, and changes its subcontractors in order to minimise its costs, whereas the district can remain independent of dominant firms only as a result of local organisation of the entire productive cycle. The industrial district is in short a very particular case which must in other words be distinguished from other models of economic and spatial development.

16.3.2 The reorganisation of mass production

We have already summarised Coriat's view that dynamic flexibility and oligopolistic markets stand alongside flexible specialisation and monopolistic competition as possible adaptations to the new technologies and new market conditions. Schamp's account of the development of new production concepts in the West German car industry lends considerable support to Coriat's case. The German car producers achieve market flexibility and cost reduction through the assembly of differentiated products from standardised mass-produced components. The use of flexible machines increases capital costs and increases the inertia of plants. Vehicle manufacturers do establish new relations with their suppliers splitting off some production operations. Vertical integration does not decline, however, as the German car companies simultaneously integrate into the provision of services related to the use and production of cars: what the car producers are doing is redefining their field of direct action as a result of decisions to focus on research and development and product design, on final assembly, and on a range of commercial, financial and marketing activities.

Schamp also questions the view that the disintegration of production activities will prompt a new spatial concentration of the suppliers to car manufacturers and the development of a new polarised production complex. In the West German case a very small proportion of suppliers concentrate around assembly plants. The need to amortise investments in plant and equipment is, he argues, a source of inertia and a major factor in shaping the development and locational structure of the industry, while the new needs of the car manufacturers are met through the development of new forms of logistic and transport organisation between suppliers and car makers. Indeed in Schamp's view the opposite is the case: in the German car industry there is an increase in the 'interregional and international division of labour . . . [and] a reduction in the density (Ausdünnung) of the map of local interdependencies between car makers and the system of suppliers' due to the car makers' strategies of single and global sourcing. His suspicion is that the spatial instabilities in the resulting network of interdependencies will be extended to the whole of Europe with the creation of the Single European Market.

In the semiconductor industry there is similarly an international division of labour. Geneau de Lamarlière's concern is with its locational structure and the adequacy of the theory of the 'new international division of labour' with its emphasis on the scope for a technical separation of different production operations and the advantages of locating assembly and testing operations in cheap labour areas where secondary articulations emerge. Whilst this model does help explain the early internationalisation of American merchant chip firms, it does not explain more recent tendencies of producers to locate near the markets they serve. To explain these phenomena she develops a rationalist model in which all firms optimise a complex objective function subject to a set of shifting constraints.

What these arguments highlight is the fact that there is not a simple relation between a particular mode of economic organisation and particular modes of spatial organisation and the development of territorial complexes. In the era of Fordism Renault adopted strategies of spatial decentralisation, while Fiat concentrated its activities in Turin. An account of the locational order therefore requires a specific analysis of spatial factors and of conjunctural and structural conditions as well as an account of the dynamics of industrial organisation.

16.3.3 Technopoles and high-tech industries

There is a view that technopoles and the development of high-tech areas is a product of a deverticalisation of production and the development of small and specialised firms. While there is no doubt that these processes do occur especially in the early phases of the revolution in electronics and computers, the view that predominates in this collection (see Dunford and Manzagol and also Schoenberger and Martinelli) is that these zones often depend critically on the development of major public organisations and large groups and on the strategies of subcontracting/partnership that they adopt. In central Scotland and Grenoble some of the most important actors are vertically integrated global corporations, while the meteoric development of Phoenix was associated with a global division of functions within major semiconductor, computer, communications equipment and aerospace companies: extra-regional investments in research laboratories and technical branch plants in an area with low wages and an absence of unions, and spatially dispersed subcontract networks and markets were important characteristics of growth.

Within these sectors there are powerful processes of concentration and centralisation in the shape of mergers and acquisitions, equity investments by large firms in smaller partners, joint ventures, and technological agreements due to high research and development and fixed costs. At the same time the need for communication and integration is leading towards moves in the direction of standardisation (and not differentiation).

The development of these zones of high-tech activities is however not just a

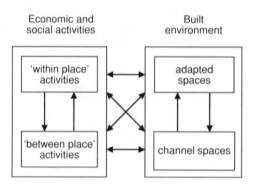

Figure 16.2 The urban and regional systems

function of the development of 'within-place' economic (productive and periproductive) activities and 'between-place' exchanges, movements, communications and logistic operations. It also depends on the development of 'adapted spaces' (buildings adapted for particular uses) and 'channel spaces' (networks for the transport of people and goods, computer and telecommunication networks for the transmission of information, and networks for the distribution of water, gas and so on) (see Figure 16.2 in which urban spatial structures are interpreted as the outcome of a two processes which allocate physical infrastructures and other built forms on the one hand and activities on the other to specific sites). There is therefore a need to consider the property development side of high-tech activities as Malézieux does in his account of the development of new industrial spaces in the Paris region. Malézieux shows how image-conscious zones of multi-purpose developments were established at nodes of the region's communications networks. At first these zones were set up in line with demand in areas designated for these uses in structure plans. However from the mid-1980s, supply-side factors assumed a leading role, supply started to exceed demand, and a whole series of imbalances were created between the development of economic activities zones and infrastructural provision. Several factors explain these changes: controls were relaxed, competition amongst local authorities increased, and an industrial property development system assumed the leading role. In short there was an absence of adequate planning which led to overproduction and jeopardised the development of zones that were more remote or less well equipped. At the same time imbalances were created between the distribution of economic activities on the one hand and the development of communications and other infrastructures on the other. Congestion and environmental degradation are among the not-unexpected consequences.

It is interesting to note that in Phoenix economic growth was accompanied by an unplanned and speculative real-estate boom, and that in recent years

Phoenix failed to attract two major research laboratories partially as a result of the absence of adequate public action and planning. In the end *laissez-faire* approaches, speculative and unplanned urbanisation, a lack of investment in social and physical infrastructures, a lack of environmental protection, low taxes and a lack of industrial policies generate, it seems, imbalances and disequilibria that will act as major obstacles to the economic 'success' of those regions that have tied their destinies to them (see Scott 1980).

What these examples highlight is the fact that the character and direction of development also depends on the social and institutional conditions in which it occurs. We shall return to this point in the final section. First, however, the spatial consequences of the communicative and integrative character of the new technologies requires attention.

16.4 Networks, metropolises and global cities

In section 16.2 we indicated that one of the main implications of the new technologies was to promote integration and the development of systems. In the view of Veltz these developments will favour locations on major computer and telecommunications networks and on major road, rail and air transport infrastructures. What results is a new kind of polarisation which depends on the resources of nodes, their connectivity and connectedness, and the scope for the appropriation of rents.

The particular geographical shape of these developments will depend on the distribution of major infrastructural investments as these investments are the precondition for any kind of diffusion of the activities structured in accordance with the principle of what Leborgne and Lipietz call vertical near-integration. Included are planned investments in means of transport and communication required to run organisations at a distance and allow interaction of geographically separated units (a national fibre-optic grid) as well as investments in support services and cultural and residential facilities.

In the French case, however, the location of these investments in activities and infrastructures reinforces the growth of a metropolitan network and is at the root of new kinds of spatial polarisation. The opposition between Paris and the French desert has, Veltz suggests, been superseded by an opposition between the network-metropolis and the French desert. This new division is reflected in two processes. One is the ever weaker relations between the development of large cities and their hinterlands, which stems from the weakness of spread effects and the decline in the extent to which cities depend on the exploitation of activities located in their hinterlands. The other is the ever closer integration of the leading sectors of second-rank centres with the activities in the Parisian pole on which they depend: examples include electronics in Rennes and aerospace in Toulouse.

In his contribution Beckouche provides empirical support for this proposition. He focuses on high-tech activities which he defines in terms of sectors and functions/occupations (research, design, manufacture, etc.). Two major cleavages are identified. In the first place there is an immense gap between Paris and the provinces. The capital accounts for over 50 per cent of 'abstract functions' and of French high-tech jobs. This polarisation of industrial jobs is a product of a set of mechanisms which reserve for Paris the key jobs within and among sectors and functions. Beckouche points out that industrial employment in Paris is over-dependent on the military and industrial complex. At the same time, however, there is also a strong concentration in Paris of design-function jobs in periproductive services. Second, there is a north-south divide between the other northern metropolises and the southern metropolises. In particular a substantial share of design and research jobs in the sophisticated state-controlled sectors of the French economy are located in the southern metropolises (Toulouse, Grenoble and Bordeaux).

There are in short powerful processes of hierarchisation and polarisation at work within a network of metropolitan areas, while the gap between the metropolises themselves and the rest of the French space economy widens.

In West Germany there is a lesser but nonetheless high degree of centralisation of management and control functions in major cities, and as Krätke shows West German spatial restructuring also centres around the differential development of the main urban agglomerations. Inertia plays a major role, while changes are in essence modifications of the existing regional structure and urban hierarchy. Krätke identifies several major causal processes. The first is the growth of high-tech activities and related direct producer services in selected central and suburban enclaves within the major urban and industrial cities.

Second, there is a correspondence between the hierarchical structure of cities and the distribution of the command functions of transnational capitalist companies: major global cities (such as Frankfurt and Hamburg) are the centres of world-wide networks and of headquarters functions and indirect (commercial and financial) producer services connected with the control of global processes of production and valorisation of capital. In recent years this gap between centres of control and the rest of the urban system has been reinforced. (It should be noted that one cannot measure this gap with employment or demographic indicators.) Three factors account for this divergence: the recent delinking of the real and financial spheres (due to the overaccumulation of capital), the emphasis of the corporate sector on financial investments, and the increase in the centralisation of capital.

In the third place there is differential growth of (high-tech and global) cities with the South gaining from the concentration of new industrial growth sectors in southern cities. In addition there have been significant processes of intra-urban polarisation and differentiation: the cultural revival of some inner areas, the development of exclusive shops and gentrification have occurred to meet the needs of highly paid, skilled workers, yet these upgraded inner city zones coexist with survival zones and reservations for low-paid, service-sector workers, for impoverished and socially marginalised groups, and for ethnic minorities. In part these processes of differentiation stem from the accentuation of the dual structure of advanced capitalist societies, but these tendencies have been reinforced by the increase in intra-urban competition and the development of entrepreneurial local politics.

There are two lessons, which Claval independently identifies in his contribution, that one should draw from this evidence. What Claval argues is that, first, the new inequalities are not so much between centres and peripheries as between metropolitan zones well linked to key physical and telecommunications infrastructures and the areas around them. These inequalities as well as the inequalities between metropolitan zones suggest one new research focus. Second, large firms have internationalised and are major determinants of the international division of labour, yet have as a result escaped the control of national governments and succeed in playing one state and one area off against another. The emphasis in much work on new industrial spaces on small and medium-sized firms and on processes of vertical disintegration seems, as Claval points out, paradoxical. If large corporations and industrial and financial groups are the dominant actors in the world economic system, more attention must be paid to their actions.

16.5 Neo-Fordism or post-Fordism?

In some respects Krätke's account of spatial and social restructuring in West Germany identifies a series of regressive tendencies which in the past were connected with neo-Fordism: a defensive reaction to the crisis of Fordism in which its (proto-socialist in form but paternalistic in content) social and economic guarantees were eroded, and a new development path centred around what the West German political scientist Hirsch identified as 'hyper-industrialisation', 'social dualism and segmentation', and an 'authoritarian state' (see Amin and Robins 1990, pp.25–6). What is significant is that these trends are identified not with the development of the United States or the United Kingdom where these trends are widely held to exist (see, for example, Davis 1986) but with the more advanced and more progressive West German case.

With the publication in 1984 of Piore and Sabel's *The Second Industrial Divide: Possibilities for Prosperity*, however, a new discourse appeared which emphasised the scope for a more enlightened way out of the crisis of Fordism and a new progressive model of capitalist development.

In order to cut through these debates it is essential to disentangle the different dimensions of social and economic change as Leborgne and Lipietz and as Boyer (1989) do. In essence Leborgne and Lipietz identify two sets of relations: *capital–capital relations*, which were considered in an section 16.2 where there are choices between strategies of subcontracting (vertical near-integration) and strategies centred on partnership (horizontal near-integration), and *capital–labour relations*. What Leborgne and Lipietz do not consider are the *relations between capital and the state* and the developmental role of the state which Dunford attempted to add into their framework in Chapter 3 of this volume. In a full analysis attention would also have to be paid to the macroeconomic order (see, for example, Leborgne and Lipietz 1990). In this collection however most attention is given to capital-labour relations.

Two characteristics (see Figure 16.3) of Fordist industrial relations are identified (Taylorism as a principle of work organisation, and a rigid wage and employment contract) and two ways out of the crisis are defined (a neo-liberal path which identifies wage and employment flexibility as solutions for the full-

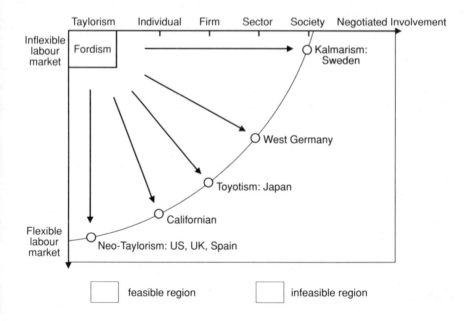

Figure 16.3 From Fordism to ...? Alternative work and employment relations

Source: adapted from Leborgne and Lipietz 1990.

employment profit squeeze, and non-Taylorist strategies of responsible involvement of workers aimed at increasing the productivity and functional flexibility of workers, improving demand response and overcoming the inefficiency of Taylorism). (The dimension of responsible involvement draws on the distinction that Friedman (1977, pp.48–50) made between direct and responsible autonomy control strategies.) In the case of the horizontal axis Leborgne and Lipietz distinguish the level at which the involvement of workers and the concessions made by employers are negotiated (if at all): not negotiated (Taylorism), individual, firm, sector and societal level negotiation. As the level at which agreements are made increases, more solidaristic, more organised, less hierarchical, less market-oriented and more rigid wage, employment and social security arrangements prevail. And as one moves around the arc from bottom left to top right the size of the group included in the social compromise increases and the size of the marginalised stratum of a dual society diminishes as does the extent of income polarisation (see Leborgne and Lipietz 1990 for these developments of the ideas set out in Chapter 2).

In this way several alternative models are identified. Neo-Taylorism is Taylorism without the social advantages of Fordism, while the combination of rigid wage and employment relations with negotiated involvement is named after the Volvo plant at Kalmar in Sweden where the assembly line was first dispensed with. The situation in any country will be a complex combination of these elements: in the Third Italy, for example, there are systems that depend on low wages, multiple job holding, irregular work, the employment of children, and the evasion of taxes and social security contributions, and there are others where a significant proportion of the workers are skilled, well-paid and provided with good collective services.

In the view of Leborgne and Lipietz the regional economies and societies that have been most successful are the ones that have chosen strategies of involvement. But the possibilities of making choices have declined. At present the differences in productivity and competitiveness between regions are great: areas whose elites chose increased work and employment flexibility and have below average productivities may not therefore have the extra surplus value to pay for more progressive social compromises and will find it very difficult to change course.

This approach does require further refinement. On the one hand there is a need to consider in more detail the question of worker involvement. The goal of Leborgne and Lipietz is to increase the job quality, job security and rights of co-determination of the workforce. Increases in the range and complexity of jobs, increases in job satisfaction and increases in skill may, however, not go with increases in job autonomy (control over the scheduling, speed and inspection of work), while increases in autonomy may not mean increases in control over working and employment conditions (see Badham and Mathews 1989, pp.200–2). On the other hand the question as to whether the initiatives and the constantly renegotiated compromises flow from management or the workforce and their implications needs to be addressed as the objectives and content of worker- and management-oriented strategies differ in significant ways.

Nonetheless the method allows one to identify the stakes and the issues around which social and political mobilisation occurs and permits a much more differentiated analysis of neo-Fordism and post-Fordism. Leborgne and Lipietz (1990) do insist that the diagram does not indicate the 'relative positions of different countries' but 'directions out of Fordism'. The 'real Fordist starting points' are different and so 'a diagram of relative positions' would look different. The interpretative question that arises, however, is the following: are these different situations in fact different paths out of Fordism, or are the differences Leborgne an Lipietz identify due in the main to the existence of different starting points (and of differences in rates of growth in the 1980s)?

Some neo-Schumpeterians and writers of flexible specialisation see a new technological divide, while Leborgne and Lipietz see a political divide with possibilities for prosperity. All contributors to this debate would accept that the direction of change depends on politics and on struggles among social classes and that the situation that results will be a mixed one. The writers who see neo-Fordist tendencies are simply less optimistic about current trends. In the view of some West German and Japanese writers their national variants of Fordism embodied more progressive compromises. Trends towards socio-economic differentiation, deregulation and commercialisation, and increases in the independence and dominance of financial and speculative capital are also found in these countries (see, for example, Krätke) and are therefore common to all. In the words of Itoh (1990):

'scaling up of the units of investment in plant and equipment, strengthening the social position of workers and trade unions, and increasing economic roles of the state were mutually related ... and formed a basic tendency in capitalist societies [which differentiated] the postwar age of Keynesianism or Fordism from earlier eras. The post-Fordist regime of accumulation reversed all these ... tendencies especially in the 1980s under the neo-conservative policies [adopted] in major capitalist countries'.

The differences that still exist between the proponents of neo-Fordism and post-Fordism rest on different evaluations of the relative weight of neo-conservatism on the one hand and movements for democratic social control, deeper solidarities, greater equality and ecologically sustainable development on the other.

Bibliography

Abernathy, W. J. (1978) *The productivity dilemma: roadblock to innovation in the automobile industry*, Baltimore and London, The Johns Hopkins University Press.

Abernathy, W. J. and Wayne, K. (1985) 'La Courbe d'expérience et ses limites', *Harvard — l'Expansion*, Numéro spécial 'Stratégie I', Paris.

Abernathy, W. J., Clark, K. B. and Kantrow, A. M. (1983) *Industrial renaissance: producing a competitive future for America*, New York, Basic Books.

Abraham-Frois, G. (1977) *Problématique de la croissance*, 2 vols, Paris, Economica.

Aganbegyan, A. (1988) 'New directions in Soviet economics', *New Left Review*, no. 169, May–June, pp.89-95.

Aglietta, M. (1976) *Régulation et crises du capitalisme*, Calmann-Lévy, Paris.

—— (1979) *A theory of capitalist regulation*, London, New Left Books.

Ambrosini, M. (1985) *'Crisi' delle relazioni industriali e innovazione tecnologica nell'esperienza Italiana*, Milano, Università Catholica, Documento di lavoro.

Amin, A. (1989) 'Flexible specialisation and small firms in Italy: myths and realities', *Antipode*, vol.21, pp.13-34.

Amin, A. and Robins, K. (1990) 'The re-emergence of regional economies? The mythical geography of flexible accumulation', *Environment and Planning D: Society and Space*, vol.8, pp.7-34.

Aoki, M. (1986) 'Horizontal vs vertical information structure of the firm', *American Economic Review*, vol.76, no. 5, December, pp.971-983.

—— (1990) 'A new paradigm of work organisation and co-ordination. Lessons from Japanese experience', in Marglin, S.A. and Schor, J. B. (1990) pp.267-93.

Arizona Gazette (1987) 'The Neal Pierce Report', 8 February 1987.

Arrow, K. (1962) 'The economic implications of learning by doing', *Review of Economic Studies*, vol.XXIX, pp.155-73.

Association Bureau-Province (1983) *Les Nouveaux Toits de la matière grise*, Paris, Association Bureau-Province.

Atkinson, J. (1984) *Flexibility, uncertainty, and manpower management. Report of a study conducted under the co-operative research programme of the I.M.S.*, Falmer, Brighton, University of Sussex, Institute of Manpower Studies, Report no.89.

—— (1987) 'Flexibility or fragmentation? The United Kingdom labour market in the 80s', *Labour and Society*, vol.12, no.1.

Audier, F. (1981) *Les Emplois tertiaires des entreprises industrielles*, Paris, Centre d'Etude et de Recherche des Qualifications (CEREQ), Dossier no.29.

Auerbach, P., Desai, M. and Shamsavari, A. (1988) 'The transition from actually existing capitalism', *New Left Review*, no.170 (July–August 1988) pp.61–78.

Augoyard, A. M., Champ, J. and Fradet, H. (1982) *L'électronique Grenobloise*, Grenoble, SIEPARG, Notes Economiques: Agglomération Grenobloise, no.1 (April).

Auguste Thouard et Conseils (1987) *Le Marche des locaux d'activite: Paris et région parisienne*, Paris, Auguste Thouard et Conseils.

Autzen, R. and Becker, H. (1988) *Wohnungsbestandssicherung, Teil 2: Engpässe in der Wohnungsversorgung*. Ein Städtevergleich, Berlin, Deutsches Institut für Urbanistik.

Avinieri, S. (1971) *The social and political thought of Karl Marx*, Cambridge, Cambridge University Press.

Aydalot, P. (ed.) (1984) *Crise et espace*, Paris, Economica.

—— (ed.) (1986a) *Milieux innovateurs en Europe*, Paris, GREMI.

—— (ed.) (1986b) *Technologies nouvelles et développement régional*, Paris, GREMI.

Ayres, R. U. (1985) 'A Schumpeterian model of technological substitution', *Technological Forecasting and Social Change*, no.27, pp.375–83.

—— and Miller S.N. (1983) *Robotics: applications and social implications*, Cambridge, Mass., BPC.

Azoulay, N. (1987) 'De la firme multiproduit à la théorie de marché contestable. Quels enseignements pour l'analyse de la flexibilité technologique', Paris, Université de Paris VII, *Cahiers du GERTTD*, no.87–09.

Bachet, D., Laury, C., Leborgne, D. and Ortsman, O. (eds) (1986) *Mutations technologiques, changements socio-culturels, et systèmes de travail*, Paris, Centre d'Etude des Systèmes et Techniques Avancées.

Bade, F. J. (1983) 'Large corporations and regional development', *Regional Studies*, vol.17, no.5, pp.315–25.

—— (1986) 'Funktionale Arbeitsteilung und regionale Beschäftigungsentwicklung', *Informationen zur Raumentwicklung*, nos 9 and 10 (Bonn, Bundesforschungsanstalt für Landeskunde und Raumordnung).

Badham, R. and Mathews, J. (1989) 'The new production systems debate', *Labour and Industry*, vol.2, no.2 (June) pp.194–246.

Bagnasco, A. (1977) *Tre Italie. La problematica territoriale dello sviluppo economico italiano*, Bologna, Il Mulino.

—— (1983) 'Il contesto sociale', in Fuà, G. and Zacchia, C. (eds) (1983) *Industrializzazione senza fratture*, Bologna, Il Mulino.

—— (1985) 'La costruzione sociale del mercato: strategie di impresa e esperimenti di scala in Italia', *Stato e mercato*, no.13 (April).

Bagnasco, A. and Pini, R. (1981) 'Sviluppo economico e trasformazioni sociopolitiche dei sistemi territoriali a economia diffusa. Economia e struttura sociale', Milan, Feltrinelli, *Quaderni della Fondazione G. Feltrinelli*, no.14.

Bagnasco, A. and Trigilia, C. (1985) *Società e politica nelle aree di piccola impresa: il caso della Valdelsa*, Milan, Franco Angeli.

Bagnasco, A. and Trigilia, C. (eds) (1984) *Società e politica nelle aree di piccola impresa: il caso di Bassano*, Venezia, Arsenale.

Bailey, E. and Friedlander, A. (1982) 'Market structure and multiproduct industries', *Journal of Economic Literature*, vol.20, no.3, September, pp.1024–48.

Baran, B. (1985) 'Office automation and women's work: the technological transformation of the insurance industry', in Castells, M. (ed.) (1985) pp.143–71.

Baumol, W., Panzar and Willing, (1982) *Contestable markets and the theory of industry structure*, New York, Harcourt Brace Jovanovich Inc.

Beaud, M. (1987) *Le système national-mondial hiérarchisé*, Paris, La Découverte.

Becattini, G. (1979) 'Dal "settore" industriale al "distretto" industriale: alcune considerazioni sull'unità di indagine dell'economia industriale', *Rivista di Economia e Politica Industriale*, vol.V, no.1, January–April.

—— (1984a) 'Ispessimenti localizzati di esternalità', *Banca Toscana Studi e Informazioni*, no.1.

—— (1984b) 'L'economista e l'ambiente', *Giornale degli Economisti e Annali di Economia*, vol.XLIII, nos 3–4, March–April.

—— (1987) 'Introduzione. Il distretto industriale marshalliano: cronaca di un ritrovamento', in Becattini, G. (ed.) (1987) pp.7–34.

—— (ed.) (1987) *Mercato e forze locali: il distretto industriale*, Bologna, Il Mulino.

—— (ed.) (1988) *Modelli locali di sviluppo*, Bologna, Il Mulino.

—— (cd.) (1990) *Il pensiero economico: temi, problemi e scuole*, Torino, UTET.

Becattini, G. and Bianchi, G. (1982) 'Sulla multiregionalità dello sviluppo economico italiano', *Note Economiche*, nos.5–6.

—— (1984) 'Chi ha paura della regionalità', *Il Ponte*, January–February.

Beckouche, P. (1988) *L'industrie électronique française: les régions face à la transnationalisation des firmes*, Paris, Université de Paris I, Thèse de Doctorat.

Beckouche, P. Savy, M. and Veltz, P. (1987) *Nouvelle economie, nouveaux territoires*, ERTES-Caisse des Dépots et Consignations. (See also the shortened version in *La Lettre de la DATAR*, no.118, July 1988).

Bellandi, M. (1982) 'Il distretto industriale in Alfred Marshall', *L'Industria*, vol.III, no.3, July–September.

—— (1988) 'Capacità innovativa diffusa e sistemi locali d'impresa', in Becattini (ed.) (1988) pp.149–172.

—— (1989) *Small firms and industrial districts in Italy*, London, Routledge.

Benedetti, E. (1989) *Mutazioni tecnologiche e condizionamenti internazionali*, Milan.

Benko, G. (1988) 'Technologies nouvelles, dévelopement urbain et changement social', in Benko, G. (ed.) *Les nouveaux aspects de la théorie social*, Caen, Paradigme, pp.123–27.

—— (1991) *Geographie des technopôles*, Paris, Masson.

Berthelot, J. M. (1988) 'La domination des services', *Le Monde*, 6 December.

Bertram, H. and Schamp, E. W. (1989) 'Räumliche Wirkungen neuer Produktionskonzepte in der Automobilindustrie', *Geographische Rundschau*, vol.41, no.5, pp.284–90.

Besson, P., Savy, M., Valeyre, A. and Veltz, P. (1988) *Gestion de production et transports: vers une nouvelle economie de la circulation*, Caen, Paradigme.

BIPE (1988) *Prévisions glissantes détaillées: Horizon 1988*, Brussels, BIPE.

Blackburn, P. and Sharpe, R. (eds) (1988) *Britain's industrial renaissance*, London, Routledge.

Blaug, M. (ed.) (1958) *Economics of education*, 2 vols, Harmondsworth, Penguin Books.

Bluestone, B. and Harrison, B. (1988) *The great U-turn: corporate restructuring and the polarising of America*, New York, Basic Books.

Boisgontier, P. and De Bernardy, M. (1986) *Les 'µe' Grenobloises ou les transformations d'un territoire industriel sous l'effet de l'innovation en micro-électronique*, Grenoble, Université des Sciences Sociales de Grenoble, CEPS, February.

Bonamy, J., Bonnet, J. and Philippe, J. (1986) 'Mutations tertiaires et dynamiques spatiales', in Plan Urbain, DATAR and CGP, *Mutations economiques et urbanisation*, Paris, La Documentation Française, pp. 251–92.

Booz-Allen and Hamilton (1988) *Cross Border Acquisitions*, Paris, Booz-Allen and Hamilton.

Borries, H. W. v. (1969) *Ökonomische Grundlagen der westdeutschen Siedlungsstrukur*, Hannover, Duncker und Humblodt.

Borzeix, A. and Linhart, D. (1988) 'La participation: un clair-obscur', *Sociologie du Travail*, no.1, pp.37–53.

Bourdais Cabinet (1988) *Le marché immobilier en France: bureaux, locaux d'activités et commerciaux*, Paris.

Bouvard, L. and Calame, P. (1988) *Le dialogue des enterprises et du territoire*, Paris, Rapport au Ministre de l'Equipement et du Logement.

Boyer, R. (ed.) (1986a) *La flexibilité du travail en Europe*, Paris, La Découverte.

—— (1986b) *La théorie de la régulation: une analyse critique*, Paris, La Découverte.

—— (ed.) (1988) *The search for labour market flexibility. The European economies in transition*, Oxford, Clarendon Press.

Boyer, R. and Coriat, B. (1986) 'De la flexibilité technique à la stabilisation macro-économique: un essai d'analyse', in Cohendet and Llerena (eds) (1986).

Boyer, R. and Mistral, J. (1978) *Accumulation, inflation, crises*, Paris, Presses Universitaires de France.

Braconnier, J. (1987) *Rapport d'information sur les Contrats Etat-régions*, Paris, Sénat, no.381, Séance 9 July 1987.

Bradbury, J. H. (1985) 'Regional and industrial restructuring processes in the new international division of labour', *Progress in Human Geography*, vol.9, no.1, pp.38–63.

Brake, K. (1988) *Phönix in der Asche: New York verändert seine Stadtstruktur*, Oldenburg, Universität Oldenburg.

Braune, E. and Macdonald, S. (1982) *Revolution in miniature. The history and impact of semiconductor electronics*, Cambridge, Cambridge University Press.

Breckner, J. and Schmals, K. (1985) *Regionalentwicklung zwischen Technologieboom und Resteverwertung. Die Beispiele Ruhrgebiet und München*, Bochum, Germinal.

Breit, W. (1987) 'Creating the "Virginia School": Charlottesville as an Academic Environment in the 1960s', *Economic Inquiry*, October, pp.647–48.

Bressand, A. and Distler, C. (1985) *Le prochain monde*, Paris, Seuil.

Bressand, A. and Nicolaïdis, K. (1988) Les services au coeur de l'économie relationelle, *Revue d'Economie Industrielle*, no.43, pp.141–63.

Bressand, A., Distler, C. and Nicolaïdis, K. (1989) 'Vers une économie de réseaux', *Politique Industrielle*, no.14, pp.155–68 (Paris, CPE).

Brusco, S. (1975) 'Organizzazione del lavoro e decentramento produttivo nel settore metalmeccanico', in FLM Bergamo (ed.) (1975) *Sindacato e piccola impresa*, Bari, De Donato.

—— (1982) 'The Emilian Model: Productive Decentralisation and Social Integration', *Cambridge Journal of Economics*, vol.6, no.2, June, pp.167–84.

—— (1986) 'Small firms and industrial districts: the experience of Italy', in Keeble, D. and Wever, E. (eds) (1986) *New firms and regional development in Europe*, Beckenham, Kent, Croom Helm.

Brusco, S. and Sabel, C. F. (1981) 'Artisan production and economic growth', in Wilkinson, F. (ed.) (1981) *The dynamics of labour market segmentation*, London, Academic Press.

Bucher, H. and Kocks, M. (1987) 'Entwicklung von Stadtregionen und Städten: empirische Analysen auf der Basis der laufenden Raumbeobachtung', *Informationen zur Raumentwicklung*, nos. 11 and 12 (Bonn, Bundesforschungsanstalt für Landeskunde und Raumordnung).

Bultel, J. (1985) 'Flexibilité de production et rentabilité d'investissements: l'exemple de la robotisation de l'assemblage en tôlerie par soudage par points', *Revue d'Economie Industrielle*, no.26, pp.1–13.

Bursi, T. (1985) *Le condizioni economico-finanziarie delle imprese dei settori maglieria e abbigliamento dell'Emilia Romagna*, Padova, CEDAM.

—— (1987) *Indagine sulle condizioni economico-finanziarie delle imprese emiliano-romagnole del tessile-abbigliamento*, Carpi, CITER-Università di Modena-Banca Popolare dell'Emilia.

Business week (1989) 'RJR Nabisco unloads some debt', *Business Week*, 19 June, p.41.

Carroue, L. (1987) 'Recherches sur les industries électriques et électroniques en Ile de France, Paris, Université de Paris I, *Notes de Recherche CRIA*, no.2.

—— (1989) *Les industries informatique, électrique et électronique en France*, Paris, Université de Paris I, Thèse de Doctorat.

Cartalas, René (1970) *L'industrie chimique et la croissance économique*, Paris, Marie-Thérèse Genin.

Casson, M. (1986) *Multinationals and world trade: vertical integration and the division of labour in world industries*, London, Allen and Unwin.

Castells, M. (ed.) (1985) *High technology, space and society*, Beverly Hills, Sage.

—— (1989) *The informational city. Information technology, economic restructuring, and the urban-regional process*, Oxford, Basil Blackwell.

Castells, M. and Henderson, J. (1987) 'Techno-economic restructuring, socio-political processes and spatial transformation: a global perspective', in Henderson, J. and Castells, M. (eds) (1987) *Global restructuring and territorial development*, London, Sage.

Cavard, J. C. (1986) 'Industries de haute technologie et politique dpartementale d'innovation dans la couronne parisienne septentrionale', *BAGF (Bulletin de l'Association de Géographes Français)*, no.3, pp.227–36.

Cavestro, W. (1989) 'Automation, New Technology and Work Content', in Wood, S. (ed.) (1989) *Work Transformed?*, London, Unwin Hyman.

CCE/BIPE (1969) *L'industrie électronique des pays de la Communauté et les investissements américains*, Brussels, CCE/BIPE.

CCI Beaubourg (1986) *Lieux de travail*, Paris, CCI.

Cecchini, P. (1988) *The European challenge. 1992: The benefits of a single market*, Aldershot, Wildwood House.

Centre d'Etudes de l'Emploi (1987) *Entreprises et Produits* no.30, Paris, Presses Universitaires de France, Cahiers du Centre d'Etudes de l'Emploi.

Centre des Nations Unies sur les Sociétés Transnationales (1983) *Transnational corporations in the international semiconductor industry*, New York, UNO.

Chamberlain, T.H. (1927) *The theory of monopolistic competition*, Cambridge, Harvard University Press.

Champ, J. and Fradet, H. (1985) 'Les structures de l'économie Grenobloise', in Joly, J. (ed.) (1985) *Grenoble et son agglomération*, Paris, La Documentation Française, *Notes et Etudes Documentaires*, no.4769, pp.43–79.

Chardonnet, J. (1953) *Les grands types de complexes industriels*, Paris, A. Colin.

CITER (1987) *Considerazioni relative all'esercizio 1986 e indirizzi programmatici per il 1987*, Carpi, CITER.

—— (1988) *Considerazioni relative all'esercizio 1987 e indirizzi programmatici per il 1988*, Carpi, CITER.

Clark, G. L. (1989) *Communities under siege Cambridge*, Cambridge University Press.

Clark, G. L., Gertler, M. S. and Whiteman, J. E. M. (1986) *Regional dynamics: studies in adjustment theory*, Boston, Mass., Allen and Unwin.

Claval, P. (1968) *Régions, nations, grands espaces*, Paris, Marie-Thérèse Genin.

—— (1978) 'La localisation des activités industrielles', *Revue géographique de l'Est*, vol.17, nos 1–2, pp.51–81.

—— (1988) 'La métropolisation de l'économie et de la société américaines', *Historiens-Géographes*, no.312, pp.447–60.

—— (1989) 'L'avenir de la métropolisation', *Annales de Géographie*, vol.98, pp.692–706.

Cockshott, P. and Cottrell, A. (1989) 'Labour value and socialist calculation', *Economy and Society* vol.18, no.1, February, pp.71–99.

Cohen, E. and Bauer, M. (1985) *Les grandes manoeuvres industrielles*, Paris, Pierre Belfond.

Cohen, J. (1987) 'Emplois de haute technologie et technopoles: Paris-Sud dans le contexte régional et national', Paris, Université de Paris I, Thèse de Doctorat.

Cohen, S. and Zysman J. (1987) *Manufacturing matters: the myth of the post-industrial society*, New York, Basic Books/Paris, Economica.

Cohen, Y, et Berry, B. (1985) *Spatial components of manufacturing change*, Chicago: University of Chicago.

Cohendet, P. and Llerena, P. (eds) (1986) *Flexibilité, information et décision*, Paris, Economica.

—— (1989) 'La flexibilité dans un regime de variété permanente', in Cohendet, P., Hollard, M., Malsch, T. and Veltz, P. (eds) *L'après-taylorisme: nouvelles normes de rationalisation dans l'entreprise en France et en RFA*, Paris, Economica, pp.55–75.

Connor, H. and Pearson, R. (1986) *Information technology manpower into the 1990s*, Falmer, Brighton, University of Sussex, Institute of Manpower Studies.

Conseil Economique et Social (1989) *L'économie française souffre-t-elle d'une insuffisance de recherche?*, Paris, La Documentation Française, Journal Officiel, séances des 25 et 26 avril 1989.

Contini, B. (1984) 'Dimensioni di impresa, divisione del lavoro e ampiezza del mercato', *Moneta e Credito*, no.148.

Contini, B. and Revelli, R. (1986) 'Natalità e mortalità delle imprese italiane: risultati preliminari e nuove prospettive di ricerca', *L'Industria*, no.2.

Cooke, P. (1988) 'Flexible integration, scope economies and strategic alliances: social and spatial mediations', *Environment and Planning D: Society and Space*, vol.6, pp.281–300.

Coombs, R., Saviotti, P. and Walsh, V. (1987) *Economics and technological change*, Basingstoke and London, Macmillan.

Coriat, B. (1979) *L'atelier et le chronomètre*, deuxième édition, Paris, C. Bourgois.

—— (1983) *La Robotique*, Paris, La Découverte.

—— (1991) 'Technical flexibility and mass production: flexible specialisation and dynamic flexibility', in Benko, G. and Dunford, M. (eds) (1991) *Industrial change and regional development*, London, Belhaven.

Costello, N., Michie, J. and Milne, S. (1989) *Beyond the casino economy: planning for the 1990s*, London, Verso.

Courlet, C. (1987) 'Développement territorial et systèmes productifs locaux en Italie', Grenoble, Institut de Recherches Economiques et Prospectives, Notes et Documents, no.22.

Crowther, D. and Echenique, M. (1972) 'Development of a model of urban spatial structure', in Martin, L. and March, L. (eds) (1972) *Urban Space and Structures*, Cambridge, Cambridge University Press, pp.175–218.

Damette, F. (1980) 'The regional framework of monopoly exploitation: new problems and trends', in Carney, J., Hudson, R. and Lewis, J. (eds) (1980) *Regions in Crisis*, London, Croom Helm.

Damette, F., Beckouche, P., Carroue, L., Cohen, J. and Scheibling, J. (1987) *La crise de l'industrie française: étude géographique*, Paris, Université de Paris I, STRATES, Rapport de recherche.

Damette, F., Beckouche, P., Cohen, J., Fischer, J-C. and Scheibling, J. (1989) *Métropolisation et aires métropolitaines - internationalisation et enjeu urbain*, Paris, Plan Urbain, DATAR, Commissariat Général au Plan/Université de Paris I, STRATES.

Dardi, M. (1990) 'Il mercato nell'analisi economica contemporanea', in Becattini (ed.) (1990), pp.51-100.

Dataquest (1985-88) *European semiconductor industry service*, vols.1-5, Dataquest.

Dataquest (1985-88) *Japanese semiconductor industry analysis*, vols.1-3, Dataquest.

David, P. (1986) 'La moissonneuse et le robot: la diffusion des innovations basées sur la micro-électronique', in Salomon, J. J. and Schmeder, G. (eds) (1986) *Les enjeux du changement technologique*, Paris, Economica.

Davis, L. E. and Taylor, J. C. (eds) (1972) *Design of jobs: selected readings*, Harmondsworth, Penguin.

Davis, M. (1986) *Prisoners of the American dream*, London, Verso.

de Blasio, G. and Riva, A. (1984) *La rilocalizzazione industriale in Lombardia*, Milan, Istituto regionale di ricerca and Franco Angeli.

de Bono, E. (1971) *The use of lateral thinking*, Harmondsworth, Penguin Books.

—— (1987) *Letters to thinkers. Further thoughts on lateral thinking*, London, Harrap.

De Roo, P. and Wachter, S. (1986) *Les dynamiques du territoire*, Paris, DATAR.

Dei Ottati, G. (1987) 'Il mercato comunitario', in Becattini (ed.) (1987) pp.117-142.

Del Monte, A. and Martinelli, F. (1987) 'The organisational structure of small and medium firms in the electronics industry: regional differentiation in Italy', paper presented at the Conference on Innovation Diffusion in the Regional Experience of Europe and the United States, Istituto Universitario Orientale, Naples, 20-21 February 1987.

—— (1988) 'Gli ostacoli alla divisione tecnica e sociale del lavoro nelle aree depresse: il caso delle piccole imprese elettroniche in Italia', *L'Industria*, no.3.

Delorme, R. and André, C. (1983) *L'Etat et l'économie*, Paris, Seuil.

Dematteis, G. (1983) 'Deconcentrazione metropolitana, crescita periferica e ripopolamento di aree marginali: il caso dell'Italia', in Cencini, C., Dematteis, G. and Menegatti, B. (eds) (1983) *L'Italia emergente*, Milan, Franco Angeli.

Dematteis, G. (1985) 'Controandurbanizzazione e deconcentrazione: un salto di scala nell'organizzazione territoriale', in Innocenti, R. (ed.) (1985) *Piccola città e piccola impresa*, Milan, Franco Angeli.

Dematteis, G. (1985) 'Controandurbanizzazione e strutture urbane reticolari', in Bianchi, G. and Magnani, I. (eds), *Sviluppo multiregionale : teorie, metodi, problemi*, Milan, Franco Angeli.

Dezert, B. (1988) 'Mutations technologiques et strategies foncières et immobilières en region parisienne', Créteil, CNG - Journées des Commissions industrielles et urbaine, September.

Dicken, P. (1986) *Global shift: industrial change in a turbulent world*, London, Harper.

Dillon, J. T. (1988) 'Levels of problem finding versus problem solving', *Questioning Exchange: A Multidisciplinary Review*, May.

Dosi, G. (1981) Technical change and survival: Europe's semiconductor industry, Falmer, Brighton, Sussex European Paper no.9.

—— (1984) *Technical change and industrial transformation*, London, MacMillan.

Drewett, R. (1980) 'Changing urban structures in Europe', *The Annals of the American Academy*, vol.451, September.

—— (1985) 'Dynamics of European metropolitan areas in the 80's', paper presented to the Seminario sulla rivitalizzazione delle aree metropolitane, Politecnico di Milano, April.

Dubois, P. and Barisi, G. (1982) 'Le défi technologique dans l'industrie de l'habillement', Paris, Université de Paris VII, Groupe de Sociologie du Travail.

Dunford, M. (1977) 'The restructuring of industrial space', *International Journal of Urban and Regional Research*, vol.1, no.3, October, pp.510-20.

Dunford, M. (1988) *Capital, the state, and regional development*, London, Pion.

—— (1988) 'Grenoble and Central Scotland's regional electronics industries', Falmer, Brighton, University of Sussex, Geography Working Paper no.18.

Dunford, M. (1989) 'Technopoles, politics and markets', in Sharp, M. and Holmes, P. (eds) (1989) *Strategies for new technology*, Oxford, Philip Allan.

Dunford, M. and Perrons, D. (1983) *The arena of capital*, London, Macmillan.

Dupuy, G. (1985) *Systèmes, réseaux et territoires*, Paris, Presses de l'ENPC.

Düll, K. and Lutz, B. (1989) *Technikentwicklung und Arbeitsteilung im internationalen Vergleich*, Frankfurt, Campus.

Emery, F. E. (1969) *Systems thinking: selected readings*, Harmondsworth, Penguin.

Emery, F. E. and Trist, E. L. (1972) 'Socio technical systems', in Davis and Taylor (eds) (1972).

Enrietti, A. (1983) 'Industria automobilistica: la 'quasi integrazione verticale' come modello interpretativo dei rapporti tra imprese', *Economia e politica industriale*, no.38

Ernst, D. (1983) *The global race in microelectronics*, Frankfurt, Campus Verlag.

Esser, J. and Hirsch, J. (1987) 'Stadtsoziologie und Gesellschaftstheorie. Von der Fordismuskrise zur 'postfordistischen' Regional- und Stadtstruktur', in Prigge, W. (ed.) (1987) *Die Materialität des Städtischen*. Basel and Boston, Birkhäuser.

Estall, R. C. (1985) 'Stock control in manufacturing: the just-in-time system and its locational implications', *Area*, vol.17, pp.129–133.

Evence, F. (1987) 'Les gourous dans l'entreprise américaine: parapsychologie et intégration du personnel', cited in *Problèmes Economiques*, no.2047, pp.31–32.

Evers, A. (1975) 'Agglomerationsprozeß und Staatsfunktionen', in Grauhan, R. -R. (ed.) (1975) *Lokale Politikforschung*, vol.1, Frankfurt and New York, Campus.

Fainstein, S. and Fainstein, N. (1987) Technology, the new international division of labor, and location: is there a qualitative discontinuity?, paper presented at the ISA Conference, Dubrovnik, 1987.

Feagin, J. R. and Smith, M. P. (1987) 'Cities and the new international division of labor: an overview', in Smith, M. P. and Feagin, J. R. (eds) (1987) *The capitalist city: global restructuring and community politics*, Oxford, Basil Blackwell.

Firn, J. R. and Roberts, D. (1984) High-technology industries, in Hood, N. and Young, S. (eds) (1984) *Industry, policy and the Scottish economy*, Edinburgh, Edinburgh University Press, pp.288–325.

Forester, T. (1987) *High tech society: the story of the information technology revolution*, Oxford, Blackwell.

Frappat, P. (1988) 'Bull ne veut plus produire à Grenoble', *Le Monde*, 23 February 1988, p.20.

Freeman, C. (1984) *Long waves in the world economy*, London, Frances Pinter.

—— (1988) 'The factory of the future: the productivity paradox, Japanese just-in-time and information technology', London, Economic and Social Research Council, *PICT Policy Research Papers*, no.3, May.

Freeman, C., Clark, J. and Soete, L. (1982) *Unemployment and technical innovation: a study of long waves and economic development*, London, Frances Pinter.

Friedman, A. L. (1977) *Industry and labour: class struggle at work and monopoly capitalism*, London, Macmillan.

Friedrichs, G. (1982) 'Microelettronica e microeconomia', in Friedrichs, G. and Schaff, A. (eds) *Rivoluzione microelettronica, Rapporto al Club di Roma*, Milan, Mondadori.

Friedrichs, J. (ed.) (1985) *Die Städte in den 80er Jahren. Demographische, ökonomische und technologische Entwicklungen*, Opladen, Westdeutscher Verlag.

Friedrichs, J., Häußermann, H. and Siebel, W. (eds) (1986) *Süd-Nord-Gefälle in der Bundesrepublik? Sozialwissenschaftliche Analysen*, Opladen, Westdeutscher Verlag.

Fröbel, F., Heinrichs, J. and Kreye, O. (1980) *The new international division of labor*, Cambridge, Cambridge University Press.

Fuà, G. (1980) *Problemi dello sviluppo tardivo in Europa*, Bologna, Il Mulino.

—— (1983) 'L'industrializzazione nel Nord-Est e nel Centro', in Fuà and Zacchia (eds) (1983).

Fuà, G. and Zacchia, C. (eds) (1983) *Industrializzazione senza fratture*, Bologna, Il Mulino.

Garofoli, G. (1978) 'Decentramento produttivo, mercato del lavoro e localizzazione industriale', in Garofoli, G. (ed.) (1978) *Ristrutturazione industriale e territorio*, Milan, Franco Angeli.

—— (1981) 'Lo sviluppo delle "aree periferiche" nell'economia italiana degli anni settanta', *L'Industria*, vol.II, no.3, July–September.

—— (1981) 'Lo sviluppo delle "aree periferiche" nell'economia italiana degli anni settanta', *L'industria*, no.2.

—— (1983a) 'Aree di specializzazione produttiva e piccole imprese in Europa', *Economia Marche*, vol.2, no.1, June.

—— (1983b) 'Le aree-sistema in Italia', *Politica ed Economia*, vol.XIV, no.11, November.

—— (1983c) 'Sviluppo regionale e ristrutturazione industriale: il modello italiano degli anni '70', *Rassegna Economica*, vol.XLVII, no.6, November–December.

——— (1983d) *Industrializzazione diffusa in Lombardia*, Milan, Istituto regionale di ricerca and Franco Angeli.

——— (1984a) 'Squilibri regionali e sviluppo del Mezzogiorno', in V Conferenza italiana di Scienze Regionali, *Preprints*, vol.I, Bari, Edizioni Levante.

——— (1984b) Modelli locali di sviluppo, paper presented at the XXV Riunione Scientifica della Società Italiana degli Economisti, Rome, November.

——— (1986a) 'Centro vs. periferia nelle politiche di valorizzazione delle economie locaii', in Garofoli, G. and Magnani, I. (eds) (1986) *Verso una nuova centralità delle aree urbane nello sviluppo dell'occupazione*, Milan, Franco Angeli.

——— (1986b) 'Le développement périphérique en Italie', *Economie et Humanisme*, no.289, May–June.

——— (1987) 'Regional inequalities and development in the Mezzogiorno', *Economic Notes*, vol.16, no.2, pp.121–40.

——— (1989) 'Industrial districts: structure and transformation', *Economic Notes*, vol.19, no.1, pp.37–54.

Gartman, D. (1979) 'Origins of the assembly line and capitalist control of work at Ford', in Zimbalist, A. (ed.) (1979) *Case Studies on the Labour Process*, New York and London, Monthly Review Press, pp 193–205.

Gatzweiler, H.-P. (1985) 'Die Entwicklung in den Regionen des Bundesgebiets', in Friedrichs, J. (ed.) (1985) *Die Städte in den 80er Jahren*, Opladen, Westdeutscher Verlag.

Geneau de Lamarlière, I. (1988) 'L'industrie des semi-conducteurs: les facteurs internationaux de localisation', Paris, Université de Paris I, Mémoire de DEA d'économie internationale.

George, P., Guglielmo, R., Kayser, B. and Lacoste, Y. (1964) *La géographie active*, Paris, Presses Universitaires de France.

Georgescu Roegen, N. (1966) *Analytical economics*, Cambridge, Mass., Harvard University Press .

Gertler, M. S. (1988) 'The limits to flexibility: comments on the post-Fordist vision of production and its geography', *Transactions of the Institute of British Geographers*, New Series, vol.13, pp.419–32.

GERTTD (1985) 'Intégration, flexibilité et gestion prévisionnelle d'emploi', Paris, Université de Paris VII, Groupe d'Etude et de Recherche sur les Techniques, le Travail et le Développement, Cahiers du GERTTD, no.2.

Gerwin, D. and Leung, T. K. (1980) 'The organisational impacts of FMS: some initial findings', Trondheim, Norway, Institute of Social Research in Industry Discussion Paper.

Getzels, J. W. (1988) 'Problem finding and creative thought', *Questioning Exchange. A Multidisciplinary Review*, May.

Gille, C. (1988) Médiation et espace urbain, Montpellier, IDATE, mimeo.

Gilly, J. P. (1987) 'Innovation et territoire: pour une approche eso-économique des technopôles', *Revue d'Economie Régionale et Urbaine*, no.5, pp.788–95.

Glasmeier, A. (1986) 'Spatial differentiation of high technology industries: implification for planning', Berkeley, University of California, Department of City and Regional Planning, PhD Dissertation.

Glasmeier, A. (1988) 'Factors governing the development of high tech industry agglomerations: a tale of three cities', *Regional Studies*, vol.22, no.4.

Glyn, A., Hughes, A., Lipietz, A. and Singh, A. (1990) 'The rise and fall of the golden age', in Marglin and Schor (1990) pp.39–125.

Gober, P. (1986) 'Why and how Phoenix households changed: 1970–1980', *Annals of the Association of American Geographers*, vol.76, pp.536–49.

Goetz-Girey, R. (1960) 'Stimulants et propagation de la croissance dans le pays de Montbéliard', *Revue économique*, vol.XI, pp.1–16.

Gold, B. (1981) 'Changing perspectives on size, scale and returns: an interpretative survey', *Journal of Economic Literature*, vol.XIX, March, pp.5–33.

Goodman, E., Bamford, J. and Saynor, P. (eds) (1989) *Small firms and industrial districts in Italy*, London, Routledge.

Gordon, D. M., Edwards, R. C. and Reich, M. (1982) *Segmented work, divided workers. The historical transformation of labour in the United States*, Cambridge, Cambridge University Press.

Gottdiener, M. (1988) 'Crisis theory and socio-spatial restructuring: the US case', in Gottdiener, M. and Komninos, N. (eds) (1988) *Capitalist development and crisis theory*, London, Macmillan.

Gottmann, J. (ed.) (1952) *L'aménagement de l'espace. Planification régionale et géographie*, Paris, A. Colin.

Grabow, B. and Henckel, D. (1986) 'Die kleinräumige Verteilung von Unternehmen der Informationstechnik in der Bundesrepublik Deutschland', Berlin, Deutsches Institut für Urbanistik, *Aktuelle Informationen*, no.3.

Granados, V. (1984) 'Small firms and rural industrialization in Spain: some results from an OECD project', in R. Hudson (ed.) (1984) *Small Firms and Regional Development*, Copenhagen, Institute for Transport, Tourism and Regional Economy.

Gravier, J.-F. (1947) *Paris et le désert français*, Paris, Flammarion.

Grieve Smith, J. and Fleck, V. (1987) 'Business strategies in small high-technology companies', *Long Range Planning*, vol.20, no.2, pp.61–8.

Grotz, R. (1979) 'Räumliche Beziehungen industrieller Mehrbetriebsunternehmen', in Borcherdt, C. and Grotz. R. (eds) (1979) *Festschrift für Wolfgang Meckelein*, Stuttgarter Geographische Studien, no.93, pp.225–43.

Groupe de Réflexion sur le Développement de l'Electronique dans la Région Grenobloise (1982) *Livre blanc sur la filière électronique dans la région grenobloise*, Grenoble, SIEPARG.

Hagey, M. J. and Malecki E. (1986) 'Linkages in high technology industries: a Florida case study', *Environment and Planning* A, vol.18, no.11, pp.1477–98.

Hakim, C. (1989) 'Workforce restructuring in Europe in the 1980s', *International Journal of Comparative Labour Law and Industrial Relations*, vol.5, part 4, Winter, pp.220–40.

Hall, P. and Markusen, A. (eds) (1985) *Silicon landscapes*, Boston, Mass., Allen and Unwin.

Harrison, B. and Bluestone, B. (1988) *The Great U-Turn*, New York, Basic Books.

Harvey, D. (1985) *The urbanisation of capital: studies in the history and theory of capitalist urbanisation 2*, Baltimore, Johns Hopkins University Press.

—— (1987) 'Flexible Akkumulation durch Urbanisierung: Überlegungen zum 'Post-Modernism' in den amerikanischen Städten', *Prokla*, no.69 Berlin, Rotbuch.

—— (1988) 'The geographical and geopolitical consequences of the transition from Fordism to flexible accumulation', in Sternlieb, G. and Hughes, J. W. (eds) (1988) *America's new market geography*, New Brunswick, NJ., Rutger.

—— (1989) *The condition of post-modernity*, Oxford, Basil Blackwell.

Häußermann, H. and Siebel, W. (1986) 'Die Polarisierung der Großstadtentwicklung im Süd-Nord-Gefälle', in Friedrichs et al. (eds) (1986).

—— (1987) *Neue Urbanität*, Frankfurt am Main, Suhrkamp.

—— (1988) 'Die schrumpfende Stadt und die Stadtsoziologie', in Friedrichs, J. (ed.) (1988) *Soziologische Stadtforschung*. Opladen, Westdeutscher Verlag.

Hautreux, J., and Rochefort, M. (1965) 'Physionomie de l'armature urbaine française', *Annales de Géographie*, vol.74, pp.660–77.

Hayes, R. H. and Wheelwright, S. C. (1984) *Restoring our competitive edge: competiting through manufacturing*, New York, John Wiley.

Henckel, D. and Nopper, G,. (1984) *Informationstechnologie und Stadtentwicklung*, Stuttgart, Kohlhammer.

Henderson, J. (1987) 'Semiconductors, Scotland and the international division of labour', *Urban Studies*, vol.24, pp.389–408.

Heuer, H. (1985) 'Die veränderte ökonomische Basis der Städte', in Friedrichs, J. (ed.), *Die Städte in den 80er Jahren*, Opladen, Westdeutscher Verlag.

Hickel, R. (1988) *Ein neuer Typ der Akkumulation?*, Hamburg, VSA.

Hirsch, J. and Roth, R. (1986) *Das neue Gesicht des Kapitalismus. Vom Fordismus zum Post-Fordismus*, Hamburg, VSA.

Hirschauer, P., Bonfanti, J. M. and Holl, S. (1988) 'La sous-traitance pour l'électronique en Région Rhône-Alpes', *TLE — Equipements*, no.2, May.

Hirschmann, W. B. (1985) 'La leçon de la courbe d'expérience', *Harvard — L'Expansion, numéro spécial 'Stratégie I'*, Paris.

Hirst, P. and Zeitlin, J. (eds) (1989) *Reversing industrial decline?: industrial structure and policy in Britain and her competitors*, Oxford, Berg.

Holmes, J. (1986) 'The organization and locational structure of production subcontracting', in Scott and Storper (eds) (1986), pp.80–106

Hounshell, D. A. (1984) *From the American system to mass production 1800-1932*, Baltimore and London, The Johns Hopkins University Press.

Houssiaux, J. (1957) 'Le concept de 'quasi-intégration' et le rôle des sous-traitants dans l'industrie', *Revue Economique*, no.3.

Howard, R. (1987) 'Parcs scientifiques et développement régional', *Bulletin ATHENA*, no.31.

Hudson, R. (1989) 'Labour-market changes and new forms of work in old industrial regions: maybe flexibility for some but not flexible accumulation', *Environment and Planning D: Society and Space*, vol.7, London, Pion.

Hurtado, R. (1984) 'Essaimage de la Télémécanique via la SEMS', *Minis et Micros*, no.216.

Hübner, K. (1988) 'Flexibilisierung und die Verselbständigung des monetären Weltmarkts. Hindernisse für einen neuen langen Aufschwung?', *Prokla*, no.71 Berlin, Rotbuch.

IAURIF (1988) 'Ile de France 2000: vers un projet régional', *Cahiers de l'IAURIF*, no.85, April.

Industry Department for Scotland (1983) Electronics manpower in Scotland in the mid-1980s, *Scottish Economic Bulletin*, no.28, December, pp.7–12.

—— (1986) 'The electronics industry in Scotland', *Statistical Bulletin*, no.C1.1, January.

ISTAT (1974) *5° Censimento generale dell'industria e del commercio, 1971*, Rome, ISTAT.

—— (1985) *6° Censimento generale dell'industria, del commercio, dei servizi e dell'artigianato, 1981*, Rome, ISTAT.

Itoh, M. (1990) 'The Japanese model of post-Fordism', paper presented at the Conference of Socialist Economists Conference, Sheffield Polytechnic, Sheffield, 13–15 July 1990.

Jacquemin, A. (1985) *Sélection et pouvoir dans la nouvelle économie industrielle*, Paris, Economica.

Jalabert, G. (1988) 'La production des bureaux dans l'agglomération toulousaine', Créteil, *CNG — Journées des Commissions industrielles et urbaines*, September.

Jeammaud, A. and Lyon-Caen, A. (1986) *Droit du travail, démocratie et crise en Europe Occidentale et en Amérique*, Arles, Actes Sud.

Jessop, B. (1990) 'Regulation theories in retrospect and prospect', *Economy and Society*, vol.19, no.2, May, pp.153–216.

Johnston, R. and Lawrence, P. R. (1988) 'Beyond vertical integration-the rise of the value-adding partnership', *Harvard Business Review*, no.4, July–August, pp.94–101.

Joint Economic Committee Of Congress (1982) *Location of high technology firms and regional economic development*, Washington DC., Joint Economic Committee Of Congress.

—— (1986) *The bi-coastal economy*, Washington DC., Joint Economic Committee Of Congress.

Jones Lang Wotton (1987) *European tenant's guide*, Paris, Jones Lang Wotton.

Junne, G. (1985) 'Reregionalisierung: Chancen regionaler Reintegration von Produkten und Konsum als Folge der Entwicklung neuer Technologien', Bonn, *Jahrbuch für Arbeit und Technik in Nordrhein-Westfalen*, pp.337–47.

Kafkalas, G. (1984) 'Small Firms and the development of a peripheral region : the case of Thraki, Greece', in R. Hudson (ed.), *Small firms and regional development*, Copenhagen, Institute for Transport, Tourism and Regional Economy.

Kaldor, N. (1961) 'Capital accumulation and economic growth', in Abraham-Frois (1977).

—— (1966) *Causes of the slow rate of economic growth in the United Kingdom*, Cambridge, Cambridge University Press.

—— (1970) 'The case for regional policies', *Scottish Journal of Political Economy*, vol.17, pp.337–48.

Kelley M. R. (1989) 'Alternative forms of work organization under programmable automation', in Wood, S. (ed.) (1989).

Kennedy, D. (1984) *Labour and reindustrialisation*, University Park, PA, The Penn-State University.

Klein, B. (1986) 'Dynamic competition and productivity advances', in Landau, R. and Rosenberg (eds) (1986).

Kleinknecht, A. (1990) 'Are there Schumpeterian waves of innovations?', *Cambridge Journal of Economics*, vol.14, no.1, March, pp.81–92.

Koepp, S. (1987) 'Sous surveillance', *Lettre Internationale*, no.14, Autumn.

Kotler, P., Fahey, L. and Jatusripitak, S. (1985) *The new competition*, Englewood Cliffs, Prentice Hall.

Krätke, S. (1988) 'Politische Ökonomie des Wohnungsbaus und der Stadtentwicklung', in Prigge, W. and Kaib, W. (eds) (1988) *Sozialer Wohnungsbau im internationalen Vergleich*, Frankfurt am Main, Vervuert.

Krätke, S. and Schmoll, F. (1987) 'Der lokale Staat: "Ausführungsorgan" oder "Gegenmacht"?', *Prokla*, no.68, Berlin, Rotbuch.

La Documentation Française (1982) *Investissement non matériel et croissance industrielle*, Paris, La Documentation Française.

Lafont, J., Leborgne, D. and Lipietz, A. (1980) Redéploiement industriel et espace économique: une approche intersectorielle comparative. Contrat CEPREMAP/Délégation à l'Aménagement du Territoire et à l'Action Régionale, in DATAR (1982) *Travaux et Recherches de Prospective*, no.85, Paris, La Documentation Française.

Lancaster, K. (1966) 'A new approach to consumer theory', *Journal of Political Economy*, vol.LXXIV, pp.132-57.

—— (1975) 'Socially optimal product differenciation', *American Economic Review*, vol.LXV, no.4, September, pp.567-85.

—— (1979) *Variety, Equity and Efficiency*, Oxford, Blackwell.

Landau, R. and Rosenberg, S. (1986) *The positive sum strategy: harnessing technology for economic growth*, Washington DC, National Academy Press.

Läpple, D. (1978) 'Gesellschaftlicher Reproduktionsprozeß und Stadtstrukturen', in Mayer, M. et al. (eds) (1978) *Stadtkrise und soziale Bewegungen*, Köln and Frankfurt am Main, Europäische Verlagsanstalt.

—— (1985) 'Internationalisation of capital and the regional problem', in Walton, J. (ed.) (1985) *Capital and labour in the urbanised world*, London, Sage.

—— (1986) 'Süd-Nord-Gefälle: Metaphor für die räumliche Folgen einer Transformationsphase: auf dem Weg zu einem post-tayloristischen Entwicklungsmodell?', in Friedrichs, J., Häußermann, H. and Siebel, W. (eds) (1986), pp.97-116.

Lassudrie-Duchène, B. (1988) 'Décomposition internationale des processus productifs et autonomie nationale', in Bourguinat, H. (ed.) (1988) *Internationalisation et autonomie de décision*, Paris, Economica.

Laumer, H. and Ochel, W. (1986) 'Adaptation des structures industrielles', *Problèmes économiques*, no.1969, pp.22-31.

Leborgne, D. (1987) 'Equipements flexibles et organisation productive: les relations industrielles au coeur de la modernisation. Eléments de comparison internationale', Paris, CEPREMAP, mimeo.

—— (1988) Modernisation: une logique des trajectoires nationales multiples, in Boyer, R. (ed.) (1988) *La seconde transformation*, Paris, Economica.

—— (1989) 'Restructuration industrielle: des formes contrastées de quasi-intégration verticale', in Coriat, B. (ed.) (1989) *L'usine post-fordienne*, Paris, Bourgois.

Leborgne, D. and Lipietz, A (1991) 'Two social strategies in the production of new industrial spaces', in Benko, G. and Dunford, M. (eds) (1991) *Industrial change and regional development*, London, Belhaven.

—— (1988) 'L'après-fordisme et son espace', *Les Temps Modernes*, vol.43, no.601, April, pp.75-114.

—— (1988) 'New technologies, new modes of regulation: some spatial implications', *Environment and Planning D: Society and Space*, vol.6, no.3.

—— (1990a) 'Avoiding two-tiers Europe', *Labour and Society*, vol.15, no.2, April.

—— (1990b) 'Fallacies and open issues about post-Fordism', Paris, CEPREMAP, *Couverture Orange*, no.9009.

Lefebvre, H. (1970) *La révolution urbaine*, Paris, Gallimard.

Legru, B. (1987) La rénovation du tissu industriel britannique: trois types d'initiatives pour favoriser la diffusion et les transfers de technologies, Paris, *Etude CPE*, no.84.

Lehoucq, T. and Strauss, J. P. (1988) 'Les industries françaises de haute technologie: des difficultés à rester dans la course', *Economie et Statistique*, no.207, February, pp.15-21.

Leinbach, T. R. and Amrhein, C. (1987) 'A geography of the venture capital industry in the U.S.', *The Professional Geographer*, vol.39, no.2, pp.146-58.

Lempa, S. (1988) 'Just-in-time-Steuerung beeinflußt Standortwahl', *Niederbayerische Wirtschaft* (Industrie-und Handelskammer Niederbayern), vol.5, pp.196-97.

Lewis, J. R. and Williams, A. M. (1984) 'The formation and role of small and medium size industrial enterprises in the Regiao Centro, Portugal', paper presented at the 24th European Congress of the Regional Science Association, Milan, August.

Liebenstein, H. (1986) 'Allocative Efficiency versus X-efficiency', *The American Economic Review*, vol.56, pp.392–415.

Lipietz, A. (1974) 'Structuration de l'espace, problème foncier et aménagement du territoire', *Environment and Planning* A, vol.7 (English translation: Lipietz, A. (1980)).

—— (1977) *Le capital et son espace*, Paris, François Maspero.

—— (1979) *Crise et inflation: pourquoi?*, Paris, François Maspero.

—— (1980) 'The structuration of space, the problem of land, and spatial policy', in Carney, J., Hudson, R. and Lewis, J. (eds) (1980) *Regions in Crisis*, London, Croom Helm.

—— (1983) *Le Monde enchanté. De la valeur à l'envol inflationniste*, Paris, La Découverte-Maspero (English translation: (1983) *The enchanted world. Inflation, credit and the world crisis*, London, Verso).

—— (1985a) 'Le national et le régional: quelle autonomie face à la crise capitaliste mondiale?', Paris, CEPREMAP, *Couverture Orange*, no.8521.

—— (1985b) *Mirages et miracles. Problèmes de l'industrialisation dans le Tiers Monde*, Paris, La Découverte. (English translation: (1987) *Mirages and miracles*, London, Verso).

—— (1985c) 'Akkumulation, Krisen und Auswege aus der Krise. Einige methodische Überlegungen zum Begriff der "Regulation" ', *Prokla*, no.58, Berlin, Rotbuch.

—— (1986) 'New tendencies in the international division of labour: regimes of accumulation and modes of regulation', in Scott, A. J. and Storper, M. (eds) (1986), pp.16–40.

—— (1988) 'Comment gérer la quatriéme phase de la crise', *Le Monde Diplomatique*, May.

—— (1989a) *Choisir l'audace. Une alternative pour le XXIème siècle*, Paris, La Découverte.

—— (1989b) 'The debt problem, European integration and the new phase of the world crisis' *New Left Review*, no.178, November–December, pp.37–50.

Locate in Scotland (1986) *Marketing and operational plan*, Glasgow, Scottish Development Agency.

Logan, J. R. and Molotch, H. L. (1987) *Urban fortunes: the political economy of place*, Berkeley, University of California Press.

Luckingham, B. (1982) *A profile history of Albuquerque, El Paso, Phoenix and Tucson*, El Paso, University of Texas.

Luttrell, W. F. (1962) *Factory location and industrial movement*, vol.1, London, National Institute of Economic and Social Research.

Lutz, B. (1984) *Der kurze Traum immerwährender Prosperität*, Frankfurt am Main, Campus.

Mahon, R. (1987) 'From Fordism to? New technologies, labour markets and unions', *Economic and Industrial Democracy*, vol.8, no.1, February, pp.5–60, London and Beverly Hills, California, Sage.

Malecki, E. (1985) 'Industrial location and corporate organisation in high technology industries', *Economic Geography*, vol.61, no.4.

Malézieux, J. (1986a) 'Une forme d'expression spatiale du changement industriel dans l'agglomération parisienne: les centres d'activités locatifs. L'exemple d'EVOLIC', in CRIA, *Mélanges offerts à J. Beaujeu-Garnier*, Paris, Université de Paris I, CRIA, pp.256–66.

—— (1986b) 'Image et aménagement d'un nouvel espace d'activité en aire métropolitaine: la ZAC Paris Nord II', *Société Géographique de Liège*, no.6, pp.122–23.

—— (1987a) 'Communication et dynamisme des espaces d'activités en région métropolitaine. L'exemple de l'agglomeration parisienne', *RECLUS Modes d'Emploi*, no.10, pp.70–3.

—— (1987b) 'Espace dynamique en Ile-de-France: le parc d'activité de Paris Nord II', *RECLUS Modes d'Emploi*, no.10, pp.74–80.

—— (1988) 'Réanimation de friches industrielles en Ile-de-France', in Milieux, villes et régions, 112ème Congrès des Sociétés Savantes, Lyon, Paris, CTHS, pp.179–94.

—— (1988) Attractivité des espaces d'activités. Recherche sur l'efficacité économique des Villes Nouvelles, Paris, Université de Paris I, CRIA, *Notes de Recherche CRIA*, no.8.

Mandel, Ernest (1986) 'In defence of socialist planning', *New Left Review*, no.159, September–October, pp.5–37.

—— (1988) 'The myth of market socialism', *New Left Review*, no.169, May–June, pp.108–120.

Marcuse, P. (1989) "Dual city": a muddy metaphor for a quartered city', *International Journal of Urban and Regional Research*, vol.13, no.4.

Marglin, S. A. and Schor, J. B. (eds) (1990) *The golden age of capitalism*, Oxford and New York, Clarendon Press.

Markusen, A. (1984) 'Defense spending and the geography of high-tech industries', Berkeley, University of California, IURD Working Paper, no.423.

—— (1985) *Profit cycles, oligopoly and regional development*, Cambridge,Mass, MIT Press.

Marshall, A. (1890) *Principles of economics*, London, Macmillan.

Marshall, M. (1987) *Long waves of regional development*, Basingstoke and London, Macmillan.

Martinelli, F. (1988) *Productive organisation and service demand in Italian textile and clothing 'districts': a case study*, Geneva, UNCTAD (MTN/RLA/CB.6).

—— (1989a) 'Une approche théorique à la demande de services aux producteurs', in Moulaert, F. (ed.) (1989) *La production des services et sa géographie*, Villeneuve D'Ascq, Presse de l'Université de Lille I, pp.45–66.

—— (1989b) 'Services aux producteurs et développement régional', in Moulaert, F. (ed.) (1989) *La production des services et sa géographie*, Villeneuve D'Ascq, Presse de l'Université de Lille I, pp.163–182.

Massey, D. (1979) 'In what sense a regional problem?', *Regional Studies*, vol.13, pp.233-43.

—— (1984) *Spatial divisions of labour: social structures and the geography of production*, London, Macmillan.

—— (1985) 'Which new technology?', in Castells, M. (ed.) (1985), pp.302-15.

—— and Meegan, R. (1982) *The anatomy of job loss: the how, why and where of employment decline*, London, Methuen.

Mathews, J. A. (1989) 'New production concepts', *Prometheus*, vol.7, no.1, June, pp.129–48.

Maurau, G. (1988) 'Formes d'emploi et flexibilité: une comparaison France, Royaume-Uni', *La note de l'IRES*, no.15, pp.1–9.

Mayer, M. (1987) 'Städtische Bewegungen in den USA: "Gegenmacht" und Inkorporierung', *Prokla*, no.68, Berlin, Rotbuch.

—— (1988) 'The changing conditions for local politics in the transformation to Post-Fordism', paper presented at the International Conference on Regulation, Barcelona.

Mayer, R. (1988) 'La traite des PMI', *Le Monde*, 31 August.

McKinsey and Company (1987) *Creating shareholder value through merger and/or acquisition*, New York, McKinsey and Co.

Medawar, P. (1969) *Induction and intuition in scientific thought, American Philosophical Society. Memoirs* vol.75 Philadelphia, Methuen.

Mensch, G. O. (1975) *Das technologische Patt: Innovationen überwinden di depression*, Frankfurt, Umschau.

Mensch, G. O. (1979) *Stalemate in technology*, New York, Ballinger.

Messine P. (1986) *Les Saturniens. Quand les patrons réinventent la société*, Paris, La Découverte.

Meyer, P. B. (1986) 'Computer-controlled manufacturing and the spatial distribution of production', *Area*, vol.18, pp.209-13.

Michalet, C. A. (1985) *Le capitalisme mondial*, Paris, Presses Universitaires de France.

Modiano, P. (1982) 'Competitività e collocazione internazionale dell'industria italiana: il problema dei prodotti tradizionali', *Economia e Politica Industriale*, no.33.

—— (1984) 'La collocazione internazionale dell'industria italiana: un tentativo di interpretazione di alcune tendenze recenti', *Economia Italiana*, no.3, September–December.

Momigliano, F. (1982) 'Determinanti ed effetti dell'attività innovativa: revisione di teorie e implicazioni di politiche pubbliche per l'innovazione industriale', *Economia e Politica Industriale*, no.35.

—— (1984) 'Revisione di modelli interpretativi delle determinanti ed effetti dell'attività, della aggregazione spaziale dei centri di R & S e della diffusione intraindustriale e territoriale delle innovazioni tecnologiche', in Camagni, R., Cappellin, R. and Garofoli, G. (eds) (1984) *Cambiamento tecnologico e diffusione territoriale*, Milan, Franco Angeli.

Monden, Y. (1981) 'What makes the Toyota production system really tick? *Industrial Engineering*, January, pp.36–46.

Morrisson Institute (1988) *Urban Growth in Arizona*, ASU.

Moulaert, F. and Swyngedouw, E. (1987) 'Regional development and the geography of the flexible production system: theoretical arguments and empirical evidence from Western Europe and the US', Lille, Université de Lille I, mimeo.

—— (1989) 'A regulation approach to the geography of the flexible production system', *Environment and Planning D: Society and Space*, vol.7, no.3, pp.327-45.

Moulaert, F., Martinelli, F. and Djellal, F. (1989) *The role of information technology consultancy in the transfer of information technology to production and service organisations*, The Hague, Report prepared for NOTA.

Mucchielli, J. L. and Thuillier, J. P. (1982) *Multinationales européennes et investissements croisés*, Paris, Economica.

Mucchielli, J. L. (1985) *Les firmes multinationales, mutations et nouvelles perspectives*, Paris, Economica.

Murray, R. (1987) 'Ownership, control and the market', *New Left Review*, no.164, July–August, pp.87–112.

Mutlu S. (1979) 'Interregional and international mobility of industrial capital: the case of the American automobile and electronics industries', Berkeley, Univerity of California, PhD dissertation.

Mészáros, I. (1978) 'Political power and dissent in post-revolutionary societies', *New Left Review*, no.108, March–April, pp.3–21.

National Economic Development Council Electronics Industry Sector Group, (1988) *Performance and competitive success. Strengthening competitiveness in UK electronics*, London, NEDO.

National Economic Development Council Information Technology Economic Development Committee (1984) *Crisis facing UK information technology*, London, NEDO.

Nelson, K. (1986) 'Labor demand, labor supply and the suburbanization of low-wage office work', in Scott, A. J. and Storper, M. (eds) (1986) pp.149–71.

Nelson, R. R. and Winter, S. G. (1982) *An evolutionary theory of economic change*, Cambridge, Mass., Harvard University Press.

New York Times (1988) 'Siemens set to pay $1.15 billion for Rolm', *New York Times*, 31 December, p.33.

—— (1989) 'Apollo Computer sale to Hewlett-Packard', *New York Times*, 13 April, p.D4.

Niada M. (1988) 'Grande è meglio', Milan, *Edizioni del Sole 24 Ore*.

NOMISMA-Laboratorio di Politica Industriale (Bianchi, P. and Gualtieri, G. (eds) (1988) *Acquisizioni, fusioni, concorrenza*, Bologna, Nomisma.

Noyelle, T. J. (1982) 'The implications of industry restructuring for spatial organisation in the United States', in Moulaert, F. and Salinas (eds) (1982) *Regional analysis and the new international division of labour*, Boston, Mass., Kluwer-Nijhoff.

—— (1988) 'Services and the world economy: towards a new international division of labor', paper presented at the Economic and Social Research Council Workshop on Localities in the International Economy, Cardiff.

Nuhn, H. and Sinz, M. (1988) 'Industriestruktureller Wandel und Beschäftigungsentwicklung in der Bundesrepublik Deutschland', *Geographische Rundschau*, no.1, Frankfurt am Main.

Nuti, F. (1983) 'Divisione del lavoro e crescita: il caso dei settori a tecnologia matura', *L'Industria*, no.1.

—— (1985) 'I distretti dell'industria tessile: problemi generali e analisi di un caso particolare', Bologna, Contribution to the CNR Project Il sistema delle imprese, mimeo.

—— (1985) 'Tecnologie emergenti, economie di scala e strategie di diversificazione delle imprese', *L'Industria*, no.1.

—— (1990) 'Rapporto al CNR sui sistemi calzaturieri in Italia', mimeo.

Oakey, R. P, Rothwell, R. and Cooper S. Y, (1988) *The management of innovation in high technology small firms*, London, Frances Pinter.

Oakey, R. P. (1985) *The regional economic impact of technological change*, London, Frances Pinter.

Oakey, R. P. (1989) 'Why Britain finds it hard to shine like Silicon Valley', *The Guardian*, 9 January.

Observatoire de l'Immobilier (1986) 'Immobilier d'entreprise: un optimisme nuancé', *L'Observatoire de l'Immobilier*, no.3.

OCDE (1985) *L'industrie mondiale des semi-conducteurs. Questions liées aux échanges*, Paris, OCDE.

Okba, M. (1988) 'Le syndicat unique dans l'entreprise et dans le système des relations professionnelles', *La note de l'IRES*, no.15, pp.53–9.

Onida F. and Viesti, G. (1988) *The Italian multinationals*, London, Croom Helm.

Paci, M. (ed.) (1980) *Famiglia e mercato del lavoro in un'economia periferica*, Milan, Franco Angeli.

—— (1982) *La struttura sociale italiana*, Bologna, Il Mulino.

Perrin, J. C. (1989) 'Milieux innovateurs: éléments de théorie et de typologie, Aix en Provence', Centre d'Economie Régionale, *Notes de Recherche*, no.104.

Perrin, M. (1938) *Saint-Etienne et sa région économique*, Tours, Arrault.

Perroux, F. (1955) 'La notion de pole de croissance', *Economie appliquée*, vol.8, no.1–2, pp.307–20.

Perroux, F. (1961) *L'économie de XXéme siécle*, Paris, Presses Universitaires de France.

Perry, R. and Wadkins, R. (1977) *The rise of Sunbelt cities*, Beverly Hills, Sage.

Peyrache, V. (1987) 'Impact social et spatial des technologies nouvelles dans le développement des régions urbaines', Paris, Communication Table Ronde DATAR.

Pike, F. Becattini, G. Sengenberger, W. (eds) (1990) *Industrial districts and inter-firm cooperation in Italy*, Geneva, International Labour Office.

Piore, M. J. (1987) Corporate Reform in American Manufacturing and the Challenge to Economic Theory, Cambridge, Mass., MIT, mimeo.

Piore, M. J. and Sabel, C. F. (1984) *The second industrial divide: possibilities for prosperity*, New York, Basic Books.

Planque, B. (1986) 'Le développement par les activités à haute technologie et ses répercutions spatiales. L'exemple de la Silicon Valley', *Revue d'Economie Régionale et Urbaine*, no.5, pp.911–41.

Polanyi, M. (1978) *Personal knowledge. Towards a post-critical philosophy*, London, Routledge and Kegan Paul.

Pollert, A. (1988) 'The 'flexible firm': fixation or fact?', *Work, Employment and Society*, vol.2, no.3, September, pp.281–316.

Porter, M. E. (1980) *Competitive strategy*, New York, The Free Press of New York.

Prévot, V. (1979) *Géographie des textiles*, Paris, Masson.

Rada, J. (1982) 'Structure and behaviour of the semi-conductor industry', New-York, a study prepared for the UN Centre on Transnational Corporations.

Radice, H. (1978) 'On the Scottish Development Agency and the contradictions of state entrepreneurship', Stirling, University of Stirling, *Discussion Papers in Economics, Finance and Investment*, no.59, May.

Ray, G. F. (1988) 'The diffusion of innovations: an update', *National Institute Economic Review*, no.122, November, pp.51–69.

Rees, J. (1979) Technological change and regional shifts in American manufacturing, *The Professional Geographer*, vol.31, no.1, pp.45–54.

Region Ile-de-France (1989) *Projet régional d'aménagement et révision du Schéma directeur de la région Ile-de-France*, Paris, Region Ile-de-France.

Riboud, A. (1987) 'Modernisation, mode d'emploi', Rapport au Premier Ministre, Paris, Union Générale d'Editions 10/18.

Richter, G. *et al.* (1988) 'Stuttgart Problemregion der 90er Jahre? Gefährdungen der Arbeitnehmer durch Umstrukturierungsprozesse in der Metallindustrie in Wirtschaftsraum Stuttgart', Munich, *IMU Studien*, no.7.

Rock M. L. (1987) *The mergers and acquisitions handbook*, New York, McGraw Hill.

Rosenberg, N. (1982) *Inside the Black Box: Technology and Economics*, Cambridge, Cambridge University Press.

Ruffieux, B. (1987) La recherche et la formation comme facteurs de développement économique local? Les technopoles, paper presented at the Jornadas on La cuidad. Instrumento de recuperacion economica y de creacion de empeo, Vitovia-Gasteiz, 9–10 April.

Sabel, C. F. (1982) *Work and politics: the division of labor in industry*, Cambridge, Cambridge University Press.

—— (1983) 'La new Italy della piccola impresa', *Politica ed Economia*, vol.XIV, no.7–8, July–August.

—— (1989) 'Flexible specialisation and the re-emergence of regional economics', in Hirst, P. and Zeitlin, J. (eds) (1989), pp.17–70.

—— and Zeitlin, J. (1982) 'Alternative storiche alla produzione di massa', *Stato e mercato*, no.5, August.

——, Herrigel, G. B., Deeg, R. and Kazis, R. (1989) 'Regional prosperities compared: Massachusetts and Baden-Württemberg in the 1980s', *Economy and Society*, vol.18, no.4 (November) pp.374–404.

——, Kern, H. and Herrigel, G. (1989) 'Collaborative manufacturing: new supplier relationships in the automobile industry and the redefinition of industrial corporations', mimeo.

SAF/LO/PTK (1982) *Convention de progrés*, Sweden, SAF/LO/PTK, 15 April.

Saint-Julien, T. and Pumain, D. (1985) 'A ville plus grande, travail plus qualifié', *Annales de la Recherche Urbaine*, no.29, pp. 105–18.

Sallez, A. (1972) *Polarisation et sous-traitance*, Paris, Eyrolles.

Salter, W. (1966) *Productivity and Technical Change*, second edition, Cambridge, Cambridge University Press.

Santo, B. and Wollard, K. (1988) 'The world of silicon: it's dog eat dog' *IEEE Spectrum*, September, pp.30–9.

Sassen-Koob, S. (1984) 'The new labor demand in global cities', in Smith, M. P. (ed.) (1984) *Cities in transformation*, Beverly Hills, Sage.

Sauvant, K. and Zimny, Z. (1987) 'Foreign direct investment in services: the neglected dimension in international service negotiations', *World Competition*, vol.31.

Sauviat, C. (1987) 'Un patronat italien chic...et choc!, *La note de l'IRES*, no. 3, 3rd quarter, pp.34–41.

Sawers, L. and Tabb W. K. (eds) (1984) *Sunbelt-snowbelt: urban development and regional restructuring*, Oxford, Oxford University Press.

Saxenian, A. (1980) Silicon chips and spatial structure: the industrial basis of urbanisation in Santa Clara Country, Berkeley, University of California, IURD Working Paper, no.345.

—— (1985) 'The genesis of Silicon Valley', in Hall, P. and Markusen, A. (eds) (1985) *Silicon landscapes*, Boston, Mass., Allen and Unwin, pp.20–48.

—— (1988) 'The new supplier relations', in *The political economy of industrial adaptation in Silicon Valley*, Cambridge, Mass., MIT, Department of Political Sciences, PhD Dissertation.

Sayer, A. (1986) 'Industrial location on a world scale: the case of the semiconductor industry', in Scott, A. J. and Storper, M. (eds) (1986), pp.107–123.

Scherer, F.M. (1970) *Industrial market structure and economic performance*, Chicago, Rand McNally.

Schoenberger, E. (1986) 'Competition, competitive strategy and industrial change: the case of electronic components', *Economic Geography*, vol.62, no.4, pp. 321–33.

—— (1988) 'From Fordism to flexible accumulation: technology, competitive strategies and international location', *Environment and Planning D: Society and Space*, vol.6, no.3, pp.245–62.

—— (1989) 'Some dilemmas of automation: strategic and operational aspects of technological change in production', *Economic Geography*, vol.65, no.3, July, pp.232–47.

—— (1989) 'Thinking about flexibility: a response to Gertler', *Transactions of the Institute of British Geographers*, vol.14, pp.109–12.

Schumpeter, J. A. (1939) *Business cycles: a theoretical, historical and statistical analysis of the capitalist process*, New York, McGraw-Hill.

Sciberras, E. (1977) *Multinational electronics companies and national economic policies*, Greenwich, Conneticut, JAC Press.

Scott, A. J. (1980) *The urban land nexus and the state*, London, Pion.

—— (1986a) 'High tech industry and territorial development: the rise of the Orange Country Complex 1955-84', *Urban Geography*, vol.7, no.1, pp.3–45.

—— (1986b) 'Industrial organization and location: division of labor, the firm and spatial process', *Economic Geography*, vol.62, no.3, June, pp.214–31.

—— (1987a) 'The semiconductor industry in South-East Asia: organisation, location and the international division of labour', *Regional Studies*, vol.21, pp.143–60.

—— (1988a) 'Flexible production systems and regional development: the rise of new industrial spaces in North America and Western Europe', *International Journal of Urban and Regional Research*, vol.12, no.2, pp.171–86.

—— (1988b) *Metropolis. From the division of labour to urban form*, Berkeley, California, University of California Press.

—— (1988c) *New industrial spaces. Flexible production organisation and regional development in North America and Western Europe*, London, Pion.

Scott, A. J. and Angel, D. P. (1987a) 'The US semiconductor industry: a locational analysis', *Environment and planning A*, vol.19, pp.875–912.

—— (1987b) 'The global assembly operations of US semiconductor firms: a geographical analysis', Los Angeles, University of California, Working Paper.

Scott, A. J. and Storper, M. (eds) (1986) *Production, work, territory. The geographical anatomy of industrial capitalism*, Boston, Allen and Unwin.

—— (1987) 'Industries de haute technologie et développement régional', *Revue internationale des Sciences sociales*, no.112, pp.237–56.

Scottish Development Agency (1979) *The electronics industry in Scotland: a proposed strategy* (Booz Allen report), Glasgow, Scottish Development Agency, April.

Secchi, B. (1974) *Squilibri regionali e sviluppo economico*, Padua, Marsilio.

Segal, Quince and Partners (1985) *The Cambridge phenomenon: the growth of high-technology industry in a university town*, Cambridge, Segal, Quince and Partners.

Sinz, M. (1984) 'Perspektiven von Niedergang und Revitalisierung: Industrie und Gewerbe in der Stadtentwicklung', *Informationen zur Raumentwicklung*, nos 10 and 11, Bonn, Bundesforschungsanstalt für Landeskunde und Raumordnung.

Smith, M. P. (1987) 'Global capital restructuring and local political crises in US cities', in Henderson, J. and Castells, M. (ed.) (1987) *Global restructuring and territorial development*, London, Sage.

Smith, M. P. and Feagin, J. R. (ed.) (1987) *The capitalist city. Global restructuring and community politics*, Oxford and New York, Basil Blackwell.

Smith, N. (1986) 'Gentrification, the frontier, and the restructuring of urban space', in Smith, N. and Williams, P. (eds) (1986) *Gentrification of the city*, London, Allen and Unwin.

Stalk, G. (1988) 'Time-the next source of competitive advantage', *Harvard Business Review*, no.4, July-August, pp.41–51.

Stevens, M. (1981) *The big eight*, New York, Macmillan.

Stoffaes, C. (1984) *Politique industrielle*, Paris, Les Cours de Droit.

Storper, M. and Christopherson, S. (1987) 'Flexible specialisation and industrial agglomerations', *Annals of the Association of American Geographers*, vol.77, no.1, pp.104–17.

Storper, M. and Walker, R. (1989) *The capitalist imperative territory, technology, and industrial growth*, Oxford, Basil Blackwell.

Storper, M. and Scott, A. J. (1989) 'The geographical foundations and social regulation of flexible production complexes', in Wolch, J. and Dear, M. (eds) (1989) *The power of geography: how territory shapes social life*, Boston, Unwin Hyman, pp. 21–40.

Stöhr, W. B. (1986) 'Territorial innovation complexes', in Aydalot, P. (ed.) (1986) *Milieux innovateurs en Europe*, Paris, *GREMI*, pp.29–54.

Streeck, W. (1987) 'Skills and the limits of neo-liberalism', paper presented at the conference on Mutamenti del lavoro e trasformazione sociale, Istituto Universitario di Studi Europei di Torino, 27-28 November.

Swyngedouw, E. (1989) 'The heart of the place: the resurrection of locality in an age of hyperspace' *Geografiska Annaler*, vol.71 B, no.1, pp.31–42.

Tarondeau, J. C. (1982) *Produits et technologies. Choix politique de l'entreprise industrielle*, Paris, Dalloz.

—— (1986) 'Sortir du dilemme productivité-flexibilité, Harvard-l'Expansion, numéro spécial 'Production', Paris.

Taylor, M. (1986) 'Industrial geography', *Progress in Human Geography*, vol.10, no.3, pp.407–15.

Tertiel (1986) 'Immobilier d'entreprise', *Tertiel*, no.35, pp.81–9.

Tertiel (1988) 'Immobilier: choisir des locaux 'high tech'', *Tertiel*, nos 31-2, pp.86–90.

Thrift, N. (1987) 'The fixers: the urban geography of international commercial capital', in Henderson, J. and Castells, M. (eds) (1987).

Tiger, H. (1986) *L'Agglomération grenobloise: un développement local confronté à quels enjeux?*, Grenoble, GETUR.

Tilton, J. E. (1971) *International diffusion of technology: the case of semiconductors*, Washington D.C., The Brookings Institute.

Truel, J. L. (1980) 'Les nouvelles stratégies de localisation internationale: le cas des semiconducteurs', *Revue d'économie industrielle*, no.14, pp.171–78.

—— (1980a) L'industrie mondiale des semi-conducteurs, Paris, Université de Paris IX, Thèse de Doctorat.

Uchitelle, L. (1988) 'Labor's lost strength', *New York Times*, 10 May.

UNCTAD (1985) *Services and the development process*, TD/B/1008/Rev.1 Geneva, United Nations (Sales no. E.85.II.D.13).

UNCTC (1988) *Foreign direct investment, the service sector and international banking*, London, Graham and Trotman.

Urbanisme (1989) Sites d'entreprises - Centres d'affaires - Technopoles, Dossier spécial Urbanisme, no.228, December-January, pp.24-65.

Valeyre, A. (1985) 'La dynamique spatiale des emplois de service liés la production industrielle', *Revue d'Economie Régionale et Urbaine*, no.4, pp.703-25.

Van Den Berg, L., Drewett, R., Klaassen, L. H., Rossi, A. and Vijverberg, C. H. T. (1982) *Urban Europe: a study of growth and decline*, Oxford, Pergamon Press.

van der Pijl, K. (1984) *The making of an Atlantic ruling class*, London, Verso.

Vasquez Barquero, A. (1983) Industrialization in rural areas: the Spanish case, paper presented at OECD Intergovernmental Meeting, Senigallia, June.

Veltz, P. (1986) 'L'espace des industries électriques et électroniques', *Annales de la Recherche Urbaine*, no.29, pp.69-76.

—— (1988) *Réseaux dans l'industrie/industrie en réseaux*, Noisy-le-Grand, Ecole Nationale des Ponts et Chaussées, LATTS.

—— (1991) 'New models of production organisation and trends in spatial development', in Benko, G. and Dunford, M. (eds), *Industrial change and regional development*, London, Belhaven, 1991.

Vinay, P. (1987) 'Women, family and work: symptoms of crisis in the informal economy of Central Italy', paper presented at the Samos Seminar on Changing Labour Processes and New Forms of Urbanisation', Samos, Greece, 31 August - 5 September 1987.

Walker, R. (1985) 'Technological determination and determinism: industrial growth and location', in Castells, M. (ed.) (1985), pp.226-64.

Walker, R. (1989) 'Machinery, labor and location', in Wood, S. (ed.) (1989).

Wallerstein, I. (1988) 'The inventions of TimeSpace realities: towards an understanding of our historical systems', *Geography*, vol.73, pp.289-97.

Weber, A. (1909) *Über den Standort der Industrien, Teil I: Reine theorie des standorts*, Tübingen, Mohr.

Weissbach, H. J. and Weissbach, R. (1987) 'Logistiksysteme in der Automobilindustrie', Wissenschaftszentrum Berlin discussion papers, IIVG, pp.87-215.

Welzk, S. (1987) *Boom ohne Arbeitsplätze*, Frankfurt am Main, B. Gutenberg.

Williamson, O. (1980) 'Transaction costs economics: the governance of contractual relations', *Journal of Law and Economics*, vol.22.

—— (1986) 'Vertical integration and transaction costs', in Stiglitz, J. E. and Mathewson, G. F. (eds) (1986) *New developments in the analysis of market structure*, London, Macmillan.

Wood, S. (ed.) (1989) *The transformation of work?*, London, Unwin Hyman.

Zachert, U. (1988) 'Genèse et usage des systèmes de classification en Allemagne Fédérale', *Travail et Emploi*, no.38, January.

Zarifan P. (1987) 'La production industrielle comme production de services', paper presented at the Colloque International sur les Services, Université de Lille I, Lille.

Zeitlin, J. (1985) 'Distretti industriali e struttura industriale in prospettiva storica', in Innocenti, R. (ed.) (1985) *Piccola città e piccola impresa*, Milan, Franco Angeli.

Zinn, K. G. (1989) 'Prosperität: auf brüchigem Boden?', *Sozialismus*, nos. 7 and 8, Hamburg, VSA.

Zysman, J. (1983) *Governments, markets, and growth. Financial systems and the politics of industrial change*, Oxford, Martin Robertson.

Ó hUallachán, B. (1987) 'Regional and technological implications of the recent build up in American defence spending', *Annals of the Association of American Geographers*, vol.77, no.2, pp.208-23.

Index